CW00957711

FOREIGN
MILITARY
INTERVENTION

FOREIGN MILITARY INTERVENTION

The Dynamics of Protracted Conflict

ARIEL E. LEVITE

BRUCE W. JENTLESON

LARRY BERMAN

EDITORS

Columbia
University
Press

New York

Columbia University Press

New York   Oxford

Copyright © 1992 Columbia University Press

All rights reserved

Library of Congress Cataloging-in-Publication Data

Foreign military intervention : the dynamics of protracted conflict /

  Ariel Levite, Bruce W. Jentleson, Larry Berman, editors.

    p.   cm.

  Includes bibliographical references and index.

    1. World   politics—1945–   2. Intervention (International law)

3. Politics and war.   4. Military history, Modern—20th century.

I. Levite, Ariel.   II. Jentleson, Bruce W., 1951–

  III. Berman, Larry.

ISBN 0-231-07294-5

D842.F58   1992

322′.5′09′04—dc20   92-735

                                                              CIP

Casebound editions of Columbia University Press books are Smyth-sewn and printed on permanent and durable acid-free paper.

Printed in the United States of America

c 10 9 8 7 6 5 4 3 2 1

To Alexander L. George,
in appreciation of an exemplary scholarly career

Contents

Preface

The idea for this book originated in the summer of 1987 when Levite (then at the Jaffee Center) joined Berman and Jentleson at UC Davis. A frequent topic for conversation, inspired by the protracted Soviet intervention in Afghanistan then winding to a close, was the apparent commonality among the Soviet case, Israel's intervention in Lebanon, and the U.S. intervention in Vietnam. These cases were all characterized by the political use of direct military force in response to political instability within another country intended not to conquer the territory but rather to install or maintain in power a local ally.

Despite the obvious profound differences among the United States, the Soviet Union and Israel, we observed some commonalities in the dilemmas and outcomes associated with these cases. We saw similarities in the patterns and dynamics of the process leading to and expanding upon the original political commitment whereby the intervening power sought support from an indigenous ally in order to stabilize or change an existing regime. These apparent similarities in what otherwise might seem *sui generis* cases proved sufficiently intriguing to stimulate our interest in looking at the phenomenon more systematically and analytically by posing several key questions. How did political-military intervention come about, proceed, and end? What could be learned from the phenomenon itself and from the several candidate cases we had identified? These all seemed issues worthy of deeper and more systematic comparative study.

What started as interesting lunchtime discussions thus quickly became a consuming dialogue of propositions, hypotheses, and theoretical guidelines. The literature on intervention provided few answers for the questions we were asking. Subsequent discussion with other scholars in the field convinced us to move ahead with a research project on protracted foreign military intervention. We identified six major cases for the study: the United States in Vietnam, the Soviet Union in Afghanistan, Syria in Lebanon, Israel in Lebanon,

India in Sri Lanka, and Cuba and South Africa in Angola. For each of these, we commissioned a case study from a noted expert in the field. We approached each case through a three-stage analytic framework: the initial commitments, or "getting in"; the duration of the actual military intervention, or "staying in"; the eventual disengagement, or "getting out." These analytic components are discussed in chapter one. As a basis for further insights, we also commissioned cross-case analyses of each of these stages as additional chapters, to be written by prominent scholars specializing in analysis of the issues characteristic of each stage.

With initial support from the University of California's Institute for Global Conflict and Cooperation and the University of California, Davis Institute of Governmental Affairs, we convened a two-and-a-half-day workshop in Davis in August 1989. The workshop brought together our case study writers, who in response to a set of original guidelines presented first drafts of their cases, as well as the authors who would be writing the cross case comparisons. The workshop served the valuable purpose of allowing us to refine and develop our analytical framework, as well as to revise the case studies in light of our theoretical interests. A year later the project participants reconvened in Tel Aviv, sponsored and partially funded by the Jaffee Center for Strategic Studies. There, the revised case studies as well as the cross-case analyses were presented and discussed with the added participation of several external reviewers. Following the Tel-Aviv workshop, the entire set of papers was revised for the final time and the introductory and concluding chapters were written. This book represents the cumulative result of this iterative process.

Acknowledgments

We have a collective intellectual debt to Professor Alexander George, who has inspired the process throughout, most notably during the UC Davis workshop in August 1989. It is with deep respect and gratitude that we dedicate this book to him.

We owe much to Alan Olmstead, Director of the UC Davis Institute of Governmental Affairs. He provided the initial seed support for seeking external funds and then hosted the workshop. Three graduate students in the UC Davis Political Science Program, Kathleen FitzGibbon, Scott Hill and Maria Courtis, provided research assistance for the project. Drew Froeliger did an excellent job on the index. We also appreciate the hard work done by IGA staff Alicia Ritter, Barbara Clemons, Flo Nelson, Donna Roggenkamp, Martha Rehrman, and Sasha Bessom.

We also appreciate the support of the staff of the UC Davis Washington Center, Melody Johnson and Fatima Mohamud, who helped organize us for our final editing meeting in March 1991 and guided the manuscript through its final stages. Linda Potoski of the UC Davis Political Science Department provided an important link between Davis and Washington. Tova Polonski, Shulamit Reich, and Orna Godai of the Jaffee Center provided invaluable assistance in the organization of the Tel-Aviv workshop.

The project could not have been undertaken without two grants from the University of California Institute on Global Conflict and Cooperation (IGCC) and the support and encouragement of John Ruggie, then IGCC Director. Likewise, the Carnegie Corporation of New York sustained the project with a significant grant that enabled the full participation of all project members in Tel-Aviv and much of the follow-up work. Dr. Frederic Mosher of Carnegie was especially responsive to our needs.

In Israel, the Federman Foundation, the Jaffee Center for Strategic Studies and its Director, Major General (Res.), Aharon Yariv, pro-

vided support, encouragement, and, most important, helped to clarify analytically our use of such terms as goals, objectives, and strategy. We also wish to thank Kate Wittenberg, Editor-in-Chief of Columbia University Press, for her support, guidance, and enthusiasm
from the outset of this project; Leslie Bialler also of Columbia Press,
for expert and collegial editing; and Doug Gentry of UC Davis Repro
Graphics for his skilled preparation of the maps.

One of the true benefits of the project was the challenging and
constructive spirit in which our authors worked. We truly appreciate
their spirit of collegiality and, of course, their willingness to engage
in numerous revisions. We also have benefitted from the insights of
several other scholars. Joining us at UC Davis were Professors Emily
Goldman and Alan Olmstead; in Tel-Aviv, Professors Itamar Rabinovich, Abraham Ben Zvi, Yair Evron, Richard Little, and Athanas-
sios Platias, Eran Lehrman, and Gideon Gera, as well as Karen Pus-
chel.

It is traditional at this point to absolve those identified above from
any errors that might appear in this volume. We do so with pleasure.
May our friends and colleagues share all that is meritorious in this
book; the three editors accept responsibility for everything else.

About the Contributors

LARRY BERMAN is currently Professor and Chairman of the Department of Political Science at the University of California, Davis. He is a Guggenheim Fellow and an American Council for Learned Societies scholar. He is the author or editor of six books, which include *Looking Back on the Reagan Presidency; Lyndon Johnson's War: The Road to Stalemate in Vietnam; The New American Presidency; Planning a Tragedy: The Americanization of the War in Vietnam; The Office of Management and Budget and the Presidency, 1921–1979*; and co-author of *Evolution of the Modern Presidency: A Bibliographical Study*.

ELIOT A. COHEN is Professor of Strategic Studies at the Paul H. Nitze School of Advanced International Studies, Johns Hopkins University. His most recent book, co-authored with John Gooch, is *Military Misfortunes: The Anatomy of Failure in War*. He has served on the Defense Department's policy planning staff and is the director of the Gulf War Air Power Survey, the United States Air Force's official study of the implications of the Gulf War of 1991 for Air Force organization, force structure, and doctrine.

GEORGE W. DOWNS is the Class of 1942 Professor of Peace and War at Princeton University and a member of the Politics Department, the Woodrow Wilson School, and the Center of International Studies. His recent publications include *Tacit Bargaining, Arms Control and Arms Races* and articles on the rational deterrence debate, arms race models, tacit bargaining, and U.S. defense policy after the Cold War.

SHAI FELDMAN is Senior Research Associate and Director of the Middle East Arms Control project at the Jaffee Center for Strategic Studies, Tel Aviv University. His numerous publications include *Israeli Nuclear Deterrence: A Strategy for the 1980s, Consensus, Deception and War: Israel in Lebanon* and articles in *Foreign Affairs, International Security*, and numerous other journals and books.

CAROLINE HARTZELL is a Ph.D. student at the Department of Political Science at the University of California, Davis. She has co-authored chapters in other books with Donald Rothchild on war termination in the Sudan and Angola was a Fulbright Dissertation Fellow, in Bogotá, Colombia, and is currently working on her doctoral dissertation on the political economy of development in the Latin American context.

MAHNAZ ISPAHANI is Director of Research at the National Democratic Institute for International Affairs (NDI) and Manager of the Soviet Union Program. She has written on a wide range of international security issues, South Asian politics and literature, Soviet democracy, and Islamic politics. Her publications include *Roads and Rivals, Pakistan: Dimensions of Insecurity*, as well as articles in *International Security, The Wilson Quarterly*, and *The New Republic*.

BRUCE W. JENTLESON is Associate Professor of Political Science and Director of the Washington Center of the University of California, Davis. He is the author of *Pipeline Politics: The Complex Political Economy of East–West Energy Trade* as well as articles in numerous books and such journals as *International Organization, International Studies Quarterly*, and *Political Science Quarterly*. He currently is writing a book on post-Cold War U.S. foreign policy.

CHARLES KUPCHAN is Assistant Professor at Princeton University. He is the author of *The Persian Gulf and the West, The Vulnerability of Empire* (forthcoming), and numerous articles on strategic and international affairs.

ARIEL E. LEVITE is Senior Research Associate at the Jaffee Center for Strategic Studies, Tel-Aviv University. He is the author of *Intelligence and Strategic Surprise, Offense and Defense in Israeli Military Doctrine*, as well as numerous articles and monographs. His current research focuses on Middle East regional security issues.

ROBERT LITWAK is Director of International Studies at the Woodrow Wilson International Center for Scholars in Washington, D.C. His publications include *Detente and the Nixon Doctrine, Security in the Persian Gulf*, and *Superpower Competition and Security in the Third World*.

YOSSI OLMERT was previously head of the Syria and Lebanon Department at the Dayan Center for Middle Eastern and African Studies and Lecturer at Tel-Aviv University. He is the author of numerous publications on the Middle East. Currently, he is Director of the Government Press Office, State of Israel.

DONALD ROTHCHILD is Professor of Political Science at the University of California, Davis. He has been a member of the faculty at Universities in Uganda, Kenya, Zambia, and Ghana. His books include *Racial Bargaining in Independent Kenya,* co-author of *Scarcity, Choice and Public Policy in Middle Africa* and co-author of *Politics and Society in Contemporary Africa.* He is the co-editor of *Eagle Entangled, Eagle Defiant,* and *Eagle Resurgent?* and *Eagle in a New World..* He is currently writing a book on conflict management in Africa.

FOREIGN
MILITARY
INTERVENTION

1

The Analysis of Protracted Foreign Military Intervention

BRUCE W. JENTLESON
ARIEL E. LEVITE

Foreign military intervention (as with so much else in international politics) goes all the way back to the Pelopponesian Wars, when Athens and Sparta intervened in the civil wars and other internal political conflicts between democrats and oligarchs in other city-states. "It became a natural thing," according to Thucydides, "for anyone who wanted a change of government to call in help from outside."[1] And, of course, as Hans Morgenthau characteristically points out, those being "called in" were motivated by more than just altruism. "From the time of the ancient Greeks to this day," writes Morgenthau, "some states have found it advantageous to intervene in the affairs of other states on behalf of their own interests."[2]

Foreign military interventions, in fact, have not always turned out to be so helpful or advantageous. Consider some salient cases from recent years: *Vietnam*, the quagmire from which the United States could not extricate itself for more than a decade; *Afghanistan*, which became a "bleeding wound" (the term was Mikhail Gorbachev's) for the Soviet Union; *Lebanon*, where Israel suffered its first military defeat, and where Syria only now, after more than fifteen years of civil war, has been able to begin to consolidate political control; *Angola*, where both Cuba and South Africa sent troops, with aid and support from the Soviet Union and the United States, respectively, in what was one of Africa's longest and most destructive wars; and *Sri Lanka*, where India sent its peacekeeping forces, only to have them become another party to a brutal war.

Many of the differences among these six cases are readily evident. The intervenors include superpowers and regional powers, democracies and non-democracies. The target countries have been both distant ones and neighboring ones. The local allies have been both incumbent regimes and insurgent movements. But their key commonality is that each involved a *protracted* foreign military intervention—longer, more costly, and less successful than anticipated. This study originated, as noted in the Preface, out of an interest in exploring the similarities that such otherwise diverse cases might have. Our implicit hypothesis is that such common patterns do exist, and while we do not deny uniqueness, through this comparative analysis we can gain insights about not only the individual cases themselves but also foreign military intervention in general.

In designing this study, we have sought to be self-conscious about both its scope and its limits. The universe from which we draw our case set of protracted foreign military interventions is a much larger one indeed. There are other cases in which military force has been used but for different goals and according to different strategies; others in which similar objectives were pursued but through different forms of intervention; others in which the foreign military interventions were quicker, more decisive, and more successful. Each of these suggests its own research design, with insights and conclusions to be drawn with their own scope and limits. However, our primary interest in this study is to determine the extent to which common patterns exist among cases in which the interventions did become protracted military ones.

We also have sought to distinguish between the similarities of process and any imputing of a single causal path; i.e., the "equifinality problem," as identified in general systems theory, of automatically taking common outcomes as evidence of common causes. Accordingly, distinct from the aggregate data analyses, macrohistorical approaches, or single-case studies that are more common in the intervention literature, our research design follows what Alexander George has called a "structured, focused comparison."[3] The structuring is in terms of three analytic stages: "getting in," from the initial political commitments to the threshold shift to a major involvement of troops in hostilities within the target state; "staying in," the duration of the military involvement; and "getting out," the military, albeit not necessarily political, disengagement. Within each of these stages we focus on three clusters of factors: the international (strategic, regional), the domestic (intervening state) and the indigenous (target state).

In this initial chapter we have three principal objectives. First, we clarify key concepts and definitions to establish the basis for the comparative analysis. Second, we discuss the significance of the study. Third, we introduce the three-stage analytic framework that provides the comparative structure.

Conceptualization and Criteria for Selection

Part of the problem inherent to the study of any type of intervention is the difficulty in defining the concept. In its most abstract form, intervention is, as noted by Stanley Hoffmann, "practically the same thing as international politics, from the beginning of time to the present."[4] We offer three initial observations to focus our study:

- Foreign military interventions represent only one type of use of military force.
- Only some foreign interventions become military ones.
- Not all foreign interventions end up being protracted ones.

Using these distinctions we then delineate the criteria that define our case set.

Foreign Military Intervention and Classical War

When in January 1991 the Bush administration launched Operation Desert Storm in retaliation for Iraq's invasion of Kuwait, protesters in Lafayette Park across from the White House carried signs saying "Stop the U.S. *Intervention* in the Middle East: No More Vietnams." But as more than a semantical point, this equating of these two most recent major U.S. uses of military force blurs the distinction between classical wars and foreign military interventions. This distinction is based on three factors: the principal domain of conflict, the central objective being pursued and the basic strategy by which military force is being used (figure 1.1).

The difference in the principal domains of conflict can be seen in the essential dictionary definitions of the key terms. War is defined as "armed hostile conflict *between* states or nations," intervention as "to interfere usually by force or the threat of force in another nation's *internal* affairs" (emphases added). The one is an interstate conflict intended to transform the international order. The other is an attempt, as Hoffmann puts it, to "try to affect, not the external activities, but the domestic affairs of a state."[5] Both have consequences and reverberations beyond their principal domains—from the outside in and the inside out, respectively—but the point is not to define their limits so much as differentiate their epicenters.

Figure 1.1
Classical Wars and Foreign Military Interventions

	Classical Wars	Foreign Mil. Interventions
Principal Domain	Interstate	Intrastate
Central Objective	Territorial Conquest	Political authority structure
Basic Strategy	Military-Political	Political-Military

All military conflict, as Clausewitz has so often been paraphrased, is continuation of politics by other means. But classical wars and foreign military interventions also differ in the particular type of politics that constitute the central objective being pursued through these other means. Wars generally seek conquest: direct physical control over territory, destruction of military capabilities, often also destruction of the adversary's economic infrastructure. In foreign military interventions the objective is less to control the territory than shape what Oran Young calls "the political authority structure" of the target state.[6] This is to be done in large part coercively, but nevertheless indirectly, through a local ally who is to be assisted in gaining or maintaining power.

With respect to strategy, all wars are not politics by the same "other means." Classical wars tend to be fought with strategies that are primarily military and secondarily political. The armed forces of the attacking state seek to defeat the armed forces of the target. Military forces vs. military forces, decided on the battlefield by the capacity of one side to prevail militarily over the other. Special operations, psychological warfare, counter-terrorism and other unconventional and more political strategies have roles to play, but these are largely supplementary and supportive ones. In foreign military interventions the relative balance is reversed, becoming what can be analytically characterized as a political-military strategy: the goals being pursued are much less readily translatable into operational military objectives, while prevailing militarily is less of a sufficient basis for achieving these objectives. The intervenor thus must seek not only to defeat the adversary on the battlefield, but also to build political support for his local ally. Moreover, although conventional military capabilities have some utility, the fighting goes more to the unconventional, particularly counterinsurgency guerrilla warfare and anti-terrorism.

Thus, the U.S. uses of military force in the Persian Gulf and in Vietnam constitute fundamentally different uses of military force, classical war and foreign military intervention, respectively. The war with Iraq was, in the tradition of World War I and II, fundamentally an interstate war. It began with a naked act of aggression, an attempt by one state (Iraq) to conquer another (Kuwait). The central (albeit not the only) objective pursued by the U.S.-led multinational coalition was to reverse this conquest and to restore internationally recognized territorial boundaries. The principal strategy for achieving this objective was a military one: to directly engage the enemy in combat, and to defeat him by prevailing on the battlefield. In fact,

Operation Desert Storm was consciously stopped short of assuming the role of remaking the internal political order in Iraq (although this objective was at least partially pursued by other means).

In Vietnam, as Larry Berman shows in his chapter, the U.S. strategy was, in contrast, principally a political one: less to directly defeat the adversary than, in Secretary of Defense Robert McNamara's memorable phrase, to win "the hearts and minds" of the people. The central objective had more to do with politically shaping the internal order and less to do with militarily altering the international order. Prevailing on the battlefield thus was both less central in and of itself and more contingent on the other and more political aspects of the overall intervention strategy. As one noted Vietnam veteran (namely General H. Norman Schwarzkopf) later reflected,

> When you commit military forces, you ought to know what you want that force to do. You can't kind of say, "Go out and pacify the entire countryside." There has got to be a more specific definition of exactly what you want that force to accomplish. . . . But when I harken back to Vietnam, I have never been able to find anywhere where we have been able to clearly define in precise terms what the ultimate objectives of our military were.[7]

It also is in this sense that the Syrian and Israeli interventions in Lebanon have something in common with each other and with India's intervention in Sri Lanka that they don't have with the 1948, 1956, 1967 or 1973 Arab–Israeli interstate wars, or that the India–Sri Lanka case doesn't have with India's 1965 and 1971 wars with Pakistan. The other Arab–Israeli wars and the India–Pakistan wars were interstate ones. The objectives were direct military defeat of the adversary, and the strategies largely conventional military ones. But for both Syria and Israel in Lebanon, and for India in Sri Lanka, as our case studies will show, the objectives were much more political and the strategies much more unconventional—in effect, very different uses of military force than either country had ever before attempted.

A related distinction can be made between the Angolan case, with its stakes of political control, and other recent African cases that have involved attempts at territorial conquest, such as the Libyan–French conflicts in the 1970s and 1980s over the Aouzou Strip in Chad. While there was some intermeshing of the internal and interstate conflicts, as Libya and France each sided with already warring factions in the ethnically driven Chadian civil war, Dominique Moisi points out that the defining characteristic of French military involvements in Africa over the past twenty years has been a shift from its earlier immediate post-colonial efforts "aimed at stabilizing leaders of regimes" to defending francophone African states from "external threats."[8] France thus withdrew its troops once an accord was reached with Libya, even though the Chadian government remained embattled from within as the internal political conflict persisted.

Military and Other Forms of Intervention

Military interventions are neither the only nor even the most frequent strategy of intervention. According to Richard Little, they represent "only a small segment of the intervention field."[9] In one study, for example, of thirty-two cases of superpower intervention between 1945 and 1987, only eight involved direct commitments of combat troops.[10] Other possible alternative interventionary strategies range from what Little calls the "verbal intervention" of demarches and other declaratory diplomacy, to economic carrots and sticks of aid and sanctions, to intelligence activities and covert actions, to military strategies short of full-fledged direct intervention (aid, training, advisers, even sporadic incursions).[11] All of these constitute efforts to coercively influence the internal political order of another state. And any or all may be pursued prior to or in addition to crossing the threshold of the direct, continuous, and massive involvement of national military forces.

There are two distinct analytic advantages, methodological and qualitative, to positing this threshold and focusing on cases which cross it. The methodological advantage is that the conceptual boundaries problem, which has plagued more general and inclusive studies of intervention, is mitigated. There never has been agreement—as a matter of analysis, let alone of international law—as to where the lines of state sovereignty are to be drawn. Therefore, it is difficult to determine which actions cross those lines as to become interventionary, or whether particular circumstances (e.g., emergencies, crises, wars) or espoused justifications (ideological, moral, humanitarian) matter.[12] Consequently, as James Rosenau laments, "so many diverse activities, motives, and consequences are considered to constitute intervention that the key terms of most definitions are ambiguous and fail to discriminate empirical phenomena."[13] It even has been argued that nonintervention, or what Hoffmann terms "non-acts," if assessed in terms of effects rather than processes, can be considered

intervention. This, according to Rosenau, "is the height of defini-
tional vagueness."[14]

With the military intervention subset, however, the empirical ref-
erents are much more reliable. "It is relatively easy," as Frederic
Pearson points out, "to identify troop or force movements, and this
definition avoids the ambiguities of others." Pearson further distin-
guishes between cases in which "troops undertook some direct military action, as opposed to longer term relatively inactive encamp-
ment on bases," focusing in his studies only on the former.[15] In a
somewhat similar manner, Melvin Small and J. David Singer use the
commitment of one thousand troops to the battle zone as one of their
criteria for "internationalized civil wars."[16] There is some range to
the levels of troop commitments in our cases, ranging as high as the
550,000 troops the United States committed in Vietnam, but little
ambiguity to the fact that significant numbers of combat troops were
committed in all six cases.[17]

The qualitative advantage is that of the inherently greater importance, in terms of both salience and impact, of military interventions.
"Issues which are present" in other types of intervention, as Little
notes, "become critical" when troops are directly involved.[18] As is
quite evident in our six cases, there is a difference of kind, not just
degree, when the intervenor sends his own troops in. It reverberates
globally and regionally in an entirely different way than other forms
of intervention. It also poses particularly sharp issues within the
domestic politics of the intervening state, with riskier potential costs
that may be imposed and constraints that may be activated. It also
interacts within the target state in ways, and with the potential for a
negative synergy, that are much less likely with other types of intervention.

Protracted and Quick-Decisive Foreign Military Interventions

As acknowledged at the outset, not all foreign military interventions
become protracted ones. Other cases, such as the U.S. interventions
in the Dominican Republic (1965), Grenada (1983) and Panama (1989),
and the Soviet interventions in Hungary (1956) and Czechoslovakia
(1968), are more aptly characterized as "quick-decisive" foreign military interventions.[19]

The question of why some military interventions become protracted and others do not cannot be conclusively answered based on

this study, although in our final chapter we do offer some propositions for further testing. As a matter of conceptualization, the distinction between protracted and quick-decisive military interventions can be operationalized in terms of three descriptive factors: (a) the duration of the military intervention, as measured from the introduction of combat troops to their final withdrawal or draw-down to pre-intervention levels of noncombat stationed forces; (b) the severity of the intervention, as measured by casualties suffered by the intervenor; and (c) the net outcome, in terms both of the intervenor's intended vs. realized objectives, and of the costs he incurred.

The patterns are striking ones indeed. The differences in the duration of the military interventions are between years and even decades, vs. matters of months, weeks, and even days. The shortest of our cases were the 1982–85 Israeli intervention in Lebanon and the 1987–90 Indian intervention in Sri Lanka. The other four cases (U.S. in Vietnam, Soviet Union in Afghanistan, Syria in Lebanon, Cuba and South Africa in Angola) were all of 10 years duration or more. On the other hand, in Panama, for example, the U.S. forces landed in the middle of the night on December 21, 1989 and had achieved most of their objectives by the time the American public woke up the next morning (although it did take about another week to actually capture Manuel Noriega). Similarly, in the Dominican Republic, within five days of the April 28, 1965 invasion, U.S. troops had achieved their objectives. Troop withdrawals from the Dominican Republic began by late May; by mid-June, all Marines had been withdrawn; by mid-November, only one airborne brigade remained.[20] And in Hungary, according to Condoleeza Rice and Michael Fry, the "outcome was secured within 24 hours" of the November 4 invasion.[21] Some strikes, demonstrations, and violent resistance continued, but the situation was sufficiently stabilized four months later for the Soviets to begin to draw down their troops. In Czechoslovakia the first Soviet troops were withdrawn within four months, and within eight months the "decisive result" of Gustav Husak's election as party secretary had been achieved.[22]

The intervenor casualty levels also strike a strong contrast.[23] Compare the 23 casualties the U.S. suffered in Panama, and the 230,398 it suffered in Vietnam; or the 0 Soviet casualties in Czechoslovakia and an estimated 75,000 in Afghanistan. In the other four protracted cases, casualties also were considerable. The Israeli absolute number was lower than the others, but both on a per capita basis and in comparison to Israel's 1967 and 1973 interstate wars, it takes on much greater significance.

While less strictly quantifiable, the differences in net outcomes also strike a strong and discernible pattern. This is *not* to make a simple dichotomy of successes and failures. In one of the protracted cases, Cuba in Angola, the intervenor paid a stiff price but did achieve some of its objectives. In another case, Syria in Lebanon, while at a substantially higher cost and much larger duration, political control eventually was imposed. Nor were there absolutely no gains for India in Sri Lanka, or even arguably for the Soviets in Afghanistan and the U.S. in Vietnam. And on the other side, the successes achieved by the Soviet Union in Eastern Europe and the United States in Latin America were less than total: a "Prague Autumn" ultimately came, some twenty-one years later; even without Noriega Panama is far from stable. The overriding point, however, is to assess the relative gains weighed against the relative costs on an intra-case basis, and to draw cross-case comparisons accordingly.

Summary: Criteria for Case Selection

These three conceptual delimitations yield three key criteria that define and delimit our case set. Our focus is on cases in which (a) political influence was pursued by one state within another by attempting to install or maintain in power a local ally, (b) through a variety of strategies culminating in the direct use of military troops, (c) in an intervention that proved to be protracted. This set of cases, of which the six included herein are representative, can be distinguished from classical wars, other strategies of intervention and quick-decisive military interventions.

Why Study Foreign Military Interventions

The rationale for studying foreign military intervention is essentially twofold. First is the salience of the phenomenon. When foreign military interventions become protracted, as our cases show, they tend to be seminal events. They come to involve considerable investment of human and material resources and affect the fate of individual leaders as well as the political, social, and economic fortunes of both the intervening and the target countries as a whole. Moreover, quite often their consequences transcend the bilateral context and reverberate throughout the regional and even the international system. In many cases the process, let alone the outcome of the intervention continues to affect policies and destinies long after the intervention itself has ended. In this respect, as noted, protracted foreign military interventions have much in common with major interstate wars.

Second is its persistence over time. It is true, as numerous studies have shown, that foreign military interventions were undertaken with particular frequency during the Cold War, and that this could at least be partially attributed to certain system specific factors characteristic of the Cold War era. First, to use Morton Kaplan's term, the "loose bipolar structure" made for zero sum calculations in which each bloc had interests both in "preventing internal changes within the political systems of its members that would move the state out of the bloc or, what is worse, into the other bloc . . . [and in] attempting to bring about changes in the political life of the members of the other bloc that would remove them from that bloc and that might possibly produce a switch in bloc affiliation."[24]

Second, the nuclear balance for its part is also frequently cited as a facilitator if not instigator of military interventions, although there is some disagreement as to whether its instability or stability best explains the link between strategic nuclear deterrence and foreign military interventions in the Third World. Thomas Schelling, among others, has argued that because perceptions of resolve are such a crucial component of the credibility of nuclear deterrence and since you can never be sure when an adversary is taking your measure, the avoidance of nuclear war often required the use of military force at lower levels of violence. Stanley Hoffmann sees it more as "compensation," that it was the very stability of strategic nuclear deterrence that left "ample room for interventions aimed at changing the international milieu by affecting the domestic political make-up of other countries."[25] Either way, a link is postulated.

A third factor was ideology. Even Hans Morgenthau acknowledged that for all the need for realpolitik, the Cold War was "a revolutionary age," in which not just power but also fundamentally conflicting views of the social order were at stake.[26] While ideological arguments have never held up as a sufficient basis for explaining either U.S. or Soviet interventions, the pronouncements of American doctrines (Truman, Eisenhower, Reagan) and of Soviet Marxist-Leninist solidarity were not to be discounted totally. Nor did ideology only come into play for the great powers. It clearly was a key motivation for Cuban intervention in Africa. French interventions in ex-colonies also had their ideological dimensions, although less about communism-anticommunism than about fulfilling this next stage of what in colonial days was considered the national "mission civiliatrice."[27]

There are, however, alternative explanations for the recurrence of foreign military interventions in the Cold War era. These largely center around other factors which came into play during this period that interacted with but were not attributes per se of the Cold War system. The most ubiquitous such factor was the end of colonialism and the creation of many new nation-states. With more nations the opportunities for military intervention, of course, increased. In addition, the difficulties of the early stages of nation-building, especially when combined with economic development and overcoming poverty, meant that many of these new nations also were highly unstable. This is evident in the data collected by J. David Singer and Melvin Small, who identify only 62 civil wars from 1816 to 1945, but 43 from 1945 to 1980; by Luigi Sensi, who puts the number of civil wars at 59 for 1945–1987; by Evan Luard, who characterizes 73 of the 127 wars since 1945 as "internal"; and by Istvan Kende, who finds an increase in the percentage of "not frontier wars" from 73 (1900–1940) to 85 percent.[28]

Moreover, even if these alternatives to the Cold War explanation of the frequency of foreign military intervention in recent decades did not exist, one could validly argue that foreign military intervention is neither a uniquely modern phenomenon, *nor necessarily one that may be a matter of the past now that the Cold War is behind us.* As Oran Young stresses, intervention in the domestic affairs of other states "has been a recurrent fear of the history of international politics." Young cites some of the examples noted earlier from the Pelopponesian era, as well as imperial Rome, which "occupied a position of such dominance in the international system that it could intervene in the affairs of most of the lesser actors in the system with virtual impunity"; from Europe in the 16th and 17th centuries and especially in the Napoleonic and post-Napoleonic periods, in which "the continuing ideological appeal of the French Revolution combined with the power of Napoleonic France to produce a state of ferment in Europe in which intervention and counterintervention became the order of the day."[29] Military interventions were a crucial component in Metternich's design for maintaining the stability of the multipolar Concert of Europe, the way to make compatible a renunciation of conquest with the need to maintain ancien regimes against internal revolution.[30] Also, in the late nineteenth century, even when the balance of power was operating effectively, it was able to "dampen" interventions but not to stop them. In fact, Hoffmann argues that military interventions were inherent in the very logic of the balance:

> The very indifference of the balance towards domestic regimes made it perfectly possible at times for one particular country to intervene in the domestic affairs of a state without being stopped by the others . . . [Thus] when the Russians came in to help the Austrians crush revolutions in Austria or in Hungary, and when the Russians again intervened to crush revolutions in Poland, nobody did anything about it.[31]

Additional examples also can be cited from the early twentieth century, such as the Spanish Civil War, in which Nazi Germany and Fascist Italy intervened (including with elite military units) on the side of Franco.

A further point is that foreign military interventions have not been uniquely characteristic of any particular type of state. The Kantian link between democracy and war proneness does not hold for foreign military interventions.[32] The range of domestic political systems among the intervenors in this study, for example, is quite broad. There are democracies (the United States, Israel, India), partial democracies (South Africa), totalitarian political systems (the Soviet Union) and highly personalized dictatorships (Cuba, Syria). When one also considers that historically the United States has undertaken more military interventions than any other single country, the agnostic nature of the relationship between the type of domestic political system and a propensity for military intervention is further reinforced. And it surely is not the case, late 1980s Soviet behavior toward Eastern Europe notwithstanding, that there is something about non-democracies that disposes them not to be intervenors.

Rather foreign military intervention is one of those phenomena endemic in the quasi-anarchic nature of the international system, irrespective of its particular structure and the particular types of domestic political systems of its major actors. Thus there is no international system structure known in the past or imaginable in the future which is either reassuringly preventive or comfortably non-conducive. Foreign military interventions are even consistent with idealist, realist, and Marxist interpretations of state behavior, which only differ in the attribution of the relative weights to the specific incentives driving the intervention. And while no definitive answer can be given to the question of the frequency at which foreign military interventions might recur now that the Cold War is finally over, there does not appear to be sufficient reason to believe that the future will be any different from the past. They have more to do with the capabilities to intervene, which always have been there and are likely to increase in the future, and with the opportunities to do so. Both have been present within all past system structures—and as we will discuss in the concluding chapter, are likely to be so within any future system structure.

Taken together, the persistence and the salience of the foreign military intervention phenomenon, thus provide a rather solid rationale for studying it. This rationale is further reinforced by certain limitations of earlier studies in this area, which have looked at foreign military intervention using different perspectives and research strategies.

Design of the Study

"Scholarly writings on the problem of intervention," James Rosenau observed more than twenty years ago, "are singularly devoid of efforts to develop systematic knowledge on the conditions under which interventionary behavior is initiated, sustained and abandoned."[33] Our study seeks to contribute to this broader theoretical development through its "bounded generalizability." Previous sections of this chapter have sought to be explicit about the boundedness; i.e., about what our cases are not. The generalizability has three bases.

First, as a comparative study, we are able to identify patterns rather than just single-case phenomenon. The existing body of empirical research is rich in single-case studies. These have considerable virtues, notably depth and richness of detail; but for purposes of theory building single-case studies also suffer from profound limitations, most prominently in overemphasizing the unique features of each case.[34] Thus, while past case studies of intervention have provided rich insights into individual historical instances of intervention, their overall contribution to the study of the intervention phenomenon has been circumscribed by their limited generalizability. Our study takes a broadly based comparative perspective, similar to the one adopted by George and Smoke for the study of deterrence, and by Katzenstein and his collaborators for the study of foreign economic policy.[35]

Second, while limited in their "type" to protracted military interventions, our cases are inclusive of substantial variations among the who, what, when, where, why, and how. The intervenors included superpowers (the United States, Soviet Union), regional powers (Syria, Israel, South Africa, India) and revolutionary powers (Cuba). They were both democracies (United States, Israel, India, South Africa at least partially) and non-democracies (Soviet Union, Syria, Cuba). The target countries were both distant countries (Vietnam, Angola for Cuba) and neighboring ones (Afghanistan, Lebanon for both Israel and Syria, Angola for South Africa, Sri Lanka). The local allies were incumbent regimes in need of buttressing (Ky-Diem in Vietnam, Karmal-Najibullah in Afghanistan, MPLA in Angola), insurgents seeking power (the Lebanese Maronite Phalange for Israel, the Angolan MPLA initially and UNITA throughout), and in some cases the intervenor switched local allies over the course of the intervention (Syria in Lebanon, India in Sri Lanka).

Third, adapting Alexander George's comparative case methodology, there is both a "structuring" and a "focusing" to the design of our study. The three analytic stages—getting in, staying in and getting out—provide the structuring. The focusing is in terms of a common set of questions asked of each case at each stage of three levels of analysis: the international system, the domestic context of the intervening state, and the "indigenous terrain" of the target state. This three-stage analytic framework gives the study depth and richness. Much of the existing literature, as noted by Rosenau, principally focuses on the initiation of military interventions, with much less attention to the staying in and getting out stages. Yet the dynamics cannot be fully understood and the dilemmas revealed without this more systematic analytic approach. In fact, our three stages correspond rather well to Rosenau's initiation, sustaining, and abandoning. It is thus the very "protractedness" of our cases that gives them the multidimensionality necessary for such a comprehensive approach.

The "Getting In" Stage

Taking stock of what we know about why and when states initiate military interventions reveals, in fact, how little we know. It has been said to be "implicit in the logic of the situation. . . . that every internal war creates a demand for foreign intervention."[36] Yet, as noted, states do not always intervene in internal wars, and when they do, military intervention is not the most frequent form. Nor do we get much further via the concept of "vital interests," as in the proposition that states intervene when "vital interests are unmistakably and imminently threatened."[37] Perceptions may then be introduced, as in Morgenthau's even more general proposition that statesmen are "guided in their decisions . . . by what they regard as their respective national interests."[38] There is, however, circularity here in that intervention is said to occur when a vital interest is at stake, and that we know an interest is vital when intervention occurs. Moreover, one of the points that is clear from the historical literature is that decisions to intervene militarily tend to be arrived at gradually and reluctantly. Even in cases which turned out quick and decisive, decision makers opted for military intervention only after other options had been attempted and, seemingly at least, exhausted as well.[39] Yet ultimately some rationale was accepted as compelling, and the decision to "get in" was made.

We thus have posed a number of key questions about the getting in stage of all of our cases: What alternative strategies for exerting political influence were attempted prior to the commitment of combat troops? Why, how, and when was the decision taken to escalate to military intervention? In particular, to what extent was it prompted by an inability to attain the objectives through alternative strategies, a change in the assessment of the threats being posed, and/or a change in the objectives being pursued? Which other considerations (domestic, international) other than the immediate problem posed by the civil strife in the foreign country influenced the decision how and when to intervene? Finally, what were the key tenets of the initial military intervention strategy, in terms of the translation of political goals into military objectives, risk assessments, and the relationships with the local ally?

In answering these questions for each case and then drawing the cross-case comparison, as Charles Kupchan does in his chapter, we are interested in understanding the dynamics of the process by which the critical threshold is crossed from other forms of intervention to the direct and massive commitment of combat troops. We approach this not as a single decision but as a process—as a series of small steps and as the result of a complex interaction of forces. Moreover, as George Downs also discusses in his chapter, it is a process in which uncertainties are inherent .

It is especially the similarities but also the differences, among the cases which interests us both with respect to the paths by which they moved to a direct massive military involvement and in the relative importance of international, domestic, and indigenous factors. What was the relative importance of such international factors as broader global and/or regional interests? What were the key alignments in the domestic politics and decision-making processes of the intervening states among elites (in particular along civil-military lines), as well as from other domestic forces? What assumptions did the intervenor make about his local ally, the adversary and other key aspects of the local political terrain? How accurate did these prove to be?

The "Staying In" Stage

Between getting in and getting out, there is what Eliot Cohen calls "the middle game," or the "staying in" stage. To date there has not been sufficient appreciation of the particular structural dilemmas posed at this stage. Perhaps the Hungary-Czechoslovakias and Dominican Republic-Grenada-Panamas made it all look too easy militarily. Yet as others have argued, even these cases may be unconditionally regarded as brief and successful military interventions only if one evaluates them solely in terms of success in attainment of the short term operational objectives, and takes into account only the duration of the military operations and not the military presence in the foreign country that may have followed it.

In other cases, however, within a few weeks of the culmination of the getting in stage, the staying in begins. This stage is characterized by numerous additional factors—indigenous, domestic, and international—which then come into play and affect the course, duration, and ultimately the fortunes of the military intervention. The staying in stage typically goes through a few phases in the course of which the military commitment and expectation of success are initially high but gradually diminish. It usually ends at a point in which the frustrated leadership of the intervening country lowers its expectations and decides to recalibrate the size of its military commitment with what it reassesses to be its intrinsic value, further costs, and other options. It may then limit or scale back its commitment and/or search for a way of extricating itself entirely from the foreign country by way of a negotiated settlement (preferably), or a unilateral withdrawal (as a last resort).

These present a number of important analytic questions. How and why did the interventionary strategy change over time, particularly with respect to both the relationship between political goals and military objectives and in tactical terms? What were the key dilemmas posed institutionally and organizationally for the military? How were foreign military interventions fought? What strategies and tactics worked better than others? These are highly important questions for each individual case, and a comparative basis provide insights into the dynamics of this "middle game."

The "Getting Out" Stage

As with the staying in stage, we know less about the dynamics of disengagement from foreign military interventions than about their initiations. In certain respects this "getting out" stage is characterized by many of the features typically associated with the termination of war, such as bargaining tactics and escalation of military operations in order to acquire negotiating leverage.[40] However, there are two salient differences. First is that in foreign military interventions the option of disengagement through unilateral withdrawal, while not likely to be considered optimal, is usually a more viable alternative than it is in classical wars, where such a move would equate with surrender of the homeland. Second, and somewhat conversely, while troops may be withdrawn alternative strategies may be more readily employed: military aid, advisers, and other strategies of "troop-less" intervention. Thus disengagement can mean different things in different cases; getting the troops out does not mean getting all the way out. Nevertheless, for the same reasons of magnitude and repercussions that the massing of combat troops is such a critical initial threshold, the military withdrawal of troops also represents a critical transition.

We thus are interested in such key questions as the conditions that lead to consideration of the disengagement option, the factors most conducive to this option being chosen, and the procedures and mechanisms most likely to facilitate its actual implementation. At what point, and prompted by what reasons, do states finally acknowledge that the military intervention has not proven decisive, and that their interests can then be best served by disengaging militarily either partially or completely? Even then, what problems and dilemmas are inherent to the disengagement process? And again, in terms of cross-case analysis, how do international, domestic, and indigenous factors compare in their relative effects on the form, timing, and consequences of the disengagement? In his chapter, George Downs addresses these questions directly as they pertain to the disengagements, as well as linking the disengagement stage back to the earlier stages by assessing the question of uncertainty as it pervades the entire life of the intervention.

Our purpose in this chapter has been to introduce and frame the case studies and cross-case analyses which follow. In the final chapter we consider the conclusions which can be drawn from the study.

Notes

1. Thucydides, *History of the Pelopponesian War*, trans. by R. Warner (Penguin: Hammondsworth, U.K., 1954), p. 208. Thanks also to Andreas Panagopoulos of the University of Athens for elaboration on Thucydides' treatment of the subject.

2. Hans J. Morgenthau, "To Intervene or Not to Intervene," *Foreign Affairs*, 45 (April 1967):425.

3. Alexander L. George, "Case Studies and Theory Development: The Method of Structured, Focused Comparison," in Paul Gordon Lauren ed., *Diplomacy: New Approaches in History, Theory and Policy* (New York: Free Press, 1979), pp. 43–68.

4. Stanley Hoffmann, "The Problem of Intervention," in Hedley Bull ed., *Intervention in World Politics* (Oxford: Clarendon Press, 1984), p. 7.

5. *Ibid.*, p. 10.

6. Oran R. Young, "Intervention and International Systems," *Journal of International Affairs*, 22, no. 2(1968):177–78.

7. C. D. B. Bryan, "Operation Desert Norm," *The New Republic*, March 11, 1991, p. 26.

8. Dominique Moisi, "Intervention in French Foreign Policy," in Bull, *Intervention in World Politics*, pp. 72–73.

9. Richard Little, *Intervention: External Involvement in Civil Wars* (London: Martin Robertson, 1975), p. 11.

10. Luigi Sensi, "Superpower Interventions in Civil Wars, 1945–1987," paper prepared for the 1988 Annual Meeting of the American Political Science Association, Washington, D.C.

11. Little, *Intervention*, pp. 8–11.

12. On the international law and normative debate, see Louis Henkin, et al., *Right v. Might: International Law and the Use of Force* (New York: Council on Foreign Relations, 1989).

13. James N. Rosenau, "Intervention as a Scientific Concept," *Journal of Conflict Resolution* 13 (June 1969):154–155.

14. Hoffmann, "The Problem of Intervention," p. 8; Rosenau, "Intervention as a Scientific Concept," p. 153.

15. Frederic S. Pearson, "Foreign Military Intervention and Domestic Disputes," *International Studies Quarterly* 18 (September 1974):259–289. A number of ambitious efforts to compile data bases on military intervention suffer from the blurring of this distinction, as well as the others discussed in this chapter. See Frederic S. Pearson and Robert A. Baumann, "International Military Intervention, 1946–1988," presented at the 1989 annual conference of the American Political Science Association, Atlanta, Georgia, and Herbert

K. Tillema, "Foreign Overt Military Intervention in the Nuclear Age" (1989), 2:179–195.

16. Melvin Small and J. David Singer, *Resort to Arms: International and Civil Wars* (Beverly Hills: Sage Publishers, 1982), p. 219.

17. The combat troops factor also sets off these cases from others that do involve such military instrumentalities as military and military advisers, intelligence sharing, and other more limited and less direct forms of military involvement. For example, Alex Schmid makes 11 distinctions of types of military assistance and 11 distinctions of limited direct military involvements; A.P. Schmid (with E. Berends), *Soviet Military Interventions Since 1945*, C.O.M.T. Research Report No. 17, W1984–85 (State University of Leiden, The Netherlands), p. 123.

18. Little, *Intervention*, p. 11.

19. The term "quick-decisive" is adapted from a similar use made by Alexander L. George; see his *The Limits of Coercive Diplomacy* (Boston: Little, Brown, 1971), pp. 15–21.

20. Abraham Lowenthal, *The Dominican Intervention* (Boston: Harvard University Press, 1972); Jerome N. Slater, "The Dominican Republic, 1961–66," in Barry M. Blechman and Stephen S.Kaplan, *Force Without War: U.S. Armed Forces as a Political Instrument* (Washington, D.C.: Brookings Institution, 1978), pp. 289–347.

21. Condoleeza Rice and Michael Fry, "The Hungarian Crisis of 1956: The Soviet Decision" in Jonathan R. Adelman ed., *Superpowers and Revolution* (Boulder, Co.: Praeger, 1986); Schmid, *Soviet Military Interveners Since 1945;* Michel Tatu, "Intervention in Eastern Europe," in Stephen S. Kaplan, *Diplomacy of Power: Soviet Armed Forces as a Political Instrument* (Washington, D.C.: Brookings Institution, 1981), pp. 205–264.

22. Philip Windsor, "Yugoslavia, 1951, and Czechoslovakia, 1968," in Barry M. Blechman and Stephen S. Kaplan, *Force Without War: U.S. Armed Forces as a Political Instrument,* (Washington, D.C.: Brookings Institution, 1978), pp. 440–512; Jiri Valenta, *Soviet Intervention in Czechoslovakia, 1968: Anatomy of a Decision* (Baltimore: Johns Hopkins University Press, 1979); Schmid, *Soviet Military Intervention;* Tatu, "Intervention in Eastern Europe."

23. Casting this measure strictly in terms of the casualties suffered by the intervenor is not to imply any moral judgment about the casualties suffered by other forces being any less important. Rather it is reflective of our primary focus in this study being on the policy pursued by the foreign intervenor.

24. Morton A. Kaplan, "Intervention in Internal War," in James N. Rosenau, ed., *International Aspects of Civil Strife* (Princeton: Princeton University Press, 1967), pp. 110–111.

25. Hoffman, "The Problem of Intervention," pp. 17–18.

26. Morgenthau, "To Intervene or Not to Intervene."

27. D. Michael Shafer, *Deadly Paradigms: The Failure of U.S. Counterinsurgency Policy* (Princeton: Princeton University Press, 1988), pp. 135–165.

28. Singer and Small, *Resort to War;* Sensi, "Superpower Interventions; Evan Luard, *The Blunted Sword* (New York: New Amsterdam Books, 1988),

pp. 61–68; Istvan Kende, "Wars of Ten Years," *Journal of Peace Research,* 15(3).

29. Young, "Intervention and International Systems," pp. 178–179.

30. Henry A. Kissinger, *A World Restored: Metternich, Castlereagh and the Problems of Peace, 1812–1822* (Boston: Houghton, Mifflin, 1979).

31. Hoffmann, "The Problem of Intervention," p. 18.

32. Michael W. Doyle, "Liberalism and World Politics," *American Political Science Review* 80 (December 1988):1151–1169; Doyle, "Kant, Liberal Legacies and Foreign Affairs: Part I," *Philosophy and Public Affairs* 12 (1983):205–235, and "Part II," *Philosophy and Public Affairs* 12 (1983):323–353.

33. Rosenau, "Intervention as a Scientific Concept," p. 149.

34. George, "Case Study and Theory Development"; Harry Eckstein, "Case Study and Theory in Political Science," in F. I. Greenstein and N. W. Polsby, eds., *Handbook of Political Science* (Reading, Mass.: Addison-Wesley, 1975), 7:79–138.

35. Alexander L. George and Richard Smoke, *Deterrence in American Foreign Policy: Theory and Practice* (New York: Columbia University Press, 1979); Peter J. Katzenstein ed., *Between Power and Plenty; Foreign Economic Policies of Advanced Industrial States* (Madison: University of Wisconsin Press, 1978).

36. George Modelski, "The International Relations of Internal War," in Rosenau, *International Aspects of Civil Strife,* p. 20.

37. Herbert Dinerstein, *Intervention Against Communism* (Baltimore: Johns Hopkins University Press, 1967), p. 53.

38. Morgenthau, "To Intervene or Not to Intervene," p. 430.

39. In the Hungary case, for example, Khrushchev initially led a majority within the Soviet Politburo opposed to intervention. Efforts were made at compromise as late as October 27–31. Only when Nagy further escalated his challenge by abolishing the one-party system and announcing withdrawal from the Warsaw Treaty Organization did the Soviets invade. In the Czechoslovakia case, Jiri Valenta argues that as late as August 3, 1968 the Soviet Politburo had decided not to intervene militarily.

40. Gordon A. Craig and Alexander L. George, *Force and Statecraft: Diplomatic Problems of our Time* (New York: Oxford University Press, 1990), pp. 229–246.

2

From Intervention to Disengagement: The United States in Vietnam

LARRY BERMAN

China

Nanning

Maoming

Railroad

Loa Cai

NORTH
VIETNAM

Zhanjiang

Hoa
Binh

★ Hanoi

Haiphong

Gulf of Tonkin

Haikou

Louangphrtabang

Thanh
Hoa

HAINAN
(China)

LAOS

Vinh
Ha Tinh

Dongfang

Vientiane

Huong Khe

Nong Khai

Khammoua

Dong Hoi

DMZ

South
China
Sea

Sakon Nakhon

Quang Tri

Khon Kaen

Loa Bao

Hué

THAILAND

Da Nang
Hoi An

Ubon
Ratchathani

Quang Ngai

Khourat

Surin

Sisaket

Cong Tum

Play Cu

Qui Nhon

Song Cau

Battembang

CAMBODIA

SOUTH
VIETNAM

Phnom
Penh

Me Thuot

Pursat

Nha Trang

Da Lat

Phan Rang

Tay Ninh

Ben Hoa

★ Saigon

Long Xuyen

Vung Tau

My Tho

Gulf of Thailand

Ca Mau

Indochina

This article explores the dynamics of foreign military intervention—in this case the gradual escalation of the U.S. commitment to Vietnam from a relatively limited supportive role to covert operations to the utilization of direct but limited military force, which ultimately evolved into protracted and significant military intervention. I am interested in the process by which a set of limited political objectives in an area of regional political instability proved to be elusive, so that the United States was drawn into a major international intervention with divisive domestic consequences. The United States moved incrementally from 23,000 American advisory personnel in Vietnam in January 1965 to an open-ended commitment of American fighting forces on July 28—a commitment that in three years was to reach a half million troops. By 1973 the nation had disengaged its military forces without accomplishing the original objectives of intervention. How did it happen? Why was the policy of intervention pursued for so long and with such intensity? How and why did the United States disengage when it did?

Stage I: Getting In

In May 1950, a month before the outbreak of hostilities in Korea, Secretary of State Dean Acheson announced the first increment of American aid to the French for the Indochina war. The bitter recriminations in the United States over "Who lost China?" produced a compelling domestic incentive for the Truman administration to do what it could to prevent a Communist victory in Indochina. The Korean conflict amplified the concern of American policy makers about Communist advances in Asia, persuading them that "world communism" was bent on dominating that portion of the world.[1]

In December 1950 the United States joined France, Vietnam, Cambodia, and Laos in signing the Mutual Defense Assistance Agreement. The United States agreed to provide military supplies and equipment through an American military advisery group. This small contingent of U.S. advisers provided limited logistical services; all supplies and equipment were dispensed through the French Expeditionary Corps. Year by year, American aid to the French Indochina military effort mounted: from $130 million in 1950 to $800 million in 1953.

The loss of Southeast Asia was defined as threatening the security of the United States and the collectivity of Free World nations. The sovereignties of Vietnam as well as other Southeast Asian countries were valued not for their own merit, but rather as a test of U.S. global position and credibility—a perception that would have a profound impact on the nature of the decision to intervene. Vietnam, or more specifically not losing Vietnam, became an increasingly important component in U.S. global interests.

As a consequence of the Korean War the political climate became profoundly antagonistic to further use of American troops on the Asian mainland. Nevertheless, Eisenhower and his associates were as convinced as the Truman administration had been of Indochina's strategic importance. What inhibited the new president from pressing the French to grant independence to the Indochinese was the fear that the war-weary French would simply withdraw, removing the "cork in the bottle," which in the American view prevented Communist forces from spreading throughout Southeast Asia, if not further. Moreover, the French might thwart American policy by failing to ratify the European Defense Community (EDC) Treaty and thus block the administration's preferred means of bringing about German rearmament.

In May 1953, the French government appointed General Henri Navarre commander in Vietnam and charged him with mounting a major new offensive against the Viet Minh. Two months later the new French government of Joseph Laniel promised to "perfect" Vietnamese independence. The Navarre Plan called for a significant infusion of Vietnamese recruits and French regulars into the anti-Communist military force and a change in strategy to large-force actions that would inflict major casualties on the Viet Minh. One of the Navarre's first moves, late in 1953, was to dispatch a major French unit of crack troops to Dien Bien Phu, the juncture of a number of roads in northwestern Indochina about 100 miles from the Chinese border. He viewed the site, a valley surrounded by 1000-foot hills, as ideal to trap the Viet Minh into engaging in a bloody assault. Navarre had barely fortified Dien Bien Phu when the Viet Minh took the bait, but moved in with such force that they made Dien Bien Phu a trap for the French.[2]

By early January 1954, Eisenhower and his advisers recognized that the situation in Dien Bien Phu was serious and that a French defeat might topple the Laniel government, lead the French to sue for peace, and probably also lead to a French government that would reject EDC. From January through early April, the administration grappled with the crisis produced by the siege of Dien Bien Phu. In doing so it explored two broad policy options: a surgical air strike and the formation of a multinational coalition to resist the Communist advance. Meanwhile it played an intricate game of coordination and accommodation with domestic political leaders and the French. Yet, given the opportunity to assist France by intervening militarily, President Eisenhower decided not to enter a French colonial war that the United States had backed with funds but no military commitment.

On May 7, 1954, the French forces were defeated at Dien Bien Phu and shortly thereafter concluded the "Final Declaration of the Geneva Conference on the Problem of Restoring Peace in Indochina." The Geneva agreements primarily settled military and not political issues. They provisionally divided Vietnam at the Seventeenth Parallel pending free unifying elections in the North and South that were to have been held by July 1956. Neither the United States nor the Vietnamese government signed the accords, although the U.S. issued a declaration committing itself to refrain from using force to disturb the cease fire and stating that it would view any aggression as a serious threat to international peace and security.[3]

Three months following Dien Bien Phu, President Eisenhower convened his National Security Council in order to review U.S. policy in the Far East. The president was already on record that "strategically South Vietnam's capture by the communists would bring their power several hundred miles into a hitherto free region. The remaining countries in Southeast Asia would be menaced by a great flanking movement. The freedom of 12 million people would be lost immediately and that of 150 million others in adjacent lands would be seriously endangered. The loss of South Vietnam would have grave consequences for us and for freedom."[4] Not losing Southeast Asia became the goal of the United States in the region. The NSC meeting resulted in one of the most important "early" decisions of America's initial involvement: the United States replaced France as the direct supplier of financial and military assistance to South Vietnam.

In September 1954 the United States, the United Kingdom, France, Australia, New Zealand, Thailand, Pakistan, and the Philippines signed the Southeast Asia Collective Defense Treaty (which created SEATO). Each of the signatories accepted an obligation to assist one another against "aggression by means of armed attack;" South Viet-

nam, Laos, and Cambodia were protocol states to SEATO. Where
SEATO involved multilateral relations, the United States solidified its
commitment in several bilateral agreements with South Vietnam and
also began sending military personnel for purposes of training a
South Vietnamese Armed Forces and mobile civil guard. In a letter to
the President of South Vietnam, Ngo Dinh Diem, President Eisenhower was exceedingly clear: "I am, accordingly, instructing the
American Ambassador to Vietnam to examine with you in your
capacity as chief of Government, how an intelligent program of
American aid given directly to your Government can serve to assist
Vietnam in its present hour of trial, provided that your Government
is prepared to give assurances as to the standards of performance it
would be able to maintain in the event such aid were supplied. The
purpose of this offer is to assist the Government of Vietnam in
developing and maintaining a strong, viable state, capable of resist-
ing attempted subversion or aggression through military means."[5]
The U.S. Operations Mission was established in 1955 as an adjunct
to the U.S. Embassy. The mission was charged with channeling
advice and financial support to help Diem solve South Vietnam's
economic problems. In 1955 alone the United States provided more
than $322 million in economic aid and played a major role in estab-
lishing the National Bank of Vietnam.

Diem, who initially appeared to be making successful strides in
rehabilitating the economy of South Vietnam, failed to cultivate broad
popular support. In consolidating power, Diem's regime became
increasingly repressive. By brazenly favoring Vietnam's Catholic minority with respect to political patronage and basic freedoms, Diem
alienated the far larger Buddhist population. Diem, whose authoritarian techniques included the abolition of all opposing political parties, strictly enforced press censorship, and brutal repression of the
Buddhists, destroyed the chance to build a democratic nationalism as
a counterbalance to Vietnamese communism. By 1959 Hanoi committed its political and military apparatus in the South to the struggle for
unification. Thousands of trained military leaders were sent into the
South for purposes of overthrowing the Diem government. These
cadres provided the core for the Viet Cong military. Infiltration into
the South increased substantially in 1959 and on September 10, 1960,
guidelines were established for what would become the National
Front for the Liberation of South Vietnam.

Vietnam loomed as a test of the Kennedy administration's inau-
gural commitment "to pay any price, to bear any burden, in the
defense of freedom." By October 1961 mounting Viet Cong pressure

led President Diem to *request military support* from the United States—specifically, ground troops to bolster the South Vietnamese army. Before acting on this request, President Kennedy dispatched General Maxwell Taylor and Walt Rostow (deputy special assistant to the president for national security affairs) to Vietnam to investigate the question of U.S. troop requirements. Following two weeks of survey work, Taylor confirmed the gloomy military situation. Taylor recommended that an *8000-man logistical task force* of engineers, medics, and infantry be sent to the South for purposes of base security. The task force would operate under the guise of providing such humanitarian effort as flood relief operations in the delta, but would really serve as a *"visible symbol of the seriousness of American intentions."* General Taylor believed that these troops might be forced to engage in combat to protect themselves or their working parties. "As a general reserve, they might be thrown into action (with U.S. agreement) against large, formed guerrilla bands which have abandoned the forests for attacks on major targets." Taylor was unperturbed about "the risks of backing into a major Asian war" which he acknowledged were *"present"* but *"not impressive."* [6]

The object of U.S. policy was still to do all that was possible without use of combat forces. This was most evident in the Kennedy administration's embrace of the doctrine of counterinsurgency—which involved a range of overt and covert activities by special forces, psychological warfare, intelligence collection, technical assistance, propaganda campaigns, etc. Covert operations in Vietnam now assumed a new level of intensity. Unmarked U.S. bombers operating under the code name "Operation Farmgate," for example, began attacks on the enemy's rearbase and infrastructure. According to Paul Kattenburg, State Department Director of Vietnam Affairs during 1963–64, "from Saigon, the CIA was masterminding elaborate intelligence collection nets and, in collaboration with Diem's security services and Ngo Dinh Nhu's political cadres and special forces, endeavoring to uncover and remove recalcitrant elements and to stimulate support for the Diem regime." [7]

The United States continued to have a great deal of trouble dealing with its local ally. Diem's government had evolved into a family oligarchy, which governed through force. To nationalists like Bui Diem, "it seemed absurd to us that the United States would place its influence and prestige behind such a man. Among ourselves, we said that the Americans must be blind, that they had their heads in the sand, that despite their immense strength, they were allowing themselves to be manipulated in their own worst interest." [8] The

American policy makers soon reached the same conclusion: on November 1, 1963, Diem was removed from office and murdered in the back of an American-built personnel carrier. The coup was planned and implemented by officers in the South Vietnamese Air Force (RVNAF), but U.S. Ambassador Henry Cabot Lodge and the CIA were certainly involved. President Kennedy, given the opportunity to instruct Lodge that the coup be stopped, issued no such orders.

Diem's death was followed by a period of great instability in Saigon, but it was also a period of great hope. The removal of Diem was viewed by many Vietnamese as a positive step toward the goal of building democratic institutions in Vietnam. Yet, the United States failed to articulate its true national interest in Vietnam. The factors which motivated support of French colonialism and later Diem stood in stark contrast with the idealism surrounding the flourishing of democratic institutions, free elections, and self-determination.

Indeed, three weeks following Diem's murder, President Kennedy was assassinated in Dallas. Reporting from Saigon on December 21, 1963, Secretary of Defense McNamara noted that "the situation is very disturbing. Current trends, unless reversed in the next 2–3 months, will lead to neutralization at best and more likely to a communist-controlled state. The new government is the greatest source of concern."[9] Ambassador Taylor cabled President Lyndon Johnson that the situation in Vietnam was so bad that perhaps U.S. policy makers had not appreciated their local ally: "Until the fall of Diem and the experience gained from the events of the following months, I doubt that anyone appreciated the magnitude of the centrifugal political forces which had been kept under control by his iron rule. The successive political upheavals and the accompanying turmoil which have followed Diem's demise upset all prior U.S. calculations as to the duration and outcome of the counter-insurgency in South Vietnam and the future remains uncertain today. There is no adequate replacement for Diem in sight."[10]

American complicity in the coup not only undermined U.S. political standing in Vietnam but also tied it to succeeding regimes. President Johnson believed that the United States was responsible for the fate of successive governments in South Vietnam. Moreover, with Diem removed there would be little future leverage in credibility with our local ally. According to Ambassador Taylor, "Diem's overthrow set in motion a sequence of crises, political and military, over the next two years which eventually forced President Johnson in 1965 to choose between accepting defeat or introducing American combat forces."[11] General Westmoreland's assessment was even more acute:

"The young president, in his zeal, made the unfortunate mistake of approving our involvement in the overthrow of President Diem in South Vietnam. This action morally locked us in Vietnam."[12]

Momentum was building in favor of any action which might change the disintegrating political outlook in South Vietnam. The Joint Chiefs of Staff now prepared a contingency bombing program of graduated military pressure against North Vietnam and covert operations along the North Vietnamese coast. These operations included U.S. patrol boat missions against North Vietnamese coastal installations. The U.S. Navy also began De Soto patrols by sending destroyers up the Gulf of Tonkin for intelligence-gathering purposes. On August 2, 1964, the destroyer *Maddox* was returning from one of these electronic espionage missions when North Vietnamese torpedo boats fired on her. Rather than withdrawing U.S. ships from this danger zone, the president ordered another destroyer, the *C. Turner Joy*, to join the *Maddox* in the Gulf of Tonkin. On August 4, both the *Maddox* and the *C. Turner Joy* reportedly came under attack.[13]

The president later met with congressional leaders and sought assurance that his action would be supported. On August 10, 1964, Congress passed the Southeast Asia Resolution, which authorized Johnson "to take all necessary measures to repeal any armed attack against the forces of the United States and to prevent further aggression." With the election against Barry Goldwater less than three months away, however, President Johnson had no desire of being portrayed as planning for war. Instead, he left the rhetoric of war to Goldwater and the planning with his Joint Chiefs and Defense Department.

Instability in Saigon served as a catalyst for the communists' goal of overthrowing the government in the South. By late 1964 the Viet Cong were increasing their terrorist attacks on U.S. installations. In a top secret December 1964 cable to Ambassador Maxwell Taylor, the president went to unusual lengths in communicating the limits of his policy options: "I have never felt that this war will be won from the air." Johnson informed Taylor that he was "ready to look with great favor" on an increased ground effort "although I know that it may involve the acceptance of larger American sacrifices . . . we have been building our strength to fight this kind of war ever since 1961, and I myself am ready to substantially increase the number of Americans in Vietnam if it is necessary to provide this kind of fighting force against the Viet Cong."[14]

The bombing of U.S. Army barracks at Pleiku triggered a sequence of events that quickly led to placing American combat forces on the ground in South Vietnam. Eight Americans were killed and more than one hundred wounded in the attack. On February 7, the day after the Viet Cong attack at Pleiku, Johnson issued a prophetic public statement: "We have *no* choice now but to clear the decks and make absolutely clear our continued determination to back South Vietnam in its fight to maintain its independence." From Pleiku, McGeorge Bundy (on his initial visit to Vietnam) cabled LBJ that "the prospect in Vietnam is grim . . . the situation in Vietnam is deteriorating and without a new U.S. action defeat appears inevitable . . . the stakes in Vietnam are extremely high. The American investment is very large . . . the international prestige of the United States, and a substantial part of our influence, are directly at risk in Vietnam . . . and there is no way of negotiating ourselves out of Vietnam which offers any serious promise at present . . . any negotiated U.S. withdrawal today would mean surrender on the installment plan." [15]

In response to the attack at Pleiku, Johnson announced the deployment to South Vietnam of a HAWK air defense battalion and rather casually observed that "other reinforcements, in units and individuals may follow." These reinforcements, sent within the next month, consisted of fully equipped ground combat units to protect air bases and proved to be the first step in an American commitment to a ground war in Vietnam. Within hours of the attack, LBJ ordered Flaming Dart reprisal air attacks against preselected North Vietnamese targets. Flaming Dart did not deter the enemy and on February 10 the Vietcong struck again, attacking a hotel at Qui Nhon, a coastal city 85 miles east of Pleiku. Twenty-three members of the 140th Maintenance Detachment of an Army aircraft repair unit were killed, more than twenty-one others wounded. This time the U.S. response would not be characterized as tit-for-tat. On February 13, 1965 President Johnson authorized ROLLING THUNDER, the systematic and expanding bombing campaign against North Vietnamese targets. As suggested by the code name, the bombing would come and go, at first mostly south of the 20th parallel, but soon moving with increasing frequency over all North Vietnam and boundaries with Laos and Cambodia. By 1967–68, the Hanoi-Haiphong region became the focus of Rolling Thunder attacks.

As the pace of the air war quickened, the decision to introduce American combat forces simultaneously evolved. General Westmoreland soon requested that two battalion landing teams of Marines—3500 men—be assigned to guard the key air base at Da Nang. The initial decision to intervene received extraordinary favorable public response and was also praised on Capitol Hill. Ambassador Taylor later wrote, "it was curious how hard it had been to get authorization for the initiation of the air campaign against the North and how relatively easy to get the Marines ashore." [16]

Within two weeks of the Marines' arrival at Danang, U.S. Army Chief of Staff Harold K. Johnson requested an additional deployment of three divisions to Vietnam. At an April 1, 1965 National Security council meeting, LBJ approved two additional division deployments (as well as 20,000 support troops) and extended their role beyond mere base security. This appears to be the "break point"; the U.S. had moved from Rolling Thunder air strikes to passive base defense to aggressive base defense. Only a general combat role remained. On June 7, 1965 General Westmoreland ("acutely aware of the gravity of my conclusions") informed Washington that South Vietnam would fall unless the United States committed forty-four battalions to Southeast Asia (at the time there were approximately 75,000 U.S. troops in Vietnam). "I made up my mind," Westmoreland recalled, "that if the United States intended to achieve its goals of denying the enemy victory in South Vietnam, Washington had to face the task realistically. Without substantial American ground combat troops, I concluded the South Vietnamese would be unable to withstand the pressure from combined Viet Cong and North Vietnamese forces." Westmoreland viewed the military crisis as a byproduct of Saigon's internal political problems: "With governments coming and going as if Saigon was a revolving door, I could see little possibility of the South Vietnamese themselves overcoming the military crisis." [17]

The introduction of troops on foreign soil was premised on U.S. policy makers' belief in the unattainability of achieving a political objective without military intervention. "The Americanization of the Vietnam war, which took place so abruptly and imperiously in the spring of 1965, had a long, significant history," wrote Bui Diem. "It was a history of the perennial failure of American diplomacy to foster a vital South Vietnamese democracy capable of handling its own affairs and worthy of partnership in the common struggle against communism. . . . The first eleven years of the United States' relationship with an independent South Vietnam set a deadly pattern. The Americans first watched the rise and fall of civilian and military dictators without attempting to use their influence decisively for something better. Then, horrified by the resulting mess, they took the whole ball of wax into their hands, intervening with massive military might. They did this suddenly and unilaterally, without consulting their ally in any meaningful way. In effect, they had worked themselves into a corner from which they could only escape—or so they thought—by making the war American. Later they would discover that Americanization, too, was a cul-de-sac." [18]

Stage II: Staying In

Throughout June and July of 1965 the question of Americanizing the war was at the center of all foreign policy discussion. [19] Undersecretary of State George Ball first attempted to influence President Johnson's future ability to control events. In a June 18 memo he titled "Keeping the Power of Decision in the South Vietnam Crisis," Ball argued that the United States was on the threshold of a new war. "In raising our commitment from 50,000 to 100,000 or more men and deploying most of the increment in combat roles we were beginning a new war—the United States directly against the Viet Cong. The President's most difficult continuing problem in South Vietnam is to prevent 'things' from getting into the saddle—or, in other words, to keep control of policy and prevent the momentum of events from taking command."

The president needed to understand the effect of losing control: "Perhaps the large-scale introduction of American forces with their concentrated fire power will force Hanoi and the Viet Cong to the decision we are seeking. On the other hand, we may not be able to fight the war successfully enough—even with 500,000 Americans in South Vietnam we must have more evidence than we now have that our troops will not bog down in the jungles and rice paddies—while we slowly blow the country to pieces." Ball tried to review the French experience for Johnson, reminding the president that "the French fought a war in Vietnam, and were finally defeated—after seven years of bloody struggle and when they still had 250,000 combat-hardened veterans in the field, supported by an army of 205,000 South Vietnamese. To be sure, the French were fighting a colonial war while we are fighting to stop aggression. But when we have put enough Americans on the ground in South Vietnam to give the appearance of a white man's war, the distinction as to our ultimate purpose will have less and less practical effect."

Ball urged the president to act cautiously—make a commitment to the 100,000 level—but no more. The summer would then be used as a test of U.S. military performance and South Vietnam's resolve. Ball focused on the political context in South Vietnam. "We cannot be sure how far the cancer has infected the whole body politics of South

Vietnam and whether we can do more than administer a cobalt treatment to a terminal case." [In a later memo Ball wrote "politically, South Vietnam is a lost cause. The country is bled white from twenty years of war and the people are sick of it. . . . Hanoi has a government and a purpose and a discipline. The 'government' in Saigon is a travesty. In a very real sense, South Vietnam is a country with an army and no government. In my view, a deep commitment of United States forces in a land war in South Vietnam would be a catastrophic error. If ever there was an occasion for a tactical withdrawal, this is it."] Ball recommended that the President direct his top advisors to prepare a plan for accelerating the land war, a plan for a vigorous diplomatic offensive designed to bring about a political settlement; and, perhaps most difficult plans for bringing about a military or political solution—"short of the ultimate U.S. objectives—that can be attained without the substantial further commitment of U.S. forces." Ball recognized that his last proposal should "be regarded as plans for cutting losses and eventually disengaging from an untenable situation."

Ball's arguments would have little influence on policy makers.[20] In retrospect there was a remarkable cogency to his position which fell on deaf ears. Ball was isolated from the majority opinion among policy makers, an Undersecretary of State taking on the highest ranking officials in government—beginning with the Secretary of Defense, Robert McNamara, and Ball's own superior, Secretary of State Dean Rusk. On June 26 McNamara circulated his "Program of Expanded Military and Political Moves with Respect to Vietnam." McNamara admitted that the Viet Cong were clearly winning the war and "the tide almost certainly cannot begin to turn in less than a few months and may not for a year or more; the war is one of attrition and will be a long one." McNamara defined winning as "to create conditions for a favorable settlement by demonstrating to the VC/DRV that the odds are against their winning. Under present conditions, however, the chances of achieving this objective are small—and the VC are winning now—largely because the ratio of guerrilla to anti-guerrilla forces is unfavorable to the government." Secretary McNamara developed three options for the president: (1) cut U.S. losses and withdraw with the best conditions that can be arranged; (2) continue at about the present level, with U.S. forces limited to about 75,000, holding on and playing for the breaks while recognizing that the U.S. position will probably grow weaker; (3) expand substantially the U.S. military pressure against the Viet Cong in the

South and the North Vietnamese in the North. At the same time launch a vigorous effort on the political side to get negotiations started.

McNamara unequivocally supported the third option—a series of expanded military moves as prerequisites for a negotiated settlement on U.S. terms. The secretary recommended that US/GVN ground strength be increased to whatever force levels were necessary to show the VC that they "cannot win." The increases would bring U.S. and third-country troop levels to forty-four battalions and be accomplished by a call-up of 100,000 Reserves. McNamara's military recommendations included a quarantine on the movement of all war supplies into North Vietnam, the mining of North Vietnam's (DRV) harbors, the destruction of all rail and highway bridges from China to Hanoi, armed reconnaissance of communication lines from China, destruction of all war-making supplies inside of North Vietnam, and destruction of all airfields and SAM sites.

Writing directly to McNamara on June 30, National Security Advisor McGeorge Bundy quickly criticized the secretary's position, deriding it as "rash to the point of folly." Bundy was critical of tripling the U.S. air effort "when the value of the air action we have taken is sharply disputed." It was also preposterous to consider mining "at a time when nearly everyone agrees the real question is not in Hanoi, but in South Vietnam." Bundy was extremely critical of McNamara's proposed deployment figure, arguing that a 200,000 man level was based "simply on the increasing weakness of Vietnamese forces. But this is a slippery slope toward the U.S. responsibility and corresponding fecklessness on the Vietnamese side." Bundy noted that McNamara's paper "omits examination of the upper limit of U.S. liability." Bundy asked, "If we need 200 thousand men now for these quite limited missions, may we not need 400 thousand later? Is this a rational course of action? Is there any real prospect that U.S. regular forces can conduct the anti-guerrilla operations which would probably remain the central problem in South Vietnam?" Bundy concluded with a question: "what is the real object of the exercise? If it is to get to the conference table, what results do we seek there? Still more brutally, do we want to invest 200,000 men to cover an eventual retreat? Can we not do that just as well where we are?"

Assistant Secretary of State William Bundy joined the battle with a memo and position paper titled "A Middle Way Course of Action in South Vietnam." The plan involved moving ahead slowly and testing military capabilities and limits. Bundy believed that his plan avoided the pitfalls of either Ball or McNamara's alternatives. "It may not give us quite as much chance of a successful outcome as the major military actions proposed in the McNamara memo, but it avoids to a major extent the very serious risks involved in this program in any case, and the far more disastrous outcome that would eventuate if we acted along the lines of the McNamara memo and still lost South Vietnam." William Bundy's program rejected withdrawal or negotiating concessions and equally rejected a decision to raise U.S. forces level above 85,000. In Bundy's carefully selected words the program provided "a fair test" since we simply do not know, and probably cannot know, whether raising the U.S. force level and combat involvement would (1) cause the Vietnamese government and especially the army to let up (2) create adverse public reactions to our whole presence on 'white men' and 'like the French' grounds."

Johnson next heard from his Secretary of State, Dean Rusk. In a rare personal memorandum to the president on July 1, which had not been circulated to the other principals, Rusk argued that "the central objective of the United States in South Vietnam must be to insure that North Vietnam not succeed in taking over or determining the future of South Vietnam by force, i.e. again defined as denial. We must accomplish this objective without a general war if possible." The war aim of the United States was not and could not be concerned with hypothetical issues such as what the South Vietnamese people would do if left alone: "The sole basis for employing U.S. forces is the aggression from the North." If this aggression was removed, the U.S. forces would also leave. Rusk rejected Ball's position by casting the issue within a much broader context with significant consequences. "There can be no serious debate about the fact that we have a commitment to assist the South Vietnamese to resist aggression from the North. . . . The integrity of the U.S. commitment is the principal pillar of peace throughout the world. If that commitment becomes unreliable, the communist world would draw conclusions that would lead to our ruin and almost certainly to a catastrophic war."

At this stage in the process, McGeorge Bundy wrote directly to President Johnson on July 1, "I think you may want to have pretty tight and hard analyses of some disrupted questions like the following: 1) What are the chances of our getting into a white man's war with all the brown men against us or apathetic? 2) How much of the McNamara planning would be on a contingency basis with no decision until August or September? 3) What would a really full political and public relations campaign look like in both the Bundy option and the McNamara option? 4) What is the upper limit of our liability if we now go to 44 battalions? 5) Can we frame this program in such a way as to keep very clear our own determination to keep the war limited? (This is another way of stating question 4.) 6) Can we get a cold, hard look at the question whether the current economic and political situation in Vietnam is so very bad that it may come apart even before this program gets into action? (I don't believe that it is that bad, but no one seems to be really sure of the facts today.)"

President Johnson now decided to send Secretary McNamara to Vietnam, ostensibly to meet with General Westmoreland and ascertain force requirements. McNamara's trip received much public attention and the president's public statement hinted at the possibility of major escalation. On the second day of McNamara's visit to Saigon, he received a back channel cable of the utmost importance from his deputy, Cyrus Vance. "Yesterday I met three times with highest authority [President Johnson] on actions associated with 34 battalion plan," the cable read. (The remaining ten battalions of the forty-four-battalion request were to come from Korea and Australia.) Vance went on to summarize what Johnson had told him [this is perhaps the most significant declassification available to scholars]:

1. It is his current intention to proceed with 34 battalion plan.
2. It is impossible for him to submit supplementary budget request of more than $300-$400 million to Congress before next January.
3. If larger request is made to Congress, he believes this will kill domestic legislative program.
4. We should be prepared to explain to the Congress that we have adequate authority and funds, by use of deficit financing, $700 million supplemental [appropriation] and possible small current supplemental to finance recommended operations until next January, when we will be able to come up with clear and precise figures as to what is required.

I asked highest authority whether request for legislation authorizing call-up of reserves and extension of tours of duty would be acceptable in the light of his comments concerning domestic program, and he said that it would.

I pointed out that we would have great difficulties with Senator Stennis concerning this course of action. He said that he recognized that but we would just have to bull it through. He requested that I talk to Senator Russell Monday and I will.

Johnson had clearly made his decision to Americanize the war by changing the entire context of commitment. When McNamara returned to Washington on July 20, he presented the president with a report warning of the incipient collapse of South Vietnam. McNamara elaborated and defended an option of "expand[ing] promptly and substantially the US military pressure . . . while launching a vigorous effort on the political side. . . ." McNamara called for approval of Westmoreland's request for 100,000 more American troops, which would bring the American troop level up to thirty-four battalions (175,000 troops), or forty-four battalions (200,000) if "third country" troops (principally Korean) proved unavailable. He indicated that a twenty-seven-battalion second-phase increase of 100,000 further men might be needed by early 1966, with further increments thereafter. McNamara also urged the president to ask Congress to permit calling up 235,000 reservists to active service and to provide a supplemental appropriation to cover the increased costs of the war.

The McNamara proposal became the focal point of extensive White House deliberations over the next few days. At both the NSC meeting of July 21 and the Joint Chiefs meeting of July next day, Johnson provides ample evidence of his awareness that an upper limit deployment might very well be in the range of 600,000 men. At one meeting he turned to McNamara and asked "now let Bob tell us why we need to risk those 600,000 lives." The declassified minutes from the meetings of July 21 show that Johnson challenged Ball to prove a case which could not be proven—that the consequences of nonengagement (really disengagement via neutralization) would be better than military engagement. "You have pointed out the danger," President Johnson told Ball, "but you haven't really proposed an alternative course." To illustrate just how intent policy makers had become in molding their local ally during the meeting, Henry Cabot Lodge noted that "there is not a tradition of a national government in Saigon. There are no roots in the country. Not until there is tranquility can you have any stability. I don't think we ought to take this government seriously. There is simply no one who can do anything. We have to do what we think we ought to do regardless of what the Saigon government does. As we move ahead on a new phase, we have the right and the duty to do certain things with or without the government's approval."

Ball's final day in court came that afternoon when he faced the president and peers. Ball told the group that "we cannot win, Mr. President. The war will be long and protracted. The most we can hope for is a messy conclusion. There remains a great danger of intrusion by the Chinese. But the biggest problem is the problem of the long war. The Korean experience was a galling one. The correlation between Korean casualties and public opinion showed support stabilized at 50 percent. As casualties increase, the pressure to strike at the very jugular of North Vietnam will become very great. I am concerned about world opinion. If we could win in a year's time, and win decisively, world opinion would be alright. However, if the war is long and protracted, as I believe it will be, then we will suffer because the world's greatest power cannot defeat guerrillas." Reprinted below is part of the dialogue which followed Ball's recommendation:

THE PRESIDENT: But George, wouldn't all these countries say that Uncle Sam was a paper tiger, wouldn't we lose credibility breaking the word of three presidents, if we did as you have proposed? It would seem to be an irresponsible blow. But I gather you don't think so?

BALL: No sir. The worse blow would be that the mightiest power on earth is unable to defeat a handful of guerrillas.

THE PRESIDENT: Then you are not basically troubled by what the world would say about our pulling out?

BALL: If we were actively helping a country with a stable government, it would be a vastly different story. Western Europeans look upon us as if we got ourselves into an imprudent situation . . .

MCNAMARA: Ky will fall soon. He is weak. We can't have elections there until there is physical security, and even then there will be no elections because as Cabot said, there is no democratic tradition.

MCGEORGE BUNDY: To accept Ball's argument would be a radical switch in policy without visible evidence that it should be done. George's analysis gives no weight to losses suffered by the other side. The world, the country, and the Vietnamese people would have alarming reactions if we got out.

RUSK: If the communist world found out that the United States would not pursue its commitment to the end, there was no telling where they would stop their expansionism.

LODGE: I feel there is greater threat to start World War III if we don't go in. Can't we see the similarity to our indolence at Munich? I simply can't be as pessimistic as Ball. We have great seaports in Vietnam. We don't need to fight on roads. We have the sea. Let us visualize meeting the VC on our own terms. We don't have to spend all our time in the jungles. If we can secure our bases, the Vietnamese can secure, in time, a political movement to, one, apprehend the terrorists, and two, give intelligence to the government. The procedures for this are known . . . The Vietnamese have been dealt more casualties than, per capita, we suffered in the Civil War. The Vietnamese soldier is an uncomplaining soldier. He has ideas he will die for.

The following day President Johnson met with the Joint Chiefs to hear their responses to McNamara's program. The Chiefs were in a position similar to Ball, in the sense of advocating a policy extreme. The President began the meeting by identifying the three options: "The options open to us are: one, leave the country, with as little loss as possible; two, maintain present force and lose slowly, three, add 100,000 men, recognizing that may not be enough and adding more next year. The disadvantages of number three option are the risk of escalation, casualties high, and the prospect of a long war without victory. I would like you to start out by stating our present position as you see it, and where we can go."

The chiefs warned Johnson that the time had arrived to increase the ante. "If we continue the way we are now," warned Admiral McDonald, "it will be a slow, sure victory for the other side. But putting more men in it will turn the tide and let us know what further we need to do. I wish we had done this long before." When Johnson asked if 100,000 men would be enough, McDonald responded that "sooner or later we will force them to the conference table." Johnson then asked about the chances for success, Paul Nitze answered "if we want to turn the tide, by putting in more men, it would be about sixty-forty." Nitze told Johnson that another 100,000 would be needed by January 1966. When Johnson asked what type of reaction this would produce, General Wheeler noted "since we are not proposing an invasion of the North, the Soviets will step up material and propaganda, and the same with the Chicoms. The North Vietnamese might introduce more regular troops. . . . the one thing all North Vietnam fears is the Chinese. For them to invite Chinese volunteers is to invite China taking over North Vietnam. The weight of judgment is that North Vietnam may reinforce their troops, but they can't match us on a buildup."

The discussion soon turned to the real crux of the matter for LBJ— the costs of escalation and the change in mission. When Admiral McDonald recommended giving Westmoreland all he needed as well as mobilizing the reserves and increasing draft calls, President Johnson asked "do you have any ideas of what this will cost? Do you have any idea what effect this will have on our economy?" Secretary McNamara responded "twelve billion dollars in 1966. It would not require wage and price controls in my judgment. The price index ought not go up more than one point or two." The President asked "doesn't it really mean that if we follow Westmoreland's requests we are in a new war? Isn't this going off the diving board?" Secretary McNamara answered, "if we carry forward all these recommendations, it would be a change in our policy. We have relied on the South to carry the brunt. Now we would be responsible for satisfactory military outcome." President Johnson next heard General Greene report that to accomplish the U.S. objectives it would take "five years, plus 500,000 troops. I think the American people would back you." Johnson asked, "how would you tell the American people what the stakes are." "The place where they will stick by you is the national security stake," responded Greene. The dialogue was without optimism or short-run terms of reference. President Johnson asked, "do all of you think the Congress and the people will go along with 600,000 people and billions of dollars being spent 10,000 miles away . . . if you make a commitment to jump off a building and you find out how high it is, you may want to withdraw that commitment." The president's military advisors emphasized that it would take hundreds of thousands of men and several years to achieve military goals. The Joint Chiefs urged Johnson to call up the Reserves and National Guard and seek public support on national security grounds.

But President Johnson decided that there would be no public announcement of a change in policy. Johnson also rejected Mc-George Bundy's proposal that he go before a joint session of Congress or make his statement in a fireside address. Instead, he simply called a midday press conference. The content as well as the forum of Johnson's message downplayed its significance. The expected call-up of the reserves and request for new funds was absent. Moreover, Johnson also used the afternoon news conference to announce John Chancellor's nomination as head of the United States Information Agency and Abe Fortas' as associate justice of the Supreme Court. JCS Chairman Wheeler cabled General Westmoreland and informed him that McNamara's recommendation for troop increases had been approved and would be announced the next day. "Do not be surprised or disappointed if the public announcement does not set forth the full details of the program, but instead reflects an incremental approach," Wheeler advised. "This tactic will probably be adopted in order to hold down international noise level."

In announcing the troop increase, Johnson did not fully reveal the levels he had now authorized—175,000 to 200,000. Instead, he noted only the immediate force increment—fighting strength would grow from 75,000 to 125,000. Nor did he tell the American people that just a few days earlier Clark Clifford had warned against any substantial buildup of U.S. ground troops. "This could be a quagmire," warned the president's trusted friend. "It could turn into an open-ended commitment on our part that would take more and more ground troops, without a realistic hope of ultimate victory."

Instead, Johnson chose to deceive the American people with respect to the goals of military involvement and their anticipated costs. "Additional forces will be needed later, and they will be sent as requested," LBJ observed at his afternoon press conference. He made a seemingly passing remark that correctly indicated that the American commitment had become open-ended: "I have asked the Commanding General, General Westmoreland, what more he needs to meet this mounting aggression. He has told me. We will meet his needs."

President Johnson traveled to Honolulu in February 1966, seven months after the fateful decision, for a first-hand assessment on the war's progress from General Westmoreland and to secure additional commitments for political reform from South Vietnam's President Nguyen Cao Ky. At Honolulu, Johnson heard that the July deployments had staved off defeat in the South, but additional troops would now be needed to take the military initiative. Johnson agreed to another dramatic increase in U.S. troop strength from the 184,000 currently deployed to 429,000 by the end of the year. In exchange for the increase, LBJ utilized his favorite exhortation, that Westmoreland "nail the coonskin to the wall" by reaching the crossover point by December 1966.[21]

Nailing that coonskin proved to be elusive. U.S. policy was directed at a war of attrition. The promised "light at the end of the tunnel" in Vietnam—the point at which North Vietnam would seek peace negotiations—was to be achieved primarily by inflicting losses on the enemy forces. Johnson and his advisors, expecting the enemy to seek negotiations when this crossover point was reached, became fixated on statistics. They employed such terms as kill-ratios, body counts, defectors, order of battle, weapons-loss, ratios, bombing, pacification, died-of-wounds, and population-control data in order to show that progress was being made. The computers could always demonstrate such progress; statistically the United States could always win the war.

At President Johnson's behest Secretary McNamara visited Vietnam in October 1966. It had been twelve months since McNamara's last visit—a period during which U.S. troop deployments had more than doubled. Signs of a military stalemate were already evident.

Military defeat had been prevented, but little progress had been made in rooting out Communist forces and destroying their infrastructure. Moreover, while unremitting but selective application of air and naval power had inflicted serious damage to war-supporting targets in North Vietnam, it had not reduced Hanoi's capacity to support or direct military operations in the South. The introduction of more than two hundred thousand ground forces had not moved the United States any closer to its political objectives.

On October 14, 1966 Secretary McNamara wrote LBJ that despite significant increases in U.S. troop deployments and in the intensity of targets in the bombing campaign, Hanoi "knows we can't achieve our goals. The prognosis is bad in that the war can be brought to a satisfactory conclusion within the next two years." The U.S. military escalation had blunted communist military initiatives, but had not diminished the enemy's will to continue. "Any military victory in South Vietnam the Viet Cong may have had in mind 18 months ago has been thwarted by our emergency deployments and actions. And our program of bombing the North has exacted a price. My concern continues, however, in other respects. This is because I see no reasonable way to bring the war to an end soon."

The war in Vietnam was now a fully Americanized one. The public's perception of the war, particularly of the lack of military progress, was creating additional burdens for the administration. Nothing symbolized the potential bankruptcy of a guns-and-butter policy more than the outbreak of racial violence throughout urban America during the summer of 1967. Rioting in late July left 26 dead in Newark; 40 killed in Detroit, where for the first time in twenty-four years federal troops were needed to stop the rioters. Federal paratroopers ultimately restored order, arresting over 7000 looters and snipers.

In the words of Senator J. William Fulbright, the Great Society had become a "sick society." The president refused to abandon his guns-and-butter strategy, but his political coalition in Congress and credibility with the general public began unraveling. The president's overall job rating, as reported in the Gallup poll, dropped from 47 percent in mid-July to 39 percent in early August. His job rating on Vietnam showed 54 percent disapproval, an all-time high disapproval rating.

During a September 29, 1967, address to the National Legislative Conference in San Antonio, Texas, President Johnson sought a way out by restating his administration's position on negotiations and the conditions under which he would agree to stop bombing North Vietnam. The president certainly hoped to find the right lever which might bring both sides to the conference table before the 1968 presidential election. LBJ now made public his proposal to North Vietnam for peace: "The United States is willing to stop all aerial and naval bombardment of North Vietnam when this will lead promptly to productive discussion. We, of course, assume that while discussions proceed, North Vietnam would not take advantage of the bombing cessation or limitation." The San Antonio formula represented a modification in the Johnson administration's demand that Hanoi halt infiltration into the South as a precondition for a bombing halt. Now, all Hanoi had to do was show an interest in productive discussions and the bombing would be halted. The president was almost desperately looking for a way out, but Ho Chi Minh had nothing to gain by negotiating with an American president facing reelection. Knowing that LBJ had more to lose, Ho rejected the San Antonio proposal.

During the early morning hours of January 31 (the Vietnamese New Year, Tet) approximately 80,000 North Vietnamese regulars and guerrillas attacked more than 100 cities through South Vietnam. Tet involved enemy attacks on 35 of 44 province capitals, 36 district towns and many villages and hamlets. For weeks before the offensive, enemy forces had been infiltrating into Saigon in civilian clothes in preparation for a well-planned campaign of terror. The goal was to achieve a popular uprising against the GVN and to show the American public that the very notion of security in the South was null and void.

From a military point of view, the VC suffered a major defeat at Tet. More than half of their committed force was lost and perhaps a quarter of their whole regular force. Moreover, the Communists failed to bring about the diversion of U.S. forces from Khe Sanh or elsewhere. Nevertheless, as reported by the American news media, the psychological impact of Tet had a demoralizing effect on the American public. The enemy had demonstrated a capability to enter and attack cities and towns and had employed terrorism for doing vast damage. Ambassador Ellsworth Bunker cabled Johnson on February 8: "Hanoi may well have reasoned that in the event that the TET attacks did not bring the outright victory they hoped for, they could still hope for political and psychological gains of such dimensions that they could come to the negotiating table with a greatly strengthened hand. They may have very well estimated that the impact of the TET attacks would at the very least greatly discourage the United States and cause other countries to put more pressure on us to negotiate on Hanoi's terms." [22]

The Tet offensive set in motion a remarkable sequence of events.

On February 1, General Wheeler cabled Admiral Sharp and General Westmoreland raising the possibility "whether tactical nuclear weapons should be used if the situation in Khe Sanh should become that desperate." While Wheeler considered that eventuality unlikely, he requested a list of susceptible targets in the areas "which lend themselves to nuclear strikes, whether some contingency nuclear planning would be in order, and what you would consider to be some of the more significant pros and cons of using tac [tactical] nukes in such a contingency." Westmoreland responded, "The use of tactical nuclear weapons should not be required in the present situation." However, should the situation change, "I visualize that either tactical nuclear weapons or chemical agents would be active candidates for employment." [During an emotional February 16 news conference, Johnson vehemently denied that nuclear weapons had ever been considered, adding even more fuel to the credibility gap fire.]

TET revealed that despite the presence of 525,000 men, billions of dollars, and extensive bombing, the United States had not stopped the enemy from replacing his forces. The rate of the war and the capacity to sustain it were controlled not by America's superior technology, but by the enemy. In effect, the United States faced stalemate in Vietnam. General Westmoreland again needed more troops and he requested an additional 206,000 from the President. The reinforcements would bring the total American military commitment in ground forces to three-quarters of a million—yet the United States was no closer to achieving its political objective than at the outset of Americanization in 1965. It was becoming increasingly evident that no amount of military power would bring North Vietnam to the conference table.

On February 27, 1968 General Wheeler sent LBJ a major report on military requirements in Vietnam. The report was based on three days of conferences with Westmoreland and the senior American commander in each of the four Corps areas. The president appointed his new secretary of defense, Clark Clifford, to head a task force to evaluate General Westmoreland's request. The president's initial instructions to Clifford were "give me the lesser of evils." Clifford questioned the Joint Chiefs and those advisors who knew the most about Vietnam. He later recorded his questions: " 'Will 200,000 more men do the job?' I found no assurance that they would. 'If no, how many more might be needed—and when?' There was no way of knowing. 'What would be involved in committing 200,000 more men to Viet Nam?' A reserve call-up of approximately 280,000, an increased draft call and an extension of tours of duty of most men then in service. 'Can the enemy respond with a build-up of his own?' He could and he probably would. 'What are the estimated costs of the latest requests?' First calculations were on the order of $2 billion for the remaining four months of that fiscal year, and an increase of $10 to $12 billion for the year beginning July 1, 1968. 'What will be the impact on the economy?' So great that we would face the possibility of credit restrictions, a tax increase and even wage and price controls. The balance of payments would be worsened by at least half a billion dollars a year. 'Can bombing stop the war?' Never by itself. It was inflicting heavy personnel and materiel losses, but bombing by itself would not stop the war. 'Will stepping up the bombing decrease American casualties?' Very little, if at all.' "[23]

Clifford also asked the Joint Chiefs, "What is the best estimate as to how long this course of action will take? Six months? One year? Two years? Not only was there no agreement, I could find no one willing to express any confidence in his guesses. Certainly, none of us was willing to assert that he could see 'light at the end of the tunnel' or that American troops would be coming home by the end of the year. After days of this type of analysis, my concern had greatly deepened. I could not find out when the war was going to end; I could not find out the manner in which it was going to end; I could not find out whether the new requests for men and equipment were going to be enough, or whether it would take more and, if more, when and how much; I could not find out how soon the South Vietnamese forces would be ready to take over. All I had was the statement, given with too little self-assurance to be comforting, that if we persisted for an indeterminate length of time, the enemy would choose not to go on." Clifford finally asked, "Does anyone see any diminution in the will of the enemy after four years of our having been there, after enormous casualties and after massive destruction from our bombing?" The answer was that there appeared to be no diminution in the will of the enemy.

Johnson received the Clifford task-force report on March 4. The report recommended meeting Westmoreland's immediate military situation by deploying 22,000 additional personnel (approximately 60 percent of which would be combat and three tactical fighter squadrons). The task force also recommended approval of a 262,000 Reserve call-up in order to help restore the strategic Reserve. But the report contained none of Clifford's private doubts or questions. Instead, it called for a major new study designed to give Westmoreland "strategic guidance" for the future. It was quite possible that an additional 200,000 American troops or double or triple that quantity, would not be enough to accomplish U.S. objectives.

It was also evident that American public opinion would no longer accept a long drawn out military campaign with high casualties. By March 1968, the Gallup Poll reported that 49 percent of the American population believed the United States had been wrong to get involved militarily in Vietnam. While seven out of ten of those calling themselves doves thought the country was wrong ever to have become involved, four in ten who considered themselves to be hawks thought so as well.

On March 13, Senator Eugene McCarthy startled the nation with his strong showing in the New Hampshire primary. The New Hampshire primary became, in retrospect, the loose thread which, when pulled, unraveled the Johnson presidency. Senator Robert Kennedy had previously announced that he would not challenge LBJ because to do so would split the Democratic party; McCarthy had none of those reservations. Campaigning as an unabashed peace candidate and assisted by thousands of young college students who came to New Hampshire to dump LBJ, McCarthy's grass-roots candidacy came to symbolize hope, the light at the end of the dark tunnel of endless escalation.

The president's name was not on the New Hampshire ballot; he was not a declared candidate; and delegates could not pledge themselves to a noncandidate. Johnson supporters were banking on a heavy write-in campaign. The timing could not have been worse for Johnson. News of Westmoreland's 206,000-man request broke on the Sunday before the New Hampshire primary. Speculation was rampant that the troop request would help McCarthy. This proved to be the case: Johnson received 49.5 percent (27,243 votes) to McCarthy's 42.4 percent (28,280 votes). When all write-ins were tabulated, the President of the United States had won the primary by all of 230 votes, and McCarthy had captured twenty of twenty-six delegate votes. The McCarthy vote was deceptive. Not all was for peace, as many self-proclaimed hawks had voted for McCarthy to protest Johnson's handling of the war. Hawks and doves finally found a common ground in their dissatisfaction with Lyndon Johnson's war.

Upon receiving the Clifford task-force report, Johnson convened a meeting of his principal foreign policy advisors. Now, for the first time, the president heard Clifford outline the problems he faced. "Your senior advisers have conferred on this matter at very great length. There is a deep-seated concern by your advisers. There is a concern that if we say yes, and step with the addition of 206,000 more men that we might continue down the road as we have been without accomplishing our purpose—which is for a viable South Vietnam which can live in peace. We are not convinced that our present policy will bring us to that objective."[24]

Clifford emphasized that the 206,000 request was not just another call for more troops. The new request brought the president to the clearly defined watershed of going down the same road of "more troops, more guns, more planes, more ships?" And, "do you go on killing more Viet Cong and more North Vietnamese and killing more Vietcong and more North Vietnamese?" Clifford now shattered any illusions the president may have held with respect to military progress. "There are grave doubts that we have made the type of progress we had hoped to have made by this time. As we build up our forces, they build up theirs. We continue to fight at a higher level of intensity. Even were we to meet this full request of 206,000 men, and the pattern continues as it has, it is likely that by March he [General Westmoreland] may want another 200,000 to 300,000 men with no end in sight. The reserve forces in North Vietnam are a cause for concern as well. They have a very substantial population from which to draw. They have no trouble whatever organizing, equipping, and training their forces." Clifford's next words must have convinced Johnson that the United States needed to disengage from Vietnam. We seem to have a sinkhole. We put in more—they match it. I see more and more fighting with more and more casualties on the US side and no end in sight to the action."

The erosion of public support threatened to overwhelm Johnson. United Nations Ambassador Arthur Goldberg now wrote Johnson in support of a bombing halt. Goldberg had resigned from the Supreme Court to accept the ambassadorship in hopes that he could forge a negotiated settlement in Vietnam. The March 15 cable represented one of his final attempts; Goldberg would submit his resignation in April. The cable reached LBJ at the Ranch. Goldberg pointed toward "a growing public belief that the war in South Vietnam is increasingly an American war, not a South Vietnamese war which the U.S. is supporting, and, further, that the war cannot be won on this basis without evermounting commitments not worth the costs . . . It is my considered opinion that the very best way to prevent further erosion of public support from taking place is to make a new and fresh move toward a political solution at this time." Goldberg recommended a total bombing halt in the North: "We would 'stop' the aerial and naval bombardment of North Vietnam for the limited time necessary to determine whether Hanoi will negotiate in good faith." Johnson was furious; he would not stop the bombing. "Let's get one thing clear," Johnson told his aides. "I'm telling you now I'm not going to stop the bombing. Now I don't want to hear any more about it. Goldberg has written to me about the whole thing, and I've heard every argument. I'm not going to stop." [25]

Stage III: Getting Out

On March 31, 1968, Lyndon Johnson finally announced a partial suspension of the bombing against North Vietnam, but he warned that if Hanoi did not demonstrate similar restraint the bombing would be accelerated. In Johnson's words, "there is no need to delay talks that could bring an end to this long and this bloody war. Tonight, I renew the offer I made last August—to stop the bombardment of North Vietnam. We ask that talks begin promptly, that they be serious talks on the substance of peace. We assume that during those talks Hanoi will not take advantage of our restraint. We are prepared to move immediately toward peace through negotiations. So tonight, in the hope that this action will lead to early talks, I am taking the first step to de-escalate the conflict. We are reducing—substantially reducing—the present level of hostilities. And we are doing so unilaterally, and at once."

The president then stunned the nation by announcing, "I shall not seek, and I will not accept, the nomination of my party for another term as your President." The leader who committed forces abroad thereby removed himself from the disengagement process. The battle over disengagement and its meaning would now preoccupy domestic political debate in the United States.

Ending the war honorably became a major issue in the 1968 presidential campaign. Republican candidate Richard Nixon stressed that the road to a negotiated peace ran through Moscow, not necessarily Hanoi. In seeking broad political accommodation with the Soviet Union, Nixon hoped that leaders in the Kremlin would exert pressure on their ideological allies in Hanoi to negotiate an end to the conflict.

Toward the end of the campaign Nixon claimed to possess a secret plan to end the war, which he would unveil following the election. Once in office, however, Nixon presented no such plan, although it was clear to the new president that the United States could no longer support an open-ended commitment in Southeast Asia. He and National Security Adviser Henry Kissinger wanted to end the war on terms acceptable to U.S. honor and prestige. On April 10, 1969 the administration issued NSAM 36, directing the Secretary of Defense Melvin Laird to prepare "a specific timetable for Vietnamizing the war." Vietnamization was a two-pronged effort involving unilateral withdrawal of American troops from South Vietnam while simultaneously turning over greater military responsibilities to South Vietnamese forces. All previous U.S. withdrawal plans had been based on a reduction in enemy forces. Vietnamization was premised on the realization that there would be no imminent political settlement involving voluntary reduction in enemy forces.[26]

Whereas President Johnson had established the preeminence of an independent and stable non-communist government in Vietnam, President Nixon redefined the political objective to an American withdrawal that did not abandon South Vietnam to a quick defeat. But Nixon was also determined not to be sucked into Hanoi's diplomatic sidesteps. He would not repeat LBJ's mistakes. Nixon chose to back up diplomatic initiatives with the most massive bombings of the war. Beginning in March 1969 the United States, under the code name MENU, secretly began bombing Viet Cong and North Vietnamese Army (NVA) sanctuaries in Cambodia. In May 1970, the air strikes on Cambodia moved from covert to open support of ground operations against the North Vietnamese [the secret bombing of Cambodia would later be one of five proposed Articles of Impeachment against Nixon].

On May 8, 1969 Hanoi announced its own ten-point proposal for ending the war, the centerpiece of which involved a complete U.S. withdrawal and abolition of the government of South Vietnam. On May 14, 1969, in a nationally televised speech, President Nixon answered Hanoi's proposal with an eight-point plan for peace that called for the simultaneous withdrawal of U.S. and communist forces (a major concession by the U.S. from its previously stipulated requirement of six months). The United States was also willing to accept participation of the NLF in the political life of the South with free supervised elections.

The May 14 speech shocked the South Vietnamese allies who now feared they would be abandoned by the new administration's need to extricate itself from Vietnam.Meeting on Midway Island, Nixon and South Vietnam's President Thieu agreed that under Vietnamization, 25,000 American troops would be withdrawn immediately and a steady exodus would follow. The Midway meetings revealed schisms between the U.S. and their Vietnamese allies. Thieu came to Midway committed to the four "No's." (1) No recognition of the enemy; (2) No neutralization of South Vietnam; (3) No coalition government and (4) No surrender of territory to enemy. According to Ambassador Bui Diem, "Nixon and Thieu played political poker [at Midway Island]. Thieu tried to get as much as he could without giving way to a plan for total American withdrawal. He hoped for a gradual American withdrawal that would end with a residual American force in South Vietnam. Visualizing a Korean-type solution with the demilitarized zone as a buffer between North and South Vietnam, Thieu hoped that two divisions of American troops, about 40,000 men, would be stationed there to act as a deterrent to a North Vietnamese invasion."[27]

Nixon left the Midway meeting jubilant. American troops were to start withdrawing from Vietnam and, of special significance, Nixon had received Thieu's acquiescence for starting secret talks between Hanoi and the United States. "Thieu agreed, provided he was informed about any political discussions. Thieu believed that private American talks would be aimed at bringing the North and South to the conference table, not that the Americans would have the South's proxy to create a settlement on American terms."[28] Thieu soon learned that the United States would formulate a negotiating strategy which did not involve consultation with their Vietnamese allies. American withdrawal and South Vietnam's survival became two separate ends for the allies.

Vietnamization ultimately proved counterproductive to what Nixon sought politically from negotiations; the more U.S. troops departed without any progress in negotiations, the less incentive Hanoi had to reach any agreement at all. Conversely, the more the U.S. diminished its military presence, the more intensely Nixon sought a negotiated settlement. As Hung and Schecter observed, "Richard Nixon's strategy was to complement negotiations with the strengthening of South Vietnam through Vietnamization. In theory, the two tracks would be parallel and complement each other. In practice, they competed with and undercut each other. To Saigon, Vietnamization was the key to survival and reaching the capability for self-defense against the North. The more Vietnamization took hold, the less willing Thieu was to negotiate with the North and accept a coalition with the Provisional Revolutionary Government. For Hanoi, there was no incentive to make concessions in the negotiations as long as American withdrawals were being accelerated as part of Vietnamization. The U.S. policy softened domestic political pressures to end the war, but was counterproductive. The policies of Vietnamization and negotiation neutralized each other instead of enhancing goals both parties sought."[29]

These lack of linkages between the objectives of disengagement and Vietnamization wrought other serious consequences. Congressional opposition increased and the antiwar movement began organizing a series of demonstrations across America. In a secret letter to Ho Chi Minh, Nixon warned that if no progress in negotiation occurred by November 1, 1969, he would resort to "measures of great consequence and force."[30] On August 15, 1969 Ho rejected all of Nixon's conditions and insisted that peace would come only when the United States removed all its troops from Vietnam and disassociated itself from the Thieu government.

In 1970 Nixon made perhaps the most controversial decision of his presidency—he sent U.S. forces to Cambodia to shore up the Lon Nol regime with hopes of keeping Cambodia out of communist control. "Nixon decided that the strategic advantages to be gained from the Cambodian incursion outweighed its political liabilities, particularly the domestic controversy that he knew would be aroused by the action. He also hoped that the invasion would put pressure on Hanoi to consider negotiations as an alternative to facing a wider war. Nixon also put the Cambodian crisis in a larger context. He saw it as one of those decisive moments in the Cold War, when the will and character of the American people and its leaders were being tested by events and by their enemies."[31] As Nixon told the nation during an evening broadcast, "I would rather be a one-term president than be a two-term president at the cost of seeing America . . . accept the first defeat in its sound 190-years' history,' " Nixon told the nation. In vintage Cold War hyperbole: "If, when the chips are down, the world's most powerful nation acts like a pitiful, helpless giant, the forces of totalitarianism and anarchy will threaten free nations and free institutions throughout the world."

In reaction to the U.S. action into Cambodia, the NLF and North Vietnamese delegates walked out of the Paris negotiations and mass antiwar demonstrations erupted in the United States. When Nixon (tying to placate public opinion and defying his field commander's wishes) announced that another 150,000 troops would soon be out of Vietnam, Hanoi hardened its resolve not to negotiate; the talks remained deadlocked. With little room to maneuver politically, Nixon (much like Johnson) found that military action provided his only base for maintaining credibility—he approved ground operations into Laos to destroy enemy logistics systems.

By 1971 American battle deaths in Vietnam since the Americanization of the war in 1965 were at all time low (of 1380); yet the military intensity of the war was at an all time high. The North Vietnamese were using the Paris talks as another mode of fighting. "The war had now entered what communist theoretrians called "danh va dam, dam va danh,"—fighting and talking, talking and fighting." [32] In the spring, Henry Kissinger began secret talks with Xuan Thuy and Le Duc Tho in Paris (later described as "walks in the night" by Thieu). Kissinger first offered a seven point peace plan that contained two very important concessions: In exchange for the return of all POWS, a date (December 31, 1971) would be set for the complete withdrawal of U.S. forces and for the first time the U.S. would not insist that the North do the same. Mutual withdrawal was replaced only by insistence that the North cease its infiltration. The proposal also separated the military issue from political issues. Under these terms, there could be a negotiated cease-fire without settling the major political question—what kind of government would South Vietnam have in the postwar period?

In March 1972 North Vietnam initiated a massive conventional invasion of South Vietnam spearheaded by more than 120,000 North Vietnamese troops, who crossed the DMZ, in the Central Highlands and Cambodian border. The attack caught U.S. intelligence by surprise and for a moment it looked like Saigon might fall. Nixon responded with force. "The bastards have never been bombed like they're going to be bombed this time," Nixon promised. [33]

At the time of the attack President Nixon had been preparing for a summit meeting in Moscow to discuss strategic arms limitations. Divisions within the Nixon administration now manifested themselves. Secretary of Defense Laird and Secretary of State Rogers warned that the bombing program (Linebacker) would ruin the summit; but when Commanding General Creighton Abrams cabled Nixon that "the whole thing may be lost," the President approved the mining of Haiphong, a naval blockade, and the B-52 Linebacker air campaign. According to Nixon, "If we were to lose Vietnam there would have been no respect for the American President . . . because we had the power and didn't use it. . . . we must be credible." Nixon gambled that the Soviets would not risk detente over Vietnam. Moreover, if South Vietnam went down the drain, detente would be lost anyway since the North's offensive would be spearheaded by Soviet military equipment. Nixon would hardly be in a politically acceptable position for welcoming a thaw in superpower relations.

The dramatic escalation in the bombing program evoked only mild criticism from Moscow and China, neither of whom were willing to risk reapproachment for their ally in Hanoi. Moreover, the North's casualties from the offensive were staggering; it lost more than one half of the two hundred thousand troops it committed. It would take two or three years to replace these forces and Hanoi's leaders now wanted to end the fighting part of the war. Several weeks before the scheduled summit, Kissinger met secretly with Soviet leader Brezhnev and offered major concessions to North Vietnam: the U.S. would accept a cease-fire in place, in exchange for the removal of only North Vietnamese forces that had entered South Vietnam since the March 31 offensive (which meant that 20,000 could stay).

The Moscow summit was held: Nixon and Brezhnev signed the SALT treaty as well as a new Berlin treaty. According to Arnold Isaacs, "the US intervened in Vietnam initially with ideas of defeating a communist insurgency, containing what it then saw as a menacing and expansionist China, and disproving theories of liberation, among other reasons. By the time the Nixon administration came to power, however, what mattered fundamentally to the US leadership was not what happened to the Vietnamese, much less to the Laos or the Cambodians, but what happened to the World's—and particularly the Soviet Union's—impression of American capability and resolve. Nixon's rapprochement with the Chinese leadership made much of the war's original rationale meaningless and thus made its actual outcome a matter of even less concern to him or to the American government. If some form of settlement on America's minimum terms could be reached, so much the better."[34]

In September 1972 Kissinger and Le Duc Tho began another series of meetings in Paris, which resulted in a two track agreement that separated military from political issues—again deferring for the future the question of who would rule South Vietnam. The negotiations produced a tentative agreement, but the terms proved unacceptable to Thieu who, according to Bunker, appeared "genuinely afraid of peace."[35] Under the proposed treaty, (A) Hanoi agreed to allow Thieu to remain in power in exchange for a grant of political status in South Vietnam to the PRG-Provisional Revolutionary Government; (B) All POWS would be returned within 60 days of cease-fire; (C) the U.S. would withdraw its remaining troops from the South; (D) All NVA troops currently in the South would be permitted to remain (Washington's greatest concession); (E) a tripartite commission would be created to supervise elections and administer the agreement; (F) all decisions of the commission would have to be unanimous—giving each delegate an absolute veto.

Nixon was apparently swayed by Thieu's fierce lobbying that the proposed Kissinger-Tho pact was tantamount to selling out the government in South Vietnam. Thieu would accept nothing less than the removal of all North Vietnamese troops in exchange for a role for the NLF (now the Provisional Revolutionary Group) in the Saigon government. Kissinger later described this as a "Greek tragedy . . . the imperatives on him [Thieu] were almost diametrically opposite of ours." [36]

A week before the 1972 presidential election, Kissinger stated that "peace is at hand," but the talks again stalled and Nixon turned to "jugular diplomacy." Nixon decided that no treaty would be signed until after the November 1972 election, when Nixon's position would be strengthened by what most observers expected to be an overwhelming election victory over George McGovern. Reelected by just such a landslide, Nixon moved swiftly against North Vietnam. During the Christmas 1972 period the United States initiated the most intensive and devastating air attacks of the war, "dropping more than 36,000 tons of bombs and exceeding the tonnage during the entire period from 1969 to 1971 . . . the destruction in parts of Hanoi and Haiphong was heavy, and as many as 1600 civilians were killed." [37]

The bombing certainly gave the North Vietnamese reason to resume negotiations; on December 28 Hanoi consented to negotiations and on December 29 the bombing stopped.

The Accord signed in Paris was not much different from the one drafted the previous October. The agreement settled only one real issue—American involvement, not who would rule South Vietnam. Nixon had threatened Thieu with cutting off all aid if he didn't go along, but gave Thieu written assurances that if North Vietnam violated the peace, the U.S. would not abandon South Vietnam. The president promised "swift and severe retaliatory actions," if the North moved against South Vietnam. Thieu told his cabinet: "The United States leaves us without any alternative except that if we sign, and will continue and there is a pledge of retaliation if the agreements are violated . . . Kissinger treats both Vietnams as adversaries. He considers himself as an outsider in these negotiations and does not distinguish between South Vietnam, as an ally, and North Vietnam, as an enemy. The Americans let the war become their war; when they liked the war they carried it forward. Then they want to stop it, they impose on both sides to stop it. When the Americans wanted to enter, we had no choice, and now here they are ready to leave we have no choice." [38]

Few of the provisions from the Accords were ever carried out. The North concluded that diplomacy, rather than military means, would

be the way to rid their country of an American military presence—
even if it meant accepting the temporary existence of a government
in South Vietnam. As North Vietnam Colonel Bao noted: "Hundreds
of billions of dollars and a half-million United States troops have
failed to subdue the Vietnamese people, $300 million more to Saigon
can in no way change the situation." Indeed, between 1973 and 75
Hanoi pressed forward in its goal of overthrowing the South. On
March 25, 1975 Thieu wrote President Gerald Ford, "Hanoi's intention to use the Paris Agreement for a military takeover of South
Vietnam was well known to us at the very time of negotiating the
Paris Agreement. You may recall that we signed it, not because
we naively believed in the enemy's good will, but because we
trusted America's solemn commitment to safeguard the peace in
Vietnam."[39]

Abbreviations

ARVN	Army of the Republic of Vietnam (South Vietnam)
CHICOM	Chinese Communist
CIA	Central Intelligence Agency
CINCPAC	Commander in Chief, Pacific Command
CIDG	Civilian Irregular Defense Group (South Vietnam)
DIA	Defense Intelligence Agency
DMZ	Demilitarized Zone
DRV	Democratic Republic of Vietnam (North Vietnam)
GVN	Government of Vietnam (South Vietnam)
JCS	Joint Chiefs of Staff
KIA	Killed in Action
MACV	U.S. Military Assistance Command, Vietnam
MIA	Missing in Action
MP	Military Police
NATO	North Atlantic Treaty Organization
NIE	National Intelligence Estimate
NSC	National Security Council
NVA	North Vietnamese Army
OB	Order of Battle
POL	Petroleum, Oil, and Lubricants [depot]
POW	Prisoner of War
RVN	Republic of Vietnam (South Vietnam)
RVNAF	Republic of Vietnam Armed Forces
SAM	Surface-to-Air-Missile
SEATO	Southeast Asia Treaty Organization
SIG	Senior Interdepartmental Group

USIS   United States Information Service
VC   Viet Cong

A Vietnam Chronology

1954

March 13–May 7: French Forces are defeated at the battle of Dien Bien Phu.

May 8–July 21: The Geneva Conference on Indochina fixes the seventeenth parallel as a provisional military demarcation line between the Democratic Republic of Vietnam (North Vietnam) and the State of Vietnam (South Vietnam). The Final Declaration of the Geneva Conference, issued July 21, prescribes a general election for North and South Vietnam, to be held in July 1956.

1955

October 26: Ngo Dinh Diem assumes the presidency of the Republic of Vietnam (South Vietnam).

1959

January: The North Vietnamese Communist Party Central Committee issues "Resolution 15," authorizing "armed struggle" against South Vietnam.

1960

December 20: Establishment of the National Liberation Front of South Vietnam is announced in Hanoi.

1962

February: United States forms MACV (Military Assistance Command, Vietnam) under General Paul D. Harkins.

March–April: United States initiates strategic hamlet program.

December 31: Approximately 11,300 U.S. military personnel are now in Vietnam.

1963

August 12: Henry Cabot Lodge replaces Frederick E. Nolting as U.S. ambassador to South Vietnam.

November 2: Diem is assassinated in military coup.

November 22: President Kennedy is assassinated. Vice President Johnson assumes the presidency.

December 31: Approximately 16,300 U.S. military personnel are now in Vietnam.

1964

June 20: General William Westmoreland is appointed MACV Commander.

July 2: Ambassador Lodge is replaced by Maxwell Taylor

August 2–4: The U.S. destroyer *Maddox* reports an attack by North Vietnamese patrol boats in Tonkin Gulf. A second attack by the North Vietnamese is repulsed by the U.S. destroyer *Turner Joy*. The U.S. launches first air strikes against North Vietnamese targets.

August 7: The Gulf of Tonkin resolution, supporting actions necessary to protect U.S. forces and to "prevent further aggression," passes the U.S. Congress.

November 2: Lyndon Johnson is elected 36th President of the United States.

1965

February 7: The U.S. base at Pleiku is attacked. Eight Americans are killed, and more than a hundred others are wounded. In Operation Flaming Dart, United States bombs North Vietnam in retaliation for attacks on American military installations in South Vietnam.

February 24: Operation Rolling Thunder, a sustained bombing campaign against North Vietnam, begins.

March 8: The first American combat troops land in Vietnam to defend the U.S. air base at Danang.

April 7: In a major policy address at Johns Hopkins University, Johnson declares that "we will not be defeated."

June 24: Air Vice Marshal Nguyen Cao Ky becomes prime minister of South Vietnam.

July 8: Henry Cabot Lodge is reappointed ambassador to South Vietnam.

July 28: The war in Vietnam is Americanized.

November 14–16: Battle of Ia Drang Valley, the first major engagement between U.S. and regular North Vietnamese troops.

1966

February 4: U.S. Senate Foreign Relations Committee, under the chairmanship of J. William Fulbright, begins televised hearings on the war.

February 6–8: Johnson meets South Vietnamese leaders in Honolulu.

October 25: Johnson meets with South Vietnamese leaders in Manila.

December 31: Approximately 385,300 U.S. military personnel are now in Vietnam. American casualties, 6,644.

1967

April 12: Ellsworth Bunker becomes new ambassador to South Vietnam.

August 25: Testifying before the Senate Preparedness Committee, McNamara asserts that the U.S. bombing campaign cannot win the war.

September 3: Nguyen Van Thieu is elected president of South Vietnam. Ky is elected vice president.

September 29: In a major policy address in San Antonio, Johnson promises to halt bombing in return for Hanoi's agreement to begin peace negotiations.

November 29: Johnson announces that McNamara will step down as Secretary of Defense.

December 31: Approximately 485,600 U.S. military personnel are now in Vietnam. American casualties, 16,021.

1968

January 21: The siege of Khe Sanh begins.

January 23: U.S.S. *Pueblo* is seized by North Korea.

January 30: Viet Cong and North Vietnamese troops launch major offensive during Tet holiday.

February 10–17: All-time weekly high of U.S. casualties is set: 543 killed in action, 2,546 wounded.

February 28: General Earle Wheeler requests 206,000 additional troops.

March 1: Clark Clifford is sworn in as Secretary of Defense.

March 25—26: Meeting to reevaluate America's Vietnam policy, a group of elder statesmen—the Senior Advisory Group or "Wise Men"—recommend de-escalation of the war.

March 31: In a nationally televised address, Johnson declares a partial bombing halt, calls for peace talks, and announces he will not seek reelection.

May 3: Johnson announces North Vietnamese agreement to begin peace talks in Paris.

October 31: Johnson announces full bombing halt.

November 5: Richard Nixon is elected 37th President of the United States.

December 31: Approximately 536,100 U.S. military personnel are now in Vietnam. American casualties, 30,610.

1969

January 25: The first plenary session of the four-way Paris peace talks among the Americans, the North Vietnamese, the South Vietnamese, and the National Liberation Front occurs.

March 18: President Nixon orders the secret bombing of communist base camps and supply depots in Cambodia to commence.

June 8: President Nixon announces that 25,000 U.S. troops will be withdrawn by the end of August and that they will be replaced by South Vietnamese forces.

November 15: In the largest antiwar demonstration to date, more than 250,000 come to Washington.

1970

May 4: National Guard troops fire into a group of student demonstrators on the campus of Kent State University, killing four and wounding eleven.

June 24: The Senate, by a vote of 81-10, repeals the Gulf of Tonkin Resolution.

1971

February 21—27. President Nixon makes his historic visit to China.

June 13: The *New York Times* begins publication of the leaked portions of the forty-seven volume Pentagon analysis of the U.S. involvement in Vietnam through 1967.

1972

May 8: Nixon announces that he has ordered the mining of all North Vietnamese ports.

May 20: The summit conference between President Nixon and Leonid Brezhnev takes place in Moscow.

October 8–11: Lengthy secret meetings in Paris between Henry Kissinger and Le Duc Tho produce a tentative settlement of the war.

October 22: President Thieu rejects the proposed settlement.

November 7: Richard Nixon is reelected president by a landslide margin, promising "peace with honor" in Vietnam.

December 18: The most concentrated air offensive of the war begins, mostly aimed at targets in the vicinity of Hanoi and Haiphong.

December 28: Hanoi announces that it is willing to resume negotiations if the U.S. will stop bombing above the 20th Parallel.

December 31: The bombing ends.

1973

January 8–18: Henry Kissinger and Le Duc Tho resume negotiations in Paris.

January 23: Nixon announces that the Paris Accords will go into effect at 7:00 p.m. EST, January 27, 1973. "Peace with honor" has been achieved.

January 27: The draft ends.

February 12-27: American POWs begin to come home.

March 29: The last U.S. troops leave South Vietnam.

1975

January 28: President Ford requests an additional $722 million in military aid for South Vietnam. Congress refuses his request.

March 24: Hanoi launches its Ho Chi Minh Campaign to "liberate" South Vietnam before the rains begin.

April 8–21: The last major battle of the Vietnam War is fought at Xuan

Loc, about 30 miles from Saigon. After hard fighting, the communists win.

April 23: President Ford pronounces the Vietnam War "finished as far as America is concerned."

April 29–30: The last Americans and eligible South Vietnamese are evacuated from Saigon.

April 30: The Communists conquer Saigon.

Major Sources for the Chronology

Bowman, John, general editor. *The World Almanac of the Vietnam War.* New York: Bison Books, 1985.

Davidson, Phillip B. *Vietnam at War: The History 1946–1975.* Novato, California: Presidio, 1988.

Gravel, Mike, ed. *The Pentagon Papers: The Defense Department History of U.S. Decision Making in Vietnam,* 4 vols. Boston: Beacon, 1971.

Moss, George Donelson. *Vietnam: An American Ordeal.* Englewood Cliffs, N.J.: Prentice Hall, 1990.

Summers, Harry G., Jr. *The Vietname War Almanac.* New York: Facts on File, 1985.

Notes

1. For an extensive analysis of the period see Lloyd Gardner, *Approaching Vietnam: From World War II through Dienbienphu* (New York: W. W. Norton, 1988).

2. For an expanded analysis of these events see John Burke and Fred Greenstein with the collaboration of Larry Berman and Richard Immerman, *How President's Test Reality: Decisions on Vietnam, 1954 and 1965* (New York: Russell Sage Foundation, 1989).

3. The de-facto division of Vietnam by the Geneva Accords had guaranteed a French controlled zone (the State of Vietnam). Vietnam nationalists envisioned the establishment of a sovereign, non-communist government. Ambassador Bui Diem later wrote, "the Communist victory at Dienbienphu aroused mixed feelings—a reluctant pride that Vietnamese had defeated France so decisively, even if the victors were our deadly enemies. But the division of the country that followed Dienbienphu, that was nothing but a blessing full of promise." See Bui Diem with David Chanoff, *In the Jaws of History* (Boston: Houghton Mifflin, 1987), p. 113.

4. See NSC, "Review of U.S. Policy in the Far East," August 1954. U.S. Congress, House, Committee on Armed Services, United States–Vietnam Relations, 1945–1967: A Study Prepared by the Department of Defense

(Washington, D.C.: U.S. Government Printing Office, 1971), Book 10, pp. 731–41. Hereafter cited as USVN.

5. Eisenhower to Diem, October 1, 1954, in George M. Kahin and John W. Lewis, *The United States in Vietnam* (New York: Dell, 1969), pp. 456–57; *Public Papers, Dwight D. Eisenhower, 1954* (Washington, D.C.: 1960), p. 383.

6. *The Pentagon Papers: The Defense Department History of the United States Decisionmaking on Vietnam*, edited by Senator Gravel (Boston: Beacon Press, 1971), 2 (sect. B.4): 84–96, 245–46, 258–59, 291–96. See also Maxwell Taylor, *Swords and Plowshares* (New York: W. W. Norton, 1972), pp. 242–44.

7. Paul Kattenberg, *The Vietnam Trauma in American Foreign Policy, 1945–75* (New Brunswick, N.J.: Transaction Books, 1980).

8. Bui Diem, *In the Jaws of History*, p. 137, 156.

9. McNamara to President Johnson, December 21, 1963. See *Vietnam: A History in Documents*, edited by Gareth Porter (New York: New American Library, 1981). Willaim Appleman Williams, Thomas McCormick, Lloyd Gardner, and Walter LaFeber, eds., *America in Vietnam: A Documentary History* (New York: W. W. Norton, 1989).

10. See Larry Berman, *Planning a Tragedy: The Americanization of the War in Vietnam* (New York: W. W. Norton, 1982), pp. 28-29.

11. Taylor, *Swords and Plowshares*, pp. 301–2.

12. Gen. William C. Westmoreland, "Vietnam in Perspective," *The Retired Officer*, October 1978, pp. 21–24.

13. Edward Moise, "Tonkin Gulf Reconsidered," in William Cogar, ed., *New Interpretations in Naval History* (Annapolis: Naval Institute Press, 1989). Joseph Goulden, *Truth is the First Casualty: The Gulf of Tonkin Affair* (Chicago: Rand McNally, 1969), p. 160; See "Chronology of Events, Tuesday, August 4, and Wednesday, August 5, 1964, Tonkin Gulf Strike," National Security File, Country File: Vietnam. See also Eugene Windchy, *Tonkin Gulf* (New York: Doubleday, 1971); *Pentagon Papers*, 3:150; "The Gulf of Tonkin: The 1964 Incidents," Hearings before the Senate Committee on Foreign Relations, 90th Cong., 2d sess. (Washington, D.C.: U.S. Government Printing Office, 1968).

14. Telegram, President Johnson to Ambassador Taylor, January 13, 1965, *Secret*, NSC History—Troop Deployment. On January 14 the Secretary of State's name replaced the president's and the telegram was sent to Taylor (see telegram, Rusk to Taylor, priority 1477, NSC History—Troop Deployment).

15. Memo, Bundy to the President, February 7, 1965, "The Situation in Vietnam."

16. Taylor, *Swords and Plowshares*, p. 327.

17. Cable, General Westmoreland, June 7, 1965, "US Troop Deployment to SVN," *Top Secret—LimDis*, #19118, NSC History—Troop Deployment (emphasis added). "A broad review of force requirements has been conducted in light of changing situation in Southeast Asia and within RVN." Westmoreland, *A Soldier Reports* (New York: Doubleday), p. 139.

18. Bui Diem, *In the Jaws of History*, p. 181.

19. See Berman, *Planning a Tragedy: The Americanization of the War in Vietnam* for an expanded analysis. All documents regarding the July decision are located in the National Security Council History file at the Lyndon Baines Johnson Library, Austin, Texas.

20. See David DeLeo, *Vietnam and the Rethinking of Containment* (Chapel Hill: University of North Carolina Press, 1991); George Ball, *The Past Has Another Pattern* (New York: W. W. Norton, 1982).

21. See Larry Berman, *Lyndon Johnson's War: The Road to Stalemate in Vietnam* (New York: W. W. Norton, 1989).

22. See National Security Council History, "The March 31st Speech," (LBJ Library). See Don Oberdorf, *TET!* (Doubleday, 1991).

23. See Clark Clifford, "A Vietnam Reappraisal," *Foreign Affairs*, July 1969, pp. 608–10.

24. Ibid.

25. See Stanley Karnow, *Vietnam* (New York: Viking, 1983); Townsend Hoopes, *The Limits of Intervention* (New York: W. W. Norton, 1987).

26. See Jeffrey J. Clarke, *Advice and Support: The Final Years, 1965–1973*, Center for Military History, United States Army, Washington, D.C. 1988.

27. Bui Diem, *In the Jaws of History*, pp. 259–262.

28. Nguyen Tien Hung and Jerrold L. Schecter, *The Palace File: Vietnam Secret Documents* (New York: Harper & Row, 1986), pp 32–34.

29. Ibid., pp. 96–97.

30. Ibid., p. 57.

31. George Donelson Moss, *Vietnam: An American Ordeal* (Englewood Cliffs, N. J.: Prentice Hall, 1990), pp. 318–320.

32. Bui Diem, *In The Jaws of History*, p. 262.

33. See Mark Clodfelter, *The Limits of Air Power: The American Bombing of North Vietnam* (New York: The Free Press, 1989), chapters 5 and 6.

34. Arnold Isaacs, *Without Honor: Defeat in Vietnam & Cambodia* (Baltimore: Johns Hopkins University Press, 1984).

35. Bui Diem, *In the Jaws of History*.

36. See Seymour Hersh, *The Price of Power: Kissinger in the Nixon White House* (New York: Summit Books, 1983).

37. See Clodfelter, *The Limits of Air Power*, pp. 194–95.

38. See Hung and Schecter, *The Palace File*, chapters 20–21.

39. Ibid.

3

The Soviet Union in Afghanistan

ROBERT S. LITWAK

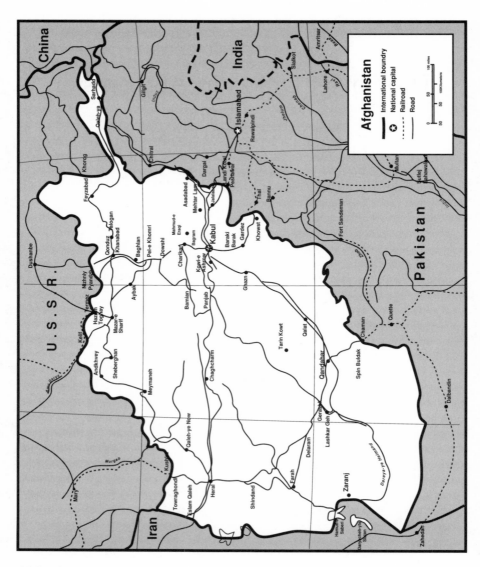

Afghanistan

Introduction

After more than eight years of bitter counterinsurgency warfare, the April 1988 Geneva accords paved the way for the withdrawal of Soviet forces from Afghanistan. By mid-May, two weeks before the Reagan-Gorbachev summit in Moscow, approximately one-quarter of the USSR's "limited contingent" of 115,000 troops had been withdrawn. On February 15, 1989, Lieutenant Boris V. Gromov, the commander of Soviet forces in Afghanistan, completed the process when he walked across the "Friendship Bridge" into Soviet Uzbekistan. In the wake of the Soviet withdrawal, the Afghan conflict again reverted to the civil war that had existed prior to, and indeed precipitated, the December 1979 invasion.

The Soviet move into Afghanistan culminated a decade of unprecedented activism by the USSR in the Third World. While America underwent the traumas of post-Vietnam retrenchment, the 1970s witnessed successive advances by Soviet clients in Africa and Asia— a geographical zone characterized by U.S. National Security Adviser Zbigniew Brzezinski as the "arc of crisis." Unlike earlier episodes such as Angola and Ethiopia, in which the Soviet role had been limited to logistical and materiel support, the Afghan crisis marked the first large-scale deployment of Soviet forces outside the Warsaw Treaty area.[1] President Jimmy Carter called the invasion "the greatest threat to peace since the Second World War" and enunciated the doctrine now bearing his name that designated the Persian Gulf a region of vital American interest.[2]

In the West, Soviet policy in Afghanistan has been considered a key litmus test of the Kremlin's broader foreign policy intentions. Some observers cast the invasion as a continuation of Moscow's historical policy of southward expansionism in pursuit of a warm-water port. Others characterized the move as essentially a defensive action to preserve a Marxist-Leninist regime in a neighboring country. Whether offensively or defensively motivated, the Soviet invasion was a major factor underlying the final demise of detente and the Reagan administration's return to a more militarized form of containment. Since November 1982, three changes of leadership in the Kremlin, culminating in the rise to power of Mikhail Gorbachev in March 1985, have radically altered the domestic context of Soviet policy. If the December 1979 invasion of Afghanistan was instrumental in shaping the image of an expansionist Soviet Union in the United States during the Reagan years, what conclusions about Soviet foreign policy intentions should be drawn from Moscow's decision to withdraw? Was it a tactical retreat in the face of military stalemate or the most dramatic manifestation of Gorbachev's "new thinking"?

This article will explore the origins, dynamics, and consequences of the Soviet military intervention in Afghanistan. In keeping with the comparative case approach employed in this project, attention will initially focus on the transition from political commitment to military intervention. In the Afghan case, this period (Stage I) was that between the "April Revolution" of 1978 that brought the Soviet-backed People's Democratic Party of Afghanistan (PDPA) to power and the December 1979 invasion. This discussion, in turn, will lead to an assessment of the USSR's twin military and political strategies within Afghanistan during the period (Stage II) between the introduction of troops and March 1985, when Gorbachev assumed power and initiated a sweeping policy review. The following section will focus on the dynamics of disengagement (Stage III)—a process that culminated in the February 1989 withdrawal of all Soviet combat forces.

Before proceeding to the detailed case analysis, one must underscore the perennial difficulty in the Soviet studies field of obtaining adequate and reliable source materials to permit rigorous foreign policy analysis. Here one must distinguish between the pre- and post-*glasnost'* eras. Before the Gorbachev revolution, available written sources fell into three broad categories: official pronouncements, presumably the most authoritative, by top party and governmental officials, such as Politburo members; analyses in scholarly journals from the various foreign policy institutes of the Soviet Academy of Sciences; and, finally, newspaper articles and the output from other organs of the Soviet mass media. In studying Soviet declaratory policy, one got very little sense of the dynamics of decision-making. The USSR, for all intents and purposes, was the classic "black box"; unlike America, where reports of the inner workings of government are routine front-page news, one could expect no leaks from Politburo meetings to shed light on Soviet deliberations. To offer a plausible interpretation of Soviet decision-making, analysts would work back and forth between Soviet declaratory policy and actual behavior, using the latter as a check on the former.

In the era of *glasnost'*, the situation has changed substantially.

Soviet publications are taking up Gorbachev's challenge to fill in the "blank spots" of the USSR's history on issues ranging from arms control to Soviet policy in Eastern Europe. With respect to Afghanistan, the period following the announcement in February 1988 of Gorbachev's proposal to withdraw all Soviet forces from the country within twelve months was followed by the publication of a number of articles that shed further light on the Brezhnev regime's decision to invade in December 1979.[3] These writings include interviews with current and former officials, both civilian and military, as well as academic specialists from various institutes of the USSR Academy of Sciences. In some instances (e.g., a detailed account of Soviet decision-making during 1978–79 in the newspaper of the Soviet military, *Kransnaya zvezda*),[4] the articles are reportedly based, in part, on archival research. These products of *glasnost'* offer unprecedented detail on the roles played by the major institutional actors and key policymakers (e.g., which sub-group within the Politburo was involved in the December 1979 decision to invade). They also occasionally challenge Western conventional wisdoms about Soviet decision-making on Afghanistan. For example, a March 1989 interview in the weekly *Ogonek* with General Valentin Varrenikov, Deputy Minister of Defense and commander of USSR ground forces, casts doubt on the view widely held by Western analysts that the Soviet military advocated intervention, while the KGB advised against it.[5]

In integrating these new source materials into our analysis of Soviet Afghan policy, one must bear in mind that these new accounts are, at best, selective and may well be self-serving justifications by those surviving officials who would rather shift blame onto those now deceased. Even in an era of *glasnost'* there is yet no Soviet counterpart to the *Pentagon Papers*. The recently published accounts in the Soviet media contain many gaps, ambiguities, and contradictions. A special commission of the Supreme Soviet has been created to address these outstanding questions and provide an authoritative accounting of Soviet policy in Afghanistan. Even with fuller archival access, however, the fact that most of the key decision-makers are deceased may make it impossible to fill in this particular "blank spot" in Soviet history.

As will be examined below, Soviet decision-making on Afghanistan during the decade between invasion and withdrawal was shaped by an amalgam of domestic, regional, and international factors. Soviet policy at the key decision points cannot be explained by any single factor in isolation. Just as the invasion was not solely the product of the Brezhnev political system or concerns about an incipient Islamic threat on the USSR's southern border, so too was the decision to leave not exclusively due to the military impact of Stinger anti-aircraft missiles or the influence of Gorbachev's "new thinking" in foreign policy. In this article, an attempt will be made to assess the *relative* importance of domestic, regional, and international influences on Soviet decision -making—while taking full account of the inherent methodological dilemmas of foreign policy analysis and the particular research problems, briefly touched upon above, related to the study of contemporary Soviet foreign policy.

Stage I: Getting In

Soviet interests in Afghanistan have their historical antecedents in the Czarist period when Russia and Britain competed in the "Great Game" for control over the territory between Central and South Asia.[6] Following the 1917 revolution, the Bolshevik leadership feared the danger of British intervention in Central Asia via Afghanistan. Moscow's desire to maintain Afghanistan as an effective buffer to British military power led to the establishment of diplomatic relations in May 1919 and the conclusion of a Treaty of Friendship in February 1921.

In the aftermath of World War II, the primary Soviet interest in Afghanistan continued to be a strategic one—namely, the prevention of any hostile power's use of that state as a base of operation against the USSR. To this end, the Soviet Union found it useful to encourage the Kabul regime's avowed policy of nonalignment.[7]

During the 1960s, Soviet–Afghan relations appreciably increased in scope. The USSR's economic, technical, and military assistance were widely in evidence and permitted the Soviet leadership a position of unrivalled influence *vis-à-vis* the Afghan regime. This rather uncritical reliance on economic assistance by the regime of King Zahir Shah fostered an Afghan foreign policy that was generally more accommodating to Soviet preferences and interests. In January 1965, an underground communist party—the People's Democratic Party of Afghanistan (PDPA)—was founded under the leadership of Nur Mohammed Taraki. In July 1967, in a development which would have major ramifications during the period of communist rule after the so-called "Great *Saur* [April] Revolution" of 1978, the PDPA split into two main factions: *Khalq* ("The Masses"), led by Taraki, and *Parcham* ("Banner"), headed by Barbrak Karmal, the man who would later lead the PDPA regime in Kabul after the December 1979 invasion.

The schism within the party reportedly resulted as much from personal differences within the PDPA's Central Committee as from substantive disagreements over policy.

King Zahir Shah was overthrown by former Premier Mohammed Daoud in June 1973, leading to the establishment of Afghanistan as a republic. While some of the participants in the 1973 coup reportedly had PDPA links, the weight of informed opinion judges Daoud to have acted in his own right. Daoud, once in power, adopted a foreign policy intended to reduce Afghan reliance on the Soviet Union. The consequent cooling of relations was reflected in the communiqués issued during the visit of Soviet President Nikolai Podgorny to Kabul in December 1975 and Daoud's return visit to Moscow in April 1977. Daoud's attempt to broaden his foreign policy options came at a time when the domestic political and economic situation was increasingly turning against him.[8]

The murder of a prominent *Parcham* labor leader triggered the chain of events that culminated in the PDPA/military coup against Daoud in April 1978. The Soviet role in this action remains an issue of contention. The reunification of the *Khalq* and *Parcham* factions in mid-1977, reportedly at Soviet insistence, paved the way for the subsequent coup. In view of the Soviet embassy's direct links with the PDPA and extensive contacts in the military, it is likely that the Soviets possessed foreknowledge of the coup. During the action itself, some of the 350 Soviet military advisers then in Afghanistan were observed with Afghan armored units; Soviet advisers also assisted at Bagram air base outside Kabul, where they helped with the servicing of MiG-21s and SU-7s.[9] Most informed observers now agree that the coup was precipitated by the murder of the *Parcham* labor leader and the Daoud regime's bungled attempt to arrest the PDPA leadership; the subsequent Soviet actions in support of the PDPA simply occurred as the coup unfolded and were not part of a preplanned coordinated plot.

The Soviet Union, dismissing Western press reports of involvement in the coup, moved quickly to consolidate relations with the PDPA regime headed by Taraki. Within three months, more than twenty bilateral agreements had been signed and the number of Soviet military advisers had doubled to 700. In Soviet public pronouncements, Afghanistan under PDPA rule was lauded along with other states of a "socialist orientation," such as Angola, Mozambique, and Ethiopia. The penetration of Soviet advisers into the key governmental, military, and economic sectors complemented a political strategy that emphasized the creation of Leninist institutions.

The Soviet stress on institution-building along Marxist-Leninist lines was a legacy of its experience in the Third World. Major policy reversals in Ghana, Egypt, and Chile during the 1960s and 1970s had convinced the Soviet leadership of the necessity of such institutions in order to prevent setbacks and ensure a relationship of long-term influence. In the case of Afghanistan, institutionalization was not alone sufficient. As will be detailed below, domestic circumstances by late 1979—specifically, the failure of the PDPA regime to meet the growing insurgent threat to its existence—demanded a direct Soviet military role if "the gains of socialism" were to be preserved.

The Soviet decision to intervene militarily in Afghanistan in late December 1979 stemmed from an amalgam of factors. Before assessing the motivations behind Soviet decision-making, a brief consideration of the events that triggered the invasion would be useful. In the aftermath of the "April Revolution," Taraki moved aggressively to consolidate his internal position. The traditional problem of factionalism within the PDPA reemerged with a new intensity as Taraki removed *Parchamis* from positions in the government, schools, and military. Key *Parcham* leaders were exiled via diplomatic postings abroad; Babrak Karmal, for example, was named ambassador to Czechoslovakia in early July. At the same time, Taraki publicly asserted that *Khalqi* control over the government was total and that the *Parcham* faction as a political force had ceased to exist.[10]

The eclipse of the *Parcham* coincided with the rise of Hafizullah Amin within the PDPA leadership. As a politburo member and party secretary, Amin played an increasingly prominent role in the implementation of the Taraki regime's radical social program. Ideological fervor overrode pragmatism. The aim of the regime's political and economic program was to bring about a rapid transformation of the Afghan society. The social measures, including radical land reform and the banning of certain religious practices, cut across every aspect of Afghan life and bred deep resentment of the regime in both urban and rural areas. Within this context, it was no accident (as the Soviet press of that time would have put it) that reported incidents of armed resistance to the regime began to increase in summer 1978. By the end of the 1978, the first *Mujaheddin* training camps and supply routes had been established across the Durand Line in Pakistan. While the Taraki regime's domestic program generated heated opposition, Moscow took no demonstrable steps to stem its pace. Only in the post-Brezhnev era would Soviet commentators acknowledge that the Taraki regime's misguided attempt to move Afghanistan from feudalism to socialism overnight—a form of "infantile leftism" in Leninist terms—had done much to generate the widespread resistance that it faced.

The conclusion of the twenty-year Treaty of Friendship, Neighborliness, and Cooperation during the visit of Taraki to the Soviet capital in early December 1978 further cemented bilateral relations. Among its provisions, the agreement affirmed Afghan acceptance of the Brezhnev 1969 Asian collective security plan and pledged both parties to take "appropriate measures" to ensure their mutual security (Article IV). With this assurance of Soviet support, the Taraki regime continued the rapid implementation of its radical domestic program. The further deterioration of the internal security situation prompted the despatch of a senior military delegation headed by Soviet General Alexei Epishev, then in charge of the ideological and political supervision of the Soviet armed forces, to Kabul in early April 1979.[11]

During mid-1979, Vassily Safronchuk, posted to Kabul in June to be Soviet Ambassador Aleksandr Puzanov's deputy, coordinated Soviet efforts to stabilize the PDPA regime.[12] He reportedly urged Taraki and Amin to end fratricidal factionalism within the PDPA and to expand the social base of the regime by cultivating noncommunist internal political allies. Whether Safronchuk sought primarily to reform the PDPA or was genuinely open to the possibility of a noncommunist alternative to the Taraki-Amin regime remains an issue of contention. It is highly questionable whether noncommunist alternatives (e.g., former officials in King Zahir Shah's government) would have been more than a legitimizing fig leaf for continued PDPA rule.[13] Nor is it clear that such an outcome would have been acceptable to the Soviets. It should be recalled that during the late Brezhnev period, ideological considerations were accorded heightened importance under the influence of Politburo hardliners such as Mikhail Suslov and Boris Ponomarev, head of the Central Committee's International Department. As will be discussed below, these Soviet leaders viewed the creation of Marxist-Leninist regimes in the Third World, as opposed to multi-party coalition governments, as the best means of institutionalizing, and thereby preserving, a long-term influence relationship.

The Epishev military mission was followed by a larger one in August headed by Soviet Deputy Defense Minister General Ivan Pavlovskii. By September 1979 the Soviet leadership faced the options of either withdrawing and allowing events in Afghanistan to run their course or massively increasing its own military and political commitment to the Taraki regime.[14] A Soviet-backed attempt by Taraki to oust Amin from the PDPA leadership on September 14 resulted instead in Taraki's murder and replacement by Amin. The evident Soviet hope had been to bring about a reconciliation of the *Khalq* and *Parcham* through a reconstituted PDPA regime under the leadership of Taraki and Karmal.

Though the Soviet leadership ostensibly accepted the mid-September episode as a fait accompli, a decision was reportedly reached in late November to overthrow Amin,[15] whom the Soviet leadership viewed as both ineffectual and politically unreliable.[16] Amin's refusal to moderate his domestic program further intensified internal opposition to PDPA rule. In early December, Lieutenant General Viktor Paputin, a first deputy minister of interior, arrived in Kabul. His avowed mission was to further improve security measures. Evidence suggests that his real purpose was to lay the organizational basis for the subsequent coup. By this time the Soviet military contingent had increased to between three and four thousand, with control over a number of key instututions (e.g., the Bagram air base outside Kabul). Amidst these preparations, Soviet publications continued to charge large-scale Western interference in Afghan internal affairs.

During the three days before the invasion some 10,000 additional Soviet airborne troops were flown in to Bagram air base. This force carried out the coup against Amin on December 27 as seven Soviet mechanized divisions (estimated at a strength of 80,000 men) crossed the frontier and seized the major urban centers. A broadcast by Babrak Karmal from the Soviet Union announced the overthrow of Amin and asserted that Soviet forces were providing assistance in compliance with the 1978 Treaty of Friendship. The first detailed Soviet commentary on the Afghan crisis appeared in *Pravda* on December 31 under the pseudonym of A. Petrov.[17] The article stated that Amin was a "helpmate" of the forces of reaction who had overthrown the "legitimate" government headed by Taraki. The United States was castigated for attempting "to subjugate the Afghan people" so that Afghanistan might replace Iran as a base of operations on the Soviet Union's "southern border."

While Soviet posthoc rationalizations were widely dismissed, the issue of Soviet motivations remains an issue of contention—this despite the publication during 1989 and early 1990 of detailed, albeit selective, accounts of Soviet decision-making preceding the invasion. In his first public pronouncement after the invasion, Brezhnev stated that "it was not a simple decision for us to send military contingents to Afghanistan."[18]

No single factor provides an adequate understanding of Soviet policy. Indeed, the striking aspect of the Afghan case is the manner in which virtually all the factors motivating Soviet policy in the Third World—geographic, ideologic, strategic considerations, *inter alia*— were in evidence. Before assessing the relative importance of domestic, regional and global considerations in Soviet decision-making, it would be useful briefly to delineate the nature of Soviet interests at stake in Afghanistan.

The obvious starting point of Soviet security is border defense. As noted above, the Soviet frontier with Afghanistan is a legacy of Russian and British imperial competition. Russia under Soviet rule has continued the Czarist policy of seeking to foster weak, dependent states along its Middle Eastern and Central Asian frontiers as the best means of securing its southern border.[19] The dynamic of imperial power, however, is governed by a self-perpetuating logic. For the empire, all territorial acquisitions in defense of the frontier are by definition defensive. This attribute makes the debate over whether Soviet action in Afghanistan was motivated by offensive or defensive considerations particularly unenlightening. The fact that Afghanistan is contiguous to the USSR automatically placed it in a different category from other instances of Soviet involvement in the Third World.[20]

Related to border security is the Soviet Muslim factor, the importance of which to Soviet decision-making is debatable.[21] The nature of the Soviet debate did not reveal any direct evidence that this was a major source of concern. Yet, given the accelerating rate of demographic growth in Central Asia (estimates were of a Turko-Muslim population of approximately eighty million by the year 2000), and the Islamic fundamentalist orientation of the Afghan resistance, the Soviet leadership could not have dismissed the possibility that the Iranian experience might be replicated in Afghanistan. Alexandre Benningsen, noting the considerable potential for events along the northern border to have a "profound impact" on Soviet domestic politics, argued that the Soviet Muslim population is "likely to be influenced by ideas, programs, and ideologies—perhaps even by models of political warfare and guerrilla activity—moving northward from a 'destabilized' and radicalized Middle East."[22] With a Soviet-Afghan border running some 400 miles, this potential for political and religious spillover strongly militated in favor of direct Soviet intervention to maintain the PDPA regime. The "rollback" of socialism in Afghanistan would have created an unacceptable precedent with uncertain implications for the Central Asian republics.

An additional determinant of Soviet policy, although of secondary

importance relative to border security and the potential destabilza-
tion of Soviet Central Asia, was ideology. While Soviet theoretical
writings of the late 1970s acknowledged the possibility of "zigzags,"
a major objective was to prevent reversals once socialism has taken
root in a country. The proposition of irreversibility was related both
to Soviet *amour-propre* and legitimacy. The renewed emphasis on
ideology in Soviet policy during the late 1970s was a consequence of
the setbacks suffered by the USSR in the Third World during the late
1960s and early 1970s. As noted above, the overthrow or reorienta-
tion of pro-Soviet governments in Ghana, Guinea, Indonesia, Egypt,
and Chile again raised the issue of regime maintenance. Although
the Soviet Union exhibited considerable flexibility in its dealings with
Third World allies, the clear preference has been for the development
of Leninist institutions where local circumstances permit. While not
precluding the possibility of a reversal, such action appeared to create the prerequisites for a long-term influence relationship. Ideology,
in this context, was thus seen to serve both the demands of Soviet
Realpolitik and legitimacy.

Soviet policy on Afghanistan was framed within the context of this
structure of interests. What is our current understanding of the Soviet decision-making process—and the relative importance of domestic, regional, and global considerations within it? According to a
variety of sources, the specific decision to overthrow Amin and invade Afghanistan on December 27, 1979 was made by a Politburo
commission on Afghanistan that included President and CPSU General Secretary Leonid Brezhnev, Soviet Premier Alexei Kosygin, KGB
chief Yurii Andropov, Defense Minister Dmitrii Ustinov, chief ideo-
logue Mikhail Suslov and Foreign Minister Andrei Gromyko.[23] Soviet
Foreign Minister Edouard Shevardnadze, then a candidate member
of the Politburo, who would later become Foreign Minister, stated in
a speech to the Supreme Soviet that he and Mikhail Gorbachev
"happened to be together at the time, and we learned about it from
the radio and newspaper reports. A decision which had grave consequences for our country was made behind the party's and people's
back. They were presented with a fait accompli."[24]

The decision was also taken evidently without serious consultation
with either academic specialists from the USSR Academy of Sciences
or officials such as Safronchuk, who had substantial experience within
the country. The role of academic specialists in Soviet decision-making on Afghanistan was the focus of a lively exchange between
novelist Aleksandr Prokhanov and Academician Oleg Bogomolov in
Literaturnaya Gazeta in early 1989. Prokhanov charged that the spe-

cialists at the relevant USSR Academy of Sciences institutes and government ministries had provided incorrect assessments of the Afghan situation; in response, Bogomalov asserted that expert advice had been ignored.[25] In the case of Safronchuk, he stated in a strikingly candid and prescient conversation with the U.S. Chargé d'Affaires J. Bruce Amstutz that the deployment of Soviet forces in Afghanistan would have adverse internal and international repercussions; Safronchuk approvingly cited the Leninist dictum that "every revolution must defend itself."[26]

The attitude of the military toward intervention remains contentious despite the publication of revealing *glasnost'* era articles exploring this issue. As noted above, the conventional wisdom in the West prior to 1989 had been that the military had supported the action. This conclusion had been based on the testimony, now discredited, of a KGB defector, Major Vladimir Kuzichkin, who reportedly stated that the KGB high command had opposed further Soviet entanglement in Afghan affairs, while the military complained about events having been allowed to "get out of hand."[27] In his *Ogonyek* interview of March 1989, General Valentin Varrenikov reports that both Chief of the General Staff Nikolai Ogarkov and Marshal Sergei Akhromeev opposed the invasion. These objections were overruled by the civilian Minister of Defense, Dmitrii Ustinov, who reportedly directed the General Staff to prepare for military operations in Afghanistan on December 10.[28]

The resort to military intervention came after the death of Taraki in September 1979 and the failure of the Safronchuk mission to politically stabilize the PDPA regime through a negotiated rapprochement between the rival *Parcham* and *Khalq* factions, as well as the broadening of the regime's social base. At that point, Soviet political options within the country appeared exhausted. This sequence of events is consistent with the "slippery slope" model. It is not known whether the leadership requested estimates from the military on the expected duration of the anti-insurgency mission in Afghanistan. The prevailing belief, according to Shevardnadze, is that "the people who made the decision . . . did not plan to stay in Afghanistan for any length of time, nor to create the sixteenth or seventeenth Soviet republic."[29]

To what extent did regional and global considerations affect Soviet decision-making? On the strategic level, Soviet relations with its great power adversaries during 1978–79 were at a nadir with little prospect for improvement. The visit of Chinese Vice Premier Deng Xiaoping to Washington in January 1979 augured still closer cooperation between Washington and Beijing. The political context was shaped by three other events: the NATO decision in early December to deploy new medium-range systems; the declining political fortunes of the SALT II treaty in the U.S. Senate; and, finally, the American naval build up in the Persian Gulf and Arabian Sea in response to events in Iran. The significance and purpose of American military deployments in Southwest Asia is particularly salient because Soviet declaratory statements following the invasion cited these moves as evidence of a direct U.S. military threat against Iran and Afghanistan.[30] Although the view that large-scale American military intervention against Iran in 1978–79 was seriously considered by the Carter administration is widely discounted in the West, with some Soviet officials and analysts it remains a major theme.[31]

The preceding analysis suggests that the Soviet decision to intervene militarily in Afghanistan was influenced by a confluence of factors, especially the desire to prevent the collapse of a Marxist-Leninist regime in a bordering state. In the political environment of the late 1970s, the Soviet leadership evidently believed that the imperatives of border required Afghanistan to be not merely a buffer state, as it had been for most of its modern history, but a country under Moscow's direct influence. This rationale was buttressed by two factors: first, the recognition that the likely alternative to a PDPA regime in Kabul was an Islamic one (which, given the uncertain consequences of such an eventuality for the stability of Soviet Central Asia in the wake of the Iranian revolution, was particularly unattractive) and, second, the evident belief within the Politburo that there was little left to forfeit in its relationship with Washington.

Stage II: Staying In

Following the death of Leonid Brezhnev in November 1982, successive Soviet leaders from Andropov to Chernenko to Gorbachev proclaimed the irreversibility of the Afghan revolution.[32] During the mid-1980s it was frequently observed that Soviet forces had fought longer in this conflict than they had against the Axis powers during World War II. At the same time, however, it was noted that some ten years had passed after the Bolshevik revolution before the area now comprising the Soviet Central Asian republics had been pacified. Many observers of Soviet foreign policy questioned whether this latter perspective might suggest the time frame within which the Soviet leadership viewed the Afghan war. While the UN-sponsored

negotiations remained stalemated in Geneva, the Soviet Union intensified military pressure on the *Mujaheddin* in order to quell domestic
opposition to the PDPA regime. To attain this objective, the size of
the USSR's "limited contingent" in Afghanistan rose during the early
1980s to 115,000 troops.[33] These forces were augmented by an additional 30,000–35,000 troops stationed in the adjacent Soviet Central
Asian republics.

The Soviet military proved surprisingly slow in adapting to the
challenge of counter-insurgency warfare within Afghanistan. Although the term "counter-insurgency" has a pejorative connotation
in the Soviet politico-military lexicon (as something only imperialists
practice), the Red Army did have well-developed doctrines of mountain and desert war. Despite this doctrinal base, Soviet military operations during the early years of the war appeared better suited to
conditions along the European central front than those in Afghanistan. In the immediate aftermath of the invasion, the evident belief,
as articulated by the commander of the Turkestan Military District,
General Yuri Maksimov, was that the presence of Soviet forces in
relatively large number would "permit the stabilization of the situation in Afghanistan, will allow the democratic forces to consolidate
and the gains of the revolution to be secured, and will permit cooling
the ardor of those who initiated military adventures."[34]

Soviet military strategy emphasized control over the major urban
centers and the road network linking them. The extensive use of
airpower against civilian targets led to the depopulation of strategic
areas in the country. The security of Kabul—the seat of the PDPA
regime—was the centerpiece of Soviet strategy. This feature prompted
the *Economist* to quip editorially that Afghanistan was becoming a
good example of socialism in one town. Apart from Kabul, Soviet
control was most effective in the relatively flat northern area, which
was of high priority because of its adjacency to the USSR and its rich
natural gas deposits.

With Kabul run as a PDPA city state, the Karmal regime governed
an estimated 20 percent of the Afghan population. Soviet casualties
for the 1979–1984 period were estimated at between 20,000 and 25,000
(with roughly one-third killed). The economic costs for the Soviet
Union over the same period were placed at $12 billion. It is striking
that, in contrast to the escalating American involvement in Vietnam
during the 1960s, the Soviet leadership did not choose to augment
substantially the size of its "limited contingent" in Afghanistan. Yuri
Gankovsy, a top Soviet specialist at the USSR Academy of Sciences'
Institute of Oriental Studies, stated that from the outset "we had no

reason to control all Afghanistan territory" and that 100,000 troops were sufficient to control "the main administrative centers and two or three economic and strategic centers."[35] Although capable of forestalling a *Mujaheddin* victory over the PDPA, this force was insufficient to achieve Soviet long-term political objectives of quelling the insurgency movement and stabilizing the situation within the country.

Karmal's elusive quest for domestic legitimacy led to the repeal of many of the draconian social measures introduced by his *Khalqi* predecessors. The regime's "hearts and minds" campaign yielded only limited results because of the PDPA's continuing identification with the Soviet occupiers. An effort was also made to increase the trappings of autonomous civilian rule. In early 1985, for example, the Revolutionary Council announced forthcoming parliamentary elections for a grand assembly, or *loi jirga*; critics noted that this body was intended to be the functional equivalent of the Supreme Soviet. These cosmetic political changes aside, the main focus of attention for the regime was its two institutional underpinnings: the armed forces and the party. The DRA Army remained both militarily ineffective and politically unreliable. The size of the force dropped from a prewar total of 90,000 to an estimated 35,000–40,000, largely because of desertions and defections over to the guerrillas. As a result, the regime was forced increasingly to rely on Soviet troops.

As the regime attempted in vain to revitalize the armed forces, the PDPA itself continued to be plagued by factionalism. Despite Soviet efforts to foster party unity, political differences between *Parcham* and *Khalq* led to frequent violent incidents. Karmal's ruling *Parcham* faction comprised only 40 percent of the PDPA membership and its adherents came primarily from non-Pushtun ethnic groups. The *Parcham* enjoyed predominance over the major party and governmental organs (notably KHAD, the Afghan intelligence service). The *Khalq* faction's membership is primarily of Pushtun ethnic origin. While more ethnically representative of Afghanistan, *Khalq* policies also tended to be more nationalistic and socially radical than those of the *Parcham*. As in the past, the shuffling of personnel at the top was a mechanism to ameliorate factional tensions. In December 1984, for example, the *Parchami* Minister of Defense, Abdul Qadar, was replaced by the *Khalq*-oriented Chief of Staff, Nazar Mohammed, following an incident in which a *Khalqi* general assaulted Qadar for preferentially promoting *Parcham* members within the military.

During the 1979–1985 period, the creation of institutions along Leninist lines was a central component of Soviet political strategy in

Afghanistan. These institutions (specifically the party, armed forces, and intelligence service) were viewed as an essential prerequisite for a long-term influence relationship. A related aspect of Soviet policy was the enforced dispatch of some 20,000 Afghan students to the Soviet Union for education. Just as Mongolians were sent to the USSR for indoctrination in the 1930s, these Afghan students were depicted as the loyal cadre of a new generation. The persistent shortage of Afghan workers who were both technically competent and politically reliable had pervasive consequences. In the economic sphere, this situation led to heavy dependence on the Soviet Union. This reliance was accompanied by an accelerating integration of the Soviet and Afghan economies. By 1984, for example, some sixty percent of Afghanistan's foreign trade was with the Soviet Union alone.

Although the Afghan resistance movement has been divided since its inception along ethnic and religious lines, military coordination among its disparate elements improved over time. The fragmentation of the resistance movement into an estimated 200–300 guerrilla groups operating within Afghanistan permitted the Soviet Union to employ a classic divide-and-rule strategy. Many of the guerrilla groups developed affiliations with the seven major political parties based across the Durand Line in Peshawar. These parties divided into two loose coalitions along traditionalist and fundamentalist lines. Political suspicion was a major factor preventing increased unity. Indeed, there were periodic reports of violent clashes between rival groups.

Relations between the resistance movement and the Pakistan government were good but somewhat problematic. With some three million refugees quartered in camps across the Durand Line, the Zia regime expressed occasional disquiet over Afghan efforts to establish a more enduring presence in Pakistan's Northwest Frontier Province (e.g., land purchases, involvement in local politics). From the resistance side, there were complaints that not all the arms supplied by the resistance's international supporters were reaching Peshawar after their arrival in Pakistan; in some instances the weapons were reportedly not delivered or were substituted with inferior arms from the Pakistani military. American military assistance to the *Mujaheddin* during the 1979–1984 period has been estimated at $625 million; aid for 1985 was reportedly set at $280 million.[36]

During the period between Brezhnev's death in November 1982 and Gorbachev's assent to power in March 1985, there were no public indications of any reevaluation or serious debate over Soviet Afghan policy within the ruling oligarchy. When meeting with Pakistan President Zia ul-Haq at the Brezhnev funeral in November 1982,

CPSU General Secretary Yuri Andropov did hint at some flexibility in the Soviet position, reportedly telling Zia that the Soviet Union would leave "quickly" if Pakistan ended its support for the *Mujaheddin*.[37] This suggestion of a possible shift, however, was contradicted by the weight of Soviet policy pronouncements, which stated that the changes within Afghanistan were "irreversible." In his address to the Central Committee Plenum in June 1983, Andropov did express irritation with client regimes whose commitment to socialism appeared more rhetorical than real: "It is one thing to proclaim socialism, but another to build it."[38] Although a reference to Afghanistan could only be intimated in the Andropov speech, others were more direct in their criticism of the PDPA. Soviet commentaries during the post-Brezhnev period began to acknowledge that the harsh political and social measures adopted by the Taraki-Amin regime during 1978–79 had done much to create the widespread popular opposition that necessitated the costly Soviet military intervention. This criticism of the excesses of Taraki and Amin did not extend to the ineffectual rule of Babrak Karmal, nor did it challenge the political bases of continued Soviet involvement in Afghanistan.

The two and a half years between Brezhnev's death and Gorbachev's assumption of power became a crucial transition period between old and new. It is now known (although it was far from clear at the time) that Andropov, the former KGB chief who knew the full extent of the Soviet Union's dire economic state, initiated many of the domestic and foreign policy changes that later became *perestroika* and "new thinking" under Gorbachev. Gorbachev himself has acknowledged the important role played by Andropov in decisively breaking with the past. Andropov's tenure, however, was brief; he lived little more than a year after assuming the position of CPSU General Secretary and it is not known the degree to which Andropov's progressive illness affected his exercise of power. One can only speculate whether Andropov would have gone as far and as fast as Gorbachev in implementing radical reforms in Soviet foreign and domestic policies. Andropov's "anti-corruption" campaign now appears to have been a disguised purge perhaps designed to prepare the political ground for just such a push.

Instead, Andropov's death brought to power one of Brezhnev's closest cronies—an individual who epitomized what Soviet commentators now call the era of "stagnation" under Brezhnev. During the year-long rule of Konstantin Chernenko, the reform process remained on hold, while the supporters of genuine change, championed by Gorbachev, positioned themselves for the next succession struggle. The Afghan war was a symptom of much broader problems facing Soviet society by the early 1980s—a provocative foreign policy that had generated an anti-Soviet coalition ringing the country from Norway to Japan, a closed foreign policy decision-making process lacking adequate checks and balances, an ideological conception of international relations that generated Soviet activism in distant regions where important Soviet national interests (defined in more orthodox terms) were not at stake. Under Gorbachev, the Afghan war came under scrutiny as part of the sweeping reevalution of Soviet foreign policy and the advent of "new thinking." Clearly the relative importance of Afghanistan in Soviet strategy takes on a different light in a world in which Soviet forces are withdrawn from Eastern Europe and Germany is unified.

These radical changes would await the ascension of Gorbachev to power in March 1985. During this hiatus following Brezhnev's death, Soviet policies in Afghanistan were in a state of political inertia. Moscow maintained its firm commitment to the preservation of the PDPA regime in Kabul. Although Taraki and Amin came under strong criticism, no doubts were expressed about the manifest inadequacies of Babrak Karmal. Soviet military strategy remained centered on the control of urban areas and the roadways connecting them; no effort was made to control the countryside nor mount offensive operations behind *Mujaheddin* lines. With the Soviet ruling oligarchy preoccupied during 1982–85 with a drawn out succession struggle, Afghanistan was an important, albeit secondary issue. This steady-state policy toward Afghanistan kept Moscow's political and economic costs within tolerable limits. To be sure, the war was unpopular with certain segments of the Soviet population—notably the youth and the intelligentsia. In the pre-Gorbachev period, however, public opinion was simply not a major factor affecting Soviet decision-making. It was only with the advent of *glasnost* and Gorbachev's moves toward democratization (as manifested in the creation of a free press) that public opinion and the media became significant forces in Soviet political life.

Stage III: Getting Out

In mid-February 1988, as the UN-sponsored negotiations in Geneva entered their final phase, Gorbachev acknowledged that "[f]ollowing the CPSU Central Committee April [1985] Plenum, the Politburo conducted a hard and impartial analysis of the position and started even at that time to seek a way out of the situation."[39] In the wake of Gorbachev's assumption of power in March 1985, however, there were no clear indicators that such a policy review was underway. Indeed, Gorbachev's initial public statements on Afghanistan indicated an intention to stay the course. Following the Chernenko funeral, for example, he sternly lectured Zia on the dangers of Pakistani assistance to the *Mujaheddin* and affirmed that Afghanistan's transition to socialism was "irreversible." While maintaining this public posture, Gorbachev initiated significant changes in Soviet military and political strategies within Afghanistan.

The change in military strategy was symbolized by the appointment of General Mikhail Zaitsev, the young and energetic former commander of Soviet forces in East Germany, to command the USSR's "limited contingent."[40] Under his leadership, Soviet military performance improved quite significantly.[41] Particularly effective use was made of helicopter gunships (e.g. the Hind Mi-24 and Mi-25) and special forces units (*spetznaz*), often operating behind *Mujaheddin* lines. Prior to that time, Soviet forces remained largely in their garrisons and ventured out only in armored vehicles along the highways connecting the country's few urban centers. By mid-1986 these Soviet military innovations were having a real impact on the resistance. Within the context of this deteriorating situation, the Reagan Administration decided in April 1986 to provide the *Mujaheddin* with Stinger anti-aircraft missiles. The arrival of these new American weapons marked a turning point in the war. With air losses estimated at one aircraft per day, the Soviet military command was forced to change tactics. They were no longer able to use helicopter gunships and tactical aircraft in close ground support roles. This development, in turn, adversely affected the effectiveness of the *spetznaz*. The Soviet response to the arrival of the Stingers was to place increased reliance on artillery and high-level aerial bombardment. Zaitsev's activist strategy based on mobility ground to a halt as Soviet military operations reverted back to their prior form.

While Zaitsev worked to turn around the ground war in 1985–1986, Gorbachev moved to revitalize the PDPA regime. At the same time, however, the General Secretary gave his first public hints of a possible Soviet military withdrawal. In his political report on February 25, 1986 to the CPSU's Twenty-Seventh Party Congress, Gorbachev described the Afghan war as a "bleeding wound." This dramatic characterization of the war was followed in early May 1986 by a shakeup in the PDPA leadership in which Karmal was replaced by Dr. Najibullah, a former top official in the KHAD. This change in the

PDPA's top leadership was consistent with efforts under Gorbachev to reinvigorate the regime and attempt to increase public support for it. Efforts were redoubled to give the appearance that the Afghan revolution's "social base" was being expanded.[42] In promoting these domestic changes within Afghanistan, Soviet commentators acknowledged that the "adventurous" strategy pursued by Tariki and Amin prior to December 1979 had much to do with generating large-scale public resistance to the PDPA regime. During the visit of Soviet Foreign Minister Eduard Shevardnadze and Central Committee International Department chief Anatoly Dobrynin to Kabul in January 1987, Najibullah issued proposals for an immediate cease-fire and the formation of a "national reconciliation" government with elements of the *Mujaheddin*. This renewed overture to the resistance movement was rejected out of hand.

In July 1987, Najibullah went to Moscow for a meeting with Gorbachev to review the military and political situation, at which time Gorbachev reportedly specified to Najibullah a definite timetable for the withdrawal of Soviet forces from Afghanistan.[43] A public hint of this development came in September 1987 when Shevardnadze stated that the Kremlin hoped that Soviet troops would be out of the country before the end of the Reagan administration. Despite these developments, most Western observers remained skeptical that the USSR would actually carry out a withdrawal.

The decisive shift in Soviet policy came in November 1987 during a meeting between Soviet Deputy Foreign Minister Yuli Vorontsov and Undersecretary of State Michael Armacost in Geneva. At that time, Vorontsov informed Armacost that the USSR would no longer hold the withdrawal of its forces from Afghanistan contingent to the guaranteed survival of the PDPA regime. Up to then, the UN-sponsored negotiations involving the Kabul government and Pakistan had made little progress owing to this Soviet insistence. Although much discussion during the negotiations focused on the timetable for a Soviet withdrawal, the crucial question had always been the composition of the follow-on government in Kabul. With this key shift in the Soviet position, the Geneva negotiations made rapid progress. On February 8, 1988, Gorbachev made public the Soviet plan for a phased withdrawal of its troops over a twelve-month period beginning as early as May 15, 1988. The extent of Gorbachev's desire to extricate Soviet forces from Afghanistan was highlighted when he accepted a last-minute American demand that the cutoff of military supplies to the Kabul regime and the resistance should be "symmetrical." Gorbachev and Najibullah met in Tashkent on April 7 to finalize arrangements for the withdrawal of Soviet forces from Afghanistan. One week later, on April 14, 1988, these terms were codified in an agreement signed by Afghanistan, Pakistan, the Soviet Union, and the United States. By the end of July 1988, the USSR had reportedly withdrawn some 30 percent of the total 115,000-man force.

The Politburo's decision to withdraw from Afghanistan was evidently a consensual one. As compared to Gorbachev's ambitious program of domestic reform, the Afghan war was not a major issue of contention within the Soviet leadership. The military as an institution appeared supportive of the Gorbachev move. In a speech at the Nineteenth All-Union CPSU Conference in July 1988, General B. V. Gromov, commander of Soviet forces in Afghanistan, stated simply that Soviet forces were returning from the country after fulfilling their internationalist duty.[44] Likewise, while other aspects of Gorbachev's policies (viz. *perestroika* and *glasnost'*) were publicly questioned by members of the top leadership, most notably by Yegor Ligachev, no major criticism was voiced of the withdrawal decision. It is striking that the Soviet Union has not undergone the kind of bitter debate over credibility and superpower responsibility that the United States experienced during the Vietnam era.

Before the February 1988 announcement many Western analysts believed that a primary factor militating against Soviet acceptance of a settlement was the feedback effect that a foreign policy setback in Afghanistan might have on the stability of Gorbachev's position within the ruling oligarchy. Parallels were drawn between a possible Afghan failure and Khrushchev's Cuban debacle. The accepted view is that the latter episode had much to do with Khrushchev's ouster and that, as a consequence, Gorbachev, while pursuing a domestic agenda that was already making him many enemies, would avoid handing his critics a foreign policy failure that might be used to undermine his position on the Politburo. This prevailing analysis, however, failed to take into full consideration the adverse domestic consequences of the conflict on Soviet society (e.g. drug problems, alienated veterans). To be sure, the war was universally unpopular and highly demoralizing at a time when Gorbachev was appealing to the voluntaristic spirit of Soviet youth, intellectuals, and workers to bring about a radical restructuring of the Soviet economy and governmental organs.

In assessing the Soviet decision to withdraw from Afghanistan, how important was the Gorbachev factor relative to other military and external considerations? While other factors had important bearing, the evidence supports the conclusion that Gorbachev the leader—

and the domestic revolution that he unleashed—was the critical determinant of Soviet decision-making. The non-Gorbachev (i.e. extra-Soviet) factors—the politically intractable situation within Afghanistan, the stalemated military conflict, and continuing international pressure—were necessary prerequisites for a withdrawal decision, but were not in themselves sufficient. The crucial factor was domestic change within the Soviet Union, which brought about a wholly new perspective on national security issues—and the relationship between Soviet foreign and domestic policies.

After assuming power, Gorbachev repeatedly stated that the primary objective of his foreign policy was to foster a tranquil international environment within which to pursue domestic social, economic, and political reform. This goal dictated a near-term, though not immediate, resolution of the Afghan war. His initial approach, as described above, was to reshape both Soviet political and military strategies to bring about the USSR's desired political outcome—the survival of the PDPA regime. Politically there was an effort, not dissimilar to that of Safronchuk's in mid-1979, to reform the PDPA (e.g. Karmal's replacement by Najibullah) and increase its popularity by wooing potential non-communist coalition partners. Militarily, General Zaitsev, while basically maintaining a garrison strategy, improved performance through the effective use of special forces. Gorbachev's twin political and military strategies proved inadequate. The political reforms did little to increase the appeal of the Najibullah regime and factionalism remained a problem within the PDPA. On the battlefield, the arrival of *stinger* anti-aircraft missiles derailed Zaitsev's counter-insurgency strategy.

At that point, Gorbachev faced the options of either upping the ante (perhaps a cross-border attack on *Mujaheddin* base camps in Pakistan), continuing to muddle along, or cutting his losses. The first option would have led to a crisis in relations with Washington leading to the derailment of the incipient Detente II and would have provided fresh impetus to the Reagan arms build up. Could *perestroika* be pursued at home under such international circumstances? Clearly not. And, at the same time, military escalation offered no assurance that the Islamic insurgency would be decisively put down.

"Staying the course" at the existing level of commitment was an equally unattractive option for Gorbachev as the war was alienating key constituencies (i.e., the youth and intelligentsia) of his internal reform program and was having other adverse social consequences within the country. Given the widespread unpopularity of the Afghan war, Gorbachev also had to take public opinion into account as he moved to democratize the foreign policy process. In an era of *glasnost'*, it would be impossible any longer to hide from public scrutiny the economic and human costs of the war. Soon Afghanistan would have become "Gorbachev's war."

Within this context, the withdrawal of Soviet forces with all its admitted uncertainties (*viz.* the very real danger that the PDPA regime would fall) was much more attractive than the alternatives of escalation or "staying the course." Despite the problems of the Afghan military and the PDPA, Soviet officials, contrary to American estimates, believed that the Najibullah regime would have a reasonable chance of survival after the withdrawal of the Red Army.[45] This conclusion was based on the view that the PDPA, unburdened by the political liability of an occupation army, would become the champion of all secular (i.e., non-Islamic) groups within the country and that the *Mujaheddin* would fragment in the absence of a unifying Soviet presence in Afghanistan. The Soviet Union, in short, remained well positioned to influence the course of events within Afghanistan following the withdrawal of Soviet forces.

Apart from its domestic benefits, the withdrawal promised to improve further the international position of the Soviet Union. At a time when Washington was talking about "litmus tests" and debating whether Gorbachev was "for real" or not, what better way of demonstrating the substance of "new thinking" than defusing the regional conflict that had been the precipitant of the revitalized Cold War of the 1980s. In the wake of the Red Army's withdrawal, the Soviets, to the surprise of many, including evidently the Bush administration, did not simply cut their losses in Afghanistan and permit events to run their course. Gorbachev sought more than just a "decent interval" between the withdrawal of Soviet forces and whatever political fate might await Najibullah. Within Afghanistan, the PDPA, freed of the political liability of Soviet occupation forces, has improved its popular standing—particularly with those secularly oriented Afghans fearing the specter of a *Mujaheddin*-run Islamic republic. Najibullah has benefited from the lack of political cohesion ad military coordination within the guerrilla movement, as well as its political identifiction with a foreign power—Pakistan.

The context of Soviet decision-making on Afghanistan has been transformed by the USSR's deepening economic and political crisis. The failed coup of August 1991 resulted in the demise of the Communist Party and enhanced authority for the various republic leaders, such as Boris Yeltsin, at the expense of Gorbachev's central government. On September 13, 1991, Secretary of State James Baker and Soviet Foreign Minister Boris Pankin agreed to a mutual arms cutoff to the various Afghan factions by January 1992 and called upon the United Nations to sponsor free elections inside the country. With the conclusion of this bilateral agreement the final vestige of superpower involvement in the Afghan civil war has been removed. It marks the final reversal of the expansionist Third World policies pursued by Moscow in the late 1970s and early 1980s. While the leadership in Moscow, whatever its political orientation, will not be indifferent to the outcome in Afghanistan, the Kremlin will remain preoccupied for the indefinite future with events and problems closer to home.

Abbreviations

CPSU — Communist Party of the Soviet Union
DRA — Democratic Republic of Afghanistan
KGB — Committee for State Security; Soviet intelligence service
KHAD — The Afghan intelligence service
Khalq — Literally "The Masses"; one of two factions of the PDPA
Mujaheddin — Afghan resistance movement
Parcham — Literally "Banner"; one of two factions of the PDPA
PDPA — People's Democratic Party of Afghanistan
Spetznaz — Soviet Special Forces

Chronology

1960s

January 1965: People's Democratic Party of Afghanistan (PDPA) founded by Nur Mohammed Taraki
July 1967: PDPA splits into rival Parcham and Khalq factions.

1970–1977

June 1973: King Zahir Shah overthrown by Mohammed Daoud; establishment of Afghanistan as a republic.
mid-1977: Reunification of Parcham and Khalq factions.

1978

April: Daoud overthrown in PDPA coup headed by Taraki.
December: Soviet-Afghan Twenty-year Treaty of Friendship concluded.

1979

March: Hafizullah Amin named prime minister; Taraki remains president and defense minister.

April: Mission of General Alexei Epishev.

August: Mission of Deputy Defense Minister Ivan Pavlovskii.

September: Taraki murdered and replaced by Amin.

Early December: Mission of General Viktor Paputin; Soviet military presence within Afghanistan augmented.

December 27: Amin killed in coup and replaced by Barbrak Karmal; Soviet force of 80,000 crosses into Afghanistan.

1982–1985

June 1982: UN-sponsored indirect negotiations between Afghanistan and Pakistan begin in Geneva.

November 1982: Brezhnev dies and is replaced as General Secretary of the CPSU by KGB chief Yuri Andropov. Andropov tells Pakistan President Zia that Soviet forces would leave "quickly" if Pakistan would cease its support for the Afghan resistance.

April 1984: Konstantin Chernenko becomes General Secretary of the CPSU following the death of Andropov.

March 1985: Following the death of Chernenko, Mikhail Gorbachev takes office as General Secretary of the CPSU.

July 1985: General Mikhail Zaitsev assumes command of Soviet forces in Afghanistan.

1986

February: During 27th Soviet Party Conference, Gorbachev calls the Afghan war a "bleeding wound" and expresses the hope that Soviet forces will be withdrawn "in the nearest future."

April: U.S. begins to supply Afghan resistance with Stinger antiaircraft missiles.

May: Moscow engineers a leadership change in Kabul in which Babrak Karmal is replaced by Najibullah.

December: During a secret Kremlin meeting, Gorbachev reportedly informs Najibullah that Moscow hopes to withdraw its forces by mid-1988.

1987

January: During the visit of Foreign Minister Eduard Shevardnadze to Kabul, Najibullah issues proposals for an immediate cease-fire and the formulation of a "national reconciliation" government with elements of the Afghan resistance.

July: Najibullah visits Moscow and is told that Soviet forces will be withdrawn from Afghanistan within 12 months.

September: During a meeting with U.S. Secretary of State George Shultz,

Shevardnadze states that Soviet forces may be withdrawn from Afghanistan before the end of the Reagan Administration.

November: In a major policy reversal, Deputy Foreign Minister Yuli Vorontsov, meeting with Undersecretary of State Michael Armacost in Geneva, states that Soviet forces will withdraw from Afghanistan without any guarantee that the PDPA will remain in power in Kabul.

December: During the U.S.–Soviet summit meeting in Washington, President Reagan states that the U.S. military assistance to the Afghan resistance will continue until Moscow ends its aid to the Kabul regime.

1988

February 8: Gorbachev announces that the Soviet troop withdrawal will begin on May 15 pending the conclusion of a UN-sponsored agreement.

April 7: Gorbachev and Najibullah meet in Tashkent; Moscow reluctantly accepts the U.S. policy of "symmetry," linking the continuation of American support to the Afghan resistance to Soviet military assistance to the Kabul regime.

April 14: The UN-sponsored Afghan accords are signed in Geneva by Afghanistan, Pakistan, the Soviet Union, and the United States.

1989

February 15: The Soviet Union completes the withdrawal of its forces from Afghanistan.

Notes

1. For a comparative assessment of Soviet involvement in Third World conflicts see Bruce D. Porter, *The USSR in Third World Conflicts: Soviet Arms and Diplomacy in Local Wars 1945–1980* (Cambridge: Cambridge University Press, 1984).

2. The declaration of the Carter Doctrine was contained in the President's 1980 State of the Union Address to Congress; see *Department of State Bulletin* 88, no. 2035 (February 1980), special section A–B.

3. For a comprehensive survey and analysis of these articles see Cynthia Roberts, in "Soviet Foreign Policy: Setting the Record Straight?," *Report on the USSR* 1, no. 50 (December 15, 1989):4–8.

4. A. Oliinik, "Vvod voisk v Afganistane: kak prinimalos' reshenie' ("The introduction of troops in Afghanistan: how the decision was taken"), *Krasnaya zvezda*, November 18, 1989, pp. 3–4.

5. *Ogonek*, no. 12, March 1989; reported in Michael Dobbs, "Soviet Cites Dissent on Afghan War," *Washington Post*, March 20, 1989; see also Roberts, "*Glasnost'*," pp. 5–6.

6. For a comprehensive historical account of Soviet-Afghan relations see

Ludwig W. Adamec, *Afghanistan's Foreign Affairs to the Mid-Twentieth Century* (Tucson: University of Arizona Press, 1974).

7. Alvin Z. Rubinstein, *Soviet Policy Toward Turkey, Iran and Afghanistan: The Dynamic of Influence* (New York: Praeger, 1982), pp. 134–135.

8. Opposition to Daoud came not only from the Left but also from Muslim traditionalists, alienated by Daoud's efforts to centralize authority. In 1975 a fundamentalist Muslim group, Hizb-i-Islami, began military operations against the Kabul government with the reported support of Pakistan and Libya; see Raymond L. Garthoff, *Detente and Confrontation: American-Soviet Relations from Nixon to Reagan* (Washington: Brookings Institution, 1985), p. 893.

9. Henry S. Bradsher, *Afghanistan and the Soviet Union* (Durham, NC: Duke University Press policy Studies, 1984), pp. 83.

10. When those Parcham leaders posted to embassies were recalled by Taraki in early September 1979 to face treason charges, they were provided political refuge by the Soviet Union, though no announcement was made to that effect.

11. See Jiri Valenta, "Soviet Decisionmaking on Afghanistan, 1979," in Jiri Valenta and William Potter, eds., *Soviet Decisionmaking for National Security* (London: George Allen & Unwin, 1984), pp. 218–236.

12. Garthoff, p. 902–905; Bradsher, *Afghanistan and the Soviet Union*, pp. 103–104.

13. Raymond Garthoff argues (*Detente and Confrontation*, p. 905) that the Soviets were more open to the possibility of a coalition government.

14. S. Neil MacFarlane, "Intervention and Regional Security," *Adelphi Paper* no. 196 (London: IISS, 1985):27–28.

15. Jiri Valenta, "From Prague to Kabul: The Soviet Style of Invasion," *International Security*, 5, no. 2 (Fall 1980):130–132.

16. Soviet commentaries, for example, accused Amin of developing "secret contacts" with Washington and Beijing. For a Soviet rendition of these events (published shortly after the invasion) see P. Demchenko, "Afghanistan: Ha Strazhe Zavoevaniy Naroda" (Afghanistan: Standing Guard Over the People's Gains"), *Kommunist*, no. 5 (March 1980):71–78.

17. A. Petrov, "On Events in Afghanistan," *Pravda* in *Current Digest of the Soviet Press*, 31, no. 52 (January 23, 1980):5–7.

18. Brezhnev's statement was read over Soviet television and was in response to a question about "the present international environment" submitted by a *Pravda* correspondent; *Pravda*, January 13, 1980 in *FBIS/SU*, January 14, 1980, pp. A1–A6.

19. For a discussion of this theme see, for example, "Soviet Relations with Countries of the Northern Tier" in Adeed Dawisha and Karen Dawisha, eds., *The Soviet Union and the Middle East: Policies and Perspectives* (London: Heinemann for the Royal Institute of International Affairs, 1982), pp. 32–40.

20. For a discussion of this theme see Edward N. Luttwak, *The Grand Strategy of the Soviet Union* (New York: St. Martin's Press, 1983), pp. 82–83.

21. Alexander Dallin, for example, argues: "The Soviet move was not motivated by the fear of the effect of Muslim self-consciousness abroad on the Turkic/Muslim population. . . . [T]here is no evidence of Russian fear of politically significant contagion or subversion by Islamic fundamentalists abroad in general and Afghan Muslims in particular." See Alexander Dallin, "The Road to Kabul: Soviet Perceptions of World Affairs and the Afghan Crisis" in *The Soviet Invasion of Afghanistan: Three Perspectives*, ACIS Working Paper no. 27 (Los Angeles: UCLA Center for International Affairs, September 1980), pp. 64–65. A contrasting position is taken by Helene Carrere d'Encausse who argues that "Homo Sovieticus" may well be supplanted by "Homo Islamicus"; see *Decline of an Empire: The Socialist Republics in Revolt* (New York: Newsweek Books, 1979), especially chapter VII.

22. Alexandre Benningsen, "Soviet Muslims and the World of Islam," *Problems of Communism* (March–April 1980), p. 51.

23. Reported by Anatolii Gromyko, son of the late Foreign Minister, in an interview with correspondent Igor' Belyaev in *Literaturnaya Gazeta*, September 20, 1989.

24. Speech entitled "Foreign Policy and Perestroika" by Foreign Minister Eduard Shevardnadze before the Supreme Soviet on October 23, 1989 in *FBIS/SU*, October 24, 1989, p. 45.

25. The initial Prokhanov appeared in *Literaturnaya Gazeta*, February 17, 1988; Bogomolov's response was in *Literaturnaya Gazeta*, March 16, 1988.

26. Garthoff, *Detente and Confrontation*, p. 917 cites confidential documents reconstructed by Iranian militants after the seizure of the U.S. embassy in Tehran.

27. See "Coups and Killings in Kabul: A KGB Defector Tells How Afghanistan Became Brezhnev's Vietnam," *Time*, November 22, 1982; discussed in Roberts, "*Glasnost*'," pp. 5–6; Garthoff, *Detente and Confrontation*, pp. 926–927.

28. *Krasnaya zvezda*, November 18, 1989; see note 4.

29. Cited in Roberts, "*Glasnost*'," p. 7.

30. The Soviets claimed that Brezhnev's warning against foreign intervention in Iran in *Pravda* on November 19, 1978 had deterred the Carter administration from directly intervening to prop up the Shah's regime.

31. See, for example, G.A. Trofimenko, "Rukoi neposvyashchennoi" *SShA*, no. 6 (1989):70–77.

32. For example, an editorial in *Pravda* on December 16, 1982 (less than one month after the death of Brezhnev) affirmed that the Afghan revolution was "irreversible."

33. Craig Karp, "A Five-Year Summary: Afghan Resistance and Soviet Occupation," *U.S. Department of State Special Report*, no. 118 (December 1984), p. 2.

34. Quoted in Garthoff, *Detente and Confrontation*, p. 935.

35. Quoted in Don Oberdorfer, "Afghanistan: The Soviet Decision to Pull Out" in *Washington Post*, April 17, 1988, p. A30.

36. Leslie H. Gelb, "Officials Say U.S. Plans to Double Supply of Arms to Afghan Rebels," *New York Times,* November 28, 1984.

37. Richard Cronin, "Afghanistan: United Nations-Sponsored Negotiations," report no. 85–210 F (Washington, DC: Congressional Research Service, 22 November 1985), p. 8.

38. *Pravda,* June 16, 1983; reprinted in *Current Digest of the Soviet Press* 35, no. 25, p. 8.

39. Gorbachev speech at CPSU Central Committee Plenum on 18 February 1988 in *FBIS-Soviet Union,* February 19, 1988, p. 56.

40. For additional background information see the excellent articles by Don Oberdorfer in *The Washington Post,* April 17, 1988.

41. For an analysis of the Soviet force structure in Afghanistan, as well as factors affecting morale and discipline, see Alexander Alexiev, *Inside the Soviet Army in Afghanistan,* no. R-3627-A (Santa Monica, CA: Rand Corporation, May 1988).

42. See, for example, "Za rasshirenie sotsialnoi bazy afganskoi revolyutsii" ("For the expansion of the Afghan revolution's social base"), *Pravda* (unsigned editorial), December 21, 1985.

43. Reported in *Washington Post,* April 17, 1988.

44. *Krasnaya zvezda,* July 2, 1988.

45. See, for example, the interview with Afghan expert Yuri Gankovsky in *Izvestiya,* May 5, 1989, p. 5.

4

Syria in Lebanon

YOSSI OLMERT

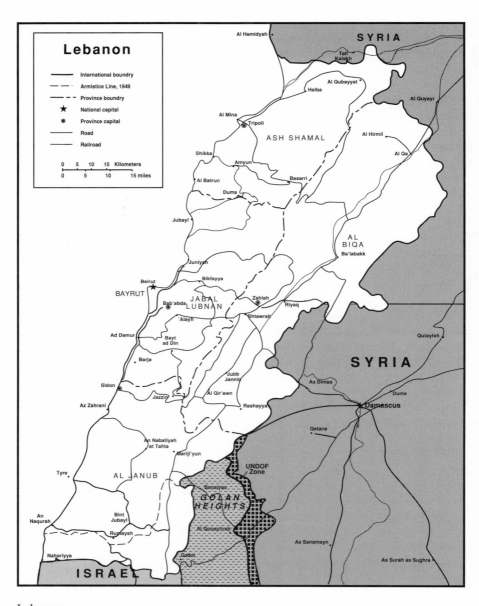

Lebanon

Introduction: Syria and Lebanon—
The Historical Dimension

On July 20, 1976, at the height of Syria's direct, all-out military intervention in the Lebanese civil war, the president of Syria, Hafiz al-Asad, delivered his most comprehensive and explicit speech ever relating to the Lebanese crisis—a speech that provided outsiders a real glimpse into the mind of a usually secretive and reticent political leader, ruling over a political system long characterized by its inaccessibility to the outside world. In the speech Asad stated, that "throughout history, Syria and Lebanon have always been one nation. This is what history shows." [1]

This and similar statements reflected a deep-rooted political tradition in Syria, focussing on the indivisibility of Lebanon from historic "Greater Syria." Lebanon's separation from Syria as of 1920 was thus perceived as a historical aberration, imposed upon Syria, the "biting heart" of Arabism, by western (particularly French) imperialism. [2]

Ideological, political, and economic considerations notwithstanding, Syrian politicians displayed a measured degree of political pragmatism when they agreed to the formal independence of Lebanon and its subsequent inclusion in the Arab League in 1944–45. This acceptance reflected Syria's own political weakness at the time, and its concern that an insistence on reintegration of Lebanon into Syria might jeopardize Syria's own independence. [3] However, Syria has never established formal diplomatic relations with Lebanon, consistently claiming that the two parts of "Greater Syria" were not separate political entities.

The Lebanese Crisis, Main Features: Up to 1975

The Lebanese crisis, which erupted in April 1975, was a multi-faceted dispute, lasting almost sixteen years (and even then, still having the potential to recur). Experts have debated whether this has been an "anomalous conflict" or a more conventional, though extremely complicated case of protracted political and social conflict. [4] Nonetheless, it is universally agreed that its longevity, intensity, and ramifications, domestically, regionally, and at times globally made it one of the most explosive conflicts of the twentieth century.

In fact, the historic roots of the conflict can be traced back to the nineteenth century, when the Lebanese fought each other for twenty years (1840–1860). The European powers intervened and forced a settlement, creating the autonomous Region of Mount Lebanon, which lasted until 1914.[5] Then came the first world war, following which the French came to the Levant in 1919, where they would remain until 1946. These were eventful years: but today, with the benefit of hindsight, we can single out the one event that overshadowed all the rest. On September 1, 1920, the French created "Greater Lebanon," the anomalous and curious political entity we now call Lebanon. The area demarcated consisted of various religious communities, mostly Sunni and Shi'i Muslims.[6] This was one reason why the new state never was an integral political unit, and thus instead of progressing toward full independence as a more or less homogeneous community, the Lebanese had to look for ways of merging communities that were reluctant to live together. This task long proved futile, making Lebanon a fragmented society in a dynamic and volatile region.

Since the mid-1960s, on top of the long-standing Muslim-Christian division, a new conflict developed regarding the role of the Palestinians. Most of the Lebanese Christians saw the country as their homeland and refused to grant a role in its affairs to the Palestinians. Most of the Lebanese Muslims identified with the Palestinian struggle against Israel and were ready to cede some of the state's sovereignty to the Palestinian organizations. This added an inter-Arab dimension to the Muslim-Christian intra-Lebanon conflict, particularly as countries like Syria, Iraq, and Libya used their own links to the Palestinian cause to themselves become increasingly involved in Lebanon's internal politics. This state of affairs set the stage for the eruption of full-scale civil war in April 1975.

The Lebanese Crisis, 1975–1990

Clearly, what has transpired in Lebanon beginning in 1975 was "essentially a civil war involving a quarrel among Lebanese nationals—more clearly so since 1982, when the Palestinian dimension to the hostilities was reduced to virtual eradication."[7] However, just as clearly, Arab and non-Arab regional parties were embroiled in the Lebanese quarrel from the very start, such that the crisis has had an "ever-growing tendency of co-opting and internalizing regional conflicts."[8] Prominent among these conflicts have been the Arab–Israeli conflict in general, and the Palestinian–Israeli conflict in particular, the Iraq–Iran war and numerous inter-Arab disputes, chief among them the chronic Iraqi–Syrian feud. Syria has had a particular and distinct role in almost all of these disputes.

The Syrian role in Lebanese politics took a sharp turn beginning with the formation of the B'ath regime in Damascus, in 1963.[9] The self-styled pan-Arabist, pro-Palestinian, and socialist regime was on an inevitable collision course with the semi-Western, Christian-dominated and capitalist Lebanon, whose support of the Palestinian cause was lukewarm, at best.[10] Hafiz al-Asad, who came to power in November 1970, did not deviate from the traditional, historical line toward Lebanon. His regime continued to support Palestinian, leftist-Lebanese and Shi'ite organizations in Lebanon, which all had strong objections to the Lebanese system. Regarding the Arab–Israeli conflict, the Asad regime asserted that "Lebanon cannot be neutral in the Arab-Israeli conflict. . . . Those who say so undermine the will of the Lebanese people, which views itself as an integral part of the Arab nation."[11]

The Asad regime, however, also displayed its pragmatic side toward Lebanon. Asad had close personal connections with the Lebanese president, Sulayman Faranjiyya.[12] Pierre Jumayyil, the leader of the largest Christian party in Lebanon, the Phalange, was officially invited to Damascus in September 1973, a visit which opened a direct line of communication between him and Asad.[13]

Thus, the Syrian regime managed to establish itself as a potential arbiter of Lebanese politics during the time in which the domestic Lebanese situation was on the verge of explosion.

Stage I: Getting In

Intially, when the Lebanese civil war broke out in April 1975, Syrian involvement in the crisis was indirect and revolved around attempts to mediate between the warring factions. The Syrian officials who carried the burden of the talks with the Lebanese were the Foreign Minister 'Abd al-Halim Khaddam, the chief of Staff, General Hikmat Shihabi, and the commander of the Air Force (who was also in charge of Syrian intelligence), General Naji Jamil.[14] (Later on, Asad would demote Jamil and eventually replace him.) Hafiz al-Asad did not engage himself extensively in the exhausting wrangling with the Lebanese.

In late October 1975 came the first confirmed reports about the involvement of Syrian-dominated Al-saiqa, a constituent of the Palestine Liberation Organization (PLO) in the fighting, alongside the leftist, mainly Muslim militias. The Syrians also supplied arms to some leftist Muslim factions and the official media in Damascus clearly sided with them. Soon afterward, the Syrians grew more concerned about the course of the crisis. There were several reasons for this increased concern.

First, the Lebanese National Movement (LNM), the umbrella organization of leftist-Muslim factions led by the Druze Kamal Jumblat, seemed to be victorious, with the support of Arab countries hostile to Syria, such as Iraq.[15]

Second, the Syrians feared that a victory for the LNM would enable its ally and backer, the PLO, to establish an independent territorial base in Lebanon, at a time when Syria was trying to create an Eastern Command, encircling Israel from Aqaba (Jordan) in the south to Tyre (Lebanon) in the north.

Third, Syria's doubled-edged nightmare was the fear that Lebanon might be partitioned, which would lead to the subsequent creation of an Israeli-backed Christian state there. Militarily, an Israeli-backed Christian state could pose a major security threat to Damascus, in addition to the Israeli–Syrian front in the Golan Heights. Ideologically, a separate Christian state was perceived as a mortal blow to the notion of Arab nationalism, which makes no distinction between Arab-Muslims and Christians.

Fourth, the deepening crisis in Lebanon could very easily spill over to Syria, itself a mosaic of ethnic, religious, and linguistic communities. Thus, the disintegration of the Lebanese state provided Syria with the chance to fulfill an age-old ambition to dominate Lebanon while confronting it with a number of risks.

When evaluating the unfolding Lebanese situation, the Syrian leadership realized that intervention in Lebanon was not risk-free politically and militarily. The Lebanese left was self-proclaimed revolutionary, anti status quo in Lebanon, in line with the revolutionary ethos of the Syrian regime. The Maronites, on the other hand, represented pro-western, pro-status quo, conservative elements. The left was backed by the PLO, and the Syrian regime was, rhetorically at least, the champion of the Palestinian struggle against Israel. Inside Syria itself, the regime was opposed by large sections of the Sunni-Muslim community, who resented the 'Alawi-dominated, secular Ba'th regime. Intervening against a largely Muslim coalition in Lebanon was therefore a major political liability to the regime in Damascus. An invasion by one Arab country to its neighbor's territory, while not totally unprecedented, was still uncommon within the framework of inter-Arab relations. Syria also had to take into account the possible reaction of the superpowers: the Soviet Union was allied with the PLO and some, at least, of the leftist Lebanese factions were strongly pro-Soviet. Also, some Arab countries that had a stake in Lebanon, such as Libya and Iraq, were pro-Soviet. The American interest was also a prime consideration: the Lebanese Christians were largely pro-West, and their cause was espoused by moderate, pro-West Arab countries.

On top of all that was the possibility of Israeli objection to any Syrian invasion. Bearing in mind Israel's military superiority over Syria, as was well exemplified in the October 1973 war, this was a formidable impediment. The possibility of an Israeli–Syrian confrontation in and over Lebanon loomed large in U.S. policy, particularly at a time when the American administration was heavily engaged in the Israeli–Egyptian process of disengagement in the Sinai. Thus, a plethora of political and military difficulties had to be overcome in order to facilitate an effective Syrian military intervention that might lead to a political settlement. Syria's response to this challenge was multidimensional, and contained political as well as military elements.

As of early 1976, pro-Syrian Palestinian units of the Palestine Liberation Army (PLA) started to infiltrate Lebanon and participate in the fighting. Still, there was no direct, overt, and formal Syrian intervention. The Palestinian proxies of Syria numbered some few thousand men, not yet an effective force in the overall configuration of forces in Lebanon. Yet, their involvement enabled the Syrian government to float a political formula to settle the crisis, supposedly a compromise between Christian and Muslim visions regarding Lebanon's future. Syria also became engaged in the search for a new president for Lebanon, one that would be ready to make concessions to the Muslims (Lebanon's president is a Maronite Christian) and would not object to granting a role for Syria in the effort to pacify and stabilize Lebanon. Thus, in the first months of 1976, limited, small-scale Syrian military intervention was aimed at facilitating a political arrangement leading to the termination of the Lebanese crisis. At the same time, Syria sought to defuse any possible tension with Israel.

The latter resented Syria's threats to annex Lebanon, warned against a unilateral Syrian intervention,[16] and was concerned about the fate of the Maronite Christians who were considered potential allies. The

Israelis, however, were not eager to intervene militarily and risk a war with Syria, particularly only three years after the October war. Instead, the Israeli government believed that Israel should "help the Christians to help themselves." In addition, the Israelis feared that the U.S. would object to any intervention and did not want to jeopardize the developing political dialogue with Egypt.[17]

Thus, a situation developed whereby Israel and Syria had, at that particular juncture, a measure of common interests in Lebanon. Consequently, in Spring 1976, Israel and Syria, helped by an American mediation effort, agreed on an arrangement known as the "Red Line" understanding. In it, Syria committed itself not to dispatch its forces beyond a line stretching from Sidon in the west to Huna in the east of southern Lebanon. Syria additionally undertook not to use its air force against ground targets in Lebanon and not to deploy ground-to-air missiles in that country.[18] The arrangement amounted, in effect, to a partial curtailment of Syria's ability to fully use its military potential in Lebanon and to a de facto partition of zones of influence in Lebanon. Syria recognized Israel's security interests in south Lebanon, while Israel recognized Syria's interests in the remaining parts of the country. This was the beginning of a relationship defined as "one of the most interesting cases of crisis management in the recent history of the Middle East," considering the profound enmity between Syria and Israel.[19]

The arrangement with Israel gave Asad the leverage he needed to deal with the leftist–Muslim–Palestinian coalition in Lebanon, which stubbornly rejected all Syrian political formulas designed to end the crisis. Syria's position was enhanced also by the election in May 1976 of a new and friendly president (Ilyas Sarkis, replacing Sulayman Faranjiyya) and statements made by Christian leaders, once Syria's bitter enemies, welcoming Syria's military intervention. Christian Lebanon, unable to defend itself, and frightened that Lebanon was slipping out of its control, was ready to accept Syrian intervention on its behalf, a readiness made unavoidable by the lack of Israeli readiness to intervene in Lebanon at the time.

Having carefully laid the political groundwork, Syria started a full-scale, direct, and open military intervention in Lebanon in late May, early June 1976. The Syrian build-up consisted of the high-level third armored division, infantry units, and commando elements belonging to the Special Forces, an elite unit of the Syrian army.[20] This intervention failed to achieve quick, decisive military gains, partly because of the limitations imposed on the Syrians by the Red Line arrangement,the difficulties of fighting in urban and mountainous regions, and the good military performance of some of the PLO factions. In Sidon alone, the Syrians lost 30 tanks and 60 soldiers, while 37 more were taken prisoners.[21]

There was also a barrage of criticism against Syria's intervention inside Syria, in the Arab world, and in the Soviet Union. Inside Syria, Asad's problem was how to explain to the Syrian people that the "heart of Arabism," Syria, had sided with the "isolationist" Maronites against the bearers of Arabism, the Palestinians. The same problem confronted Syria with regard to those Arab countries, such as Egypt, Libya, Iraq and others which supported the Muslim-leftist-Palestinian coalition in Lebanon and which resented Syria's ambitions in Lebanon. Only one Arab country, Jordan, extended public support for Syria's intervention, while Saudi-Arabia was quietly in support as well.

The Soviets, of course, resented the American mediation role which facilitated the Syrian intervention.[22] The effect of the criticism of Syria was exacerbated by Israel's inaction and Maronite support to Syria; both seemed to indicate Syria's collaboration with enemies of the Arabs. The emerging alliance between the Maronites, suspected of being isolationists and pro-Israel, and the self-styled pan-Arab, anti-Israel regime in Damascus, proved to be a major political liability to Hafiz al-Asad. Military considerations coupled with political realities forced Asad, therefore, to halt his offensive shortly after its initiation. However, Asad just wanted to weather the storm, yet he was determined to solidify Syria's position in Lebanon.

The direct military offensive was resumed only in late September, when the Syrian army achieved some quick military victories, but Hafiz al-Asad determined that Syria needed a political solution, achieved from a position of strength, rather than a complete military victory, which would be extremely costly politically. This offensive, called the Mountain offensive, lasted for 20 days, from September 28 to October 17.

It was carried out in two stages: between September 28 and 30, the Third Armored Division, aided by Christian militias, took over a Palestinian-Muslim pocket in the center of Mount Lebanon, located where it cut off the Lebanese capital from the Biq'a valley. In the second stage, between October 12 and 16, the Syrian troops advanced toward Beirut and Sidon.[23] In both stages, the Muslim-Palestinian coalition did not put up strong resistance, chiefly because of its tremendous exhaustion after the initial fighting with the Syrians. Two Arab summit conferences, convened in October 1976 in Riyadh (Saudi Arabia) and Cairo gave a seal of formality to Syria's achievements. Egypt, Saudi Arabia, and the PLO recognized Syria's hege-mony in Lebanon, while the former abandoned its struggle against the PLO leadership and was ready to somewhat qualify the formal manifestations of its central role in Lebanon.[24] By this time, the Syrian leadership, in which Hafiz al-Asad was the key decision-maker, perceived the Syrian intervention as a success story. The Lebanese imbroglio was of potentially dangerous ramifications for Syria. However, the reality of the situation in late 1976 was much more in Syria's favor.

In actual terms, Lebanon was partitioned, following the initial stages of the civil war, between Syrian, Christian, Muslim, Palestin-ian and Israeli-dominated enclaves. Syria was clearly the dominant political and military power in the fragmented country, but not the only one. Moreover, the Riyadh and Cairo conferences (see above) were seeking to lay the foundations of a lasting and binding political solution in Lebanon. Continuation of the process of political settle-ment depended, therefore, largely on cooperation between the var-ious Lebanese factions and Syria, the final arbiter of Lebanese poli-tics.

From then on, Syria's intervention in Lebanon has been deter-mined by the continuous search for a political settlement of the Lebanese crisis, based on the political and military supremacy of Syria in Lebanon. This long period can be divided roughly into three sub-periods: 1976–1982; 1982–1985 (the time from Israel's invasion to its almost complete withdrawal); 1985 to 1990–91, when Syria finally consolidated its control (at least for the moment).

Stage II: Staying In

Evolution and Complications of the Military Intervention: 1976–1982

For six years, Syria's policy in Lebanon was consistent, underlined by a set of clearly defined objectives. Chief among them were the prevention of war with Israel in and over Lebanon; resistance to any Arab interference in Lebanon; the containment of potential local hostile elements, both for the threats they posed in their own right and the risk that they could provoke troubles between Syria and Israel (particularly in the case of the PLO); and the establishment of a viable central Lebanese government linked to Syria in some form of "special relationship." In sum, Syria pushed in Lebanon a policy of consolidating the new "status quo" that had been created following its intervention.

Yet for many years Syria was unable to transform its military power in Lebanon into tangible and lasting political assets. The failure resulted from Syria's need to grapple simultaneously with mounting problems in a number of contexts: Palestinian, Lebanese, domestic Syrian, regional, and international.

With regard to the Palestinians, Syria failed to cement a viable strategic understanding with the PLO. The latter were free to operate in southern Lebanon, and their activities there ignited two rounds of fighting with Israel, in March 1978 (Operation Litani) and in July 1981.[25] Syria did not intervene in either case, and by its abstention demonstrated its determination not to fight Israel unless its own interests were at stake. Nevertheless, the PLO's activities were dangerous to Syria because of the likelihood of another confrontation in south Lebanon, which could spill over to other parts of the country. Such a situation eventually materialized in summer 1982, when Israel launched "Operation Peace for Galilee."

Syria also failed to dominate the main Christian militia, the Lebanese Forces (LF), which were taken over in the late 1970s by pro-Israeli elements, led by the charismatic Bashir Jumayyil.[26] The Syria-Christian rift reflected the changing circumstances of the post-civil war situation; first, the Syrian-PLO relations improved (see above), much to the chagrin of the Christians; second, the Christians increasingly related to the Syrian Army in Lebanon as an army of occupation. This was so largely because the Christians did not feel themselves as threatened as they had been during the civil war.

Bashir Jumayyil clearly defined the problem, arguing that "history is full of examples of foreign armies, which came to assist other nations, and soon enough were perceived as foreign armies . . ."[27]; third, there were changes within the Christian camp itself, resulting in the emergence of young, radical and pro-Israeli elements. The Syria-Christian tensions led to violent clashes, in February–June 1978, which were greatly escalated between June–October 1978, terminating without a clear military decision, in part because the Syrians felt the need to limit themselves to artillery attacks, and refrained from ground assault on East Beirut. One of the byproducts of the confrontation was that even the government of President Sarkis, initially considered Syria's stooge, became less subservient to the "big brother" in Damascus,[28] thus undermining the legitimacy of Syria's continued presence in Lebanon.

The Syrians were also unable to peacefully cooperate with some of the leaders of the leftist coalition in Lebanon. The most notable example was the Druze leader, Kamal Jumblat, who was murdered by the Syrians in March 1977. This murder denied the Lebanese left its most charismatic and capable leader. Jumblat was perceived by the Syrian regime as a threat because of his potential influence over Syria's own Druze community, and his traditional independent positions with regard to Lebanon's future and Syria's standing there.[29] His murder, by agents of Syria's intelligence, was to be the first of many such murders of Syria's rivals in Lebanon in years to come.

At home, in a rather ironic twist, the Syrian regime faced mounting opposition from the Muslim Brotherhood, who were supported by elements hostile to the Syrian regime in Lebanon.[30] This was a good example of the unintended consequences military intervention can have.

In the regional context, Syria was increasingly isolated in the late 1970s, and the Jordanian-Iraqi *rapprochement* and the Egyptian-Israeli Peace Treaty were particularly detrimental to Syria's interests.[31] More globally, Syria's relations with the U.S. were seriously damaged by its objection to the Israeli–Egyptian peace process. Relations with the Soviet Union were friendly; nevertheless, the Syrian-Soviet Treaty of Friendship and Cooperation concluded in October 1980 did not contain any Soviet commitment to protect Syria's interests in Lebanon.[32]

By far the greatest challenge to Syria's position in Lebanon was the change in Israel's perception of its own Lebanese policy and Syria's role there, following the establishment of the right-wing Likud government led by Menachem Begin. This change was gradual, and was part of a more comprehensive reappraisal of Israel's foreign policy. Especially after the conclusion of the Egyptian-Israeli Peace Treaty, Israel adopted a more militant posture, which reflected a growing self-confidence and a realization that the strategic balance in the Middle East had swung in its favor.

The new Israeli policy toward Lebanon consisted of three fundamental elements. First, Israel should expand and diversify its support of the Christians in the north of Lebanon. Christian leaders, for their part, persistently agitated for greater Israeli support. However, the change of policy in Israel was primarily the outcome of an Israeli reassessment and not only in response to Christian pressures, although the Israeli leadership was eager to accommodate the Christians if only to have another pretext to deepen Israel's involvement in Lebanon. Second, the PLO presence in Lebanon was intolerable. Finally, Syria's role in Lebanon was negative. Overall, this was clearly a revisionist policy, and Israel was increasingly viewed in Damascus as a belligerent country. This impression was boosted by Israel's December 1981 decision to extend Israeli law to the Golan Heights, essentially annexing it.

In response to the Israeli challenge, Syria adopted a two-pronged strategy. It sought to avoid war with Israel while taking various steps to indicate to Israel that Syria was still a key actor in Lebanon and an important one in the regional context. Damascus adopted the policy of pursuing "strategic parity" with Israel, dramatically increased its military build-up[33] and, as early as 1979, took a 'historic and important' decision to curtail Israel's aerial activity over Lebanon.[34] Thus, between 1980 and 1982, there was a series of aerial confrontations in which the Syrian forces were always defeated by the superior Israeli air force. The most serious incident took place in April 1981, when the Israelis intervened in the fighting between the Syrians and the LF in Zahla, and Syria reacted by deploying ground-to-air missiles in the Biq'a valley. By so doing, and by not avoiding air-battles, despite their poor results, Syria clearly indicated its determination to signal to Israel that it would not acquiesce in an Israeli policy intended to force Syria from Lebanon.

The outcome was that two out of the three components of the Red Line understanding were violated: the politics of crisis management had been replaced by the politics of brinkmanship. Still, Syria proved its point; it demonstrated a resolve to stay in Lebanon, after it seemed at one point during 1980 that the Syrian regime contemplated a massive redeployment of its troops in Lebanon.[35] However, this determination, taken in conjunction with Israel's own resolve to change the status quo in Lebanon, set the stage for the war of 1982, and dramatically demonstrated a change of emphasis in Syria's policy in Lebanon. Whereas through 1979 Syria's involvement in Lebanon was mainly designed to solidify a new political order in Lebanon, based on Syria's hegemony, in the years leading up to the 1982 war Syria's main effort in Lebanon was focussed on dealing with the Israeli challenge, not only to Syria's position in Lebanon, but to its position in the entire region.

The 1982 War: Actors, Objectives, Results

The fighting of June–August 1982 was in effect a war that took place inside Lebanon virtually without the participation of the Lebanese. While Israel fought Syria and the PLO, local forces—whether Christian or Muslim—remained passive. Israel fought in Lebanon in order to achieve three goals. The first was to defeat the PLO military, eliminate its presence in Lebanon, and cut it down to size politically (i.e., to remove the PLO from the political agenda of the Middle East). The second objective was to establish a strong government in Beirut which would be friendly toward Israel and sign a peace treaty with it. Such a government could only be Christian-dominated and led by Bashir Jumayyil, the commander of the LF, who was Syria's principal enemy in Lebanon. And the third goal was to create conditions which would either force Syria to abandon Lebanon without a war or, in the event of Syrian resistance, force the troops out by inflicting a serious military blow on Syrian forces in Lebanon.

The PLO fought for its very survival, both as a military force and as a potent political factor. Syria had made it clear, even before the war, that it would distinguish between an Israeli strike against the PLO and an all-out attack on Lebanon. In the first case, Syrian intervention would be limited; in the second, Syria would help the Palestinians and Lebanese to turn the "occupiers' life into an unbearable inferno."[36] The Israeli–PLO war developed after three or four days into a limited, controlled clash between Israel and Syria. The confrontation was limited, because in Israel there was no one opinion about the desirability of a major confrontation with Syria. Defense Minister Ariel Sharon strongly advocated such a move but Prime Minister Begin, Chief of Staff Eytan, and the rest of the government were opposed. What happened was that in no instance was the Israeli army fully geared up toward an all-out battle with Syria. The Syrian forces, for their part, were at pains to refrain from such a battle. In the first three days of the fighting the Syrians took some defensive measures, especially in the Biq'a valley, but did not reinforce their build-up in Lebanon, which was based on an infantry brigade in Beirut and an enlarged brigade in the Biq'a.[37]

It was not until June 8, 1982, two days after the first Israeli foray, that the Syrian forces entered into battle with the invading Israelis in the Jizzin area, a strategic location on the southern slopes of Mount Lebanon. Their troops there consisted of an infantry battalion, as well as commando and armored elements.[38] The fighting in Jizzin opened a three-day period of Israeli–Syrian battles, in the air and on the ground. The Syrians lost most of their ground-to-air missiles systems, 100 aircraft, the First armored division and the 47th armored brigade. Altogether, they lost 345 tanks, 70 armored personnel carriers, 45 artillery pieces, and 400 soldiers.[39] This was a defeat, but not a complete rout. The Syrian strategy of an attempt to avoid a full-scale battle with Israel in and over Lebanon seemed to be working. Yet there were some political explanations to be made.

The regime explained that "a war, if it takes place with the current imbalance . . . will never realize our aims . . . a war that could achieve our aims is one that we ourselves choose, and whose time and place are fixed by us and not by the enemy . . . it is unreasonable that we should leave the Golan in front of us . . . and fight the enemy from Lebanon."[40] This was, clearly, an apologetic announcement, but it was also fairly representative of Syria's policy in Lebanon since 1976, and after 1982.

There were other reasons as well for the limited nature of the Israeli–Syrian confrontation. The Arab world was remarkably passive. Although Arab media and spokesmen had predicted a massive Israeli invasion of Lebanon, "Arab capitals were unprepared and inter-Arab bodies slow to react."[41] Arab attention was focused on the Iran–Iraq war and other regional issues. Some Arab countries, such as Iraq, Jordan, and Egypt, resented Syria's policies with regard to Lebanon, the Gulf, and other regional problems, and were not unduly distressed at Syria's humiliation. In fact the only actual external support Syria received during the crisis was in the form of several hundred Iranian Revolutionary Guards, who were allowed by Damascus to cross its territory on their way to Lebanon.[42]

Syria had always objected to any Arab interference in Lebanon, other than its own. This policy proved detrimental during the fighting because no Arab country felt obliged to come to Syria's help. Yet, the lack of Arab interference neutralized much of the possible regional ill-effects of the war in 1982. It remained a local affair, and not another full-scale round of the Arab–Israeli conflict.

The lack of super-power involvement also contributed to the neutralization of much of the potential volatility of the 1982 war. The Soviet Union was not committed to protect Syria's interests in Lebanon, and Syrian territory proper was not in danger. The U.S., while not in complete agreement with Israel's war aims, was not greatly concerned about the destruction of the PLO and the humiliation of Syria, both Soviet clients. As for the various Lebanese factions, both the pro-Israeli LF and the pro-Syrian and pro-PLO LNM and other elements, such as the Shi'ite al-Amal militia and the Druze Progressive Socialist Party (PSP), refrained from actively taking part in the fighting. While the overall military weight of all these factions was in any event insignificant, this was not the case with regard to their political importance and the ability of some of them to cause the type of "inferno" that Syria had earlier predicted would come Israel's way. The impact of this was later to be dramatically demonstrated (see below).

The war officially ended early in September when the PLO's evacuation from Beirut was completed. By then, Israel was the clear victor, Syria and the PLO the losers. In Lebanon itself, the Christians, under the newly elected President Bashir Jumayyil, were the clear beneficiaries of the Israeli victory. However, this phase constituted only "the end of the beginning" of the war and its ramifications. In September 1982, a new phase of war between proxies started that was to last for almost three years.

Bashir Jumayyil was elected President of Lebanon on August 23, 1982. On September 14, 1982 he was murdered. In retaliation, on September 17 and 18 the LF carried out massacres in the Palestinian refugee camps of Sabra and Shatila. On September 21 a united Lebanese Chamber of Deputies voted almost unanimously in favor of Amin Jumayyil, Bashir's brother, as the new President of Lebanon. About the same time, the USSR started new shipments of sophisticated arms to Syria which boosted the self-confidence of the Syrian rulers.[43] This sequence of events signaled the beginning of the end of Israel's ambitious plans with regard to Lebanon. The unceremonious end came in June 1985, when Israel completed its unilateral withdrawal from Lebanon. This was clearly a defeat for Israel and a victory for Syria. During this period, Israeli and Syrian policies in Lebanon followed diametrically opposed courses both in terms of the definition of their aims and their success in implementing them.

Israel first wanted to sign a full, formal peace treaty with Lebanon. Following Bashir's death, Amin Jumayyil ruled out a peace treaty. Instead, on May 17, 1983 the Israelis and Lebanese signed an agreement terminating the state of war between the two countries, devised security arrangements along their border, and called upon all foreign forces to leave Lebanon.[44] The agreement fell short of the initial Israeli demand for a peace treaty, but even in its limited form it was rejected by Syria. This was due to Syria's principled resistance to any political accord between any Arab country and Israel, as well as Syria's objection to be put on a par with Israel with regard to the legitimacy of their military presence in Lebanon. On March 5, 1984, the agreement was unilaterally abrogated by the Lebanese government.[45] On November 8, 1984, Israel and Lebanon started talks about a unilateral Israeli withdrawal and the establishment of security arrangements between the two countries. These talks soon broke down and on January 14, 1985 the government of national unity in Israel voted in favor of a complete, unilateral, three-phase withdrawal from

Lebanon. Israel left a small contingent in Lebanon, whose task was to help the Israeli-backed South Lebanon Army (SLA) to monitor a small security zone that Israel regarded as absolutely vital to its security interests.[46]

Israel's withdrawal was brought about by the cumulative effect of two factors, the dissent in Israel regarding the situation in Lebanon and the activities of Syria and its proxies there. Back in the summer of 1982, Syria's position in Lebanon seemed abysmal, having fallen from the hegemonic power in Lebanon to suffering military defeats there at the hands of the Israelis. Asad was determined to reverse this state of affairs. Yet he also was well aware of Syria's military inferiority with regard to Israel, especially its vulnerability in the Biq'a valley where the Israelis were dangerously close to Damascus. Syria therefore decided to wage its war against Israel through Lebanese proxies. This decision reflected a major change of policy.

Before 1982, Syria had been at pains to contain local Lebanese elements, in particular to prevent them from initiating unmanageable troubles between itself and Israel. Under the new circumstances, Syria reversed its policy and it soon paid off. The Syrians established a coalition consisting of a wide spectrum of Lebanese and Palestinians whose common denominator was their opposition to Amin Jumayyil, the LF, and Israel. The murder of Bashir Jumayyil was Syria's first success in Lebanon after the war, and was another example of its ability to use terrorism.

More such use of proxies was to come over the next three years. Syria's Palestinian clients drove Arafat's PLO out from the Biq'a and then from Tripoli. Serious blows were inflicted on the LF and the government, particularly the Maronite defeat in the Shouf Mountains in September 1983 and the Shi'ite takeover of West Beirut in February 1984. Shi'ite militias, backed by Iran as well as Syria, launched a series of spectacular suicidal attacks against Israeli targets in south Lebanon and the Multi-National Force (MNF) in Beirut.[47] The results of all this were obvious; Israel's allies were defeated, Amin Jumayyil's government adopted the "Syrian option," and the MNF was evacuated. During 1984 the focus of Syrian activities was in southern Lebanon where the local population, helped by Syria and inspired by Shi'ite militias, rose up against Israel. Thus, the Israelis were, indeed, subjected to the threatened intolerable "inferno." The politics of proxies proved to be a major success, enabling Syria to undo Israel's initial achievements in Lebanon without involvement in a full-scale military confrontation.

This success once again whet its appetite to attain hegemony in

Lebanon. Moreover, it also lent credibility to Syria's ambitions to become a pivotal power-broker in the Middle East. Syria's success was doubly impressive when seen against the backdrop of a lack of substantial Soviet and Arab support, while fighting not only against Israeli interests but also the interests of the U.S. in Lebanon.

Staying in and Not Getting Out: Crisis Management with Israel and Pax Syranica in Lebanon, 1985–91

Even after the Israeli withdrawal from Lebanon, there was intermittent tension between Israel and Syria. This was the case because the Syrian military build-up continued unabated, because Asad continued his belligerent rhetoric and because Syria was behind some terror attacks against Israeli targets in Europe, notably the attempt to plant a bomb on board an El-Al aircraft in London in April 1986. The Israelis responded with their own war of words and their attention was increasingly focused on Syria's intentions, especially because of their respect for Asad's consistency and motivation. Yet, the tension did not unleash any clash between the two countries in Lebanon. Paradoxically enough, the circumstances of Israel's withdrawal contributed to this state of affairs. In the absence of any binding understanding between Israel and Syria over Lebanon, the Syrians were careful not to provoke direct hostilities with the Israelis in Lebanon, being uncertain of Israel's likely reaction. Israel's failure in Lebanon somewhat diminished its power of deterrence toward Syria, but not enough to make Syria feel that a confrontation with Israel was desirable.

In this respect the situation represented a continuation of Syria's policy since 1976 that Lebanon was not to become the arena of a military clash with Israel. Syria's regional policies were still totally opposed to Israel's, and in terms of rhetoric Syria gave unqualified support to anti-Israeli actions in south Lebanon. However, a careful examination of these actions reveals that many of them were perpetrated by elements not subservient to Syria, such as Shi'ite militants and Palestinian factions. Moreover, the Israeli concept of a security zone arguably has justified itself, since the area has in practice provided an effective buffer between south Lebanon and Israel. Not one Israeli citizen had been killed in Galilee since the completion of Israel's withdrawal. The security zone also has enjoyed relative economic stability as opposed to the rapid economic decline in the rest of Lebanon.

Thus, with no imminent danger of a Syrian–Israeli collision in Lebanon, there was no incentive for either side to reactivate the Red Line understanding. This was not a risk-free situation, yet the reality of the Lebanese situation was that both Syria and Israel were at pains to prevent a collision in and over Lebanon. This state of affairs was dramatically highlighted in November 1987, following the hang-glider attacks from Syrian-controlled Lebanese territory on an Israeli military base in Galilee, culminating in six Israeli victims, and the tension emerging between the Syrians and General Michel 'Awn in late 1989 (see below).

All along, though, Syria never wavered from the objective of consolidating its hegemony in Lebanon. Its failure to do so until October 1990 served to highlight the ambitious nature of the undertaking and the realities of Syria's position in the battered country, as well as the regional and international contexts prior to Iraq's invasion of Kuwait in August 1990. Syria was successful in precipitating the Israeli and American withdrawals from Lebanon and could put effective pressure on Yasir Arafat's PLO. It was also able to establish a local coalition to fight Syrian enemies in Lebanon. However, all this was not enough when Syria had to find a positive formula to settle things in Lebanon. During most of the period the Lebanese situation confronted Syria with difficult policy dilemmas and few attractive options. The Syrians were keen to preserve their dominant position in Lebanon but reluctant to employ significant additional military forces (beyond their now permanent presence in Eastern and Southeastern Lebanon) to implement their plans.

Accordingly, the Syrians had to rely heavily on their intelligence network in Lebanon, led by Brigadier Ghazi Kana'an, a distant relative of Asad, who controlled a web of pro-Syrian militias and civilian organizations. Kana'an, a ruthless officer who made a name for himself as an able observer of the Lebanese scene, was the overall Syrian supervisor of the situation in Lebanon itself, while Khaddam, now vice-president, was in charge of the Lebanese portfolio in Damascus. However, their activities proved insufficient, and the Lebanese domestic configuration shifted gradually against Syria. The PLO infiltrated back to various areas of Lebanon and in the process inflicted severe blows on Syria's ally, the Shi'ite militia al-Amal.

The other Shi'ite militia, Hizballah, continued to be backed by Iran, which was intensifying and diversifying its activities in Lebanon in a number of ways. First, it increased its support of Hizballah, in its competition with Amal for the hearts and minds of the Shi'ite community. The Shi'ite militants came forward with a comprehensive message that touched the social, economic, spiritual, and political aspirations of the average Shi'i. What made it all the more attractive was the fact that Iran, despite its own economic problems, proved capable of channeling substantial funds to Lebanon. The exact amount is hard to come by, but it is safe to assume that payments were in the range of $80 million per year through the late 1980s. Consequently, both Hizballah's political and military strength grew considerably. Estimates were of 4,000 Hizbollah fighters, of whom 2,500 were in the Biqa, 1,000 in Beirut, and 500 in the south. There was a gradual shift from small clandestine units to large semi-regular military formations.[48]

Second, Iran and Hizballah together intensified their campaign against Arab and Western individuals and institutions. This was particularly damaging to Syria's interests for three reasons: a) it proved how unstable Syria's hold over Lebanon still was; b) it happened at a time when Syria was trying to improve its international image, which had suffered considerably following revelations that Syria was involved in terrorist operations in Europe in 1986; c) Iran managed to use the hostage situation as leverage against western countries, as was exemplified in the Irangate scandal. It is of significance, that the first leaks about the American-Iranian-Israeli arms-for-hostages deal appeared in a pro-Syrian weekly in Beirut (Al-Shira).

Third, Hizballah stepped up its attacks against the SLA and the Israeli forces in the "Security Zone." These were not necessarily contrary to Syria's interests. However, because of the sensitivity of the Israeli-Lebanese border situation, Syria preferred to be in complete control of anti-Israeli activities in order not to be drawn, at the wrong time, into a dispute with Israel in and over Lebanon. Such a confrontation might result from uncontrolled Hizballah activities.

Fourth, Iran intervened diplomatically in the "war of the camps," in late 1986, between Amal and the anti-Syrian Arafat loyalists in the PLO.[49] It mediated a cease-fire which Hizballah was supposed to observe as well. The latter had argued that Amal's war against the Palestinians pitted Muslim against Muslim, whereas the true effort of all Muslims should be the "Liberation of Jerusalem."[50] This was a challenge not only to Amal but also to their Syrian patrons, the self-styled champions of Arab nationalism.

Fifth, Iran extended its support to segments of the Sunni community, most notably the Tawahid Movement in Tripoli, led by Shaykh Sa'id Sha'ban, an avowed enemy of Syria. Syrian–Iranian relations with regard to Lebanon reflected profound contrasting visions regarding its future, a state of affairs that was played down by both countries during the years 1982–1985, but surfaced soon after the Israeli withdrawal in 1985. Iran wanted a Muslim, revolutionary Lebanon, whereas Syria has always wanted a Syrian-dominated Lebanon.

Syria also had problems with the Christian camp in Lebanon, basically because it was unable to completely dominate Amin Jumayyil, the legally elected president and its failure to determine the election of a new Lebanese president in September 1988. Consequently, the presidency became vacant, competing governments emerged in East and West Beirut, and after so many years of a civil war and a regional conflict, Lebanon finally came close to a formal partition.

All this was happening against the backdrop of a deterioration of Syria's economic situation, as well as of its regional and international standing. Military expenditures, including funds to maintain the military presence in Lebanon, were one of the main reasons leading to Syria's economic predicament in the second half of the 1980s.[51] This crisis, while not precipitating a Syrian change of heart with regard to its continued presence in Lebanon, nevertheless further impeded Syria's ability to exert its control over Lebanon, itself suffering from a terrible economic crisis.

Regional developments were still militating against Syria's position in the inter-Arab system in general, as well as in Lebanon. Most notable among these developments was the Iran-Iraq war, and its subsequent termination, which enabled Syria's arch-enemy Iraq a freer hand in its drive to settle scores with the Syrian regime. Indeed, Iraq's involvement in the Syrian-'Awn dispute during 1989, on the part of the latter, served notice to Asad about his vulnerability in Lebanon at that time. Egypt's readmission into the Arab League and the PLO diplomatic offensive following the Palestinian uprising further isolated Syria in the Arab system, a situation which started to change even before the Iraqi invasion of Kuwait, with some bilateral efforts toward an Eyptian-Syrian *rapprochement*.

Also, developments in the international arena caused troubles to the Asad regime, particularly the new Soviet policy of *glasnost* and *perestroika* and its application in the Middle East. The repeated Soviet call to Syria to abandon its policy of achieving "strategic parity" with Israel was one significant element of the new posture of Soviet policy.

The cumulative effect of all this on Syria's policy in Lebanon was telling. In dealing with the Lebanese situation, Syria applied its now familiar two-pronged strategy of combining attempts at political reconciliation with military pressure. The first comprehensive Syrian effort to achieve a political settlement of Lebanon's crisis following Israel's withdrawal in 1985, was the "Damascus Agreement."

On December 28, 1985, three Lebanese—Walid Jumblat, leader of the PSP and the most prominent leader of the Druze community; Nabih Barri, leader of the Shi'ite militia, al-Amal; and Elie Hubayka, Chairman of the Lebanese Forces Executive Committee—signed a "national agreement to solve the Lebanese crisis."[52] It was a detailed and comprehensive agreement consisting of elements relating to all aspects of life in Lebanon. It stressed the point that Lebanon's identity and affiliation were Arab, as Lebanon was an active founding member of the League of Arab States. The agreement also stressed absolute adherence to Lebanon's unity. All partition plans, all forms of discrimination, and all proposals for political decentralization, such as federations and cantons, were rejected. This was in line with traditional Syrian policy, as well as with Druze and Shi'ite policies. The Lebanese Forces toyed with the idea of a federal regime, but it was never their declared choice. This was the case with other Christian elements, who agreed that in order to build Lebanon's future and establish a modern state, it was necessary to dismantle the sectarian system and replace it with a new Constitution, drafted within one year at most.

It was abundantly clear that the Damascus Agreement was qualitatively different from other such agreements, not only for what it contained but also for the fact of who its signatories were. The agreement was signed by the leaders of the three most powerful militias, rather than by leaders of political parties. This was a complete change from the Lebanese reconciliation conferences at Geneva and Lausanne (in 1983–84) and from agreements reached before and after these conferences. Walid Jumblat had indicated that the established Christian leadership had lost its control over its constituents and that a meaningful agreement could be signed only with their armed elements.

His reasoning was that, although there would be inevitable objections to the Damascus Agreement, indeed to any agreement, only powerful military forces would be effective in dealing with them. In the past, the Lebanese Forces had played a secondary role to the traditional Maronite political leadership and so did not have an interest in being part of an agreement, let alone in preserving it.

Neither the President nor the Prime Minister, the two highest-ranking political figures in the country, were partners to the agreement, and this put its legitimacy and legality in doubt. It was Jumblat's and Barri's traditional policy to ignore the President, who, they charged, was a partisan figure and not a symbol of national unity. That the Syrians eventually agreed to this agreement was an indirect admission of a change in their policy, which was initially designed to elevate Amin Jumayyil as the embodiment of legitimacy in the country. The President was seen as a puppet of Syria, but for a number of reasons Syria's interest in maintaining Jumayyil's position weakened.

First, as the Israelis completed their withdrawal from the South, the Syrians did not need Amin Jumayyil's anti-Israel rhetoric as much as they previously had. Jumayyil played his role in the Syrian-inspired script, but once that script progressed beyond a certain point he was less important. Second, the President was in command of one of the weakest military forces in the country, the official Lebanese Army, and even this command was under constant pressure. Third, he had lost ground even inside his own community, as the Lebanese Forces under Elie Hubayka had gained influence and had become ready to participate in Syrian-led settlements. Fourth, it became clear to Damascus, after so many futile attempts, that its strongest allies in Lebanon, the Druze and Shi'ite militias, could not come to a viable and lasting arrangement with the much-hated President. From the point of view of Hubayka and his men, abandoning the President—although it would run contrary to traditional Christian regard for the Presidency—would make it possible to consolidate their own dominant position in the Christian community, with the backing of the other powerful forces on the Lebanese scene.

Not only the Maronite President but also the Sunni Prime Minister was snubbed in Damascus. It was not just a personal humiliation for Rashid Karami, a devoted and loyal supporter of Syria; it was a snub to the entire Sunni community, which ceased to be important in decision-making. The exclusion of the Sunnis reflected profound developments among the non-Christians in Lebanon. The Shi'ites and Druzes had become military and politically more powerful than the Sunnis; Syria, the natural hinterland of Lebanon's Muslim population, was controlled by a largely non-Sunni elite and the Arab world, largely Sunni, was unable to help Lebanon's Sunni population because it was preoccupied with other, more pressing problems and because of the extent of "Syrianization" of the Lebanese problem.

The weak link in the Damascus connection proved to be the Christian community. Just two days after the signing of the agreement, various quarters questioned it. Hubayka himself, while defending the agreement, said that it should be supported by other steps inasmuch as it was only a statement of primary principles. On December 31, signaling that the real battle over the agreement had begun in earnest, there were assassination attempts on President Jumayyil and one of Hubayka's main advisers. The attempts began a short-lived but decisive battle in East Beirut. Amin Jumayyil and Camille Chamoun led the anti-agreement elements and tried to mobilize the support of the Maronite Church and the Vatican delegate in Beirut. On January 8 there were reports of armed clashes between elements inside the Lebanese Forces, as men loyal to Samir Ja'ja' attacked Hubayka's loyalists, thus highlighting the fact that the Forces, usually Hubayka's power base, were split down the middle. On January 10, sources close to Amin Jumayyil revealed his reservations about the agreement, which actually amounted to a total rejection.

On January 13, while President Jumayyil was in Damascus to iron out his differences with the Syrians,[53] forces loyal to Hubayka attacked the Jumayyil stronghold in Al-Matn and East Beirut. When Jumayyil returned, he resorted to his remaining means of help by meeting secretly with his arch-rival Samir Ja'ja', who also resented Hubayka's policies. This almost unimaginable alliance produced an unexpected military result: the combined forces of Jumayyil and Ja'ja' defeated Hubayka's supporters,[54] taking from the Damascus alliance its Christian component. Notwithstanding the overall Christian decline, defeats, and disunity in Lebanon, there could be no meaningful peace agreement in the country without Christian participation. Syria had suffered a setback, but it remained the final arbiter of Lebanon's politics. Elie Hubayka fled Lebanon, and for the moment President Amin Jumayyil and the young and militant Samir Ja'ja' dominated Lebanon's Christian community.

The other attempt at a comprehensive political settlement came later on, in the summer of 1988, and revolved around the possible election of a new Lebanese president. The failure of this attempt, emanating mainly from disunity within the Maronite community, signalled the beginning of a new round of fighting in Lebanon, this time between General Michel 'Awn, Amin Jumayyil's designated successor, and the Syrian army. On March 14, 1989, 'Awn declared a "war of liberation" against Syria, while hoping to mobilize Arab (especially Iraqi), and international (especially French) support. By September 22, when a cease-fire finally went into effect, more than 800 people had died in the indiscriminate artillery barrages between 'Awn's forces and the Syrians and their allies in West Beirut and around the capital.[55] Among these allies were Shi'ites, Sunni and Druze militias. The fighting precipitated another round of peace talks, this time not only under Syrian patronage but also with the participation of the Arab League. The Syrians applied a military as well as a political pressure on 'Awn, and they mobilized their political clients in Lebanon to participate in the anti-'Awn coalition.

The battle against 'Awn developed into another example of the traditional Lebanese linkage between domestic and regional conflict. Iraq sided with 'Awn, and the two main Shi'ite organizations, Hizballah and Amal, which had previously hesitated to take part in the battle against 'Awn, were now motivated to do just that, in response to the Iraqi involvement. The ferocity of the fighting in Beirut focussed international and Arab attention on the situation, unlike previous rounds of fighting in Beirut, which had involved mainly Muslim factions. (Examples of such inter-Muslim skirmishes are those of February 1987 and February–May 1988, both of which culminated in Syrian intervention.)

This time, however, 'Awn's strategy of introducing the fighting as a "war of liberation" launched by a legitimate Lebanese government seemed to work. Early in the fighting, President Mitterand and other French officials made statements openly supporting 'Awn, and in April 1989 France sent two naval vessels with relief supplies for the Christians, and also appealed to heads of state of European and Arab countries to join France in concerted action to end the conflict. The Soviet Union took its own action in early July 1989 when its first deputy Foreign Minister visited both Baghdad and Damascus. On July 5, 1989 the French president and Mikhail Gorbachev met in Paris and issued a joint statement expressing their "profound preoccupation" with Lebanon. The very existence of international pressure on Syria was a novel element of the Lebanese situation, which as of 1983–84 ceased to attract international attention. This pressure, plus the Arab mediation efforts, were much to the displeasure of the Syrians. The pressures reflected Syria's overall weakness at this time, which prompted 'Awn's action. 'Awn came to the conclusion that the Lebanese problem has been left dormant by everyone—Israel, France, the U.S. His conclusion was to create the "Intifada Effect," reintroducing the problem by breaking the status quo. 'Awn's gamble almost paid off in August 1989, when there was mounting international pressure on Syria to halt the fighting and refrain from penetrating into East Beirut. This was the time when diplomatic mediation efforts played a major role, and culminated in the October 1989 Arab League-sponsored Ta'if Accord.[56]

This plan provided for the election of Lebanon's first president since Amin Jumayyil's departure from office, for political reforms aimed at giving the Muslims a greater share of power, and for continued Syrian influence over the country's affairs, as well as continued military presence. Although the Taif accord attracted Arab and international support, 'Awn bitterly objected, particularly because it legitimized the continued presence of Syrian troops in Lebanon. For this reason Syria could relate to the Accord as an achievement, since it yet again gave a seal of approval to its special status in Lebanon. The problem was that Lebanon was the symbol of a no-state state. Its newly elected president, Rene Muawad, was murdered; his successor, Elias Harawi, would not even set foot in the Christian areas for quite some time; and fighting, particularly within the Christian and Shi'ite communities continued unabated until October 1990, bringing further havoc on the battered country.

This situation further weakened the Christian community, traditionally the main pillar of resistance to Syria's designs in Lebanon. Many Lebanese Christians became passive and indifferent, and 'Awn's war of liberation deteriorated into an internal communal feud. This feud played into the hands of Asad, but his moment came only after Iraq's invasion of Kuwait, on August 2, 1990.

Iraq then ceased its support of 'Awn, its attention obviously distracted. After a few months of hesitation and wrangling with the United States, Syria joined the anti-Saddam Hussein coalition, thus gaining an ability to extract a price from the U.S. American policy makers were convinced that Syria's support of the coalition was essential, perhaps even crucial. Syria was the self-styled champion of Arab radicalism, therefore its opposition to Saddam neutralized much of the latter's attraction in the Arab world. The Gulf crisis also proved that the Soviet Union was unable to conduct a policy contrary to that of the U.S., and the developing crisis also put a burden on Israel. The Israelis, who maintained a low profile during the Gulf crisis (the reasons for which are beyond my scope here), agreed not to take any actions that could have undermined the Arab coalition against Saddam.

Taking advantage of its newly acquired "free hand" in Lebanon, on October 13, 1990, Syria's army in Lebanon, backed by its air force (which was being used for the first time since the beginning of the Lebanese crisis), smashed 'Awn's forces in a quick and decisive battle. The U.S. acquiesced in the operation. The Arab members of the anti-Saddam coalition did likewise. Iraq and the PLO's objections were irrelevant and Israel, by choice and with the lessons of 1982–1985 in mind, stayed out. Although before the Syrian operation the

Israelis had stated publicly that they reserved the right to retain their freedom of action, the emphasis was on Israel's vital security interests in South Lebanon, not in Beirut.[57] Without admitting as much, Israel helped keep Syria within the coalition.

Following its major military victory in October 1990, Syria's policy in Lebanon has been characterized by a series of achievements, the foremost of which have been the Treaty of Brotherhood and Cooperation, signed on May 12, 1991, and the Security Pact of September 1, 1991. These two agreements clearly defined Syria's historic interest in Lebanon and cemented the special, preferential relationships between the two countries.

Hafiz al-Asad was thus eventually in a position to reap the fruits of his patient and determined strategy.

Conclusions

Syria, in words and deeds, has made it abundantly clear since the crisis began in 1975 that it has never had any intention of getting out of Lebanon. In this case, therefore, there has been no "getting out" stage of disengagement.

From Syria's standpoint, its presence in Lebanon is a fulfillment of historical rights. More practically, Syria has perceived its huge investment in Lebanon as crucial to its own political stability, its ability to determine Palestinian politics, and its overall standing in the pan-Arab system. This combination of domestic and external factors has made the Lebanese question a litmus test for the ability of the Syrian regime to survive domestically and play a meaningful role in Middle East politics. While Syrian rhetoric claims that the Palestinian–Israeli question is uppermost on Syria's national agenda, in practice it is the Lebanese crisis, that has engaged Syria's political attention, and its military and economic resources, more than any other issue.

For several reasons, however, Asad repeatedly has been forced to delay his grand scheme. First, Syria failed to commit all its resources to the Lebanese issue until 1990–91 despite its priority, since it could not handle many crises simultaneously. Asad also had to contend with the Israeli challenge in the Golan Heights and the growth of a fundamentalist Islamic movement at home, and has had to keep an eye on the border with Iraq, a long-time foe he chose to further antagonize by aiding Iran in the Iran-Iraq war. Syria thus was long hesitant to expose its army to a full-scale military confrontation in and over Lebanon. Asad instead tried to achieve his goal by threatening to use his power, by using power through proxies, and then, only as a last resort, by doing it himself.

Second has been the problem of alliance-building in Lebanon. Traditionally Asad has coopted the Shi'ites, as well as some Palestinian factions, the Druzes, some Sunnis, and at times, some Christians. However, until October 1990 there were always enough hostile forces remaining to combine together against a common foreign enemy, i.e., Syria, only to fight each other later on. Lebanese factions repeatedly have proven to possess their own formidable manipulative skills.

Finally, third-party intervention by those other than Syria with interests at stake and scores to settle has served to complicate matters further: Israel, of course; Iran, which chose to strike out at the West by backing the hostage-taking mechanism of Hizballah; Iraq, which vented its anger on Syria by first backing some Palestinian factions in the 1970s and then 'Awn's forces in 1988–1990; and, to a lesser extent and at various points, France and the United States.

In sum, Asad's strategy with regard to Lebanon has consisted of a three-stage policy. Stage one was the pacification of the Lebanese political-military cauldron, going back to 1975. Stage two was the consolidation of Syrian hegemony, although not annexation in the formal sense, and at least tacit acceptance of this fait accompli by key regional and international actors. This took more than fifteen years, and was achieved only under the unusual circumstances created by the Iraqi invasion of Kuwait. But Asad once again proved his ability to make full use of opportunities as they appear.

In the third stage, as yet still in progress, Syria will turn its attention to creating strategic parity with Israel, in which case, Lebanon is to be used as part of the overall Syrian build-up. To wit, on September 1, 1991, Syria and Lebanon signed a new security pact that, according to Syria's General Talas, gave his country the right to prevent Israeli attacks against Lebanon.

When evaluating the balance-sheet of Syria's intervention in Lebanon after sixteen hectic years, it is clear that Syria has been successful in implementing two of the three objectives of its policy in Lebanon—a state that nevertheless remains an inherently fragile and unstable political entity. This state of affairs, coupled with Syria's deep-rooted commitment to Lebanon and its desire to incorporate it within its build-up against Israel made it clear that in this case there is not likely to be any disengagement. Nor, however, can Syrian control be as assured in the future as it may have appeared to have been in 1990–91.

Abbreviations

LF	Lebanese Forces
LNM	Lebanese National Movement
MNF	Multi National Force
PLA	Palestine Liberation Army
PLO	Palestine Liberation Organization
PSP	Progressive Socialist Party
SLA	South Lebanon Army

Chronology

1840–1946

1840–1860: Lebanon's Great Civil War of the nineteenth century.

1861–1914: The Autonomous Region of Mount Lebanon

1920: The establishment of "Greater Lebanon"

1946: Lebanon and Syria become fully independent as two sovereign states.

1950–1975

May–July 1950: A short-lived Lebanese civil war.

March 1963: The rise of the B'ath party to power in Syria.

November 1970: The rise of Hafiz al-Asad to power in Syria.

April 13, 1975: The beginning of the Lebanese civil war.

1976–1981

May–June 1976: Syria invades Lebanon.

October 1976: Riyadh and Cairo Arab Summit Conferences, formally terminating the Lebanese civil war.

May 1977: Likud comes to power in Israel.

March 1978: Israel begins Operation Litani in South Lebanon.

June–July 1981: A round of hostilities between Israel and the PLO in South Lebanon.

1982–1985

June 5, 1982: Israel invades Lebanon.

June 8–11, 1982: Israeli-Syrian clashes in Lebanon.

September 17, 1982: President-elect Bashir Jumayyil is assassinated; his brother Amin is subsequently elected in his place.

May 17, 1983: The abortive Israeli-Lebanese agreement is signed.

March 1984: Lebanon abrogates the May 1983 agreement.

May–June 1985: The final stage of Israel's withdrawal from Lebanon.

December 28, 1985: The "Damascus Agreement" is signed; it will shortly be undone by events in East Beirut.

1987-1991

February 1987: Syrian troops enter West Beirut to put an end to communal strife there.

May 1988: Syrian troops enter South Beirut, to put an end to infighting betwen the Shi'is there.

September 1988: Syria fails to bring about the election of a successor to Amin Jumayyil.

March–September 1989: General 'Awn's "war of liberation" against Syria.

October 1989: The Ta'if Accord, another unsuccessful attempt to resolve the Lebanese crisis.

August 2, 1990: Iraq invades Kuwait.

October 1990: Syria militarily consolidates its control in Lebanon.

May 12, 1991: Lebanese–Syrian Treaty of Brotherhood and Cooperation signed.

September 1, 1991: Lebanese–Syrian Security Pact signed.

Notes

1. The full text of Asad's speech, *Al-b'ath*, July 21, 1976.

2. P. S. Khoury, *Syria and the French Mandate: The Politics of Arab Nationalism* (London: I. B. Tauris, 1987), pp. 44–71.

3. Y. Olmert, *British Policy Towards the Levant States, 1940–1945*, PhD thesis (London School of Economics, 1983), pp. 270–283.

4. E. E. Azar and R. F. Haddad, "Lebanon: An Anomalous Conflict?" *Third World Quarterly*, 8, no. 4 (October 1986):1337–1350.

5. On the Autonomous Region, see J. P. Spagnolo, *France and Ottoman Lebanon: 1861–1914* (London: Ithaca Press, 1977).

6. On the creation of "Greater Lebanon," see M. Zamir, *The Formation of Modern Lebanon* (London: Croom Helm, 1985), pp. 38–97.

7. K. Salibi, Lebanon and the Middle Eastern question, *Papers on Lebanon*, no. 8, (Oxford: Center For Lebanese Studies, 1988), p. 4.

8. Azar and Haddad, "Lebanon," p. 1337.

9. I. Rabinovich, *Syria Under the Ba'th 1963–66: The Army-Party Symbiosis* (Jerusalem: Israel Universities Press, 1972), pp. 49–75.

10. On these aspects of the Lebanese state, see K. Salibi, *Crossroads to Civil War: Lebanon 1958–1976* (Delmar, N.Y.: Caravan Books, 1976).

11. R. Damascus, April 2, 1974.

12. R. Avi-Ran, *Syrian Involvement in Lebanon (1975–1985)* (In Hebrew) (Tel-Aviv: Ma'arakoth, 1986), p.19.

13. For an account of this visit and its implications see, *Al-Anwar*, November 1, 1976.

14. Khaddam and Shihabi visited Lebanon three times during 1975, and Jamil once.

15. On the LNM, and its internal composition, see A. al-Azmeh, "The progressive Forces," in R. Owen ed., Essays on the crisis in Lebanon (London: Ithaca Press, 1976), pp. 59–73: S. Zabian, *Al-Haraka Al-Wataniyya Al-Lubnaniyya* (in Arabic), (Beirut: Dar al-Masira, 1977).

16. See Israeli statements to this effect, *Ma-ariv*, January 8, 11, 12, 21, 1976. On the Syrian threat to annex Lebanon, see interview with Khaddam, *Al-Ra'y al-'Amm*, January 7, 1976.

17. On the Israeli deliberation, see Y. Rabin, *A Service Notebook* (in Hebrew), (Tel-Aviv: Ma'ariv, 1979), 2:502–507.

18. Ibid., p. 503. On the U.S. role in Lebanon, see R. W. Stookey, "The United States," in P. E. Haley and L. W. Snider, eds., *Lebanon in Crisis* (Syracuse: Syracuse University Press, 1979), pp. 225–248.

19. I. Rabinovich, "Controlled Conflict in the Middle East— The Syrian-Israeli Rivalry in Lebanon," unpublished paper, presented to the International Conference on Crisis Management in the Middle East, York University, Toronto, October 1985, p. 1.

20. D. Asher, *Mountain Armoured Warfare: Syria Military Intervention in Lebanon (1975–1976)* (in Hebrew), (Tel-Aviv: Ma'arakoth, 1985), pp. 25–26.

21. See the Report of AFP, June 13, 1976.

22. On the Soviet role, see P. O. Freedman, "The Soviet Union and the civil war in Lebanon, 1975–76," *The Jerusalem Journal of International Relations*, 3, no. 4 (1978):63–74.

23. Asher, *Mountain Armoured Warfare*, pp. 32–46.

24. R. Avi-Ran, *Syrian Involvement in Lebanon*, p. 75.

25. On the complex nature of the Syrian–PLO relationship, see M. E. Selim, "The Survival of a Nonstate Actor: The Foreign Policy of the Palestine Liberation Organization," in B. Korany and A. E. Hillal Dessouki, *The Foreign Policies of Arab States* (Boulder: Westview, 1984), pp. 197–241; R. Khalidi, "The Asad Regime and the Palestinian Resistance," *Arab Studies Quarterly*, 6, no. 4 (1984):259–266.

26. On the LF and the rise of Bashir Jumayyil, see L. W. Snider, "The Lebanese Forces: Their Origins and Role in Lebanese Politics," *Middle East Journal*, vol. 38, no. 1 (1984):1–33.

27. *Monday Morning*, April 18–24, 1977.

28. See an interesting though biased description in K. Pakradouni, *Al-Salam Al-Mafkud* (in Arabic), (Beirut: Dar al-Sharq Lilmanshurat, 1984).

29. On Jumblat's anti-Syrian feelings, see his *I Speak For Lebanon* (London: Zed Press, 1982).

30. On Muslim Brotherhood activities, see D. Kehat, "Syria," in C. Legum, H. Shaked, D. Dishon, eds., *Middle East Contemporary Survey* (Hereafter Known as *MECS*), vols. 2, 3, 4, pp. 729–730, 803–808, 759–766 (respectively). On connections between the Muslim Brotherhood and the LF in Lebanon, see N. Nasr, *Faillite Syrienne Au Liban 1975–1981* (Beirut: Dar al-Amal, 1983), 2:541; Z. Schiff and E. Ya'ari, *A False War* (in Hebrew), (Tel-Aviv: Schoken, 1984), pp. 66–67.

126   YOSSI OLMERT

1. On Syria's isolation since Sadat's visit to Israel, see D. Kehat, "Syria,"
MECS, 2:735–739.
32. On the Treaty, see A. J. Becker and F. Fukuyama, "The USSR and the
Middle East," *MECS*, 4:63–66. D. Kehat, "Syria," *MECS*, 4: 777–780.
33. M. A. Heller, D. Tamari, Z. Eytan, eds., *The Middle East Military
Balance-1983* (in Hebrew), (Tel-Aviv: Jaffee Center For Strategic Studies, 1983),
pp. 174–180.
34. See an official Syrian publication entitled *The Israeli Invasion of Lebanon*
(in Arabic), by a group of researchers supervised by the Defense Minister,
General Mustafa Talas, Damascus, 1983, pp. 179–184.
35. R. Avi-Ran, *Syrian Involvement in Lebanon*, p. 128.
36. Louis Fares on R. Monte Carlo, February 12, 1982. Fares is known for
his contacts with the highest echelons of the Syrian regime.
37. *Israeli Invasion of Lebanon* , p. 206.
38. Ibid., p. 140.
39. This is actually an Israeli estimate, see R. Eytan, *The Story of a Soldier*
(in Hebrew), (Tel-Aviv: Ma'ariv, 1985), p. 273. (R. Eytan was Israel's Chief-
of-Staff during the Lebanese war).
40. The full text of the Syrian communique, B. Damascus, June 19–22,
1982.
41. D. Dishon and B. Maddy-Weitzman, "Inter Arab Relations," *MECS*,
6:247.
42. Y. Olmert, "Syria," *MECS*, 6:866.
43. Ibid., pp. 866–868.
44. Y. Olmert, "Lebanon," *MECS*, 7:664–668. For full text of the agreement, see ibid., pp. 690–696.
45. Ibid., pp. 545–546.
46. The SLA had been formed in 1976 under Major Sa'ad Haddad. In
1985, its commander was General Antoine Lahad.
47. Y. Olmert, "Lebanon," *MECS*, 8:551–557. The MNF was created, in
summer 1982, as a temporary force to provide a security net allowing the
evacuation of the PLO and Syria forces from West Beirut. It later assumed
other functions.
48. Zeev Schiff, a prominent Israeli analyst, in *Ha'aretz*, September 22,
1986.
49. Y. Olmert, "Lebanon," *MECS*, 10:482–484.
50. Ibid., p. 485.
51. See E. Kanovsky, *What's Behind Syria's Current Economic Problems* (Tel-
Aviv: Dayan Center for Middle Eastern Studies, 1985).
52. Y. Olmert, "Lebanon," *MECS*, 9:533–537.
53. *Ma'ariv*, January 14, 1986.
54. For a full description of the bizarre sequence of events, see *Al-Shira'*,
January 20, 1986.
55. "Lebanon," *Economist Intelligence Unit* (EIU), Country Report, no. 2,
1989, p. 10, no. 3 (1989), pp. 7–10.

56. For the full text of the Ta'if Accord, see *Al-Nahar*, October 23, 1989.

57. For the text of the Israeli announcement, made by Uri Lubrani, Coordinator of Israel's policy in Lebanon, see the Israeli newspapers—e.g., *Yedioth Aharonot, Ma'ariv, Ha-Aretz*—of October 12, 1990.

58. For the full text of the "Brotherhood and Cooperation" Agreement, see *Voice of the South*, May 16, 1991. On the other agreement, see *JP*, September 2, 1991.

5

Israel's Involvement in Lebanon: 1975–1985

SHAI FELDMAN

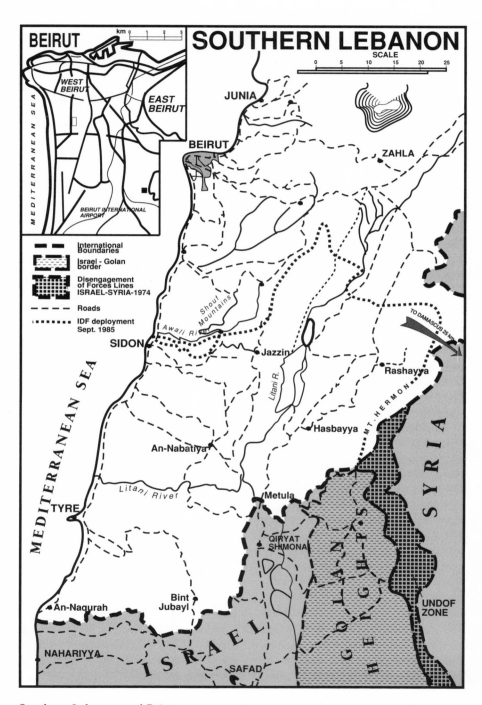

Southern Lebanon and Beirut

Introduction

Israel's decade-long involvement in Lebanon, followed by a period of more focused activity in the country's south, provides fertile ground for theorizing about the causes and effects of military intervention. An introduction to a volume devoted to Israel's invasion of Lebanon proposed that ". . . Israel's decision to go to war in June 1982 was not made by Begin and Sharon, but was the outcome of a long and painful attempt by Sharon's predecessors to find a solution to the problem through less drastic means."[1] It is difficult to imagine a more flawed assessment of the nature of Israel's involvement in Lebanon. Thus, a central proposition to be advanced here is that the escalation of Israel's intervention in Lebanon, leading to the 1982 invasion, resulted primarily not from a gradual exhaustion of less drastic means for addressing the problem but rather from a fundamental redefinition of the problem presented to Israel by the Lebanese scene. In turn, this redefinition of the problem led to a drastic reformulation of Israel's purposes in Lebanon. Without comprehending these more demanding purposes, the changes in Israel's strategy in Lebanon—ultimately reflected in its invasion—cannot be understood.

Thus, Israel's involvement in Lebanon does not support "slippery slope" theories of military intervention: there is no evidence that each step in Israel's climb up the escalation ladder was compelled by previous steps. Quite the contrary, decisions to escalate—whether correct or mistaken—were purposefully navigated by Israeli leaders. At no stage were the hands of the architects of Israel's involvement forced by the nature of previous action taken.

Another proposition to be advanced here is that given the nature of Lebanon's domestic and external environment, Israel could only sustain its initial limited goals in Lebanon. An added advantage associated with these limited goals is that they placed only modest demands on Israel's willpower. Indeed, Israel's success during 1976–1981 was clearly related to its ability to adjust its purposes and strategy to the opportunities and constraints presented by the Lebanese reality, as well as to the objective and subjective limitations of its own capabilities. Similarly, Israel's failure in 1982 was determined primarily by the fact that these environmental factors, and the added demands on Israel's ability and will to sustain costs, prevented the achievement of the more ambitious purposes it adopted toward the end of 1981. This became clearer as Israel encountered, during its protracted stay there, the various complexities of the Lebanese quagmire. Eventually, the difficulties involved led to the IDF's disengagement.

"Limited Goals" Strategy: Initial Success, 1975–1978

Lebanon has presented Israel with a multi-faceted challenge since 1970.[2] First, it became a central arena for the armed struggle waged against Israel by most Palestinian organizations, members and non-members of the PLO, following their expulsion from Jordan. Thus, the first of Israel's objectives in Lebanon became denial: preventing the Palestinians from making effective use of Lebanon as a launching board for terrorism against the Jewish state. In Israeli terminology, this became an important part of its "current security" policy.

Second, Lebanon became the scene—particularly as of 1975—of growing Syrian presence and involvement. Thus, in assessing the overall Syrian threat, Israel could not ignore the former's force-structure in Lebanon. Checking Syria's potential capacity to utilize Lebanese turf as a second front in a future confrontation became Israel's second purpose in Lebanon. In Israeli terminology, this became a component of its "basic security" policy.

Indeed, at various decision junctions, Israel had to compare the risks involved in Syria's presence in Lebanon with its resulting payoffs. These payoffs were especially pronounced when Syria's intervention there was directed against the Palestinians.[3] Then, Israel had to weigh the gains involved in meeting its "current security" challenge more effectively, and through less costly means, by accepting growing Syrian involvement in Lebanon at the risk of increasing the magnitude of its potential "basic security" problem posed by such involvement.

Third, as a consequence of an initiative taken by the Christian Maronites, the Lebanese arena presented Israel with a unique opportunity to forge an alliance with an important Arab community. An alliance with Arabs was a fundamental purpose of political Zionism since its inception. It also corresponded with the Israelis' psychological need to be accepted by their neighbors. Indeed, the Lebanese Christians sought Israel's support prior to its acceptance by any important factor in the Arab world. Under such circumstances, the Maronites' approach could not be easily resisted.[4]

In addition, Israel could not ignore the potential utility of the alliance with the Christians for checking the Palestinians' freedom of action, as well as in presenting a challenge to Syrian power, thus forcing Damascus to divert some of its military resources away from the Golan Heights. Such logic was consistent with Ben Gurion's concept of "the alliance with Middle East minorities," an important element of Israel's original grand strategy.[5]

Thus, during most of the past fifteen years, Israel's purposes in Lebanon were largely defensive: to diminish Palestinian power to conduct terrorism and to check the Syrian threat through the utilization of complex means, including an alliance with the Maronite Christians. Furthermore, the arena's most challenging aspect was Israel's ability to keep its combined response balanced: addressing each threat effectively without increasing the magnitude of other risks. Indeed, maintaining such balance was the key to Israel's success in the Lebanese front until 1982.

Before the 1967 war the Israeli–Lebanese border was almost completely quiet. In 1968 the PLO initiated mortar fire against Israeli settlements along the Lebanese border, and began to use Beirut as a launching board for international terrorism—notably with the October attack on an El-Al plane at Athens airport. Israeli military reprisals followed, including a commando raid on Beirut airport, where most of the passenger aircraft of Lebanon's airline were blown up. Subsequent internal Lebanese pressures led the PLO to undertake— in the framework of the 1969 Cairo agreement—to cease using Lebanon as a staging area for attacks against Israel.[6]

Palestinian terrorism escalated following the PLO's expulsion from Jordan in late 1970, and the relocation of its headquarters to Lebanon. During the first half of the 1970s, Israel's response to such terrorism remained entirely defensive: increased Palestinian terrorism simply lead to an escalation of Israeli reprisals.

When the Lebanese civil war began in mid-1975, Israel was preoccupied with the efforts to reach a second disengagement agreement with Egypt. Only after the agreement was concluded in September could Israeli leaders turn their attention to Lebanon. Having done so, they realized that the escalating civil war in Lebanon presented Israel with a mix of risks and opportunities. While the Palestinians emerged as a potent force, threatening to become a dominant factor there, the Syrians, who were just as alarmed as Israel at the prospects of Lebanon's domination by radical Palestinians, were predisposed to intervene. At the same time, the war brought about the first Christian overture to Israel—a modest request for assistance.

Israel reacted very cautiously to the specter of the civil war, the Maronites' mid-1975 approach, and the danger of Syrian intervention. In early 1976 it decided to respond to the Christian request with a modest supply of arms and ammunition, and communicated to Syria that it would not intervene unless the latter invaded Lebanon. It warned the Syrians that if they did invade, the IDF would be forced to establish defensive positions along the Litani river. In addition to its general prudence, this response made it clear that although Israel could not ignore developments in Lebanon at large, its interests were largely confined to the country's south.

When the Syrians invaded Lebanon in May 1976, they allied themselves with the country's Christians, directing their action against the increasingly powerful PLO. This led Palestinians to escape to the south, thus exacerbating Israel's "current security" problem there. Israel responded positively, in March 1976, to the request for assistance addressed to it by Christian Lebanese villagers along the border. By August, a Christian–Shi'i militia unit was established in the south: the South Lebanese Forces. It was commanded by Major Sa'd Haddad, who was commissioned by the Christian-dominated Lebanese Army in the north and was supported by Israel.[7]

In tailoring its response to the problems presented by the Lebanese scene in 1976, the Israeli government recognized its common interests with Syria in checking Palestinian power in Lebanon. Consequently, it communicated effectively its willingness to tolerate Syria's invasion provided this would not increase significantly Syria's future capacity to threaten Israel. The Israeli government defined clear criteria for assessing the potential implications of Syria's involvement, and articulated a set of "red lines" which, unless crossed, would allow Israel to accept Syria's move.[8]

Attending to its other interests in Lebanon, Israel simultaneously awarded modest assistance in arms and ammunition to the Christians in the north, and more pronounced assistance in the south. In November 1976 the IDF employed its artillery for the first time in support of the South Lebanese Forces.[9] Such action, however, was clearly defensive. Israel's increased involvement in the south did not follow a redefinition of Israel's purposes; rather, it constituted a response to the change in the nature of the threat: the Palestinians' move to the south, which followed their earlier move from Jordan to Lebanon, amplified the threat they presented along Israel's northern border. Israel's response was relatively inexpensive: instead of direct intervention similar to the Syrians' in the north, Israel opted for indirect and more modest involvement through an alliance with the Christian and Shi'i villagers in the south.

The dilemma Israel faced during this period—between its "current security" interest in having the Syrians deal with the PLO threat, and its "basic security" interest in checking Syria's capacity to threaten Israel from the north—was crystallized in early 1977 when the Syrians sought to move some of their forces to the southern town of Nabatiya.[10] While Syria's action could have contributed to curtailing the PLO threat in the south even further, such movement was in clear violation of the aforementioned red lines. Consequently, Jerusalem reacted by communicating to Damascus a clear deterrent threat. This resulted in Syria's withdrawal from Nabatiya and the restoration of the red lines.[11]

Indeed, the care Israel took in making sure that its efforts to maximize its current security did not compromise the imperatives of its basic security paid off in early 1978. President Sadat's peace overture—and Syria's decision to place itself in clear opposition to his move and to lead the so-called "rejectionist front"—led Syria to substitute its allies: the Lebanese Christians were replaced by the PLO. In mid-1978 the Syrians began to shell the Christian quarters of Beirut, leading the Maronites to request expanded Israeli assistance. Israel responded by adding another red line: the defense of Christians from massive Syrian attacks. However, the means employed for that purpose by Israel were limited to the realm of deterrence: two IAF fighters were sent to create a sonic boom over Beirut as a sign of Israel's commitment.[12]

Israel's earlier insistence that the Syrians be prevented from positioning their forces too close to the Israeli border now paid off. The PLO, first pressured by Syria in the north and later allied with the Syrians, now constituted a growing threat in the south. The situation there deteriorated in the spring of 1977: Major Haddad's forces moved to the tactical offensive, and the PLO responded by counter attacks. By September, the IDF for the first time took an active part in the fighting: its armored forces aided the Christians' attack on the village of al-Hiam. The PLO responded by a Katyusha rocket attack on Israel's northern settlements, and following pressures exerted by the Carter administration, Israel withdrew its forces.[13]

Yet the effectiveness of the sporadic Christian militia's presence in the south against PLO incursions was limited at best. The further strengthening of the PLO caused the ceasefire to collapse repeatedly.

Israel's artillery responses to PLO Katyusha attacks were ineffective, and by November 1977 the IAF was sent to bomb PLO strongholds in southern Lebanon. The bombing comprised effective active deterrence: the front remained quiet until March 1978.

While Israeli policy during the period described here did not eliminate the challenges presented to Israel by the Lebanese scene, it should nevertheless be judged as successful in containing the threats at tolerable costs. The causes of this success were complex: first, Israeli decision-making regarding Lebanon during the Rabin government was uniquely rational, orderly, and informed. Prime Minister Rabin, Defense Minister Peres, Foreign Minister Allon, and IDF Chief of Staff Mordechai (Motta) Gur, were a highly qualified group, enjoying much cumulative experience and expertise regarding the Lebanese arena, and the ability to combine political, diplomatic, and military considerations in producing balanced policy. This group was also sufficiently versed in the complexities of the Lebanese scene to avoid a common cause of intelligence failures: consumer misreading of intelligence assessments provided by their producers.

The formation of the government led by the Likud leader, Menachem Begin, in May 1977, did not result in an immediate change in Israel's policy vis-à-vis Lebanon: Israel's new Prime Minister was content with the policies of the Rabin government in this realm. Defense Minister Weizman and Foreign Minister Dayan were preoccupied by the prospects for establishing peace with Egypt. They opted for continuing a defensive posture in Lebanon while pursuing the diplomatic initiative with Egypt. As long as General Gur remained IDF Chief of Staff, continuity at all levels of policy regarding Lebanon was maintained.

Second, such decision-making demonstrated a high degree of consensus among Israel's policy elite. In particular, almost all members of the policy-making circle agreed on the absolute imperative of avoiding escalation in a region which was considered to be of only secondary importance to Israel's security and wellbeing. Israeli leaders were largely united in their satisfaction with reducing the threats to Israel to a tolerable level and agreed that the configuration of forces operating in the Lebanese arena would prevent the attainment of absolute goals such as the complete elimination of terrorism.

Third, an important principle was adhered to throughout the period: namely, that Israel would not fight the Maronites' battles and would limit its assistance to "helping the Christians help themselves." Such insistence guaranteed that the costs of Israeli strategy in Lebanon would remain low. In turn, this helped insure that the policy pursued would continue to enjoy a domestic consensus in Israel. Inexpensive policies are rarely a focus of much dissent.

Fourth, Israeli policy vis-à-vis Syria was pragmatic and sophisticated: it recognized that while Israeli and Syrian interests differed in the Lebanon conflict, they sometimes partially overlapped, thus creating the grounds for limited cooperation between them.

Fifth, the enormous caution with which Israel pursued its limited interests in Lebanon also diminished the likelihood of a clash with the United States. Indeed, while Washington was not thrilled with each of Israel's moves, it demonstrated a measure of understanding if not sympathy for Israel's right to attend to its "basic" and "current" security requirements. Moreover, Washington implicitly became an accomplice to Israeli policy by playing an active role, not only in communicating Israeli messages to Syria and vice-versa, but also in acting otherwise to smooth Israeli-Syrian relations.[14]

Finally, Israel's purposes in helping the Maronites remained defensive: namely, checking growing PLO power in Lebanon. The Rabin government—and initially the Begin government as well—carefully avoided any notions of helping the Christians reestablish their former domination in Lebanon. Indeed, most Israeli decision makers regarded the Maronites as far too weak to become dominant. Hence, Israel wisely refrained from attempting to redraw the Lebanese domestic political map.

Overall, the defensive nature of Israel's purposes in Lebanon, and its associated strategy of denial, constituted not only a measure but also a central cause of its success. Quite simply, it is far easier to deny than to construct; it is far more difficult to forge a new reality than to obstruct such a process.

The mid-March 1978 Litani operation demonstrated the causes of Israel's successful limited goals strategy. The operation followed a deadly PLO hostage-taking terrorist attack inside Israel. The Israeli government responded by sending its forces to punish the Palestinians in south Lebanon, thus establishing a measure of active deterrence and to create a 100-kilometer wide and 10-kilometer deep *cordon sanitaire* along the Lebanese-Israeli border, which would be clean of Palestinian terrorists and where Israel's southern-Christian allies would construct an effective security belt.

The military operation was accompanied by a series of steps designed to diminish its potential political-strategic costs. In order to reduce potential damage to the Egyptian-Israeli peace process, Israel informed Egypt of the operation's purposes and dimensions. In addition, Israel's intention to withdraw immediately after reaching the operation's limited goals was made crystal clear, thus diminishing the magnitude of the negative international reaction. Also, Israel communicated to Damascus clearly and credibly that the operation was not directed against Syria and its interests in Lebanon. Thus, the odds of Syrian misperception and overreaction were reduced. Finally, the IDF was instructed to stay clear of Tyre, thus avoiding the perils of controlling a large Arab population.

Judging by its results, and given the constraints of the Lebanese arena, the 1978 Litani operation must be regarded as a success. True, the punishment exerted on the Palestinian terrorists was limited; most PLO fighters were able to flee faster than the IDF's advance. However, the operation helped forge a security belt along Israel's northern border consisting of two main filters: Major Haddad's enhanced South Lebanese Forces and the units of UNIFIL (United Nations Forces in Lebanon) which were established subsequent to the operation. The two combined to reduce the terrorist threat to Israel's north.[15]

The pressures exerted on the PLO by the 1976 Syrian invasion, causing its forces to move from Beirut to the south, was now complemented by Israeli action that pushed the PLO to the north, away from the immediate vicinity of the Israeli–Lebanese border. As a result, the PLO was largely boxed in a square north of the Litani and south of the Zaharani rivers. There, it established a mini-state with its own health, education, and other social services.

More important from Israel's standpoint, the PLO gradually transformed the structure of its armed formations from terrorist groupings to conventional forces. While such forces could never pose a serious challenge to the IDF's power, they did enhance the PLO's effectiveness in some military realms, primarily the capacity to deliver artillery fire against Israel's northern settlements. At the same time, the conventionalization of the PLO and its concentration in the Litani-Zaharani region increased its vulnerability considerably.

Getting In: From Defense to Offense, 1978–1982

Begin and Eitan: Expanding Objectives, Diminishing Success

The nomination, in April 1978, of General Rafael ("Raful") Eitan to replace General Gur as IDF Chief of Staff marked the beginning of the redefinition of Israel's strategy and purposes in Lebanon. Eitan, a former commander of the IDF's Northern Command, sought an absolute response to the challenges presented to Israel by the Lebanese scene. He was also unsatisfied with Israeli strategy, which emphasized retaliation and deterrence vis-à-vis the PLO, which in his view meant yielding the initiative—and hence the capacity to determine the agenda—to the PLO.

Consequently, Raful moved to transform Israel's *modus operandi* in the north, substituting deterrence and retaliation by offense and initiative. Air bombings and land commando raids were carried out throughout the first half of 1979, focusing—but not exclusively—on the Litani-Zaharani region. More important, these activities were conducted not in response and retaliation to specific PLO action but rather as an Israeli-initiated effort to wage war on the PLO.[16]

Despite the changes in mode of operation in southern Lebanon, Israel in 1979–1980 had not yet fundamentally altered its strategy and purposes in Lebanon. Thus, while moving to the offense in the south, Israel's posture remained largely defensive vis-à-vis Syria's presence in the north. Indeed, Prime Minister Begin insisted that Israel continue to adhere to a central feature of its former strategy in Lebanon: avoiding a clash with the Syrians. Therefore, when Syria reacted to Israel's increased air-to-surface activity in mid-1979 by introducing radars for a surface-to-air missile system into Lebanon, the IAF was instructed to reduce the frequency of its bombings and to avoid such attacks north of Zahla altogether.[17]

Yet the nomination of General Eitan did signal the beginning of Israel's expanded commitment to the Christians of the north. In October 1978 Israel promised the Maronites that if the Syrian air force attacked them, the IDF would respond. This was expanded two years later; during a visit to the Christian port town of Junia, Eitan promised his hosts that Israel would support the Christians' Lebanese front should it be pressed by the Syrians. These commitments provided the Maronites, for the first time, with the capacity to catalyze an Israeli-Syrian clash. Consequently, Israel lost its capacity to maintain complete control over the level of its involvement in Lebanon.

The implications of this change were apparent during the mid-1981 clashes in Zahla. Earlier, 1980 was characterized by the growing entrenchment of the PLO in the Litani-Zaharani area, and the increasing strength of the Kataib, lead by Bashir Jumayyil, within the Christians' Lebanese Front. This resulted from Jumayyil's success in establishing his faction's dominance over the Franjiya and Chamounist factions within the Maronite Christian community. The more moderate Sunni-Muslim community had meanwhile weakened, leaving the Maronites and the Palestinians as the most powerful forces in

Lebanon, with the Druse continuing to maintain control in specific regions, and the Shi'is showing initial signs of political organization.

Jumayyil's new strength also brought about a redefinition of the Lebanese Front's own purposes: it now proclaimed its desire to unify Lebanon under the Maronites' dominance. The front added that should such unification turn out to be impractical, it would seek the partitioning or cantonization of Lebanon. By mid-1981, the Lebanese Front supplemented its political offensive with corresponding military moves. It chose to take the tactical offensive in the vicinity of Zahla by placing a Phalange unit there, and by constructing a road to its southwest. Their next step was to ambush Syrian units in the area, killing a number soldiers. Syria responded by shelling Zahla with artillery fire and launching an attack on the Christian stronghold on nearby Mount Senin. It utilized helicopter-carried infantry to support the attack, and later followed up by constructing entrenchments for a surface-to-air missile system in the area.

Seeking to aid the Christians and recalling that Syrian use of helicopters violated the red line restricting their use of airpower in Lebanon, Israel responded by sending the IAF to destroy two Syrian transport helicopters in the Mount Senin district. In turn, Damascus responded by introducing surface-to-air missiles into Lebanon. Viewing the latter act as a further violation of the 1976 understanding, Prime Minister Begin ordered an air strike against the missiles on April 30, 1981. However, bad weather brought about the bombing's cancellation; the United States had meanwhile intervened diplomatically to defuse the crisis, sending Philip Habib to mediate between Israel and Syria.[18]

Begin and Raful were extremely unhappy with the outcome of the April battles: the Syrians remained in Mount Senin and their surface-to-air missiles remained in Lebanon. On May 28, Begin approved a renewal of the offensive against the PLO mini-state in south Lebanon.[19] The PLO responded to Israel's attack by shelling the Christian enclave in the south, and, in mid-July—following additional artillery exchanges between the PLO and the South Lebanese Forces—Israel conducted a massive bombing of PLO headquarters in Beirut.

The Palestinians responded with artillery fire—this time directed against Israeli settlements along its Lebanese border. Israel reacted by sending its air force to suppress the PLO's artillery. The battle lasted some twelve days but the IAF failed to achieve effective artillery suppression. Prime Minister Begin—unwilling to risk a war with Syria and a negative American response—decided against trying to obtain such suppression by sending the IDF's ground forces into

Lebanon. Instead, he opted for diplomacy and invited Habib to mediate a cease-fire.

Judging by its outcome, Israeli policy toward Lebanon between
April 1978 and mid-1981, was less than completely successful. Israeli
deterrence *vis-à-vis* both the Syrians and the PLO eroded during this
period: the Syrians were able to establish their violation of the 1976
red line by defeating all efforts to compel them to withdraw their air-
defense system from Lebanon; the PLO was justified in viewing the
July battle as the first time Israel had failed to defeat them. A number
of causes account for Israel's diminishing success in Lebanon during
the mid-1978 to mid-1981 period. First, the composition of Israeli
decision makers changed, with General Eitan replacing General Gur
as the IDF Chief of Staff, and, later, with the departure of Ezer
Weizman and the assumption of the Defense Minister's responsibilities by Prime Minister Begin. Since Foreign Minister Dayan remained
preoccupied with the Israeli-Egyptian peace process, decisions over
Lebanon rested largely with Raful and Begin. The former was largely
incapable of integrating political, diplomatic, and military considerations, and the latter had insufficient understanding of the complex
Lebanese scene; hence, Begin's tools for controlling Israeli policy
were far from complete.

Second, the consensus among Israeli decision makers over their
policy began to deteriorate. True, both Begin and Eitan sought to
substitute Israel's strategy in Lebanon from defense to offense. But
whereas Begin was willing to apply such change only to the Palestinians, Raful extended the new policy to a strengthening of Israel's
commitment to the Maronites and to a willingness to engage the
Syrians. While Begin mostly succeeded in preventing the extension
of the new offensive doctrine to the latter realms, he did yield to
Raful at some critical junctures. In turn, this led—especially in 1981—
to growing dissent within the Israeli government, as some ministers
began to voice their discomfort at Israel's new willingness to be
manipulated by the Maronites.

Third, during this period Israel departed for the first time from its
principle of refraining from waging the Christians' battles: in Mount
Senin, the IAF intervened for the first time on the Maronites' behalf.
This taught the Christians that they could act irresponsibly and still
depend on Israel to bail them out.

Fourth, Israel lost some of its prior sophistication in reading Syrian
intentions and recognizing that the two countries enjoy some mutual
interests in Lebanon. More frequently, Israeli behavior was condi-
tioned by worst case analysis of Syrian actions and intentions. As a

consequence, it showed a propensity to overreact to steps taken by Damascus.

Sharon: Israeli Purposes and Strategy Redefined

The formation of Begin's second government, in which Ariel Sharon was appointed Defense Minister, was a watershed in terms of Israel's definition of its purpose and strategy in Lebanon. Most important, the perception of the problems presented to Israel by the Lebanese reality was fundamentally altered. The new Defense Minister was bothered not by the immediate and operational PLO terrorist threat to Israel, but rather by the *political* threat the organization had represented. Ultimately, Sharon was interested in creating conditions for the establishment of a permanent minimal autonomy in the West Bank and Gaza. His view was that as long as the PLO—seeking Palestinian state independence—remained potent, Israel was unlikely to find Palestinian partners in the territories for such autonomy, partially because the latter were deterred by PLO terrorist threats.

The evolution of the PLO mini-state in the Litani-Zaharani region exacerbated this wider political threat. By establishing the capacity to provide a wide array of social services within the territory under its control, the PLO's claim to be able to manage the responsibilities of statehood were strengthened.

This more complex definition of the problem brought about a correspondingly more demanding purpose: the political destruction of the PLO. Such destruction required eliminating the Palestinian mini-state in southern Lebanon, and—through an alliance with the Maronites—crushing the PLO in Beirut. However, such gains could not be stabilized without a restructuring of Lebanon's political map: the country had to be unified under the Maronites' domination. In turn, such restructuring required that the Syrian forces be expelled from Lebanon.[20]

The operational plan designed to achieve these objectives (the "big plan") was code named "ORANIM." It was brought to the Israeli Cabinet for approval on December 20, 1981, shortly after Israel's annexation of the Golan Heights. It called for a major assault toward the Beirut-Damascus highway and the outskirts of Beirut. The proposed operation also included the landing of IDF forces in the port of Junia (north of Beirut), and the joining of forces with Bashir Jumayyil's Lebanese Front in an attempt to surround Lebanon's capital.

The assumption was that Jumayyil's Phalangists would assault the PLO in West Beirut once the IDF's tanks reached the city's outskirts. It remains somewhat unclear whether the plan also called for an Israeli assault on the Syrians in the Beqa'a or, instead, for an effort to obtain their withdrawal by reaching their rear with overwhelming force.

Fearing that the invasion would result in a full-scale war with Syria, with heavy casualties resulting, many in the Israeli Cabinet opposed Sharon's scheme. This led Prime Minister Begin to take the proposal off the Cabinet's agenda.[21]

Sharon's conclusion from the December debate seems to have been that since his preferred strategy for Lebanon—as an integrated construct—was unlikely to gain Cabinet approval, attempts should be made to implement it piecemeal. Thus, in late January, early March, early April, and mid-May, 1982, Sharon proposed to the Israeli Cabinet a series of military operations against Palestinian targets in Lebanon, but very much scaled down from the December ORANIM plan. Sharon's most probably hoped that the dynamics created once any military operation was initiated would enable its piecemeal expansion to the dimensions envisaged by the original ORANIM plan.

The Israeli government rejected these proposals for much the same reasons it rejected ORANIM in December. However, following the shooting by a Palestinian terrorist of Israel's Ambassador to Great Britain in early June, the Israeli Cabinet approved an IAF bombing of PLO bases in Lebanon. The Palestinians responded by artillery shelling across the Lebanese border, and on June 5 the Israeli Cabinet met to determine Israel's response.

The result was a decision to conduct what may be described as a "super Litani operation": a limited invasion of southern Lebanon, with the stated purpose of creating a 25-mile deep PLO-free zone. Presenting this decision to the Israeli Knesset a day later, Prime Minister Begin pledged that once the IDF reached a line 25 miles north of the border, "our work will have been done and all fighting will cease." That day, in a letter to President Reagan, Begin committed Israel to the same limited objective. The government's decision further made it clear that Israel would do its best to avoid clashing with the Syrians.

It should be noted that in opting for a limited incursion into Lebanon, the Israeli government made use of an extremely favorable regional and international environment. The Arab world was divided to an unprecedented degree: Iraq was engulfed in a war with Iran;

Egypt had attained Israel's complete withdrawal from the Sinai only a year earlier and was in no mood to risk its recapture by the IDF in response to a harsh Egyptian response to the invasion; moreover, engaged in a bitter conflict with Syria ever since the 1978 Camp David Accords, Cairo could be expected at least to tolerate a weakening of Syria's hold in Lebanon; Jordan, in turn, could be expected to tacitly welcome any erosion of the PLO's power. There also were sufficient indications that the United States would accept an Israeli action that remained "proportional" to the challenges presented by the PLO to Israel's security and wellbeing. Finally, there was reason to believe that the Soviet Union's negative reaction would remain benign as long as Israeli action did not escalate into a direct threat to the Damascus regime.

The first five days of Israel's campaign comprised a fascinating tale of deception and insubordination.[22] Israel's Defense Minister did his best to implement the ORANIM plan despite the limitations the Cabinet's original disapproval—and its authorization of a limited plan on June 5—had now placed on his freedom of action. By the fifth day of the war, the IDF found itself positioned along some sections of the Beirut–Damascus highway, and at the outskirts of Beirut.

Following the IDF's initial thrust and its advance along certain axes to a depth of 25 miles, Sharon extracted the Cabinet's consent for further movements north by employing a number of means: (a) persuading the Cabinet that the best way to avoid the costs of a violent confrontation with the Syrians is to outflank them, since they are bound to reduce their exposure by withdrawing. The sensitivity of the Israeli Cabinet to costs made this argument highly effective; (b) by describing the IDF's positions as "exposed," thus requiring that they be "improved" if soldiers' lives were to be spared. Such presentations invariably resulted in the desired approvals from Israel's cost-sensitive Cabinet. Indeed, the Cabinet's approval for the June 9 attack on Syria's surface-to-air missile launchers in Lebanon was obtained in a similar fashion: the Israeli Air Force's ground-support operations were required if the costs to the IDF's land forces were to be kept low; in turn, the destruction of the missiles was necessary in order that the IAF could perform such missions without incurring "intolerable" costs; (c) ordering the IDF to move and later presenting such movement to the Cabinet as *faits accomplis*. Such movements were invariably justified by Sharon as required due to the development of specific circumstances on the ground; (d) finally, maneuvering the Syrians into situations in which they would be compelled to open fire, and then presenting the Cabinet with the imperative of responding to such fire. The latter two methods later led Begin to testify somewhat cynically that he was always kept informed of the steps directed by Sharon "either before or after the fact."

Thus, Israel's invasion of Lebanon did not result from any "slippery slope" and does not support such theories of military intervention. Israel found itself in the Lebanese mud not because each step in its involvement dictated that it further deepen its intervention but from a well articulated "grand design" which Israel's Defense Minister was determined to implement.

The precise degree to which Prime Minister Begin was an active and willing partner to Sharon's determination to attempt the Big Plan's implementation in June 1982, remains a mystery to this very day. It is clear that Begin was originally an ardent supporter of the plan but it may very well be that by early 1982 he understood that it could not be implemented in the absence of a supportive Cabinet and national consensus. In any event, there is ample evidence to suggest that many among the less senior members of the Israeli Cabinet indeed slid down the "slippery slope" to support Sharon's schemes.

Yet employing deception to extract Cabinet approvals for fragmented IDF advances precluded the early achievement of the invasion's objectives. Deceiving the Cabinet regarding the operation's intended scope meant that an early surprise attack on the Syrian forces in Lebanon could not be conducted. As a result, these forces could not be defeated swiftly and forcefully, and the Maronites' Syrian flank could not be secured; consequently, the Christians could not or would not assault the PLO's forces and headquarters in Beirut. Thus, the absence of consensus at the Cabinet level led to deception, while the requirements of deception meant that a major prerequisite to the Big Plan could not be fulfilled.

The lack of consensus among the IDF's rank and file had a similar effect.[23] Skepticism regarding the worthiness of the expanded invasion's goals led the IDF to attempt to avoid costs. This resulted in its cautious and slow advance. Later, IDF commanders and soldiers expressed clear dissent regarding the proposed conquest of West Beirut. This meant that the PLO's headquarters and forces there could not be destroyed.

Staying In: Constraints, Costs and Consequences

During the first part of Israel's stay in Lebanon, every effort was made by Israel's Defense Minister to obtain his original objectives: the political devastation of the PLO, secured by the expulsion of the Syrians from Lebanon and stabilized by the country's unification under the leadership of Bashir Jumayyil's Maronite Phalanges. But the manner in which its invasion was conducted—which, in turn, was largely affected by Israel's internal consensus and resolve—and the constraints imposed by Lebanon's domestic, regional, and international environment, soon made these goals extremely elusive.

Unable to defeat the Syrians early and decisively, the IDF could only push their forces northward to the Beirut–Damascus highway in the Beqa'a at the end of the first week of the war, and eastward from Beirut during the following two weeks: the so-called "crawling stage" of the war. Such IDF advances, however, were insufficient to prevent the Syrians from continuing to exercise control over Lebanon's strategic linchpin: the Zahla-Shturah-Ba'al Bek area. From there, they continued to affect the domestic Lebanese scene by maintaining a robust capacity to prevent any internal or external force—perceived as detrimental to their interests—from achieving dominance in Lebanon.

At the same time, Israel's Maronite allies refuted Sharon's prewar expectations regarding their capabilities and resolve. Better aware of their weakness than his Israeli friends, Bashir Jumayyil was determined to avoid an attrition of the Phalanges' limited power in a costly assault on Beirut. Also, assessing that once the war was over, and given the Maronites' limited power, he would be forced to form a coalition with other Lebanese factions, Bashir was equally careful to avoid undermining his legitimacy by entering Western Beirut under the Israelis' auspices. Thus, he opted for inaction, leaving the onus of eliminating the PLO forces and headquarters in Beirut to the IDF.

The Reagan administration at first seemed to have resigned itself to Israel's invasion. Partly, this resulted from its acceptance, at face value, of Israel's commitment, contained in Begin's June 6 letter to the President, to adhere to the original limited objectives it stipulated on June 5.[24] Partly, it may have been induced by the internal split within the administration: Secretary of State Haig seems to have been supportive of Israel's original limited objectives, while Secretary of Defense Weinberger was instinctively hostile to any unilateral Israeli action.[25] But since Haig initially dominated America's response, Israel was able to act fairly free of a significant superpower constraint during the first four days of the war.

This convenient global environment soon changed. The Soviet Union, which at first had made a surprisingly mild response to Israel's incursion, became increasingly nervous once the IDF tank forces began to push northward in the Beqa'a on June 10. Primarily, the Soviets became concerned that should Damascus feel threatened by the IDF's proximity, they would be faced with Syrian pressure to intervene. To avoid this, Moscow turned to Washington. The Reagan administration, interested in avoiding any pretext for Soviet intervention, impressed upon Jerusalem the urgent need to accept a cease-fire. Begin responded positively and the cease-fire was affected as of noontime on June 11.

As of that point, American policy presented serious constraints upon the IDF's freedom of action. Partly, the change in Washington's attitude can be traced to the departure of Secretary of State Haig. In any event, the United States repeatedly imposed cease-fires throughout Israel's efforts to dislodge the Syrians from the western parts of the Beirut–Damascus highway during the last two weeks of June. Hoping to avert such impositions, the Israeli Cabinet restricted the means employed by the IDF. Thus, permission to use airpower and heavy artillery against Syria's ground forces positioned along the highway was denied; and, initially, the means used to gain the PLO's expulsion from Beirut were similarly restricted.

Given the overwhelming power it deployed, Israel was destined to gain the PLO's eventual departure from Beirut. However, Israel failed to gain the organization's political destruction through a humiliating unconditional expulsion from Lebanon's capital. Largely, this failure resulted from the Israeli-PLO imbalance of resolve in Beirut. By early July, the expanded purposes of the invasion became a subject of growing dissent among all strata of the Israeli politics: the Cabinet, the IDF's rank and file, the political parties represented in the Knesset, and the public at large.[26] In order to avert further erosion, the navigators of Israeli policy were compelled to exercise even greater sensitivity to costs. Thus, an IDF ground assault, requiring complicated urban warfare, on heavily populated Western Beirut, was judged too costly and was ruled out.

On the ground, Israeli soldiers and officers demonstrated diminishing willingness to risk their lives for the sake of gaining the PLO's expulsion. Hence, the IDF was forced to employ relatively "safe" means: airpower and artillery shelling. These were complemented by less lethal methods: cut-offs of electricity and water supplies.

Conversely, the PLO fighters besieged in Beirut demonstrated impressive willingness to sustain the heavy costs entailed in withstanding Israel's firepower. Totally surrounded, they felt pressed to the wall, and in the absence of any option to withdraw, the individual PLO fighter had no choice but to resist.

Impressed by the performance of his rank and file, PLO leader Yasir Arafat stalled the efforts to compel his forces to leave Beirut. Thus, although by mid-July he had already accepted the principle of withdrawal, he accompanied his consent by a number of conditions and added new ones periodically. Primarily, Arafat sought to extract an American recognition in exchange for the PLO withdrawal.[27] Since the Reagan administration would not or could not grant such recognition, diplomatic efforts—conducted primarily by Habib, through the mediation of Lebanese Muslim leaders—failed during July to gain the PLO's departure.

The efforts to gain the PLO's "relocation" through diplomacy were also complicated by the refusal of Arab state leaders to accept the departing Palestinians. In turn, such unwillingness further reinforced the PLO fighters' conviction that they had no choice but to fight.

The resistance demonstrated by the PLO, matched by the equally impressive resolve demonstrated by the Syrian forces trapped in Beirut, forced Sharon to escalate the use of firepower employed in an effort to break their will. However, such escalation exacerbated the "global" constraints: increasingly, Washington bluntly expressed its anger regarding Israel's indiscriminate use of airpower and artillery. This process peaked on August 12 when an 11-hour bombardment of Beirut conducted by the IAF elicited an extremely angry phone call from President Reagan to Prime Minister Begin.[28]

The August 12 bombing, which was ordered by Defense Minister Sharon without the Israeli Cabinet's approval, also resulted in a heated debate within the Cabinet. As a consequence, the Israeli government undertook to cease all military activity around Beirut, thus permitting Habib to complete the negotiations for the PLO's withdrawal. At the same time, the Cabinet diminished its Defense Minister's authority by stipulating that no further military measures be taken without the approval of the Prime Minister or the full Cabinet.

Paradoxically, just as domestically and externally generated forces presented unprecedented constraints on the architect of Israel's intervention in Lebanon, the cumulative pressures exerted on the PLO and the Syrians finally yielded the desired results: Arafat and Asad accepted the withdrawal of their respective forces from Beirut. The second two weeks of August thus comprised the height of Israel's achievements in Lebanon: the PLO and the Syrians withdrew from

Beirut; the road to the election of Bashir Jumayyil to Lebanon's Presidency was paved; and tensions between Washington and Jerusalem eased considerably.[29]

The objective constraints imposed by Lebanon's internal and external environments, as well as by Israel's domestic scene, soon ended the short life of these achievements. By early September, Bashir Jumayyil's assassination demonstrated both Syria's capacity to employ creative means of attending to its interests in Lebanon, and Israel's precarious standing even among the Maronite Christians. Syria's role in the assassination proved conclusively that by avoiding decisive defeat it sustained the capacity to affect developments in Lebanon through methods well suited to the nature of the Lebanese political and cultural terrain.

For Israel, the assassination merely highlighted the growing doubts regarding the utility of the alliance with Bashir Jumayyil's Maronite Christians. By late August, assessing that he would not be able to rule Lebanon without the support of a number of non-Maronite factions and without functioning links to the Arab world, Jumayyil had stubbornly resisted Israeli pressures for the early conclusion of a formal Lebanese-Israeli peace treaty. He reasoned that such a treaty might undermine his legitimacy in the eyes of other Lebanese factions and the neighboring Arab states. Jumayyil also insisted that the South Lebanese Forces, led by Major Haddad, be brought under his government's authority.

Following Bashir's assassination, the inability to find a replacement combining his stature with a positive approach toward Israel illustrated the precarious nature of a strategy that depended entirely on the survivability and intentions of a single individual. Reluctantly, Israel had no choice but to accept the nomination to the post of Bashir's brother, Amin, who had far better relations in Damascus than in Tel Aviv.

The post-assassination massacre conducted by the Phalangists in the refugee camps of Sabra and Shatila, and the international criticism directed at Israel—which was held accountable for atrocities perpetrated in areas under its control—provided conclusive evidence regarding the fallacy of a strategy based on the assumption that the Maronites were able and responsible allies.

America's reaction to the massacre merely exacerbated U.S.-Israeli tensions which, after a very short respite, developed afresh after the September 1 announcement of President Reagan's initiative for a resolution of the Israeli-Palestinian-Jordanian conflict. At the very least, the initiative pulled the rug from under Sharon's ultimate purpose in invading Lebanon: given the President's stated preference for full autonomy for the West Bank and Gaza, ultimately leading to the establishment of a Palestinian entity linked to Jordan, Sharon could no longer hope to find credible and willing Palestinian partners for the much more limited autonomy he had in mind.

The damage suffered by Israel as a consequence of the American media's graphic accounts of the massacre multiplied the effect of the Reagan administration's sharp reaction to the IDF's post-assassination move into West Beirut. Washington's massive pressure compelled Israel to affect an immediate withdrawal of its forces from the city's western sectors. Henceforth, Israel had lost the initiative in Lebanon and its forces found themselves in a long course combining retrenchment and retreat.

The massacre at Sabra and Shatila, and the Israeli government's initial resistance to having the affair investigated by a commission of inquiry, also accelerated the erosion of Israel's domestic consensus. Subsequently, Tel Aviv witnessed the largest demonstration in Israel's history. On September 25, crowds measured in the hundreds of thousands gathered in the city's municipal square to protest their government's behavior.[30] On September 28, the Israeli Cabinet capitulated and established the Kahan Commission to investigate the events surrounding the Beirut massacre. Henceforth, the Israeli leaders' conduct in Lebanon was increasingly affected by their concerns regarding the Commission's pending report.

Thus, in every possible respect, the assassination of Bashir Jumayyil turned out to be a watershed for Israel's intervention in Lebanon. Yet it would be a mistake to see the murder as an important cause of Israel's ultimate failure. The assassination, and the developments it triggered, merely illustrated the questionable validity of the various assumptions upon which Israel's invasion was based.

In the post-Sabra and Shatila environment, Israel now found itself in triple jeopardy in Lebanon. Generally, it was considered by the various Lebanese factions as being on the defensive and as incapable of determining the course of developments in the country. As a consequence, its deterrent power within Lebanon eroded. More worrisome, it found itself at the crossfire between various Lebanese factions, primarily the Druse and the Maronites. The latter launched a major effort to regain their hold in the Shuf mountains from which they had been expelled following Kamal Junblat's assassination in 1977. But Walid Junblat's warriors proved themselves more than a match to the Maronites who failed to gain ground.

At last, the Israelis realized what had been clear to Bashir Jumayyil

and should have been clear to them much earlier: namely, that chan-
nels of communication and negotiations with other Lebanese factions
must be kept open even while fighting continues. Consequently, the
Israelis now expanded their links beyond the Maronites to include
the Druse and Shi'i leaderships. However, in the Shuf the Israelis
found themselves placed with the impossible task of attempting mediation between the Maronites and the Druse while being perceived
by the latter as allied with the former. This also increased the frustration of Israel's own Druse community and threatened the delicate
relations between the community and the organs of the Jewish state.[31]

Finally, Israel now became engaged in almost constant friction
with Washington D.C. This resulted from America's increased involvement in Lebanon. Twice within a two-month period, developments in Lebanon created a requirement for direct intervention by
U.S. Marines in Beirut. In late August, they were brought into Beirut
in order to safeguard the PLO's evacuation; following the massacre,
they were sent to replace the withdrawing IDF forces in the western
district.

But while Israel remained a party to the conflict, the U.S. Marines
were bestowed with the task of keeping the peace between the
various parties that constituted the Lebanese quagmire. While the
IDF was there to attend to Israel's interests, the Marines' ability to
fulfill their mission depended on their capacity to find a neutral
ground between the various warring parties. Thus, a conflict of interest between the IDF and the Marines in Beirut became inevitable.
Indeed, by February 1983, tensions between the IDF and the Marines
reached alarming dimensions, culminating in a dangerous incident
in Beirut's outskirts in which a Marine officer had pulled a pistol
against an Israeli tank commander in an effort to compel him to
withdraw the three tanks he commanded.[32]

Meanwhile, the costs of the IDF's presence in Lebanon continued
to accumulate: by October Israel had suffered 368 dead and 2,383
wounded.[33] In November, the IDF headquarters in Tyre exploded,
killing 89 and wounding 56 Israelis.[34] Financially, Israel's presence in
Lebanon was said to involve an average expenditure of a million
dollars a day. Consequently, criticism of the intervention in Lebanon
continued to mount as well.

It is noteworthy that one of the most significant costs of Israel's
invasion and stay in Lebanon has had relatively little effect on the
Israeli government's conduct. At the time, the most positive element
of its regional environment was the peace agreement it had signed
only three years earlier with Egypt, the largest and most populous

Arab state. While the agreement continued to be the subject of periodic attacks within Egypt's political elite—primarily from the intellectual left but also from the ultra-religious right—Israel's invasion of Lebanon undermined the position and standing of the many Egyptians who favored the accommodation process. The latter became vulnerable to the argument that the invasion demonstrated that Israel seeks only to dominate the Middle East and that if the Egyptian–Israeli peace treaty did not provide Jerusalem the confidence that its southern front was secure, Israel would not have risked such an invasion.

But while the invasion did irreparable damage to the delicate fabric of Israeli–Egyptian relations, there is no evidence that Israeli decision makers considered this a constraining factor. Indeed, while paying lip service to the critical importance of Egyptian–Israeli relations, the architects of Israel's invasion of Lebanon, and its leaders during its protracted stay there, manifested insensitivity to the damage incurred in this realm.

While public support for Israel's stay in Lebanon continued to erode, its government remained committed to its ambitious agenda. Hence, in mid-October it continued to condition any Israeli withdrawal on the establishment of a de-facto peace with Lebanon: namely, on the normalization of relations between Israel and the Lebanese state; on the prior withdrawal of all PLO and Syrian forces from Lebanon; and on a set of security arrangements within a depth of 40 km north of the Israeli-Lebanese border.[35]

After preparatory U.S. mediation between Israel and President Amin Jumayyil's government registered no progress for more than two months, Defense Minister Sharon sprung another strategic surprise in mid-December by announcing that he had reached an agreement with the Jumayyil regime on a working document that would serve as a basis for direct negotiations between the two governments. This was denied by Lebanon's new President, but on December 28 Israeli–Lebanese negotiations began.[36]

By early 1983, however, the Lebanese, the PLO, and Syria, were no longer predisposed to concede any of Israel's stipulated demands. Quite the contrary, they assessed that the cumulative costs incurred by Israel might soon lead it to withdraw unilaterally. Indeed, they had ample evidence of more frequent calls within Israel—both among and outside its government—for the IDF's disengagement from Beirut and the Shuf maintains.

Getting Out: Redefining Israel's Purposes

The beginning of Israel's disengagement from Lebanon can be traced to the Israeli government decision, in early February 1983, to accept the findings of the Kahan Commission of Inquiry.[37] Although the substance of the Commission's report was confined to the Sabra and Shatila massacre, its gruesomely detailed analysis highlighted the nature of their Phalange allies, thus further staining the Lebanese adventure in the Israelis' eyes. More important, the Commission's report led to the departure of Defense Minister Sharon and his replacement by Israel's Ambassador in Washington, Moshe Arens. Not only was Arens less committed to Sharon's ambitious objectives in Lebanon, he was also far more sensitive to America's concerns. IDF Chief of Staff Eitan, due for retirement anyway, was also strongly reprimanded by the Commission. Thus the two prime architects of Israel's invasion soon left the stage.

By this time, US-Israeli relations experienced a role reversal. Impressed by the error it had committed by sinking into the Lebanon quagmire, the Israelis became increasingly predisposed to disengage unilaterally from Beirut and the Shuf. Fearing that an uncoordinated withdrawal would result in chaos culminating in a Christian-Druze bloodbath, alarmed that the IDF's withdrawal would leave the U.S. Marines exposed to sabotage by the Syrians and their local allies, and concerned that once it reached more convenient lines Israel might entrench itself and reject a return to the international border, Washington now pressured Israel to refrain from such a withdrawal.[38]

As a consequence of Israeli threats to withdraw, and following the collapse of its efforts to re-launch the Israeli-Jordanian-Palestinian peace process based on its President's September 1 initiative, the Reagan administration turned its efforts and political clout to attaining an agreement between Israel and Lebanon. By April, George Shultz, who had replaced General Haig as Secretary of State, took personal charge of America's diplomatic efforts.[39] Following his arrival, he began to embark upon an intensive shuttle between the various interested parties.

In May, the Israeli–Lebanese agreements were concluded. But while Israel's withdrawal was still contingent upon Syrian reciprocity, Shultz committed a grave error in opting to postpone negotiations for Syria's withdrawal until after an agreement with Israel was reached. However, in the aftermath of the Israeli–Lebanese agreement, Syria became even more convinced that Israel was predisposed to withdraw. The Syrians' confidence also resulted from a perception that they had not been defeated in the war; that Israel—with its internal consensus shattered—was unlikely to attempt to dislodge them by force; and that the Soviet promise to provide them with an enhanced air-defense system would soon add to their power significantly. Hence, they saw no reason to make any concessions.

Moreover, since Syria regarded the Israeli–Lebanese agreement as providing formal recognition of Israeli security interests in Lebanon and as another milestone in the road embarked upon in 1978 at Camp David toward Arab-Israeli accommodation, it had every interest in seeing the agreement collapse.[40] So angered were the Syrians that they now made every effort to delegitimize Amin Jumayyil's regime. They orchestrated an anti-Jumayyil coalition—the National Salvation Front—comprising Walid Jumblatt, Nabih Barri, Suliman Franjia, and Rashid Karame.

Faced with Syria's refusal to cooperate, Israel became impatient and threatened again to conduct a partial unilateral withdrawal. Thus, it withdrew from its long-standing demand that its pullback be contingent upon the Syrians' simultaneous withdrawal. In late June, Prime Minister Shamir and Defense Minister Arens traveled to Washington to gain its approval for an Israeli withdrawal.[41] Reagan and Shultz approved the Israeli plan but continued to press for arrangements that might avoid chaos. Hence, Israel continued to negotiate the details of the post-withdrawal arrangements with the Lebanese Army and the Druse.

While the Druse were eager to please their Syrian supporters and to increase Israel's predicaments in the Shuf, Israel became ever more resentful of the costs entailed in its continued presence there. Indeed, it now also found itself increasingly at a disadvantage against Damascus: while their Maronites continued to demonstrate their inherent weakness, the Syrians' allies—the Druse—manifested impressive capacities. With Israel's domestic consensus manifesting continued erosion, Damascus could assess that Israel would wish to avoid another war with Syria. This encouraged the Syrians to behave increasingly boldly, suggesting that Israeli deterrence had also eroded.

Israel's effort to negotiate with the Lebanese Army and the Druse modalities for an orderly withdrawal failed repeatedly. By September 4 its government lost patience and decided to withdraw unilaterally to the Awali river.[42] A few days earlier, on August 30, it was informed by Prime Minister Begin that he had decided to resign, and on September 15 Begin had his letter of resignation delivered to the President.[43] Thus, by early fall, all the principal conductors of Israel's intervention in Lebanon were gone.

Begin's departure, following the exits of Sharon and Eitan, allowed Arens to accelerate the process of redefining Israel's purposes in Lebanon. Under his guidance, Israel returned to its pre-Sharon view of the challenge presented by the Lebanese scene: namely, that while Israel could not remain indifferent to developments in Lebanon at large, its direct interests were confined to the country's south, where "basic" and "current" security threats to Israel were to be faced.

The redefinition of Israel's purposes contributed, soon after the IDF's pullback to the Awali was completed in October, to immediate pressures for further withdrawals. These pressures were accelerated by mounting Israeli casualties. In November, a truck full of explosives was detonated near the IDF's headquarters in Tyre, killing forty soldiers. As a result of these mounting costs, leaders of the opposition Labor Party now called openly for the IDF's withdrawal to the international border. This called was echoed by the Likud's Deputy Prime Minister, David Levy.

While Prime Minister Shamir remained opposed to redeployment, Defense Minister Arens increasingly gave expression to opinions within the IDF favoring further pullbacks. By early 1984 the IDF's high command was eager to quit the Lebanese mess in order to focus its energies and resources on more fundamental threats to Israel's security, namely those involving the large conventional forces of the neighboring Arab states. Moreover, a number of senior IDF commanders also saw some advantages in Syria's continued presence in Lebanon. They pointed out that Syria's need to divert forces away from the Golan Heights, and to devote them to policing Lebanon, was not entirely detrimental to Israel's interests.

At this point the need to face the implications of further unilateral withdrawals was also propelled by the unlikelihood that an agreement with responsible parties about the modalities of an orderly pullback could be reached. Once again, the general perception among the main elements of the Lebanese equation—the Syrians, the Druse, the Shi'is—was that Israel was in any case on its way out; hence, there was no perceived need to accommodate it in any fashion.

By early 1984, developments within Lebanon took another turn to the worse from Israel's standpoint. As a consequence of the PLO's removal a year earlier, and the gradual attrition of the quarreling Druse and Christians, the Shi'is' relative position had improved dramatically. In January, Shi'i religious leaders in Lebanon were calling for a holy war against Israel, and Nabih Barri, the leader of their largest organization, al-Amal, called for political action and military strikes against the IDF.[44] In February, the Shi'is gained control over Western Beirut and began to pose a serious threat in South Lebanon. By mid-year, Shi'i terrorism there—directed against Israeli soldiers in an effort to compel their pullback from Lebanon—became the new focus of the IDF's concerns.

At the same time, Amin Jumayyil tilted increasingly toward Damascus, and in the spring of 1984 he announced the abrogation of the May 1983 Israeli–Lebanese agreement.[45] Content with their gain, the Syrians saw no need to press for an early Israeli withdrawal to the international border. Quite the contrary, they were happy to watch Israel become the victim of growing Shi'i terrorism. Also, they probably feared that the completion of Israel's withdrawal would be regarded by Washington as an opportunity to renew the efforts to relaunch the stalled Reagan initiative. Such a development was regarded in Damascus as undesirable, since it threatened to leave the Golan Heights as the last unresolved issue of the Arab–Israeli conflict. The Syrians were convinced that under such circumstances Israel would simply freeze the status quo in the Heights forever.

Thus, the Syrian factor did not comprise an immediate constraint upon Israel's ability to remain south of the Awali. Rather, the accumulating casualties suffered by the IDF as a consequence of Shi'i terrorism induced a major debate in Israel regarding the wisdom of continuing to hold south Lebanon. Israel's political and civilian ranks were divided between those arguing that Israel should not withdraw in the absence of proper security arrangements and those calling for an immediate unilateral withdrawal designed to cut Israel's losses. An important question addressed was the danger that Shi'i terrorism might be exported across the border into northern Israel were the IDF to withdraw unilaterally.

In the absence of a central party with which security arrangements for the post-withdrawal period could be concluded, Israel took some unilateral steps in mid-1984. Primarily, following the death of Major Sa'd Haddad, it created a larger South Lebanon Army and placed it under the command of a Christian retired Lebanese Army officer, Brigadier General Antoine Lahad. His army grew to include 3,000 soldiers and officers, and its composition was made to better reflect the local population.[46] Thus, separate Druse and Shi'i units were created within his forces.

Increasingly, Israelis became convinced of the need to cut their losses and to base the security of their northern settlements on a combination of IDF patrols from within Israel with the filters provided by Lahad's forces. The mid-year national elections, resulting in the creation of a national unity government headed by Labor leader Shimon Peres, who was committed to an early Israeli withdrawal, accelerated the process. On November 9, 1984, military talks between Israeli and Lebanese officers, regarding the modalities of Israel's withdrawal, were opened. But little progress was made, and in January 1985, Likud's Deputy Prime Minister David Levy broke party line and—in a special Cabinet meeting—voted in favor of withdrawal. The pullback was implemented in three stages, in February, March, and April. On June 10, 1985, the Israeli government formally announced the end of the IDF's presence in Lebanon.[47]

Abbreviations

IDF   Israel Defense Forces
IAF   Israel Air Force
PLO   Palestine Liberation Organization
UNIFIL United Nations Forces in Lebanon

Chronology

1975

Civil war in Lebanon brings about first Christian overture to Israel; Israeli reaction is cautious.

1976

Early: Israel responds to Christian overture with modest supply of arms. Message to Syria is, "we won't intervene unless you do." Syria enters conflict on side of Christians; Palestinians flee south.

August: Christian/Shi'i militia (SLF) formed, commanded by renegade Major Haddad, supported by Israel. Although sharing common interests with Syria, Israel dictates "Red Lines" as new set of conditions.

November: Israeli Defense Force (IDF) employs artillery for first time in support of SLF.

1977

Early: Syrians try to move forces to Nabatiya (beyond Red Lines) but retreat in response to Israeli deterrence. Israeli elections lead to first Likud government, headed by Menachem Begin.

September: Situation deteriorates in the South as Israel intervenes actively for the first time; PLO answers with Katyusha attack. After pressure from President Carter, Israel retreats.

November: Artillery response to Katyushas proves ineffective; Israeli Air
Force (IAF) sent in to bomb PLO strongholds. Border becomes quiet.

1978

March: *Litani Operation* (following terrorist attack on Israel) establishes 100
km wide, 10 km deep *cordon sanitaire*. Israel retreats, establishing security belt composed of SLF and UN peacekeeping force (UNIFIL).
April: Nomination of new Israeli chief of staff, General Rafael Eitan (Raful).
Middle of Year: Syria begins to shell Christian areas of Beirut; Israel
responds to Maronite requests by increasing aid and adding another
red line to defend Christians from Syrian attack.

1979

During first half of the year Israel increases bombing and commando raids
against PLO. Syrians move in SAM equipment; Israel reduces air activity.

1980

Growing entrenchment of PLO in Litani-Zaharani area.

1981

Early: Lebanese Front takes to offensive, ambushing Syrian units; this
triggers Syrian attack on Christian stronghold and preparations for
deployment of SAMs in Lebanon. Israel sends in IAF in support of
Christians, destroying two Syrian choppers; in turn Syria deploys SAMs.
April 30: Begin orders air strikes against SAMs, but bad weather forces
cancellation of the attack, and in the meantime U.S. negotiates a reduction of tension.
May 28: Begin approves renewal of offensive against PLO, which responds by shelling Christians in the South.
August: Following artillery duels between PLO and SLF, Israel launches
massive bombing of PLO headquarters in Beirut. Palestinians respond
with artillery fire against Israel's northern settlements; Israel unsuccessfully attempts to employ IAF against artillery. After 12 days, Begin
invites U.S. diplomat Philip Habib to negotiate cease-fire.
December 20: Sharon's grand plan for a military campaign to bring about
the political destruction of PLO (*Oranim*) is brought before cabinet.
Fearing costly confrontation with Syria, many in Cabinet are opposed.

1982

January–May: Sharon resubmits plan piecemeal and watered down. Cabinet is still opposed.
June 3: Israeli ambassador to Great Britain shot by Palestinian gunmen.
Cabinet approves IAF bombing of PLO bases in Lebanon. PLO responds with artillery fire.

June 5: Cabinet meets to discuss response to PLO fire and decides to launch Operation Peace for Galilee.

June 9: IAF attack on Syrian SAMs.

June 10: Israeli tank forces begin to push north in Beka'a.

June 11: Soviet pressure on U.S. leads Israel to accept cease-fire, which U.S. imposes as Israel tries to dislodge Syria.

August: Following negotiated agreement and Israeli military pressure, PLO and Syrians evacuate Beirut, reducing friction between Jerusalem and Washington. U.S. Marines are brought in to safeguard PLO evacuation.

Early September: Lebanese president elect Bashir Jumayyil assassinated by Syrians. Sabra and Shatila massacre leads to reintroduction of U.S. Marines to replace withdrawing Israel forces.

September 25: Massive demonstration in Tel-Aviv over Sabra and Shatila massacre. Cabinet capitulates and establishes Kahan Commission to investigate the massacre.

mid-October: Israeli conditions for withdrawal are de facto peace with Lebanon.

November: Israeli military headquarters in Tyre bombed; 89 dead, 56 injured.

December 28: Israeli-Lebanese negotiations begin.

1983

February: Israeli government endorses findings of Kahan Commission; beginning of Israeli disengagement.

April: Secretary of State Shultz leads U.S. efforts to control Israeli withdrawal.

May 17: Israeli-Lebanese agreement concluded successfully.

June: Foreign Minister Yitzhak Shamir and Defense Minister Moshe Arens go to Washington to get approval for partial unilateral withdrawal.

August 30: Begin announces his plans to resign.

September 4: Failing to negotiate orderly withdrawal with the Druse, Israeli government decides to unilaterally withdraw south to Awali River.

September 15: Begin resigns.

November: Another terrorist bombing of Israeli military headquarters in Tyre kills 40.

1984

Year begins with feuding between Druse and Christians, which improves conditions for Shi'is. Shi'i terrorism becomes the main concern of IDF.

Spring: Lebanon abrogates May 1983 agreement with Israel.

Early Summer: Following death of Haddad, Israel creates larger Southern Lebanese Army.

September 11: Withdrawal talks between Israeli and Lebanese officers begin.

1985

January: Israeli cabinet votes in favor of withdrawal from Lebanon.
February–April: Three stages of Israeli pullback.
June 10: Israeli government announces end of IDF presence in Lebanon.

Notes

1. Avner Yaniv, *Dilemmas of Security* (Oxford: Oxford University Press, 1987), p. viii.
2. The analysis provided here regarding the evolution of Israel's involvement in Lebanon during the period 1975–1981 relies heavily on Yair Evron's excellent account in *War and Intervention in Lebanon: The Israeli-Syrian Deterrence Dialogue* (London: Croom Helm, 1987).
3. Ibid., pp. 13–14, 30–42.
4. Ibid., pp. 42–45.
5. Shai Feldman "Israel's Grand Strategy: David Ben Gurion and Israel's Next Great Debate," paper presented to the Woodrow Wilson Center for Scholars, Washington D.C., June 15, 1988 (unpublished).
6. Evron, *War and Intervention in Lebanon*, pp. 28–30.
7. Ibid., p. 45.
8. Ibid., pp. 46–47.
9. Ibid., p. 45.
10. Ibid., p. 54–56.
11. Ibid., pp. 62–66.
12. Ibid., p. 69.
13. Ibid., pp. 69–70.
14. Ibid., p. 46.
15. Ibid., pp. 71–82.
16. Ibid., p. 85.
17. Ibid., pp. 87–89.
18. Ibid., pp. 89–97.
19. Ibid., pp. 97–100.
20. Shai Felman and Heda Rechnitz-Kijner *Deception, Consensus, and War: Israel in Lebanon* Tel Aviv University: Jaffee Center for Strategic Studies, Paper no. 27, October 1984, pp. 10–24.
21. The sequence of events to follow has been documented in detail in Feldman and Rechnitz-Kijner, *Deception, Consensus* pp. 25–30.
22. Ibid., pp. 30–34.
23. Ibid., pp. 48–61.
24. *Jerusalem Post* June 7, 1982.
25. See Itamar Rabinovich "The War in Lebanon: An Overview," in Colin Legum et al. eds., *Middle East Contemporary Survey, 1981–1982*. London and New York: Holmes and Meier, 1984, p. 116.
26. Feldman and Rechnitz-Kijner, *Deception, Consensus* pp. 37–65.

27. Rabinovich, "The War in Lebanon," p. 122.

28. Aharon S. Klieman "Israel," in Legum et al., p. 644.

29. Itamar Rabinovich "Israel and Lebanon in 1983," in Colin Legum et al. eds., *Middle East Contemporary Survey*, 1982–1983. London and New York, Holmes and Meier, 1985, p. 137.

30. Feldman and Rechnitz-Kijner, *Deception, Consensus* p. 64.

31. Rabinovich, "Israel and Lebanon in 1983," p. 138.

32. Klieman, "Israel and Lebanon in 1983" 1982–1983, p. 600.

33. Klieman, "Israel," 1981–1982, p. 647.

34. Ibid.

35. Rabinovich, "Israel and Lebanon in 1983," p. 141.

36. Ibid., p. 140.

37. Klieman, "Israel," 1982–1983, p. 598.

38. Ibid., pp. 599–600.

39. Rabinovich, "Israel and Lebanon in 1983," p. 141.

40. Ibid., p. 143.

41. Ibid., p. 146.

42. Ibid., p. 147.

43. Klieman, "Israel," p. 595.

44. Avram Schweitzer, "Israel," in Haim Shaked and Daniel Dishon eds., *Middle East Contemporary Survey*, 1983–1984 (Boulder, Colorado: Westview Press, 1986), p. 498.

45. Itamar Rabinovich "Israel in Lebanon, September 1983-September 1984," in Shaked and Dishon, 1983–1984, p. 78.

46. Ibid., p. 79.

47. Schweitzer, "Israel," pp. 487–490.

6

The Case of Angola: Four Power Intervention and Disengagement

DONALD ROTHCHILD AND
CAROLINE HARTZELL

We wish to express our appreciation to Claudia Imkamp for research assistance on this chapter and to Jeffrey Herbst and Marina Ottaway for comments on the first draft.

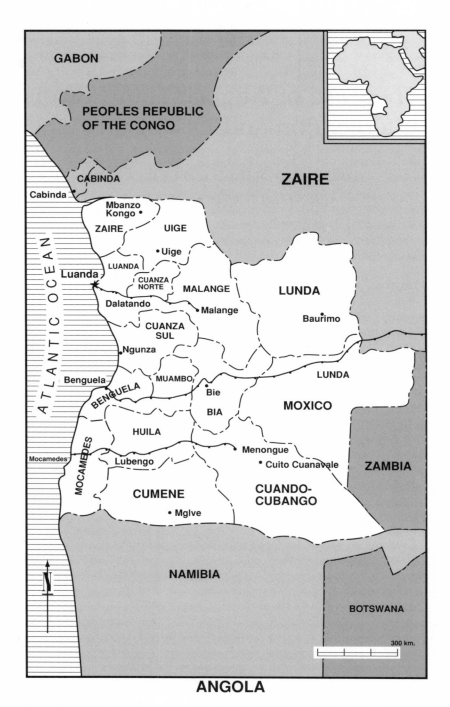

GABON

PEOPLES REPUBLIC
OF THE CONGO

ZAIRE

CABINDA

Cabinda

Mbanzo
Kongo •

ZAIRE   UIGE

• Uige

LUANDA

Luanda   CUANZA
               NORTE   MALANGE   LUNDA

Dalatando   • Malange
                                         Baurimo •
               CUANZA
               SUL

• Ngunza

                                                LUNDA
Benguela   MUAMBO
               BENGUELA   • Bie   MOXICO

                                 BIA

               HUILA

Mocamedes   • Menongue
               Lubengo   • Cuito Cuanavale   ZAMBIA

               CUMENE   CUANDO-
                               CUBANGO
                 • Mglve

ATLANTIC OCEAN

MOCAMEDES

NAMIBIA

                                              BOTSWANA

300 km.

ANGOLA

Angola

Introduction

What began as a struggle by Angolan nationalist movements against a colonial power had become, by the time of Angola's independence in 1975, an internationalized war with serious implications for East-West relations. Before and after independence, four major external actors—the Soviet Union, the United States, Cuba, and South Africa—became involved in the Angolan conflict, each seeking to shape an outcome that would advance its perceived interests. This engagement in Angolan affairs proved financially costly to the four sets of external actors; brought on a deterioration in U.S.-Soviet detente of the 1970s; entailed troop losses for Cuba and South Africa; strained the relations between sub-Saharan Africa and South Africa, the United States, and increasingly, although to a lesser extent, the Soviet Union; and led to a further weakening to any claims that South Africa might make to international legitimacy. In addition, a comprehensive picture requires full recognition of the physical, moral, social and economic devastation wrought in Angola. What caused each of these outside powers to play an active role in the Angolan conflict? And what led ultimately to their decisions to disengage? In this chapter we intend to probe the calculi adopted by the four external actors that culminated in their intervention and to examine their calculi for disengaging from the internationalized dimensions of this conflict.

The Angolan situation is unique among the cases of military intervention dealt with in this volume. In this instance two types of intervention, indirect and direct, were present throughout the conflict. The United States and the Soviet Union intervened only indirectly; South Africa and Cuba, which did dispatch troops, were the countries that intervened directly. The two great powers, wary of the potential dangers of encountering each other in combat, allowed, even encouraged, the two lesser powers to become involved; the lesser powers thus fulfilled superpower purposes as well as their own. Interaction of this nature between the intervenors, the target state and the international environment would prove critical for all three stages of the conflict in Angola. During Stage I (Getting In: 1974–76), the intervenors reacted to one another's moves in Angola (a country whose instability after years of a war for liberation was compounded by an emerging civil war) in the context of an international environment that saw major strains in detente. Stage II (Staying In: 1976–88) consisted of a stalemate in Angola as Cuba and South Africa faced off; the U.S. and USSR coexisted uneasily in a post-detente world; and the MPLA and UNITA became mired in a war of attrition. The rising costs of Stage II led to Stage III (Getting Out: 1988–89), which saw a regional settlement negotiated, in part, by the U.S. and the USSR in a much-changed international environment. As we intend to show, the interactions between such factors, and particularly the direct and indirect ways in which the intervention process occurred, had important implications for the subsequent disengagement process.

Stage I: Getting In, 1974–76

A series of uprisings in Angola during the first three months of 1961 posed the first serious threat to five hundred years of Portuguese colonial rule. As uncoordinated and lacking in an inclusive national focus as these rebellions were, they were nonetheless indicative of a generalized resentment on the part of the African population against colonial domination. Although the Portuguese were soon able to contain this insurrection, it had evolved by 1962 into a small-scale guerrilla war which would persist over the next twelve years.[1]

Leading the Angolan insurgency against Portugal were two nationalist movements, the Popular Movement for the Liberation of Angola (MPLA), led by Agostinho Neto, and the National Front for the Liberation of Angola (FNLA), headed by Holden Roberto. To these was added a third movement in 1966, the National Union for the Total Independence of Angola (UNITA), whose president was (and still is) Jonas Savimbi. Each of these movements had distinct ethnic roots in the Angolan sociopolitical landscape, different ideological inclinations, unique organizational structures, and its own ties to external actors in the international environment. These variables were key influences on the course of the Angolan conflict, and the roles the three nationalist movements played in that conflict, over the years.

The war in Angola was fought not just against Portugal but had as a major dimension a struggle for power among the three nationalist movements. The years between 1961 and 1974 saw the FNLA, MPLA, and UNITA vie for control over territory and peoples in Angola, as well as for international recognition by independent countries and multilateral organizations (the Organization for African Unity [OAU]), and the access to resources that accompanied such recognition. Unwilling to unify their forces and suffering from military and/or internal weaknesses, the three nationalist movements were unable to achieve any major successes against the Portuguese military. It was the April 25, 1974 coup in Portugal by the Movement of the Armed Forces that cleared the road to Angola's independence. Under pressure by young officers tired of fighting Portugal's costly wars in Guinea-Bissau, Mozambique, and Angola, the new president of Portugal, Antonio de Spinola, announced on July 27, 1974 the right of those three countries to independent statehood.

In Angola, the transition to African self-rule was complicated by the existence of three liberation movements with which the Portuguese had to negotiate. Responding to Portugal's suspension of all military activities in Angola, UNITA, the FNLA, and the MPLA each arranged its own truce with the Portuguese. These truces were followed by a jockeying for military and political positions on the part of the three Angolan movements. The FNLA, backed by Zaire and at this point receiving economic and military aid from the United States, moved troops into northern Angola in an effort to ensure that it would be the militarily superior power. The MPLA, although weakened by factional infighting, sought to secure control over the Angolan capital of Luanda, a Mbundu ethnic stronghold. UNITA's favored strategy during this period involved political rather than military activity; Savimbi traveled throughout Angola as well as abroad, in order to promote his proposal for a three-party coalition at the political center in which the MPLA, FNLA, and UNITA would participate.

Over the ensuing months periodic bouts of violence broke out in Luanda as troops of the three nationalist movements clashed with each other as well as with some of Luanda's white population. Meanwhile, there was progress on the political front. On January 3 to 5, 1975, Holden Roberto, Agostinho Neto, and Jonas Savimbi, meeting in Kenya, signed a trilateral accord indicating a common position among them on negotiations with the Portuguese. The three leaders then proceeded to Alvor, Portugal, where, along with the Portuguese, they worked out the Alvor Agreement. This agreement provided for October elections to a Constituent Assembly, leading to independence on November 11, 1975.

A renewal of fighting among the nationalist movements soon overshadowed the Alvor Agreement. This conflict was fueled by increasing amounts of arms received by the three movements from abroad. By July, the fighting had escalated to the point that the MPLA was able to drive the FNLA from Luanda, and UNITA withdrew into its heartland sanctuary. On November 10, 1975, the eve of Angola's independence, Portugal quietly withdrew from Angola. Its failure to hand over the reins of power to any group in effective control left them all to fight it out. On that same day the MPLA, with Cuban assistance, decisively defeated the FNLA's forces only miles from Luanda. Having ensured its control over the capital on November 11, 1975, Angola's independence day, the MPLA proclaimed an independent People's Republic of Angola (PRA). From that moment forward the conflict in post-independence Angola reached the threshold of all-out civil war; moreover, the ties of the nationalist movements to external powers made this an internationalized confrontation with implications for the southern African region and the East–West rivalry.

What incentives did the four powers have for becoming involved in Angola? Not only did those of a security, financial, and ideological nature figure in the four actors' decisions to intervene, but trade-offs between these incentives would prove to have an influence on the course of the intervention process. Perhaps the primary incentive for Cuba's direct intervention in Angola was ideology. Cuba, under Fidel Castro's leadership, had long identified with what were considered to be progressive movements and Third World causes. Not only were these movements and causes ideologically attractive to revolutionary Cuba, but international solidarity with developing and nonaligned countries was considered to be an important strategy in defense of the Cuban revolution.[2]

In contrast to the disastrous results of Cuban efforts to foment socialist revolution in Latin America during the 1960s, Havana considered Africa to be fertile ground for revolutionary change. Castro, who saw great potential for Cuban influence in a continent where some countries had yet to be decolonized,[3] set about fostering ties with nationalist movements like the MPLA which he found ideologically attractive. In doing so, Cuban policy was motivated primarily by ideology. There was certainly little Cuba could hope to gain strategically or economically by promoting revolution in Africa; that continent's underdeveloped countries were not particularly suitable trading partners for Cuba, and Havana lacked the resources to take advantage of possible strategic opportunities in Africa.

A related incentive for Cuba's Angolan intervention was the desire, particularly strong on Castro's part, to be seen by other developing and nonaligned countries as a Third World leader. It appears that Castro's aspirations in this direction may have been threatened in the early 1970s by the growth of detente and the spread of nationalism in the Third World. Cuban ties to and dependency on the Soviet Union became increasingly apparent in an age that saw its fellow Third World countries advocating autonomy from both super-powers. It seems likely that this prompted Castro to recognize that "without stature as a leader in the Third World, Cuba becomes merely one of many small island states."[4] Thus an effort to reclaim its status as a Third World leader may well have been an incentive leading Cuba to pursue an autonomous, interventionist course in Angola in 1975.

Despite Cuba's wish to demonstrate some degree of autonomy from the Soviet Union, a desire on Havana's part to secure its relationship with Moscow was another incentive for Cuba's Angolan intervention. After the turbulence of Cuban–Soviet relations in the mid and late 1960s, Cuba no doubt wished to put the relationship on firmer ground. Havana may have believed that this could best be done by proving Cuba's political worth to the Soviet Union as a socialist leader among Third World countries, and by demonstrating Cuba's military prowess on behalf of a cause to which the Soviets were sympathetic as well. Cuba's intervention in Angola apparently did succeed in gaining more leverage and bargaining power for Havana with the Soviets, at least in the short term; beginning in 1975, for example, the Soviet Union expanded its economic and military assistance to Cuba.[5]

The importance of these incentives to Cuba indicates that there were reasons for Havana to undertake an autonomous policy course with respect to its intervention in Angola. Cuba has long been adamant that its actions in Angola were in no way dictated by Moscow. In one of his major speeches on Angola, for example, Fidel Castro made this point while also giving the Soviet Union credit for its intervention in Angola: "Cuba alone bears the responsibility for taking that decision. The U.S.S.R. had always helped the peoples of the Portuguese colonies in their struggle for independence . . . , but it never requested that a single Cuban be sent to that country. . . . A decision of that nature could only be made by our own Party."[6] Indirect Soviet corroboration of Cuban autonomy was provided by Soviet defector Arkady Shevchenko, who recounts being told by Vasily Kuznetsov that the idea for Cuba's large-scale military operation had originated in Havana, not in Moscow.[7]

A major incentive leading to South Africa's direct intervention in Angola was its perceived security concerns. Pretoria worried about challenges to itself as well as to its continued control of Namibia. South Africa felt threatened by the MPLA's possible rise to power largely because of its proximity to Angola and its perception of encroaching danger. A South African defense document contended: "The threat to the R.S.A. within the ambit of the communist international battle for world domination is also related to the increase and establishment of communist influence and presence in Southern Africa, the Indian Ocean, and its littoral countries."[8] And more generally, it was concerned about a total Communist onslaught on the African continent. Prime Minister Vorster said of the Soviets and the Cubans that "the[ir] aim is not simply the establishment of a Marxist state in Angola, but to endeavor to secure a whole row of Marxist states from Angola to Dar-es-Salaam."[9]

A related incentive for South African action in Angola was domestic political pressures by certain circles to take action against the perceived Marxist threats to South Africa and Namibia. According to Deon Guldenhuys, the military was the driving force behind South Africa's involvement in Angola. Because the general public in South Africa was not informed about the Republic's involvement in Angola during the 1975–76 period, white public opinion did not play a significant role in the question of South African intervention in the Angolan conflict. Kenneth Grundy has observed the following with respect to political pressures in South African policy-making circles: "Insofar as the policy dispute can be characterized as one between hawks and doves, it was Defence arrayed against BOSS [Bureau for State Security] and Foreign Affairs (particularly Secretary Brand Fourie and Ambassador Pik Botha), and Information playing a supportive role."[10] Thus it was primarily the military, in conjunction with a few advisers close to Vorster, who pressed for South Africa's direct entry into the Angolan conflict.

In the case of the Soviets, ideology figured as an incentive contributing to the decision to intervene. The MPLA's Marxist inclinations are likely to have led the Soviets to regard it as a regime with shared values. In addition, by aligning itself at that time with a radical Third World power, Moscow could attempt to lay to rest criticism that detente with the United States had led it to become a status quo power. "A tough stand [on Angola]," argues Jiri Valenta, "could have been perceived by Brezhnev and his supporters as a convenient demonstration to critics at home and abroad that detente is not a 'one-way street,' that the U.S.S.R. does not 'betray' the revolutionary forces in the Third World."[11]

Another incentive underlying Soviet behavior in Angola was Moscow's desire to deny the United States and China the opportunity to expand their influence in southern Africa. The Soviet Union and

China had been competing for influence in Africa since the late 1950s, and China had stepped up its efforts in that area after the demise of the Cultural Revolution in 1969. China's assistance to the FNLA, and its warm relations with movements like the Front for the Liberation of Mozambique (FRELIMO), Zimbabwe African National Union (ZANU), and SWAPO, were of great concern to Moscow, which feared the future influence China could have with black-led governments in the region.[12] Moscow was particularly anxious about the possibility of a U.S.–Chinese "condominium" in southern Africa, a fear fueled by U.S. and Chinese support for the same movement, the FNLA, and by Kissinger's references to the "parallel views" held by Washington and Beijing on Angola.[13]

A third incentive behind the Soviet Union's indirect intervention in Angola may have been its interest, as a world naval power, in acquiring facilities around major oceans to improve the ability of its naval and fishing fleets to operate worldwide.[14] The Soviet Union's relationship with the MPLA led to its acquiring port rights in Luanda, Lobito, and Mocamedes.[15] These were not the equivalent of naval bases that impart treaty-based rights of sovereignty, however, a fact that imposed constraints on the nature of Soviet naval missions.[16]

The incentives behind the United States' indirect intervention in Angola were relatively clear. In the first place, the U.S. sought to put a halt to what was perceived to be Moscow's expansion of its power and influence into Angola. President Ford referred to such Soviet actions as "the Soviet-backed effort to take over the country by force."[17] Kissinger was concerned that "Angola represent[ed] the first time since the aftermath of World War II that the Soviet Union ha[d] moved militarily at long distances to impose a regime of its choice." Under these circumstances, he argued, the U.S. had to respond appropriately to the Soviet challenge.[18]

A related incentive for American behavior toward Angola was the U.S.'s desire to see the strategic status quo maintained in Africa. The U.S. wished to encourage political stability in southern Africa and to preserve that region's linkages to the international economic system. As a study by the Congressional Research Service concluded, "Kissinger perceived the Third World as a component of regional power in the larger context of a balance of global power," and "[h]e stressed the necessity of maintaining regional balances so that the larger global balance might be preserved."[19]

These different mixes of incentives help to explain why separate sets of actors chose to intervene in the conflict in various ways. In contrast to the two direct intervenors, neither the U.S. nor the Soviet

Union viewed their vital interests as closely linked to the MPLA's accession to power, allowing them to rely on a strategy of indirect intervention and encouragement of the direct intervenors to act on their behalfs. The direct intervenors, on the other hand, certainly saw the stakes in a different light. South Africa not only had immediate security interests it wished to protect (such as the giant Cunene River hydroelectric project in Angola that produces energy for uranium mining and industry in Namibia), but also was concerned about possible "terrorist" threats directed against the Republic from hostile and "Communist"-influenced neighbors such as Angola.[20]

Cuba's perceptions of and relations with the MPLA may be described as more fraternal than those of the Soviet Union, particularly given the history of long-term Cuban ties with and assistance to that movement. Havana's close relations with the MPLA regime, as well as Castro's belief that Cuban security could best be ensured through close relations with Third World regimes, appear to have been prime factors influencing the Cuban decision to intervene directly in the Angolan conflict.

The interests that the United States and the Soviet Union saw as being at stake in Angola were less salient than those held by South Africa and Cuba. This was not, however, the sole reason the superpowers chose to intervene indirectly. Washington's and Moscow's concerns about detente, continued geopolitical competition, and the potential for direct superpower confrontation also figured in their calculations. The initiation of detente between the United States and the Soviet Union did not mean the end of global competition. This connection was perhaps most apparent to the Soviets, who not only viewed Soviet military support of revolutionary movements and regimes in the Third World as compatible with detente, but also believed "peaceful coexistence" to be a means for preventing United States military assistance to counter-revolutionary forces.[21] Nonetheless, both countries recognized that they remained within the parameters of a competitive relationship.

Detente notwithstanding, there was little coordinated regulation of competition between the superpowers as it affected the Angolan conflict in 1974–75. Upset about the loss of trade privileges following the enactment of the Jackson-Vanik and Stevenson amendments and Kissinger's virtual exclusion of the Soviets from the Middle East peace process, Moscow saw little reason to exercise restraint in Angola when an opportunity arose. Although there was little regulation of competition between the superpowers when it came to Angola, there was apparently still enough interest in the detente relationship and concern about the possibilities of a direct confrontation to limit their actions to indirect intervention. According to Christopher Stevens, there were elements in the Soviet foreign and defense ministries who opposed intervention, fearing that it might threaten detente. Soviet "concern with the potential U.S. reaction," he added, "argued for a modulated intervention in order to balance its commitment to the MPLA with the risk of open confrontation with the U.S."[22]

The roles of the four powers became more clearly defined during the first eighteen months of the intervention process. In contrast to earlier efforts by the four external actors to assist the Angolan nationalist movements, Stage I involved the first extensions of military power. As it proceeded, Stage I was characterized by increasing commitment to and involvement in the Angolan conflict by the four powers. Movement from one stage in the intervention process to another occurred partly in response to the unfolding situation on the ground and partly as a result of the four intervenors' changing goals and interests.

Intervention began in Angola soon after the unexpected Portuguese coup of April 1974. This period was not altogether a quiescent one, because of incidents such as the massacres by white Angolans of Africans living in Luanda's slums.[23] However, during this time the MPLA, UNITA, and the FNLA ended their military struggle against the Portuguese and few clashes occurred for a number of months between the three movements. The first few months of this phase were characterized by relatively low levels of assistance by the external intervenors to the Angolan nationalist movements. Nonetheless, such support as there was pointed to the underlying interests that these foreign powers had in Angola.

China was the first external power to react actively to the changing political situation in Angola, sending limited numbers of military advisers and amounts of military supplies to the FNLA.[24] Although the United States had, in previous years, provided Holden Roberto with some financial assistance, it too entered the competition for influence. In June 1974 the CIA began funding Roberto without approval from the Forty Committee, a working group appointed to provide close supervision of the CIA. Resumption of Soviet assistance to the MPLA, which had been reduced because of struggles within that movement, did not take place until October 1974.

On January 22, 1975, the Forty Committee authorized the CIA to send $300,000 to the FNLA.[25] This action was significant not because of the sum of money involved, but because it came only one week after the Alvor Agreement. "The American government," John Marcum writes, "expanded an 'existing' client relationship that it was confident its 'adversaries knew about,' without either undertaking to persuade the FNLA not to seek a zero-sum victory by force of arms or signaling to Moscow a readiness to accept a coalition that would include the MPLA."[26]

After what amounted to an uneasy two month truce following the Alvor Agreement, FNLA forces attacked MPLA installations in Luanda in March 1975. FNLA troops followed this up with an assault on an MPLA training camp in Caxito, reportedly killing a number of recruits. Further fighting took place in April as the FNLA raided MPLA offices in Luanda's slums. Violence then radiated outward as towns to the north and south of Luanda became caught up in the fighting. In addition, an MPLA attack on UNITA recruits in June threatened to drag UNITA into the war, for Savimbi found himself under growing pressure to retaliate.

During this period, the external intervenors were busy as well. Soviet military supplies for the MPLA began to arrive in March 1975, funneled into Angola through Congo-Brazzaville and through Angola itself (as some Portuguese officials chose to ignore what was happening).[27] According to Raymond Garthoff, the Soviet decision to send the March shipment of arms "presumably preceded the American funding in January 1975. . . . Further Soviet increases in arms supplies to the MPLA during the summer of 1975 were, however, influenced by the active bid for power by the FNLA, supported by the Chinese and Americans, beginning in March."[28] In April, following clashes between the FNLA and MPLA, Neto sent an MPLA official to Havana requesting Cuban advisory assistance.[29] The Cubans responded to this appeal by sending 230 Cuban advisers in June who proceeded to set up four training camps in MPLA-held territory. With July came an increase in U.S. assistance to the FNLA. That month the Forty Committee asked the CIA to submit a covert action plan for an operation in Angola. It was completed quickly and submitted to President Ford who approved it and authorized the expenditure of $6 million, later supplemented by an additional $8 million. Following the release of these funds, the U.S. dispatched the first shipment of arms to Kinshasa.[30]

During the period between early August 1975 and the end of January 1976 a key turning point occurred as the direct intervenors made their first extensions of military force into Angola. At times, they confronted each other on the battlefield, adding to the tensions of the period. It was at this stage, as each external intervenor reacted to the situation incrementally and made its final decisions about the extent of its commitment to its local allies, that the intervention in Angola could have escalated into a superpower confrontation. That it did not indicates that movement from non-armed to armed intervention (i.e., the "slippery slope") was not inevitable for all actors.

The civil war in Angola reached a new height in August when UNITA entered the conflict directly by declaring war on the MPLA and forming an alliance with the FNLA.[31] While those events were taking place, South African troops crossed the Namibian border into Angola on August 11 and 12. When Pretoria finally confirmed its incursion, it stated that it had moved in to take "security precautions" in Angola to protect Namibia's northern border, as well as the hydroelectric power station on the Cunene river. However, the South Africans moved beyond these targets, seizing control of the Cunene district capital of Pereira d'Eca and the town of Rocadas. In addition, South Africa began to establish training facilities in southern Angola for the FNLA and UNITA and to supply arms to the FNLA.[32]

South Africa's limited intervention in southern Angola and the increasing U.S. and Chinese military aid to the new FNLA-UNITA coalition began to turn the tide of the civil war during August and September. The MPLA, even though supported by a small number of Cuban advisers, found it increasingly difficult to hold off the FNLA and UNITA and feared it might be defeated before 11 November, independence day. In light of this situation, the Soviet Union began to see the MPLA's position as precarious, a perception magnified by the Soviet belief that a large scale South African intervention was imminent.[33] Up to this point, the Soviets, who were still publicly advocating a coalition government for Angola, appear not to have made a decision regarding the extent of their involvement. Now, reacting to what they saw as U.S. and Chinese escalation of aid, the weakness of the MPLA, and the relatively low risks posed by a United States preoccupied with Vietnam and Watergate, the Soviets apparently decided to commit themselves as indirect intervenors.

MPLA concern over South Africa's August incursion deepened, prompting the leadership to call on Cuba for assistance. In response, Cuba sent several hundred military specialists and advisers, along with the first 700 Cuban troops. The first troopship left Cuba on September 7 and arrived in Angola three weeks later.[34] The Soviet Union's new degree of commitment to the MPLA was reflected in the use of Soviet and East German ships to transport the first regular units of Cuban combat troops from Cuba.[35]

What followed after the escalation of Cuban and Soviet assistance to the MPLA in September and October is reminiscent of a tit-for-tat strategy. On October 23 South Africa undertook an invasion of southern Angola, seeking to advance toward Luanda. The operation consisted of a mechanized column composed of about 2,000 to 3,000 South African regular troops (a number that would later double), several thousand UNITA and FNLA troops, and a number of white Angolan and European mercenaries.[36] The column advanced at a rapid rate, capturing Sa da Bandeira and Mocamedes without resistance and moving on toward Benguela before encountering Cuban rocket fire. The Cubans retreated from Benguela and Lobito on November 5, however, permitting the column to resume its advance.

The response to this successful South African invasion was "Operation Carlota," a huge expansion of Cuban military assistance to the MPLA. The first wave of Cuban troops left home aboard four or five troopships in late October.[37] Then, on November 7, Cuba began airlifting troops aboard its fleet of aged Bristol Britannias. Subsequently, in November and December, the Soviet Union provided Cuba with longer range IL-62 aircraft, and in January began directly airlifting Cuban troops to Angola.[38] The new infusion of Cuban forces enabled the MPLA to repulse a November attack by the FNLA on Luanda. Completely demoralized by a Cuban 122 mm. rocket bombardment, FNLA and Zairian forces dispersed only miles from the capital.[39]

Meanwhile, the South African column had stalled on the Queve River approximately 120 miles south of Luanda. There, in late November, the South Africans encountered an MPLA unit reinforced by the Cubans.[40] The mixed MPLA-Cuban force halted South Africa's advance in the south and by December's end had shifted the battlefield situation in their favor.

The United States reacted with dismay to the October and November Soviet-Cuban buildup and MPLA-Cuban battlefield successes. In his first public speech on the matter, Kissinger let the Soviets know that their actions in Angola might jeopardize detente. He warned: "time is running out; continuation of an interventionist policy must inevitably threaten other relationships."[41] The CIA and National Security Council responded to the increasing Soviet-Cuban military presence by attempting to create a program that would help the FNLA to "win" the war. However, because of the depletion of the CIA's Contingency Reserve Fund at that time, plans for such a program ran into difficulties.[42] In addition, members of Congress, led by Senator Dick Clark, Chairman of the Subcommittee on African Affairs, had become increasingly unhappy with the U.S.'s Angola program. Much to the dismay of Ford and Kissinger, the Senate approved the Tunney Amendment on December 19, preventing any use of 1976 defense funds in Angola except for intelligence-gathering purposes. The House also voted in favor of the amendment, and on February 9 it was signed into law.

In January 1976, South African troops pulled back to positions just north of the Angola–Namibia border. The South African government reportedly announced that it would withdraw all its forces from Angola because of the U.S. refusal to continue assistance to the FNLA and UNITA.[43] Stage I of the intervention process thus came to a conclusion with the MPLA, backed by Cuba and the USSR, poised to consolidate its power in Angola. Although unsuccessful in their efforts at limiting rival ambitions in the area, the U.S. and South Africa remained key actors in the intervention process, ready to take indirect and direct initiatives respectively when they believed action to be appropriate.

Stage II: Staying In, 1976–88

In the period after the initial turbulence accompanying independence, the Popular Armed Forces for the Liberation of Angola (FAPLA), supported by some 15,000 to 18,000 Cuban forces and Soviet-supplied military equipment, had begun the process of tightening their control over the periphery. FAPLA and its allies had triumphed over the various guerrilla elements in the field by February 1976 and, during the next month, they had compelled the South African troops to pull back from Angolan territory. Fresh from victory, the MPLA regime was in a position to gain widespread international acceptance of its legitimacy.

However, the military victory was far from complete. Because of internal and external opposition, the MPLA regime's capacity for effective governance still remained in doubt. The government's major internal opponent, UNITA, continued to mount guerrilla attacks, mainly in the rural areas but also, from time to time, in the urban centers as well. In addition, a now much weakened FNLA force continued to organize occasional forays, and a less well known Cabinda-based guerrilla faction (the Front for the Liberation of the Enclave of Cabinda [FLEC]) also launched raids from time to time. These guerrilla actions, and most particularly those of Jonas Savimbi's UNITA in the south-central part of the country, represented a challenge to the People's Republic which had to be taken seriously.

Yet what made them threatening to the government were their links with a powerful and determined regional actor, the Union of South Africa. The connections between the insurgent movements and South Africa stretched FAPLA's capabilities greatly, for it had to deal with militarily equipped and supported local oppositions as well as the South African Defence Force (SADF).

On the whole the military challenge that these internal and external antagonists posed to the Angolan government's authority during the 1976 to 1980 period remained manageable. The FNLA and FLEC, both backed secretly by Zaire's President Mobutu Sese Seko following the civil war, carried out limited attacks from time to time on village outposts and small towns in the north and in Cabinda. However, in the aftermath of Shaba II, Mobutu agreed to normalize his relations with the Angolans in an externally mediated effort in August 1978. To show his good intentions, Mobutu ended his support for these insurgencies, and thereafter the FNLA and FLEC raids became relatively infrequent and insignificant.

The challenge from UNITA proved more significant, but nonetheless containable, during this period. UNITA's contingents, with apparent support from South Africa, carried out numerous raids in the Central Highlands and along the country's southern border in 1977 and 1978. During the next two years, its area of engagement was expanded and came to include urban centers as well as the economically critical Benguela railway. The effect was to tie down FAPLA and Cuban military units and be wasteful of lives and scarce economic resources.

Yet, as Angola's President Agostinho Neto maintained at the time, "The enemy is not the poor Savimbis; the enemy is SA [South Africa]."[44] It was South Africa that had the capacity to threaten the unity and well-being of an independent Angola, and increasingly it used this power to intervene militarily. Although South African troops did withdraw from Angolan territory in March 1976, the South African presence continued to be felt in various ways. Operating from their military bases (in particular, at Grootfontein and Rundu) in neighboring Namibia, the South Africans remained in close contact with Savimbi's UNITA, supplying the insurgents with war materiel and training them in the use of modern military equipment. For the South Africans, the cost of this tie with UNITA was low, and the consequences, in terms of their objective of "neutralizing" a neighboring country, quite decisive.[45]

The continuing low-intensity conflict that marked the first five years of Angola's independence escalated noticeably in the 1980s. By the end of 1983, SADF units had undertaken a major new probe, advancing deep into southern Angola. UNITA, aided logistically as well in terms of equipment and training by the South Africans, pushed outward from its home base in central and southeastern Angola to provinces in the western and northeastern parts of the country. FAPLA found itself stretched to the limits of its abilities and relied increasingly on Cuban troops and Soviet advisers and materiel to deal with the worsening security situation.

As a difficult 1983 neared a close, the Luanda regime, in a major effort to ease its military predicament through negotiations, began to explore the possibility of reaching a cease-fire and disengagement agreement with its arch-enemies—the South Africans. It was becoming increasingly clear that FAPLA could not achieve a military victory over the SADF forces at that time. And the economic dislocations caused by the drought and continued fighting were a further impetus toward a negotiated settlement.

Initial contacts between the Angolans, the South Africans, and the U.S. interlocutors proved inconclusive, largely because the two main rivals refused to make any compromises on the issue of "linkage" (i.e., tying Namibia's independence to the withdrawal of Cuban troops from Angola). December of 1983, though, saw the South Africans propose to UN Secretary-General Javier Perez de Cuellar a month's truce and a disengagement of forces from southern Angola. The Angolans at first rejected this opening, but later advised the Secretary-General that they would accept the truce and disengagement proposal if they were joined to UNSC Resolution 435 on Namibia's independence. With these proposals on the table, American mediators, led by U.S. Assistant Secretary of State for African Affairs Chester Crocker, embarked on a major diplomatic effort to narrow the differences. These initiatives appeared to have borne results, for in mid-February delegations from Angola and South Africa met in Lusaka and agreed to a cease-fire and disengagement agreement as well as a joint Angolan-South African commission to monitor the disengagement process.

The Lusaka agreement of February 16, 1984 did not represent a comprehensive settlement of regional issues, but rather an understanding between the combatants to desist from taking advantage by entering into new military engagements in the area. Even though the first stages of the SADF withdrawal called for in the Lusaka agreement did occur as anticipated, the process dragged on inconclusively in the period that followed. These delays awakened new suspicions among Angolans and among African representatives at the United

Nations regarding South Africa's intentions in that country. By mid-1984, then, cautious expectations about regional detente had largely faded. The post-Lusaka accord reality was one of lingering hope mixed with despair over evidence of a deadlock that held Angola in its grips. South Africa, Allister Sparks asserted, had adopted "a policy of hit-and-talk": it used "its military and economic strength as the regional superpower to rough up its black neighbours, then offer[ed] them a deal they [could]n't refuse, as the price for leaving them in peace and even helping them back on their feet with aid." [46] By selectively using both positive and negative incentives it kept its neighbors off balance.

One of the two stratagems employed by South Africa toward Angola during the next three years involved the possibility of a wider peace in the region. From time to time, some evidence of movement on the diplomatic track during the mid-1984 through 1986 period did surface. For example, in March 1984 Cuba indicated a willingness to consider negotiations on the Cuban troop withdrawal issue, and in October, dos Santos reiterated his country's support for a combined Cuban troop redeployment and subsequent withdrawal provided it took place within an overall regional settlement. Carrying on a quiet shuttle diplomacy between the two sides, U.S. diplomats tried "to get the parties [to talk] around a single set of ideas." [47] However, just as Crocker was reported to be readying a compromise deal in May 1985, Angolan forces captured a South African commando reportedly dispatched on a mission to blow up oil installations in Cabinda. South Africa's good faith now became a matter of serious doubt in African diplomatic circles, and this, combined with Angolan outrage over renewed U.S. support for UNITA, contributed to a fifteen-month disruption of the negotiating process. [48]

The second stratagem of South Africa's policy toward Angola, Pretoria's continuing use of armed struggle in the late 1984–1986 period, involved two fronts: a direct challenge by the SADF in southern Angola, and an indirect challenge through connection with Savimbi's UNITA insurgency. South Africa's armed threat to Angolan stability was far broader than the cross-border violations taking place at this time, and included an economic as well as a military dimension. SADF units launched a series of deep penetrations into southern Angola in 1985 and 1986, striking against SWAPO insurgents as well as reducing pressure on the UNITA insurgents. In addition, South Africa gave active military support to UNITA's hard-pressed guerrilla forces, operating deep inside Angola alongside Savimbi's troops and providing crucial air and ground support during the September 1985 battle of Mavinga.

The 1985 battle for Mavinga was a harbinger of important events to come. In late July, FAPLA units mounted a successful offensive against the town of Cazombo, which was taken on September 19. Meanwhile an Angolan army force, backed by Cuban combat troops and employing the latest in Soviet weaponry, launched a second drive to take the strategically significant town of Mavinga, near Savimbi's central base in Jamba in southeastern Angola. As FAPLA units advanced from the north and west in an effort to encircle the embattled UNITA defenders, a major three-day battle ensued from September 27 to September 29, when FAPLA troops were ordered to pull back to the town of Cunjamba. The Angolan army offensive, one of the most determined and costly of the long civil war, reportedly brought two comparably-sized forces into direct confrontation with one another: motorized brigades of 4,000 men backed by MiG fighters and helicopter gunships on the FAPLA side, and 5,500 UNITA troops backed by a variety of South African ground and air forces on the other side.[49] The decisive factor in tipping the balance was the intervention of the South African air force which devastated the exposed FAPLA units on the ground.

From this point forward the South African-UNITA linkage became open and a basic element in the SADF military strategy in the area. As South Africa's Defense Minister, General Magnus Malan, declared at this time: "[W]e have had links with Unita, we do have links with them, and we shall have links again with them in future if the circumstances demand it."[50] Throughout this period, SADF was reported to have increased its military activities in Angola, participating alongside UNITA combat forces in attacking the strategically important town of Cuito Cuanavale in the southeastern part of the country.

UNITA represented the second front during these years of war against FAPLA's Cuban-backed troops. UNITA's guerrillas, a significant force in their own right, became a threatening rival when joined to South African military power. By 1986, UNITA had extended its operations from its base in the southeast and was active in every part of the country except for the areas around Luanda and the southwest. With many of the FAPLA contingents committed to defending the country against South African incursions into Cunene province, UNITA guerrilla elements were relatively free to attack agricultural and mining facilities, rail and transport, and dams and power lines in the rural areas. Repeated hit-and-run attacks wore down the Angolan government's capacity to exercise effective control over the country, much less to achieve its developmental objectives. Hence the war had become a stalemate: a relatively well-trained and well-equipped FAPLA army controlled the major cities and the oil-producing areas of the country, but lacked the capacity to defeat the South African-backed UNITA insurgents in any decisive manner. Unable to deliver a death blow in the direct encounter with the guerrilla force around Mavinga in 1985, FAPLA found itself during the following year responding to an escalating series of attacks throughout the country.

For many of Angola's leaders, UNITA was still not accepted as an autonomous, nationalist movement. The MPLA believed that UNITA could be defeated, as FNLA had before it, if it were not for South Africa's continuing interference.[51] In part at least, this denial of UNITA's capabilities contributed to an inability to cope effectively with its reality. This tendency to look outward, and to perceive the challenge facing the government in exogenous terms, was compounded by the decision of the U.S. Congress to repeal the Clark Amendment in July 1985 and to begin the shipment of limited supplies of weapons (mainly Stinger anti-aircraft and TOW anti-tank missiles) to the insurgents soon afterward. By deciding upon aid to Savimbi, the U.S. increased the pressure on Luanda, making Soviet–Cuban support more indispensable and the civil war more obviously a stalemate.

The Military Climax: A Transition Point to Stage III

In overcoming the stalemate on the ground, the direct military intervenors and the Angolan government had only limited choices. In essence, they could fight on in the hopes of a military victory or seek a political settlement through negotiations. Although proposals aimed at laying the groundwork for a prenegotiation stage were evident in the first half of 1988 (particularly regarding the issue of Cuban withdrawal), this diplomatic option could not go very far while the two sides still envisaged the possibility of a military triumph. Hence a decisive test of arms remained unavoidable before there could be serious talks leading up to a negotiated agreement.

By the summer of 1987, evidence of a significant arms build-up in the area pointed to the likelihood of an impending battle. U.S. intelligence sources estimated that the Soviet Union sent $1 billion in war materiel in the late 1986–early 1987 period, bringing its total military aid to the MPLA regime to $4 billion in the past decade.[52] The United States was also active in 1987, and was reported to have airlifted planeloads of weapons to an air base at Kamina, in Zaire's Shaba province, for transshipment to UNITA's insurgents in the field.

On the basis of Soviet (but not Cuban) advice, FAPLA did launch a major new offensive in 1987 against the strategically important town of Mavinga, only to encounter sharp resistance from UNITA and South African ground forces, supported by South African air power. By September it had become clear that South African–backed units had stood their ground, although at a heavy cost in terms of casualties to itself and its opponents. Moreover, it had already become apparent that South Africa's fleet of ageing Mirage III jets could no longer be relied upon to control the skies against FAPLA's MiG 23s, piloted by well trained Angolan and Cuban officers. FAPLA's emergence as an effective fighting entity able to stand up to SADF on its own turf signaled an important change in the balance of military forces in the region.

After another heavy FAPLA assault on Mavinga was repulsed in October 1987, the 18,000-man Angolan army pulled back in an orderly manner to its support base at Cuito Cuanavale. South African-UNITA troops pursued these retreating FAPLA units to the town's perimeters and began a punishing siege that lasted more than six months. Lacking superiority in the air, South Africa's G-5 and G-6 artillery subjected Cuito Cuanavale and its airbase to a daily bombardment of up to 200 155-mm. shells a day.[53] The defending force of 700 FAPLA and 100 Cuban troops (backed up by a large Angolan-Cuban contingent outside the town) dug in and absorbed the punishment.[54] Various South African-backed probes by UNITA and Namibian troops to seize the town and airbase were blunted, and the South African command, assessing the casualties resulting from a direct infantry assault by SADF combat soldiers as politically unacceptable, became mired in a static war of attrition. For many, the stalemate at Cuito Cuanavale was in fact a Cuban-FAPLA success— an "Angolan Verdun."[55] The South Africans were not defeated, but as one astute report put it, "FAPLA have taken on the SADF on terms approaching equality and have inflicted unacceptably heavy casualties. The SADF has been put at a strategic disadvantage."[56]

The extent of this strategic disadvantage became apparent as FAPLA regrouped and gradually regained the initiative in 1988. Cuba's Fidel Castro, after a meeting on November 7 with dos Santos, had agreed to send an additional force of well-trained combat soldiers to Angola in an effort to turn the tide in FAPLA's favor. By January, the number of Cuban troops had reached 40,000 and had a double mission—to relieve the garrison at Cuito Cuanavale as well as to engage the SADF units directly in southern Angola. Protected by advanced radar systems and an effective air arm, the Cubans raised the intensity of the warfare in the area, thereby altering South African perceptions of the possibilities of a military victory.

By spring 1988, the Cuban force (now enlarged to a 50,000-man contingent) went on the offensive in southern Angola. Leaving the north hostage to UNITA's spreading insurgency, the Cubans concentrated their attack on the SADF contingents in southern Angola. By late May, Cuban motorized and infantry battalions had swept down through Namibe and Cunene provinces to take up positions within 40 miles of the Angola–Namibia border. Backed by superior air power, these Cuban combatants continued their advance during June and finally clashed with the South Africans on June 26, near the important hydroelectric dam at Calueque. In the Calueque incident, the Cubans responded to a SADF artillery bombardment with an assault by an armored task force and an air attack. In the air raid, Cuban-piloted MiG-23s reportedly bombed South African positions as well as the dam itself. At least twelve white South African soldiers were killed (Luanda claimed it was twenty-six), the highest number in any one battle in the war.[57]

Pretoria protested the air raid, contending that the dam had been protected by an understanding with Angola arising from its key role in supplying water to Namibia's Ovamboland area. Taunted by the Cubans and embarrassed by the loss of most of the buffer zone, a powerful SADF counterattack was anticipated at Calueque, but it never materialized. The explanation for this, concludes Gillian Gunn, is the change in the balance of power in the area. "The Angolan-Cuban forces," she writes, "now had a significant edge in the air war and could give the SADF a good run for its money on the ground."[58] And President Botha himself asserted that the Cuban contingents were too well entrenched to risk a military offensive. For the South Africans, as well as the MPLA regime and the other intervenors, the costs of war now exceeded its anticipated benefits. This contributed to a change of perceptions on all sides that resulted in raising a negotiated peace to a preferred option.

Stage III: Getting Out, 1988–89

The battle of Cuito Cuanavale and the military encounter at the Calueque Dam represented a turning point in two respects. First, they indicated an important change in the balance of strategic forces. Cuban air superiority undermined South African pretensions to military invincibility in the region, and the ability of FAPLA units to hold on to the town and airfield at Cuito Cuanavale showed them to be worthy opponents on their own territory. Second, the heavy costs of the struggle had contributed to a sense of war weariness on the part of the MPLA regime and the direct and indirect intervenors. SADF losses in aircraft and personnel (hundreds of black troops as well as at least sixty white soldiers) brought about a new skepticism and sensitivity over casualties and financial costs in civilian circles. Cuba found that the military expenditures it was incurring in Angola were crippling its domestic development plans and that its Africa policy was exacerbating its already strained relations with the United States.[59] And in Luanda, the moderate Catate group was fatigued by an ongoing two-front struggle that had incurred thousands of war casualties and left its economy gravely weakened.[60]

When these two factors became linked to a third—increasing pragmatism in the relations between the superpowers—movement toward mutual disengagement on the part of the direct intervenors became a serious possibility. The two indirect intervenors, conscious that the "new thinking" in the Soviet Union had created unforeseen opportunities for tacit cooperation on regional conflict issues, were prepared to explore initiatives aimed at peacemaking. As these three factors converged in the summer of 1988, the perceptions of the various parties changed and a move from a military deadlock toward a negotiated settlement became realizable. Once all sides had come to recognize this military stalemate and the costs of continuing the status quo, they were able to advance at a steady pace toward a peaceful settlement of some of their important differences.

The critical negotiations to end the stalemate and bring about a regional settlement stretched across an eight-month period, from the prenegotiation talks in London in May 1988 to the signing of two accords on Namibia's independence and the withdrawal of Cuban troops on December 22, 1988. Of all the issues confronting the negotiating parties, none was more critical than the problem of Cuban troop withdrawal from Angola and a South African pullout from Namibia. As the sharp encounter at the Calueque dam was to indicate, the possibility of a major clash between the two direct intervenors was increasing. All the major actors came to realize this over time, making an agreement on a disengagement of forces essential.

New prospects for negotiations on this matter occurred in the spring of 1987, when the Angolan government decided to resume the discussions it had broken off earlier over the Reagan administration's decision to send military assistance once again to the UNITA insurgents. Subsequent meetings with Crocker in July on the question of "linkage" ended in stalemate; nevertheless, the two countries pledged to continue their efforts to find a negotiated solution to regional problems. In August Angola again took the initiative. A communique issued after talks in Havana between dos Santos and Castro promised greater flexibility in their stances. What this entailed became clearer in the following weeks as the Angolan government declared itself willing to accept the gradual and phased withdrawal of Cuban troops provided four conditions were met: the withdrawal of SADF troops from southern Angola, the cessation of South Africa's aggression, respect for Angola's sovereignty and territorial integrity, and the implementation of UNSC Resolution 435 on Namibia's independence.[61] U.S. officials responded cautiously to this proposal, promising to study it and get back to the Angolans.[62]

The pace of U.S.-Angolan diplomatic contacts began to quicken in September 1987. The Angolans reportedly accepted the U.S. position on linking a Cuban withdrawal to Namibia's independence and proposed the redeployment of Cuban troops north of the 13th parallel during the first phase, with a full withdrawal to follow.[63] Then, in March 1988, the American mediators met separately with the Angolans and Cubans in Luanda, and with the South Africans in Geneva. The parallel encounters showed the two sides to be far apart in their thinking on the timetable for Cuban withdrawal, aid for the insurgents, and the terms for South Africa's pullback from Namibia. However, with the Angolans prepared to accept a total Cuban troop withdrawal *in principle*, Crocker deemed the moment to be ripe for a major third-party mediation effort.[64]

The four powers began their formal negotiations with a series of exploratory talks in London. With Crocker in the chair, the representatives of Angola, Cuba, and South Africa met in secret to hold a very general discussion on the Angolan proposal for a four-year withdrawal of Cuban forces; the 20,000 stationed in the south were to leave within eighteen months, the 15,000 in the north to pull out in stages over a four-year period.[65] This proposal, linked to a number of other conditions such as Namibia's independence and aid to UNITA, diverged markedly from the South African call for a full Cuban withdrawal in one year's time.

During the follow-up sessions at Brazzaville and Cairo, the South Africans became more strident on the need for a quick pullout of Cuban troops and the inclusion of UNITA in Angola's ruling coalition. That the various sides maintained the necessary momentum at this juncture is attributable to the quiet but persistent efforts of the two indirect intervenors. In a case of tacit cooperation, the Soviets reportedly pressed their Angolan and Cuban allies to work constructively, while the Americans used their influence to encourage the South Africans to adopt a more conciliatory stance.[66] The extent of superpower influence on these partially autonomous states must not be overstated, but it certainly facilitated the process of exchange between bitter rivals.

It was in New York during July 1988 that representatives of the Angolan, Cuban, and South African governments were able to move from uncoordinated rhetorical stances to an acceptance of general principles for a peaceful settlement in southwestern Africa. The parties prudently dealt with broad policy outlines, discussing such issues as Namibia's independence, a phased Cuban troop withdrawal and verification, respect for sovereign statehood and nonaggression, and a recognition of the U.S. role as mediator. For all its omissions (a timetable for the Cuban troop withdrawal, the South African military pullout, the role of UNITA in Angolan politics, external assistance to UNITA, and the possible restrictions on SWAPO and ANC activities after the settlement), the agreement was highly important. It put in place an organizing framework for the next set of negotiations.

The momentum for peace in the region was now building up. At the Geneva talks a process of give-and-take emerged. In the end, the conferees at Geneva issued a joint statement announcing a *de facto* cessation of hostilities and a sequence of steps leading to peace in southwestern Africa. The four parties made a commitment to reach an agreement on a Cuban and South African troop withdrawal from Angola by September 1, 1988; they also agreed to recommend November 1 as the date for beginning the implementation of UNSC Resolution 435 on Namibia's independence. Several weeks later the three direct combatants signed an accord at Ruacana ending hostilities between them and setting up a Joint Military Monitoring Committee to resolve any conflicts that might arise in implementing the disengagement process.

The time had come when agreement on a timetable for a withdrawal of Cuban troops appeared indispensable to the success of the American-sponsored peace process. Some progress was made at Brazzaville in August and September in narrowing the wide gaps between the South African and Cuban-Angolan positions. Then, in October, the four powers reached a general compromise in New York on a 24 to 30 month withdrawal period, and met in Geneva the following month on the timing of the withdrawals. This proved a time of tense bargaining, requiring considerable accommodation. The final product was most positive, for the conferees hammered out a tentative accord providing for the withdrawal of Cuban troops over a 27-month period, with some two-thirds of these soldiers being withdrawn in the first year and the remainder being redeployed by stages to the north. Asked why this preliminary agreement was possible at just this time, one senior American official involved in the negotiations listed "[a]n element of exhaustion, mutual confidence and clearly the fact that the U.S. and the Soviets have made progress dealing with issues around the world as key factors enabling agreement to occur."[67]

The basic accord had now been arrived at, although a few issues (verification procedures and the language of the protocol) still remained on the table. The issue of verification was left for December 22, the date for the signing of the final pacts, when it was worked out between the U.N. Secretary General and representatives of Angola and Cuba. The deal had been struck. Accordingly, the four parties gathered at the United Nations in New York for the final signing of the two accords on Namibia's independence and the withdrawal of Cuban troops. The angry exchanges that marked the signing ceremony revealed the continuing misgivings that the antagonists held regarding one another's intentions. They also showed that under the right circumstances and with determined leadership, the negotiating process can sometimes surmount deeply divisive adversarial perceptions.

Although the agreement's achievements certainly were very substantial, a number of important regional matters remained unresolved: UNITA's possible reconciliation with the MPLA regime, U.S. aid to that movement, the future of the South African–held enclave of Walvis Bay inside Namibia, the closure of ANC training camps, and the implementation of an effective monitoring process. The general fragility of the accords became painfully apparent soon after the signing ceremony. President dos Santos charged that in contravention of the treaty, South Africa continued to aid UNITA, and bitter fighting broke out in April 1989 between South African territorial forces and infiltrating SWAPO guerrillas along Namibia's northern border. The tensions accompanying disengagement did not lead to an unravelling of the settlement package, however, pointing to the underlying strength of the larger process of peace leading up to the settlement.

Conclusion: The Importance of Changing Incentives for Disengagement

Certainly there were some continuities between 1975 and 1988 in the direct and indirect intervenors' incentives for being engaged in the Angolan conflict. Despite some important differences, the incentives of the 1975 intervenors tended to have a common denominator in the confrontation between East and West. The superpowers sought to gain or maintain their positions in southern Africa in order to deny the area to their rival, and they held sharply different perceptions of the nature of the MPLA regime and its implications for their respective aims in southern Africa. In this, they were joined by the two direct intervenors, the South Africans sharing the U.S.'s beliefs about the destabilizing implications of an Afro-Marxist regime in their region, and the Cubans united with the Soviets in their determination to challenge South African apartheid as well as America's overarching hegemony on the continent.

By 1988, as the cold war waned, the totalist perceptions that the East and West had of one another eased, and gradually pragmatic views gained ascendancy in Moscow and Washington. For Reagan, the "evil empire" became a state with national interests, and Gorbachev's "new thinking" encouraged Soviets leaders to reassess the costs of a substantial involvement on the side of the MPLA in Angola. This made the Soviets more prepared to experiment with joint problem-solving efforts aimed at dealing with regional conflicts. Cuba and South Africa were slower to adjust to the new detente, but in time changing regional *and* global imperatives left them with little alternative. The upshot was a settlement enabling the Angolan government and the direct and indirect intervenors to achieve some of their major objectives: the Cubans emerged as champions of Third World causes; the South Africans secured a formal agreement on Cuban troop withdrawal and an informal agreement on the closing of ANC training camps in Angola; the Soviets showed themselves to be supportive of African purposes at a critical juncture; and with the agreement on the Cuban withdrawal, the United States promoted its larger security objectives in the region.

It is naturally important to take account of the changes taking place in Angolan government circles. After all, an agreement was possible without UNITA's assent, but Luanda remained an important actor at every stage of the peace process. And the authorities in Luanda, who had experienced decades of warfare against a colonial power and against internal rivals and external intervenors, had every reason to look positively on an end to the military struggle. Despite rich lands and extensive diamond and petroleum resources, post-independence Angola was described as "teetering on the brink of famine after 12 years of war and bureaucratic rule and a two-year decline in oil prices."[68] To deal with both economic and social deterioration, Angolan government authorities came to view it as necessary to take steps to overcome the military stalemate and to begin the process of normalizing regional relations.

Of the direct intervenors, Cuba was the most determined proponent of a confrontationist stance. Having displayed "a strong internationalist spirit" and having effectively championed the Marxist-Leninist revolutionary cause in Angola, the Cubans could claim a victory (particularly after the Calueque Dam incident) and negotiate on disengagement without loss of face.[69] The alternatives would likely have proved potentially burdensome in terms of health hazards (particularly AIDS), increasing battle casualties and, with Angola unable to cover the full costs of Cuban military activities because of a drop in world oil prices, financial outlays.[70] As a result, the Cubans found themselves in a position to accept a negotiated settlement, especially one favored by the Angolan government and the Soviets.[71]

South Africa gradually altered its assessment of the external and internal situations in light of political and economic realities in 1987–88. Internationally the Soviets came to appear less adventurous and less inclined toward an expansion of their influence in southern Africa. And, the Americans seemed more determined than ever to press Pretoria to change its policies on Namibian independence and apartheid, enacting sanctions legislation and threatening to tighten these laws if necessary. Regionally, the easy military dominance that SADF forces displayed in the cross-border raids of the early 1980s now gave way to a difficult and costly war of attrition with well-armed Cuban and Angolan government forces. At home, the seemingly endless war involvement in Angola was also beginning to have psychological and economic costs and the loss of military superiority held out the prospect of increasing white casualties. To reduce its diplomatic and economic burdens (the economic growth rate in South Africa averaged only 1.4 percent annually in 1983) and to regain legitimacy in the eyes of the world community, South African leaders began to reassess their priorities and view a negotiated solution as in their long-term interests.

As the two indirect intervenors had been careful to avoid sending their own nationals into combat in Angola, it was less difficult for them to alter their priorities and to disengage than was the case with the direct intervenors. For the Reagan administration, initial U.S. goals with respect to the Angola–Namibia negotiations were clear: "to restore and advance U.S. influence in the region; to expand our cooperative relations with African states; and to deny to the Soviet Union the opportunity to use its influence to exacerbate already dangerous situations in Angola, South Africa, and the other countries of the area."[72] Subsequently, the issue of Cuban troop withdrawals and an Angolan national reconciliation that included UNITA in the ruling coalition became important aims. From the time he took office as Assistant Secretary of State for African Affairs, Crocker identified the Namibian independence issue as one of the four key areas on which U.S. policy should focus.[73] Crocker launched a diplomatic initiative that persisted throughout the Reagan presidency and ultimately, to the surprise of many, succeeded in mediating an agreement for the southern African region that reconciled the objectives of the Angolan government and the four intervenors.

If U.S. incentives for becoming involved in the Angolan conflict remained reasonably constant between 1975 and 1988 (the persistence of these incentives explained, in part, the U.S.'s decision to resume military assistance to UNITA in 1985 and afterward), the same cannot be said of the Soviet Union. Certainly Soviet strategic and economic interests in Angola were limited. With the emergence of Mikhail Gorbachev as General Secretary in the mid-1980s and his policy of *perestroika* (restructuring), there was a growing recognition of the costs to the Soviets of continuing superpower rivalries in the Third World. Determined to achieve an arms accord and to pursue their domestic developmental objectives, Soviet leaders deemphasized their roles as revolutionary leaders and opted for a more pragmatic vision of their relations with Western countries, particularly the United States.[74] In adopting this outlook, the USSR increasingly assumed the posture of a "normal" state, pursuing its interests vis-à-vis other states in the world community. Conciliation on Third World issues became a means of consolidating and strengthening its home base.[75] The effect was to place regional conflicts on a lower order of priorities, and make possible tacit cooperation with U.S. negotiators on bringing about a mutually acceptable agreement providing for the disengagement of Cuban and South African forces.

The practical consequences of the Soviet shift in incentives and perceptions of the West had important implications for conflict management in Angola. This became clear when a new strategic deadlock emerged among the direct intervenors at the time of the siege at Cuito Cuanavale and the Calueque Dam engagement. Both the Cubans and South Africans emerged slightly bruised from these encounters; nevertheless, both remained in fighting trim and prepared, if necessary, to fight an expanded war. While the Cubans, South Africans, and Angolans all displayed a degree of weariness over the seemingly unending war in Angola, all had the will and capacity to continue it, unless some face-saving alternative surfaced.

This face-saving alternative did emerge most decisively during the 1988 negotiations in the form of tacit cooperation on the part of the two indirect intervenors. As hypothesized, the nature of the intervention process did in fact give a clue about the process of disengagement, for the two great powers did, for different but overlapping reasons, act decisively in this instance to facilitate a peaceful outcome. As indirect intervenors for whom the conflict was less salient, the two superpowers were able to exert influence over the Angolan government and the two direct intervenors through the manipulation of incentives. Throughout the different stages of the 1988 negotiations, Crocker's determined efforts to mediate between the antagonists received important assistance from Soviet diplomats. As Angola's major ideological and military arms supporter, the Soviets were particularly well placed to encourage the MPLA regime to negotiate in earnest and to adopt a conciliatory stance on such issues as the timetable for Cuba's troop withdrawal, reconciliation with UNITA, and continuing covert U.S. assistance to UNITA. The importance of the Soviets' behind-the-scenes activities was apparent throughout 1988, as they helped to keep the negotiation process on track and to clarify points of contention.

Clearly it would be an overstatement to contend that the two indirect intervenors *controlled* the Angolan government or the two direct intervenors. Because the Angolans, Cubans, and South Africans were partially autonomous state actors, the U.S. and the USSR could achieve their purposes only through the use of quiet pressures or positive and negative incentives. U.S. officials reportedly described the Soviets as utilizing "cajolery and arm-twisting" to extract concessions from their Cuban and Angolan allies, especially during the tense negotiations on the timetable for a parallel withdrawal of troops.[76] Castro, who received some $5 billion a year in economic subsidies, as well as receiving logistical and materiel support from the Soviets for his African campaign, was described as "highly vulnerable to Soviet politico-economic coercion."[77] Similarly, the MPLA regime was in no position to reject Soviet pressures, having received billions of dollars in military assistance from Moscow over the years. The result was to give the Soviets considerable, but not unlimited, influence over the decision-making processes of these two allies. In a like manner, the Reagan administration exerted some leverage over the South African government, despite all the efforts of the latter to insulate itself from American pressures. Determined to achieve a Namibian settlement before leaving office, Crocker increasingly acted to affect South African affairs, implementing the sanctions legislation mandated by Congress and bypassing the South African government to give support to antiapartheid groups on the scene. In addition, he "repackaged" the linkage proposal, formerly the object of scorn on the part of the frontline states, so that Namibia would gain its independence *before* the full withdrawal of Cuban troops from Angola, something the South Africans objected to but to no avail.[78]

The Angolan civil war may well prove to be a model for the management of conflict in other such regional confrontations. In situations where the direct intervenors become locked into a conflict situation, the achievement of tacit cooperation by the superpowers may help the great powers not only to keep their roles limited but also to engage in joint problem-solving initiatives.[79] In Angola, there was a link between interventionist and disengagement behaviors. The U.S. and the USSR chose to intervene indirectly because the conflict was less salient for them than for Cuba and South Africa in terms of the nature of the interests, in particular the security imperatives, that the great powers found at stake in the region.

Clearly, an interactional dynamic was at work, for the way the various actors entered into the conflict had an effect on the way in which they ultimately disengaged. In the case of the indirect intervenors, there was some degree of detachment which enabled them, without any loss of face or credibility, to take advantage of changing incentive patterns and to play a significant role in the peace process. As superpowers, the indirect intervenors were also in a position to exert leverage over the Angolan government and the two direct intervenors through the manipulation of incentives. For example, by imposing sanctions on South Africa, by emphasizing to Cuba that a timely withdrawal from Angola would reaffirm its status as a Third World champion, and other such actions, the U.S. and Soviet Union were able to facilitate disengagement through the use of positive and negative incentives.

What this indicates is that a change in the incentives contributing to interventionist behavior need not occur across the board simultaneously for all actors in order for disengagement to take place. Where great powers can put aside their past rivalries for the moment and converge to use their influence on other intervenors, movement from intervention to disengagement may occur, as in the fortuitous case of Angola.

Postscript

With the signing of the tripartite accords in December 1988 and the redeployment and disengagement of Cuban and South African military forces, the focus shifted to the ongoing internal military encounter within Angola between the MPLA government and the UNITA insurgents. Both the international and internal conflict situations involved intense confrontations; yet they diverged in terms of the material resources that could be brought to bear on them and the levels of external involvement. Moreover, while the perceptions that the external intervenors had of one another shifted over time in such a way as to facilitate a constructive outcome, those that the internal political actors had of one another remained relatively fixed.

The conflict in the country's southeast had proved unwinnable, even when external forces had been involved in a major way. Now the internal adversaries were being left increasingly to their own devices, and a continuing struggle offered them little prospect of significant benefits. Even so, the problem following the international settlement was how to overcome the political stalemate and begin the search for a peaceful solution. Zaire's President Mobutu Sese Seko stepped into this situation resolutely.

The process leading up to the Mobutu-orchestrated Gbadolite summit began while the negotiations on the interstate agreement were underway. A perceptible softening of government and insurgent positions on the issue of a political solution to their differences became apparent in early 1989 and gathered momentum the following May when a conference of eight regional leaders met in Luanda. There, the African heads of state (from Zaire, Congo, Gabon, Zimbabwe, Mozambique, Zambia, Sao Tome and Principe, and Angola) endorsed a seven-point Angolan government peace plan. This plan, which emphasized a peace zone along the Benguela railroad, an end to foreign interference, the cessation of support to UNITA, and the application of an amnesty by the government, made only limited concessions to the insurgent movement. The gap between adversaries remained wide. Whereas the Angolan government still insisted upon Savimbi's temporary exile and the integration of UNITA's civilian and military components into the MPLA-led one-party state, Savimbi called for multiparty elections and the possibility of coalition government. Nevertheless, as Savimbi observed, fourteen years of war had shown that neither side was capable of a military victory. If they could not impose their terms, then a political settlement became the only logical alternative to continued fighting.

In an attempt to put pressure on the adversaries to negotiate in earnest, Mobutu assembled an impressive array of twenty African leaders at Gbadolite, Zaire on June 22, 1989. Throughout the seven-hour, closed-door summit meeting, the two adversaries were kept apart, while Mobutu met first with one and then the other, "cajoling and threatening" them in order to extract agreement on the summit declaration.[80] What emerged from this effort was not a carefully worked out peace agreement, but an advance in a larger negotiating process.

At the symbolic level, the first direct encounter between dos Santos and Savimbi and the handshake between these adversaries signaled a willingness to search for national reconciliation by political means. The presence of many of Africa's most respected leaders, moreover, facilitated Savimbi's emergence from the dim shadows of nonrespectability. At the substantive level, three principles emerged from the text of the final Gbadolite Declaration: the desire for an end to the war and national reconciliation, agreement on a cease-fire, and provision for a joint commission to prepare the plan for national reconciliation in Angola.[81]

Yet profound differences of perceptions and interpretations continued to divide the adversaries. Dos Santos and his supporters came away from Gbadolite convinced that Savimbi had agreed to a voluntary and temporary exile and that UNITA's military and civilian elements would be integrated into the MPLA's party, bureaucratic, and military units. Savimbi dismissed talk of his exile, refused the proposed offer of amnesty, rejected the integration of UNITA into MPLA institutions, and demanded the establishment of a multiparty system and free, open elections. Whereas MPLA viewed Gbadolite as the end of UNITA, UNITA perceived it as an opportunity to compete separately for power and to move to some form of power-sharing at the national level.

Although the parties at Gbadolite had agreed in principle upon a cease-fire to become effective on June 24, they failed to give this meaning by establishing a mechanism to determine the rules of permissible behavior or to resolve violations. Not surprisingly, the cease-fire never really took hold. At first, the hostilities between the MPLA and UNITA forces were limited and strategic in nature; soon, however, they increased in intensity, culminating in heavy fighting around Mavinga in late December 1989 and early 1990.

Despite these evidences of continuing military engagements in the field, Mobutu pushed ahead resolutely with his mediatory initiative. Following Gbadolite, a regional summit was held in Harare on August 22 where the frontline leaders criticized Mobutu for failing to secure in writing agreement on peace terms ; in their final communique, they encouraged Savimbi to retire temporarily and voluntarily from Angola and to allow the integration of UNITA into the MPLA and its state institutions. As anticipated, Savimbi firmly rejected these recommendations.

A second regional summit was held in Kinshasa on September 18. In this case, Savimbi was invited to attend, but, despite pressures from U.S. Assistant Secretary of State for African Affairs Herman J. Cohen and others, he declined to join the gathering.[82] Under these circumstances, the conferees at Kinshasa merely reaffirmed their support for the Gbadolite agreement and called upon Savimbi to sign a new draft statement on the implementation process. Savimbi refused and instead proposed the creation of a multinational force to verify and guarantee the cease-fire and to hold competitive elections.[83] What had started at Gbadolite was being complicated by a combination of historical memories, personal antagonisms, developing schisms within one of the bargaining parties(the MPLA), and the character of the stakes involved in the conflict. Taken together, such variables placed severe constraints on what the African heads of state could achieve as facilitators in Angola.

In explaining the lack of movement toward a resolution of the Angolan conflict following Gbadolite, it is important to note the parts played—or not played effectively—by the mediator, South Africa, and the two superpowers. Although acclaimed for his bid to bring an end to the Angolan fighting, Mobutu's credentials to act as a mediator were the source of his weakness. In Angola, Mobutu's long record of interference, first on the side of Holden Roberto's FNLA and then on the side of UNITA, had created doubts about how impartial he could be. Could Zaire back UNITA and at the same time act as a credible mediator? Unlike the U.S. role in the interstate negotiations, a smaller power, led by a president who was not held in high esteem in his region, was attempting to orchestrate an African initiative aimed at ending the Angolan civil war.

Mobutu's handling of the peacemaking initiative was also questioned. At the Harare summit, Mobutu was blamed for the hastiness of the Gbadolite proceedings and the consequent misunderstandings of interpretation arising out of its marathon sessions. On all sides, the frustrations of the continuing civil war were placed largely on the mediator's shoulders; his failure to secure a written and binding agreement on the modalities of the cease-fire and on the terms of the peace agreement were deemed responsible for the breakdown that followed. As Mobutu tried to respond to these charges, holding dos Santos to the accord while securing Savimbi's exile and UNITA's incorporation into the MPLA, he found himself unable to satisfy either side. The MPLA leadership, which showed increasing signs of dividing into pragmatists and hard-liners, drew back from the new initiative, and Savimbi not only rejected the Harare summit plan but also questioned the impartiality of the mediator himself.[84] The mediator, in brief, had emerged as part of the larger problem of peace.

The role of South Africa in the Gbadolite peace process was unclear. Although the Cubans withdrew their troops from Angola prior to July 1, 1991 as scheduled under the terms of the Angola–Namibia accords, the South Africans sent mixed signals regarding their intentions. On the one hand, there were charges that the South Africans were continuing to interfere in Angola's internal affairs, sending arms to the guerrilla forces;[85] on the other hand, there was evidence of diplomatic pressure by the South Africans in August and September 1989 to get the MPLA and UNITA to abide by the Gbadolite provisions on the cease-fire.[86] Other international talks between the South Africans and African presidents followed, with the South African leaders giving public support to Mobutu's mediation effort.[87] Even so, the question that remained to be answered was how much pressure the South Africans were prepared to bring to bear.

In the case of the two superpowers, both of whom had played such a significant role in the Angola–Namibia settlement, the same question pertains: what would these great powers be prepared to contribute to a successful internal settlement? At the Gbadolite meetings in June 1989, various observers concluded that Soviet pressures were a significant factor in wringing concessions from a hesitant and reluctant dos Santos, and that the Soviets pressured their clients at key junctures to keep the peace process on track. Even so, their military arms shipments to the combatants continued at relatively high levels throughout the Gbadolite negotiations and after. Thus while not underestimating the Soviet commitment to the Gbadolite initiative in principle, the subtle behind-the-scenes role that Moscow played does not seem intense enough to bring about a change of perceptions and incentives on the part of the Angolan government.

For their part, U.S. officials enthusiastically welcomed the Gbadolite summit as a positive step, but its pressures on Savimbi were not sufficient to encourage a major change in perceptions and incentives at that juncture. In backing the African initiative at Gbadolite, the U.S. combined both negative and positive incentives in an effort to push the process ahead. On the negative side, both nonrecognition of the Angolan government and continued military aid to the insurgents were viewed as means for changing MPLA preferences.[88] On the positive side, Washington also made use of incentives to promote cooperation. Not only did the Bush administration hold out the prospect of normalizing relations with the Luanda regime once it had concluded an internal settlement with the insurgent movement, but it gave "tacit assurances" that with national reconciliation it would consider ending military aid to UNITA.[89] With respect to the mediation effort itself, the U.S. played a facilitative role; it exerted pressure on Savimbi to attend Gbadolite and subsequent summits, and affirmed its support for Mobutu's role as mediator. Despite these initiatives, however, Savimbi resisted American pressures, refusing, for example, to attend the Kinshasa summit. Steadfast U.S. support of Savimbi gave the Americans sufficient influence to press for cooperation but not enough to assure movement toward a compromise agreement.

With the Gbadolite process deadlocked and Mobutu unable to bring sufficient political and economic resources to bear on the disputing parties to come to a settlement, a new approach became imperative. The two Angolan adversaries remained extremely wary and distrustful of one another. Nevertheless, neither the Angolan government nor the UNITA insurgents could muster sufficient military capacity to eliminate the opposition or force its capitulation. Moreover, the conditions for a sustained military effort were less and less encouraging. Not only were Angolans weary of the protracted civil war, but their external supporters were disengaging. Cuban forces withdrew from Angola in advance of the schedule set out in the Angola–Namibia accords, and South African assistance, reportedly extended in a clandestine manner, was obviously diminutive by comparison with former levels. Most significantly, the superpowers, having made the shift from adversarial to cautiously cooperative relations, were now quite anxious to reduce their involvement in the internal war in Angola and pursue new openings toward peace.

Recognizing that the Mobutu initiative had stalled and forthright about the need to regain momentum in the negotiations, President dos Santos called for the acceptance of a new third-party intermediary. Portugal, the former colonial power, rose to the occasion, and from mid-1990 onward chaired a series of talks between representatives of the Angolan government and UNITA. By December, the Portuguese-initiated talks were given an important boost when Secretary of State James A. Baker 3d. met publicly with the Angolan Foreign Minister, and Foreign Minister Eduard Shevardnadze conferred openly with UNITA President Savimbi. Then the United States and the Soviet Union co-sponsored a meeting in Washington D.C. of the two Angolan rivals, the Portuguese intermediary, and the two great powers. With the U.S. and Soviets present, the two antagonists managed to work out what became known as the Washington Concepts Paper, the basic framework for the serious negotiation sessions to follow. Unlike Gbadolite, where the great powers gave general support to Mobutu's peace initiative but displayed little urgency over the proceedings, the U.S. and the USSR were now brought directly into the Portuguese negotiations as official observers. As Assistant Secretary Cohen commented on their active involvement in the negotiating process: "We both played a very important role in helping to bring about compromises under the overall jurisdiction of the Portuguese mediator."[90]

The Washington agreement on basic negotiating principles gave a new impetus to the flagging talks at Estoril, Portugal. By the time the sixth round of talks took place on April 4, most of the major points of disagreement had been resolved, and the negotiators were able to focus their attention on the key remaining issues: the formation of a unified national army, the setting of dates for a cease-fire and the holding of multiparty elections, and the international monitoring of the cease-fire. The election date proved to be the most contentious point. Whereas UNITA proposed that elections be held between 9 and 12 months after the cease-fire, the Angolan government suggested a waiting period of three years. The Portuguese recommended a compromise of 18 months before the elections. Although the MPLA indicated a willingness to accept a reduction to 24 months, UNITA representatives continued to insist on a 12-month period.

This haggling over the major outstanding issues continued on through the remainder of April when, to the surprise of many, the conferees achieved a breakthrough to peace. On May 1, Lopo do Nascimento representing the Angolan government and Jeremias Chitunda of UNITA initialed the various documents making up the peace accords. Under the terms of these preliminary agreements, signed by dos Santos and Savimbi at a formal ceremony in Lisbon on

May 31, a complex package of provisions was settled upon, including a cease-fire; UNITA's recognition of the Angolan government and dos Santos as president until general elections are held; UNITA's right to take part in political activities in a multiparty democracy; free and fair elections under the supervision of international observers; the consultation of all Angolan political forces to determine the specific timetable for elections (tentatively set for late 1992); and, once the cease-fire comes into effect, the creation of a single national military organization (made up of the current Angolan government air force and navy, and an army evenly divided between government and UNITA troops).[91] Significantly, the great powers, who had helped to overcome hurdles in the way of a negotiated settlement, now agreed to take part in the implementation process.

Abbreviations

FAPLA	Popular Armed Forces for the Liberation of Angola
FLEC	Front for the Liberation of the Enclave of Cabinda
FNLA	National Front for the Liberation of Angola
FRELIMO	Front for the Liberation of Mozambique
MPLA	Popular Movement for the Liberation of Angola
OAU	Organization for African Unity
RSA	Republic of South Africa
SADF	South African Defense Force
SWAPO	South West African People's Organization
UNSC	United Nations Security Council
UNITA	National Union for the Total Independence of Angola
ZANU	Zimbabwe African National Union

Chronology

1933–1973

1933: Colonial Act in Portugal reforms administration.

1951: Portuguese colonies become "Overseas Provinces."

1955: Angola Communist Party founded.

1956: MPLA founded.

1960: Arrest of Agostinho Neto. Protest demonstration in Icolo-e-Bengo leads to the death of 30 and wounding of 200.

1961: Nationalists attack Luanda prison.

1961: Uprising in northern Angola. UN Security Council debate on Angola.

1961: UN Security Council requests Portugal "to immediately suspend the measures of repression in Angola."

1965: OAU starts funding MPLA operations.

1966: UNITA formed inside Angola. Jonas Savimbi is president.

1974

April 24: Military coup in Portugal overthrows Caetano government.

July: Portugal declares it is prepared to give independence to its African territories. Armistice between Portugal and the FNLA, MPLA, and UNITA. Violence by white settlers in Luanda and other towns against Africans. Portugal appoints a five-member military junta to govern Angola.

August: MPLA reconstitutes its guerrilla army as FAPLA. Right of Angola to self-determination is recognized by Portugal. Rosa Coutinho forms Angola Provisional Government.

1975

January 15: Alvor Agreement.

January 31: Transitional government takes office. U.S. Forty Committee votes to increase clandestine support to FNLA.

July 9–15: "Battle for Luanda." MPLA ousts FNLA and UNITA from the capital. Airlift of Portuguese settlers from Angola begins.

August: Traffic on the Benguela Railway suspended. Portugal suspends Alvor Agreement. High Commissioner in Luanda takes full control of government.

mid-September: MPLA forces hold twelve of sixteen provinces.

October 23: Invasion of Angola by South African regular troops with UNITA and FNLA forces. Cuban instructors in Angola.

November 7: Beginning of "Operation Carlota," airlift of Cuban troops to Angola.

November 10: Portugal withdraws from Angola.

November 11: Angola independent. MPLA proclaims the People's Republic of Angola (PRA).

November 12: FNLA and UNITA announce the formation of a coalition government, the Democratic People's Republic of Angola.

December 19: U.S. Senate votes to prohibit further covert aid to FNLA and UNITA.

1976–1988

1976, February: Portugal recognizes PRA.

1976, October: PRA signs a twenty-year "Treaty of Friendship" with the USSR.

1979, September 10: Death of President Agostinho Neto.

1979, September 21: José Eduardo dos Santos succeeds Neto as President of Angola and of MPLA.

1981, August: South Africa launches Operation Protea, a one-month incursion by South African army units into Cunene Province.

1984, February 16: PRA and South Africa sign the Lusaka Agreement, a commitment to abide by a disengagement accord and to desist from entering ito new military engagements in the area.

1985, April 17: South Africa completes the formal withdrawal of its troops from Angola.

1985, July: U.S. Congress repeals Clark Amendment and begins to ship limited supplies of weapons to UNITA.

1985, September: FAPLA units, backed by Cuban combat troops, try to seize town of Mavinga in southeastern Angola and are driven off by UNITA and South African forces.

1987, October: South African–UNITA attack on Cuito Cuanavale results in heavy SADF casualties as FAPLA and Cuban troops withstand siege.

1988, June: Cuban troops bomb South African positions at the Calueque Dam in southern Angola.

1988, December 22: Angola, South Africa, Cuba, and the U.S. gather in New York to sign two accords providing for the withdrawal of Cuban troops from Angola and for Namibia's independence.

Notes

1. John Marcum, *The Angolan Revolution, Vol. 2: Exile Politics and Guerrilla Warfare (1962–1976)* (Cambridge, Mass.: MIT Press, 1978), pp. 2–3.

2. Because available information on U.S. and South African decisionmaking is more reliable than that for Cuba and the USSR, we are necessarily more tentative about our conclusions and guiding rationales with respect to the latter two countries.

3. Tad Szulc, *Fidel: A Critical Portrait,* (New York: Morrow, 1986), pp. 628–629.

4. William J. Durch, "The Cuban Military in Africa and the Middle East: From Algeria to Angola," *Studies in Comparative Communism,* 11 nos. 1 and 2 (Spring/Summer 1978):72.

5. William LeoGrande, "Cuban-Soviet Relations and Cuban Policy in Africa," *Cuban Studies/Estudios Cubanos* 10 no. 1 (January 1980):20.

6. *Granma Weekly Review,* Havana, May 2, 1976. Fidel Castro made this speech on April 19, 1976.

7. Arkady N. Shevchenko, *Breaking With Moscow* (New York: Ballantine Books, 1985), p. 363.

8. Republic of South Africa, Department of Defense, *White Paper on Defence and Armament Production, 1975,* p. 7.

9. Quoted in Robin Hallet, "The South African Intervention in Angola, 1975–76," *African Affairs,* 77, no. 308 (July 1978):363.

10. Deon Guldenhuys, *The Diplomacy of Isolation* (Johannesburg: Macmillan South Africa Publishers, 1984), pp. 79–80. Kenneth W. Grundy, *The Militarization of South African Politics* (Bloomington: Indiana University Press, 1986), p. 89.

11. Jiri Valenta, "The Soviet–Cuban Intervention in Angola, 1975," *Studies in Comparative Communism*, 11, nos. 1 and 2 (Spring/Summer 1978):21.

12. David Albright, "Soviet Policy," *Problems of Communism*, 27 (January–February 1978):33–34.

13. Raymond Garthoff, *Detente and Confrontation: American–Soviet Relations from Nixon to Reagan* (Washington, D.C.: The Brookings Institution, 1985), p. 529. According to Garthoff, while Kissinger stated twice in news conferences in December 1975 that the U.S. and China had "parallel views," and even policies, on Angola, he made clear that U.S. decisions and actions were not "coordinated" with Beijing.

14. Colin Legum, "Angola and the Horn of Africa," in Stephen S. Kaplan et al., *Diplomacy of Power* (Washington, D.C.: The Brookings Institution, 1981), p. 571.

15. Arthur Jay Klinghoffer, *The Angolan War: A Study in Soviet Policy in the Third World* (Boulder, Colo.: Westview Press, 1980), p. 75.

16. Albright, "Soviet Policy," p. 31.

17. "President Ford Reiterates U.S. Objectives in Angola," text of a letter from President Ford to Speaker of the House Carl Albert, January 27, *Department of State Bulletin*, 74 (February 16, 1976):183.

18. Statement of Henry Kissinger, Secretary of State, January 29, 1976. Hearings before the Subcommittee on African Affairs of the Senate Committee on Foreign Relations on U.S. Involvement in the Civil War in Angola, January 9, February 3, 4 and 6, 1976, 94th Congress, 2nd session (Washington, D.C.: Government Printing Office, 1976).

19. This excerpt from the study by the Congressional Research Service is quoted in Klinghoffer, *The Angolan War*, p. 77.

20. Henry F. Jackson, *From the Congo to Soweto: U.S. Foreign Policy Toward Africa Since 1960* (New York: Morrow, 1982), p. 69. In describing South Africa's view of southern Africa after the Angolan "debacle," Thomas Callaghy notes that the South Africans believe that in order to attack them, the Soviets are employing a "two-pronged strategy of fostering and directing a 'terrorist' threat to South Africa while building up the conventional forces of the new socialist states." Thomas M. Callaghy, "Apartheid and Socialism: South Africa's Relations with Angola and Mozambique," in Thomas M. Callaghy ed., *South Africa in Southern Africa: The Intensifying Vortex of Violence* (New York: Praeger, 1983), p. 269.

21. Mark N. Katz, *The Third World in Soviet Military Thought* (London: Croom Helm, 1982), p. 80.

22. Christopher Stevens, "The Soviet Role in Southern Africa," in John Seiler ed., *Southern Africa Since the Portuguese Coup* (Boulder: Westview Press, 1980), pp. 48–49.

23. *Africa Confidential* 15, no. 17 (August 23, 1974):1.

24. Although China was the first to react, it did not have a sustained involvement throughout the intervention and disengagement processes and therefore is not included in our study.

25. John Stockwell, *In Search of Enemies*, (New York: Norton, 1978), p. 67.

26. Marcum, *The Angolan Revolution*, p. 257.

27. Stockwell, *In Search of Enemies*, p. 68.

28. Garthoff, *Detente and Confrontation*, p. 507.

29. Jiri Valenta, "The Soviet-Cuban Intervention in Angola, 1975," *Studies in Comparative Communism*, 11, nos. 1 and 2 (Spring/Summer 1978):11; and Durch, "The Cuban Military in Africa and the Middle East," p. 64.

30. Stockwell, *In Search of Enemies*, p. 55. The U.S.'s plan was to send arms to Zaire to replace equipment Mobutu was sending to Angola from his own stocks.

31. Valenta, "The Soviet–Cuban Intervention in Angola, 1975," p. 18.

32. Klinghoffer, *The Angolan War*, p. 44.

33. Valenta, "The Soviet–Cuban Intervention in Angola, 1975," p. 19.

34. Gerald Bender, "Kissinger in Angola: Anatomy of Failure," in René Lemarchand ed., *American Policy in Southern Africa: The Stakes and the Stance* (Washington, D.C.: University Press of America, 1978), p. 92; Garthoff, *Detente and Confrontation*, p. 511; and Klinghoffer, *The Angolan War*, p. 112. Interestingly enough, Fidel Castro would later call these forces "instructors," stating that only on November 5, 1975, after South Africa's October 23 invasion, did Cuba decide to send the first military units to Angola in support of the MPLA. See *Granma Weekly Review*, March 28, 1976. According to Durch, this Cuban distinction between "instructors" and "military units" is tenable. Durch explains: "Cuban troops in Angola before November did not appear to operate as separate, integral units. They appeared, rather, to go into the field as advisers to MPLA units. . . . Using this distinction, Cuba's account of its involvement would seem to stand up well under scrutiny." Durch, "The Cuban Military in Africa and the Middle East," p. 67.

35. Valenta, "The Soviet-Cuban Intervention in Angola, 1975," p. 26.

36. Garthoff, *Detente and Confrontation*, p. 512.

37. Edward Gonzalez, "Complexities of Cuban Foreign Policy," *Problems of Communism*, 26 (November-December 1977):11; and Durch, "The Cuban Military in Africa and the Middle East," p. 68. Both Gonzalez and Durch believe that Cuba's escalation of its intervention was a response to the South African invasion, which threatened not only Cuba's ally, the MPLA, but also the Cuban troops already in Angola. Raymond Garthoff, on the other hand, argues that given the timing of the initial Cuban response in October, Havana must already have decided to provide combat troops before October 23. Garthoff does believe, however, that additional troops sent by Cuba in November were a response to South Africa's October incursion. Garthoff, *Detente and Confrontation*, p. 513.

38. Garthoff, *Detente and Confrontation*, p. 512.

39. For a vivid account of this confrontation which became known as the Battle of Death Road, see Stockwell, *In Search of Enemies*, pp. 214–215.

40. Marcum, *The Angolan Revolution*, p. 272.

41. "Building an Enduring Foreign Policy," Address by Secretary Kissinger, Detroit, Michigan, November 24, *Department of State Bulletin*, 73 (December 15, 1975):843.

42. Stockwell, *In Search of Enemies*, pp. 216–226.

43. *BBC Monitoring Service*, ME/5117 (January 26, 1976), p. B/3.

44. Quoted in Colin Legum ed., *Africa Contemporary Record 1978–79* (New York: Africana Publishing Co., 1980), p. B489.

45. Robert M. Price, "South Africa and Afro-Marxism: Pretoria's Relations with Mozambique and Angola in Regional Perspective," in Edmond J. Keller and Donald Rothchild, eds., *Afro-Marxist Regimes: Ideology and Public Policy* (Boulder: Lynne Rienner, 1987), p. 259.

46. Allister Sparks, "Botha goes for a deal on Namibia," *Observer* (London), May 13, 1984, p. 10.

47. *Africa News* 24, 7 (April 8, 1985):3.

48. Louis Wiznitzer, "UN expected to reaffirm role in Namibia," *Christian Science Monitor*, June 14, 1985, p. 14; and Martin Lowenkopf, "If the Cold War Is Over in Africa, Will the United States Still Care?" *CSIS Africa Notes*, no. 98 (May 30, 1989):4.

49. Jonas Savimbi, press conference in *Foreign Broadcast Information Service*, Daily Report, Middle East and Africa 5, no. 196 (October 9, 1985): U3 and U4; and *Africa Research Bulletin*, Political Series, 22, no. 10 (November 15, 1985):7825–7827.

50. Quoted in Colin Legum ed., *Africa Contemporary Record 1985–86* (New York: Africana Publishing Co., 1987), p. B625. Also see his comments in BBC, *Summary of World Broadcasts*, no. 8064 (September 24, 1985):B10.

51. Quoted in Margaret A. Novicki, "Angola: Against All Odds," *Africa Report* 30, no. 1 (January-February, 1985):8.

52. David Ottaway, "Angola Gets Infusion of Soviet Arms," *Washington Post*, May 12, 1987, p. A27. U.S. government sources indicate that from 1977 to 1987 Angola imported approximately $9.23 billion in military equipment, most of it of Soviet origin. See Marina Ottaway, "The Soviet Union and Africa," in John Harbeson and Donald Rothchild eds., *Africa in World Politics* (Boulder: Westview, 1991, p.235.). With the repeal of the Clark amendment in 1985, the U.S. provided UNITA with some $15 million in aid.

53. *Africa Confidential* 29, no. 3 (February 5, 1988):2.

54. *Africa Confidential* 29, no. 3 (February 5, 1988):1–3; and Karl Maier, "Angola: The Military Stalemate," *Africa Report* 33, 3 (May-June 1988): 34–35.

55. James Brooke, "Angolans Besting South Africa in a Remote Battle," *New York Times*, May 18, 1988, p. A6.

56. *Africa Confidential*, 29, no. 7 (April 1, 1988):1.

57. Bernard E. Trainor, "Pretoria Critical of Angola Attack," *New York Times*, June 30, 1988, p. A5; and *Africa Confidential* 29, 14 (July 15, 1988):1–2.

58. Gillian Gunn, "A Guide to the Intricacies of the Angola-Namibia Negotiations," *CSIS Africa Notes*, no. 90 (September 8, 1988): 12; also see Howard Wolpe, "Seizing Southern African Opportunities," *Foreign Policy*, no. 73 (Winter 1988–89):61.

59. Pamela S. Falk, "Cuba in Africa," *Foreign Affairs* 65, 5 (Summer 1987):1077–78.

60. Obinna Anyadike, "Angola: Britain hosts secret talks," *West Africa*, May 9, 1988, p. 833; and Michael McFaul, "Rethinking the 'Reagan Doctrine' in Angola," *International Security* 14, 3 (Winter 1989/90):111–112.

61. BBC, ME/8639 (August 6, 1987): ii, and ME/8644 (August 12, 1987), p. B/6.

62. *West Africa*, August 24, 1987, p. 1667.

63. *New African*, no. 244 (January 1988):18.

64. Robert Pear, "U.S. Making New Push for Angolan Pact," *New York Times*, April 15, 1988, p. A4. On the concept of "ripeness," see I. William Zartman, *Ripe for Resolution*, 2d ed. (New York: Oxford University Press, 1989), p. 10.

65. Ray Kennedy, "Tit for tat threats precede London meeting on Angola," *Times* (London), May 2, 1988, p. 7.

66. *Africa Research Bulletin*, Political Series 25, no. 6 (July 15, 1988):8900–8902; and Gunn, "A Guide to the Intricacies," p. 11.

67. Quoted in *New York Times*, November 16, 1988, p. 1. Also see David B. Ottaway, "Cubans Agree To Withdraw Troops From Angola," *Manchester Guardian Weekly*, 139, no. 22 (November 27, 1988):18.

68. Bruno Dethomas, "Angola teeters on the brink of famine," *Manchester Guardian Weekly* 137, 14 (October 4, 1987):11.

69. Interview with Fidel Castro, *Granma Weekly Review*, March 13, 1988, p. 7.

70. Falk, "Cuba in Africa," p. 1095. Also see Jorge I. Dominguez, "Political and Military Limitations and Consequences of Cuban Policies in Africa," *Cuban Studies* 10, 2 (July 1980):25.

71. Chas. W. Freeman, Jr., "The Angola/Namibia Accords," *Foreign Affairs* 68, 3 (Summer 1989):133.

72. Chester A. Crocker, *The U.S. and Angola, a Statem... Before the Senate Committee on Foreign Relations, February 18, 1986*. (Washington, D.C.: Department of State, Bureau of Public Affairs, 1986), Current Policy no. 796, p. 1.

73. Donald Rothchild and John Ravenhill, "From Carter to Reagan: The Global Perspective on Africa Becomes Ascendant," in K. Oye, R. Lieber and D. Rothchild eds., *Eagle Defiant* (Boston: Little, Brown, 1983), p. 348.

74. Vadim A. Medvedev, the Kremlin's chief ideologist, has rejected a world struggle against the West, and Gorbachev spoke at the United Nations of "de-ideologizing relations among states." *New York Times*, October 6, 1988, p. A1, and December 8, 1988, p. A6.

75. See Gerhard Wettig, " 'New Thinking' on Security and East-West Relations," *Problems of Communism*, vol. 37 (March-April 1988):12.

76. *Time*, 132 no. 26 (December 26, 1988):25.

77. Jiri Valenta, "Comment: The Soviet-Cuban Alliance in Africa and Future Prospects in the Third World," *Cuban Studies*, 10, no. 2 (July 1980):34.

78. Pauline Baker, "The American Challenge in Southern Africa," *Current History*, 88, no. 538 (May 1989):245.

79. For an example of successful joint Soviet–U.S. initiatives in the Central American region see Michael Kramer, "Anger, Bluff—and Cooperation," *Time*, 135, no. 23 (June 4, 1990).

80. *Africa Research Bulletin*, 26 no. 6 (June 15, 1989):9316.

81. The text of the Gbadolite Declaration appeared in BBC Monitoring Service, ME/0493 (June 27, 1989): B/1.

82. Warren Clark, Jr., *National Reconciliation Efforts for Angola, a Statement Before the Subcommittee on Africa of the House Foreign Affairs Committee, September 27, 1989* (Washington D.C.: Department of State, Bureau of Public Affairs, 1989), Current Policy No. 1217, p. 2.

83. BBC Monitoring Service, ME/0574 (September 29, 1989):B/2.

84. Clark, *National Reconciliation Efforts for Angola*, p.2; and BBC Monitoring Service, ME/0565 (September 19, 1989): ii, and ME/0574 (September 29, 1989): B/2, B/3. In addition, Savimbi stated that the peace talks were not achieving their desired results "because they were not prepared properly." *The Times* (London), September 13, 1989, p. 11.

85. See Kenneth B. Noble, "Truce Imperiled, Angola Leader Says," *New York Times*, August 24, 1989, A3.

86. Christopher S. Wren, "De Klerk in Zaire to Discuss Angola," *New York Times*, August 26, 1989, p. A4.

87. See Foreign Minister Pik Botha's remarks in *Africa Research Bulletin* (Political Series), 26, no. 11 (December 15, 1989): 9477.

88. *Hearings* Before the Committee on Foreign Relations United States Senate on the Nomination of Herman J. Cohen to be Assistant Secretary of State for African Affairs, May 3, 1989 (Washington D.C.: Alderson Reporting Co., 1989), p. 26.

89. Martin Lowenkopf, "If the Cold War is Over in Africa, Will the United States Still Care?" *CSIS Africa Notes*, No. 98 (May 30, 1989):5; and Robert Pear, "U.S. and Angola Discuss Forging Diplomatic Ties," *New York Times*, January 27, 1989, p. A3.

90. Herman J. Cohen, "Ceasefire and Political Settlement in Angola," *U.S. Department of State Dispatch*, 2, no. 18 (May 6, 1991): 328. Also see Shawn McCormick, "Angola: The Road to Peace," *CSIS Africa Notes*, no. 125 (June 6, 1991):11.

91. For one participant in the mediation process, linkage was the "only available framework for a settlement." Freeman, "The Angola/Namibia Accord," p. 133. Also see Colin Legum, "Southern Africa: Analysis of the Peace Process, *Third World Reports*, L.B/1 (January 11, 1989):6; and G. R. Berridge, "Diplomacy and the Angola/Namibia Accords," *International Affairs* (London), 65, no. 3 (Summer 1989):471.

7

India's Role in Sri Lanka's Ethnic Conflict

MAHNAZ ISPAHANI

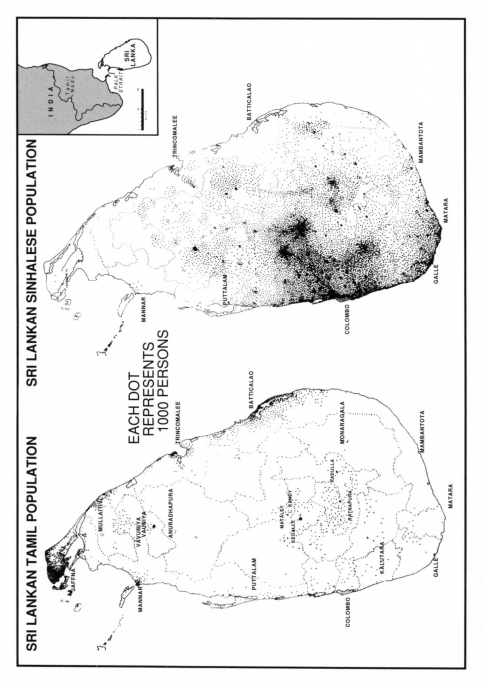

SRI LANKAN TAMIL POPULATION

SRI LANKAN SINHALESE POPULATION

EACH DOT
REPRESENTS
1000 PERSONS

Sri Lanka, showing population of Tamils and Sinhalese

Introduction

Soon after the British abandoned their empire in South Asia, Sri Lanka, a tear shaped island in the Indian Ocean, emerged as the region's most vigorous democracy. Its citizens were well-educated and well-fed. Its politics were democratic.

Today, Sri Lanka is debilitated by one of the bloodiest ethnic conflicts to blight South Asia, a region long familiar with communal violence. While the ethnic divide has imperiled democracy, competitive democratic politics have also played a role in worsening ethnic tensions.

The Sri Lankan Tamils, who are Hindu, constitute about 13 percent of the island's 18 million people. The Sinhalese Buddhists comprise about 75 percent of the population, and Muslims make up another 7 percent. There are more than one million Indian or "estate" Tamils (mainly plantation workers imported from India in the nineteenth century, who, as a group, have not been participants in the ethnic conflict). Tamils predominate in the north and in parts of the former Eastern Province, where they constitute 42 percent of the population. Muslim Moors make up 32 percent and Sinhalese 25 percent of the area's inhabitants. Tamils also inhabit the neighborhood of the capital city, Colombo.

The Sri Lankan conflict in which India intervened originated in a quarrel between the Sinhalese and the Tamils. Like most such disputes, it has been transnational, ignoring political and territorial boundaries. Its transnational nature has been evident in the ethnic war's every dimension, from the psychological to the strategic. While the Tamils view themselves as an increasingly beleaguered minority, the Sinhalese majority in Sri Lanka also considers itself to be endangered: it associates Sri Lanka's Tamils with the approximately 60 million Tamils who live across the narrow Palk Straits in the powerful southern Indian state of Tamil Nadu. The Tamil–Sinhalese feud has spawned its own myths, in which the ancient religious tales of India and Sri Lanka are intertwined.

I am grateful to the Woodrow Wilson Center for Scholars where, as a Fellow in 1989, I had the peaceful opportunity to study ethnic conflicts, and to Lise Hartman for spotting important materials that I would need in my research.

Successive Sinhalese political parties and governments prosecuted policies in the spheres of language rights, education, employment, and culture, which gradually alienated the educated Tamil minority. In 1948 thousands of "estate" Tamils were disenfranchised. In 1956, Parliament passed the Official Language Act, which made Sinhala the official language of the country. This became known as the "Sinhala Only Act." In 1958, bloody Sinhalese–Tamil riots occurred.

During the 1960s and 1970s, electoral politics led the two main Sinhalese parties—the Sri Lanka Freedom Party (SLFP) and the United National Party (UNP)—to compete for the Sinhalese vote by making increasingly chauvinist promises, thereby increasing ethnic polarization. Sri Lanka's 1972 Constitution further antagonized the Tamils. Not only did it reaffirm Sinhala's official status but it also accorded a special status to Buddhism. The electoral competition between the UNP and the SLFP made it difficult for either party to make concessions to the Tamils without risking the stoking of Sinhalese sentiment by its opponent.

In Sri Lanka's ethnically based polity the Tamils were initially represented by the Federal Party. In 1976 this party evolved into the Tamil United Liberation Front (TULF). Arguing for greater autonomy for Tamil areas, the TULF competed in the 1977 general elections, which marked a turning point in Sinhalese–Tamil politics. The SLFP, which had held power since 1970, was vanquished and the UNP, led by Junius Jayawardene, took power. The TULF ran on a platform of radical autonomy for the Tamils and became the main opposition party in Parliament.

President Jayawardene changed the direction of Sri Lanka's policies, promoting a pro-western orientation abroad and political authoritarianism and a free market at home. In December 1982, Jayawardene held an unprecedented referendum by which the UNP-dominated parliament's term was extended for six more years.

New constitutional concessions in 1978 that Tamil would be a "national" language proved inadequate to redress Tamil grievances. A Sinhalese government policy on university admissions, known as the "standardization of marks," which discriminated against Tamil candidates by deliberately lowering their grades and establishing a quota for admissions, further enlarged the ethnic divide. Tamil politicians demanded the merger of the Northern and Eastern provinces, the protection of the Tamil language, and a genuine devolution of powers to local Tamil authorities. The government's responses (which included offers of District Development Councils with delegated powers) were unsatisfactory to the Tamils. After 1978, more radical

Tamil student groups began to emerge, one of the earliest being the Tamil New Tigers. By 1983 they had become militant, raising the demand for a separate Tamil state, Tamil Eelam.

The roots of India's intervention can be traced to the events of 1983. During July and August of that year Tamil militants viciously attacked a group of soldiers. The return of the soldiers' bodies to Colombo led to anti-Tamil riots. Between 140 and 600 Tamils died and thousands were left homeless. The UNP government did not intervene for four days and the *London Times* referred to the "culpable bias of the government forces."[1] Thousands of Tamil refugees began to leave southern Sri Lanka for the north, as well as for southern India. Other Tamils fled to the West—to the U.S. and Canada— where they became both an effective lobby for their cause and, reportedly, a source of financing for Tamil militants at home. Shortly after the August troubles the UNP government passed a constitutional amendment forbidding the peaceful advocacy of separatism. All sixteen members of the TULF delegation in Parliament resigned and exiled themselves to Tamil Nadu.

Now, no Tamil representatives remained in the political process. In the coming years, many of these moderate Tamil politicians would be killed by the militants. The Liberation Tigers of Tamil Eelam (LTTE or "Tigers"), which emerged as the most effective Tamil guerrilla organization, would be their chief adversary. Estimated at between 200 and 700 in 1983 the number of Tamil militants had risen to between 2,000 and 10,000 by 1985.[2] The ethnic war had come to a boil.

Stage I: Getting In

Geography and history conspired to make India a central player in Sri Lanka's crisis. The island nation is only about 30 miles from the south Indian state of Tamil Nadu, separated by the narrow Palk Straits. Tamils on both sides of this water divide share religion and culture. Before the 1980s, the most sensitive dispute between India and Sri Lanka involved the political status of the estate Tamils, disenfranchised by Sri Lanka in 1948. Sri Lanka posed no military threat to India: except for a brief period during 1971 its army has been insignificant.

Aimed at ameliorating perceived threats to its internal and external security, and the assertion of regional dominance in South Asia, India's policies toward Sri Lanka's conflict evolved gradually. At different times and in varying combinations, three main strategies were employed: India provided sanctuary, arms, and training for Tamil guerrillas, served as mediator between the Sri Lankan government and the Tamil militants, and intervened militarily to resolve the ethnic impasse. The Sri Lankan conflict raised India's concerns about the involvement of third powers, namely Pakistan and the United States, and challenged India to act as the manager of the region's conflicts.

If we are to understand the nature of India's intervention it is important to note that during the 1980s, its capital, New Delhi, and the capital of Tamil Nadu, Madras, responded to different policy priorities. New Delhi had both a broader geopolitical perspective and a need to forge coalitions with the ruling party in Madras, while the Tamil Nadu state government was often driven by the compulsions of ethnic solidarity, a desire to assert its independence from the Indian center, and its electoral competition with rival state political parties. If Sri Lanka had been entirely peripheral to India's strategic interests, then ethnic affinity alone might not have precipitated an Indian military commitment. The Indian military intervention of 1987, however, fused the interests of the national and state capitals. Public opinion in Tamil Nadu encouraged India to act, and New Delhi was able to achieve its own regional security goals. Ultimately the strategic gains would survive the misadventure in Sri Lanka.

By the late 1970s, India had begun to view itself as an Indian Ocean power whose rights and responsibilities stretched south across the waters. An ambitious program of naval expansion had been launched. Indians fretted about the potential use of the island of Diego Garcia by extra-regional forces, and Indira Gandhi loudly supported the Sri Lankan leader Sirimavo Bandaranaika's proposal that the United Nations turn the Indian Ocean into a "Zone of Peace."

In 1977, leaders changed in Sri Lanka and India when Bandaranaike and Gandhi both lost elections. Between 1977 and 1980 India's Janata government, led by Morarji Desai, maintained a cooperative relationship with the government of Jayawardene. In 1980, however, when Indira Gandhi returned to power, Indo–Sri Lankan relations worsened.

Jayawardene's policies were not to Gandhi's liking. The Sri Lankan president reversed Bandaranaika's policy of nonalignment and embittered India by his efforts to extend Sri Lanka's relationships outside South Asia. For instance, Jayawardene asked that Sri Lanka be permitted to join ASEAN, a pro-Western and non-South Asian regional group. When the UNP government negotiated with an

American firm to build oil-storage facilities at the port of Trincomalee, reportedly after rejecting an Indian offer and a Soviet "feeler," India objected.[3] It complained, too, after Sri Lanka signed an agreement with the Voice of America to establish a transmission center in Sri Lanka, and Jayawardene embarked on a search for weapons and diplomatic support from the United States, as well as from India's adversaries, China and Pakistan. Such efforts violated a central tenet of India's regional policy, which opposes the attempts of other South Asian states to establish extraregional alliances. In 1983, Gandhi warned Sri Lanka that "any external involvement will complicate matters for both the countries."[4]

India's strategic concerns were exacerbated by the impact which the violent Sinhalese–Tamil feud inside Sri Lanka was having on transnational relations between Indian and Sri Lankan Tamils. When, in 1983, more than 100,000 Tamil refugees fled to Tamil Nadu with horrifying tales of atrocities committed against them by Sinhalese, the vagaries of the Sri Lankan conflict permeated Tamil Nadu politics. Although public opinion would vacillate in intensity throughout the 1980s, India's Tamils remained sensitive to the reports of attacks on Sri Lanka's Tamils. One chief minister of Tamil Nadu, the charismatic ex-movie star, M.G. Ramachandran—leader of the All India Anna Dravida Munnetra *Kazhagam* (AIADMK)—became a famed patron of the Sri Lankan Tamils, especially of the LTTE.

Domestic political concerns powerfully influenced New Delhi. The AIADMK was an important regional ally of Indira Gandhi's Congress Party. Its political sympathy for the Sri Lankan Tamils—rivaled only by that of its political opponent, the erstwhile pro-secession Dravida Munnetra *Kazhagam* (DMK)—and the popular support for their cause evidenced in south India could not be ignored by the Indian center. Inside Tamil Nadu, the electoral competition between the AIADMK and the DMK led both parties to try to outdo one another in their allegiance to the cause of the Sri Lankan Tamils. While the AIADMK (and later the DMK) favored the LTTE, Mrs. Gandhi also reportedly financed another armed group, TELO.[5]

Although she tried to act as a political mediator in Sri Lanka, asking the Sri Lankan government to grant greater autonomy to the Tamils, Indira Gandhi simultaneously fanned the violence by training and arming Tamil militants. In Tamil Nadu the guerrillas reportedly established arsenals for weapons as well as training camps, "Eelam information centers," and communications facilities. Reportedly, millions of dollars worth of weapons were supplied to them; India's Research and Analysis Wing (RAW) as well as Indian and foreign retired officers served as trainers; and logistics services were provided so that the Tamil militants could freely ship their arms to Sri Lanka.[6] As one writer phrased it, Mrs. Gandhi's strategy was to "harass Colombo only to the extent of forcing it to reach an agreement" with the Tamils, which would be "acceptable to New Delhi."[7]

New Delhi was pressured by Madras to go so far as to support the creation of an independent Eelam, but it desisted. Even during Gandhi's tenure it was not evident that India wanted a new Tamil state, given its own large Tamil population, and Tamil Nadu's history of opposition to New Delhi's control. Although the comparison is sometimes made, the situation was not analogous to that prevailing during the Indo–Pakistani conflict of 1971, when the flood of refugees from Bangladesh became the official rationale for Indian military intervention on behalf of the Bengali secessionists. Then, the overriding aim had been the destruction of united Pakistan. In 1987, Eelam was not India's goal. This would become quickly evident in the period following the 1987 Accord.

In this first phase of the Indo–Sri Lankan entanglement, the Indian government cooperated with Tamil militants against the Sri Lankan government. During the course of India's involvement in the conflict, however, alliance partners would change often, and in unexpected and historic ways. In 1985, the second phase began. It opened with a political strategy of negotiation and ended with a military intervention.

In 1984, leaders changed. Indira Gandhi was assassinated on October 31, 1984 and her son Rajiv Gandhi swept to power with an overwhelming electoral mandate. He began his tenure as a conciliator, signing accords in India's violence-ridden territories of Assam, Mizoram, and Punjab. Rajiv Gandhi did not want Tamil Eelam. Nor did he desire a Sri Lankan state fortified by Western partners, Chinese arms, or Pakistani and Israeli trainers. Gandhi's preferred strategy for resolving the Indian dilemma was mediation. He would use India's stature to pressure Jayawardene into negotiating greater autonomy for the Tamils, while employing the sanctuary India provided to the Tamil militants to pressure them into dialogue with Sri Lanka's government. These talks were held in Bhutan and elsewhere. New Delhi tried to walk a fine line between responding to domestic calls for allegiance to the Sri Lankan Tamil cause and denying the guerrillas the capability to secede.

From the beginning, however, India's strategy was flawed. Gandhi never had sufficient leverage over either the Sri Lankan government or the LTTE to force a favorable outcome in the negotiations. The Sri Lankan rivals would agree neither on the nature of the promised devolution of powers nor on the cessation of hostilities.

During this time, the Indian government was becoming increasingly discomfited by President Jayawardene's travels. The Sri Lankan leader sought military aid from the United States and others. The U.S. refused Sri Lanka's requests in 1984. Israel's *Mossad* reportedly agreed to provide arms and counterinsurgency training to special units of the Sri Lankan security forces (the Special Task Force) and Israel was permitted to establish an interests section in the U.S. Embassy in Colombo. (Ties had been broken in 1970.) Pakistan was said to have provided military training, and the services of Keeny Meeny, Inc., a British mercenary organization comprised of former SAS commandos, were acquired.[8]

Between 1985 and 1987, too, in one of its periodic shifts, the Tamil Nadu public's mood regarding Sri Lanka's Tamils altered. Indian Tamils were losing patience with the political intransigence and criminality of the Sri Lankan Tamil militants, whose activities now included drug-trafficking, smuggling, robberies, bombings, and assassinations. The LTTE guerrillas were especially preoccupied with slaughtering rival Tamils. The national and state authorities responded by arresting some militants and restricting their movement. Although Gandhi took advantage of the shift in public sentiment to increase the political pressure on the Tamil militants, finally, his efforts failed.

The LTTE took the initiative and severed the ties that bound it to India, and in 1987 the Sri Lankan government did the same. While negotiations remained stalled, Jayawardene opted to pursue a military offensive. These events paved the way for Gandhi's decision to involve the Indian military in his neighbor's war.

Frustrated by their harassment at the hands of Indian politicians and policemen, the LTTE abandoned its bases in Tamil Nadu and returned to northern Sri Lanka, causing the first important rupture with India. On the peninsula it set up bases, secured control of the city of Jaffna, and continued to use the Palk Strait for resupplies from India. This return of the LTTE to Sri Lanka precipitated a military confrontation between the Tamil guerrillas and the Sinhalese-dominated Sri Lankan armed forces.

The Sri Lankan army had grown rapidly since 1983 and was frequently criticized for its indiscriminate attacks against Tamil civilians. By 1987 it was better armed and trained than it had ever been, and, at 60,000 troops, nearly three times its 1983 size. Its officers were confident that they could "win" against the LTTE and resented the political restrictions on civilian casualties.[9]

On January 1, 1987, against Indian advice, the LTTE initiated efforts to usurp the civilian administration of the Northern Province. President Jayawardene, who had been considering the military option (also against Indian advice), retaliated. First, he ordered the cut-off of essential supplies and services, including kerosene and gasoline, to the Tamil areas in the north. This action severely affected the Tamil civilians of Jaffna. Immediately, public opinion in Tamil Nadu veered toward sympathy for the Tamil cause. As the Sri Lankan government had been pressured by Sinhalese public opinion to limit concessions to the Tamils, so Rajiv Gandhi came under intense domestic pressure in Tamil Nadu to stop the maltreatment of Tamil civilians in Jaffna. As the *Hindustan Times* phrased it, if the Sri Lankan government's assault on Tamil civilians led to a greater refugee exodus, "the anger that will be aroused in Tamil Nadu will severely restrict New Delhi's capacity to play a constructive role in the Sri Lanka crisis in future."[10]

Following renewed LTTE assaults (including a massacre of Sinhalese civilians in the northeast and a bomb explosion in Colombo in April 1987), and despite Gandhi's warnings, Jayawardene announced a war against the LTTE. In late May 1987, the Sri Lankan army deployed 3,000 troops, launching a major assault to retake the Jaffna peninsula, and thereby transforming Rajiv Gandhi's role once more. When it seemed as though the Sri Lankan army might actually defeat the LTTE militarily, Gandhi abandoned peaceful mediation for military intervention.

The heavy loss of Tamil civilian lives in these ensuing battles resulted in the denunciation of the Indian government at home for its "vacillating" and "inconsistent" handling of the crisis. Tamil Nadu's Chief Minister demanded that New Delhi stop Sri Lanka's military offensive. The state's support for the LTTE was particularly influential in the summer of 1987. The Chief Minister of Tamil Nadu announced a large humanitarian aid grant to the LTTE, while India warned that it could not remain indifferent to the plight of the Jaffna Tamils.[11]

On June 3, India sent an unarmed flotilla of food supplies to Sri Lanka. It was turned back by the Sri Lankan navy. The following day India sent five transport planes escorted by four Mirage fighters to drop relief supplies directly above Jaffna. The Sri Lankan army promptly curtailed its offensive. By these acts India violated international law and served notice on Sri Lanka that it would not tolerate either the obliteration of the LTTE or high Tamil civilian casualties.[12]

Although South Asia's smaller states expressed concern about India's actions, none came to Sri Lanka's assistance. Sri Lanka understood the message of the world: South Asia was India's domain. On July 29 1987, India and Sri Lanka signed an agreement to end the Tamil–Sinhalese war. It was the eighth negotiation in the search for peace.[13]

The Accord signified a reversal in President Jayawardene's anti-Indian policies. He had been extremely vocal in his condemnation of India's airdrop, even taking his complaints to regional and international fora. Now, Jayawardene was forced to accept the inevitability of India's involvement, letting it shoulder the burden of resolving the crisis. Some years later he said, "By signing the treaty India was undertaking responsibility to help solve the problem they themselves [sic] had created." The burden had grown increasingly onerous for Jayawardene. The costs of war were high: the UNP government had promulgated a "Prevention of Terrorism Act"; there were 6,000 to 8,000 political prisoners; and a state of emergency and official censorship was enforced. The financial costs of the war exceeded $500 million each year.[14]

When the Accord was signed, Nepal and Bangladesh welcomed it. Pakistan hoped that Indo–Sri Lankan relations would "continue to be governed by respect for the principles of territorial integrity, independence and sovereignty"; and the Maldives and Bhutan released no statements.[15]

To address the ethnic crisis Sri Lanka and India forged a new bilateral relationship. The negotiations leading to the accord, however, carried the seeds of its destruction. They were conducted hastily and in secret. Although the terms of the Accord directly affected the LTTE and other militant Tamil groups, they were not included in the talks. Jayawardene failed to establish even a minimal domestic consensus for the agreement. He consulted neither his Prime Minister, Ranasinghe Premdasa, nor other members of his Cabinet, nor the UNP leadership. In fact, opposition to the Accord in Sri Lanka was led by Prime Minister Premdasa who saw it as an infringement upon Sri Lanka's sovereignty and was skeptical about the Sinhalese response to the accord's concessions to the Tamils. As a strategy for peacemaking, the Accord split the UNP. In the end, neither the Tamil militants nor the Sinhalese elite actively supported it.

Although India's military intervention would have salutary consequences for its Cold War concerns, ethnopolitics played an important role in luring it into the quagmire. For India, the Accord was a measure of last resort to resolve a war whose extreme consequences—an independent Eelam or the massacre of Tamil civilians—could not be politically countenanced. Tired of the behavior of the militants, India's Tamils supported the Accord as the best strategy for safeguarding the security and rights of Tamil civilians. And New Delhi and Madras agreed that the restoration of a sense of security to the Tamil population of northern and eastern Sri Lanka was a precondition to any Tamil–Sinhalese peace.

The Accord, which was supported by an exchange of letters, gave India control over important facets of Sri Lanka's foreign policy, military, and intelligence operations. In India, the Congress (I) party gained the approval of their Tamil Nadu political allies as well as the broader populace, while Rajiv Gandhi asserted India's influence across the region and the Indian Ocean waters. In exchange for all this, India became the "guarantor" of the terms of the Accord, even if that required the induction of troops. When it signed the agreement, India became obliged to cooperate with Sri Lanka's authorities to ensure the safety and security of all the communities in the Northern and Eastern provinces, where the war was most fiercely fought.

India had two main military and political objectives: to stop the military advances of the Sri Lankan army into Tamil territories, and gain concessions for the Sri Lankan Tamils as well as for itself from the Sri Lankan government. The specific military provisions of the Accord included a prompt cease-fire which was to become effective within 48 hours of the signing, the release of Tamil political prisoners, and the return of Sri Lankan forces to their barracks within 72 hours of the cease-fire. India agreed to deny Tamil militants their bases in Tamil Nadu and to cooperate with the Sri Lankan Navy and Coast Guard to prevent gun running from Tamil Nadu.

The Accord specified that "All arms presently held by militant groups will be surrendered in accordance with an agreed procedure to authorities to be designated by the government of Sri Lanka." Further, the Accord stated that "In the event that the government of Sri Lanka requests the government of India to afford military assistance to implement these proposals the government of India will cooperate by giving the government of Sri Lanka such military assistance as and when requested."[16]

The political objectives of the Accord were to unite the Northern and Eastern provinces into a single administrative unit; hold prior to December 1988 a referendum in the Eastern province which would determine its unification with the Northern province; and hold elections to the provincial councils of the north and east before December 1987.

While the Accord did not specify the timing and conditions under which Indian troops would enter Sri Lanka, and established no particular consultative mechanisms, Rajiv Gandhi did announce to the Lok Sabha (India's lower house of parliament) on July 30, 1987, that President Jayawardene had formally requested Indian military assistance to "implement the Indo–Sri Lankan agreement for ending the ethnic crisis," particularly since the Janatha Vimukti Peramuna (JVP) had begun to disturb the peace in the south, placing increasing demands on the Sri Lankan security forces.[17]

Stage II: Staying In

In the letters that accompanied the Accord, India requested and received Sri Lanka's assurance that mutual discussions would be held about the presence of all foreign military and intelligence personnel permitted in the country, deny the use of Trincomalee to any power unfriendly to India, develop the port's oil facilities with an Indian rather than a U.S. company, and allow India to review the VOA agreement as well as all such future agreements that might be used for intelligence or military purposes.[18]

Since the improvement in U.S.–Soviet relations had diminished the geopolitical attraction of island states such as Sri Lanka, India found its regional security objectives relatively simple to achieve. For instance, the U.S. tacitly recognized India's sphere of influence by consulting it before sending spare parts for Sri Lanka's helicopters. International praise was heaped upon Gandhi: U.S. Congressman Stephen Solarz nominated him for the Nobel Peace Prize.

In all respects other than those geopolitical, however, India's peacemaking gamble went awry. Both the Sri Lankan and Indian governments took a calculated risk in signing the Accord without the support of either Sinhalese and Tamil militants. Both governments miscalculated.

What was to go wrong with the Indian troop commitment began to go wrong immediately. Critical to the success of the Accord were Gandhi's ability to make the Tamil militants and civilians feel secure and Jayawardene's ability to convince the Buddhist Sinhalese nationalists to support the Accord. Neither government was able to fulfill its part of the political bargain. Although the Sri Lankan troop offensive was curtailed, Tamil political prisoners were released, significant

concessions were wrested from the Sri Lankan government on a new
federal formula for the country, and India promised to guarantee
everyone's good behavior, Sri Lanka's Tamil militants were not reas-
sured.When the Accord was announced, the Sinhalese rioted. More
than forty persons died, and assassination attempts were made upon
the lives of both Jayawardene and Gandhi in Sri Lanka.

Only one of the Accord's tactical military objectives was speedily
achieved. Sri Lankan troops withdrew to their barracks. Although
the Accord asked all the parties to accept India as impartial guarantor
and to disarm, only five rebel groups voluntarily relinquished their
weapons. The sixth and most powerful group, the LTTE, after giving
a hesitant verbal assent, soon became recalcitrant, surrendering only
a token number of weapons.

By 1987, the LTTE's well-trained and equipped fighters had become beneficiaries of more than ten years of Indian armed support
and sanctuary. The LTTE leader, Vellupillai Prabhakaran, complained that the Accord had failed to achieve the LTTE's political
objectives and suggested that India was protecting its own regional
interests rather than the cause of the Tamils. He argued that he was
not bound by the Accord's terms since the LTTE had been informed
only after it had been signed. Following the arrival of the Indian
Peace Keeping Force (IPKF), the LTTE organized demonstrations
against its presence in the Jaffna peninsula and accused India of
"partiality" toward rival Tamil militant groups.[19] Throughout the
1980s, the Indian and Sri Lankan governments were challenged by
the LTTE's claim to be the exclusive representative of all the Tamils.

India failed to persuade the LTTE that if it surrendered its weapons, the rebel organization could be the beneficiary of an Indian-
negotiated devolution of power. The LTTE relinquished only about
20 per cent of its arms to the IPKF and remained distrustful of the Sri
Lankan army as well as of India's role as guarantor of the peace.[20]
When the LTTE refused to turn in its weapons, India became obliged
by the terms of the Accord forcibly to disarm the militants.

At different times, different wars enveloped Sri Lanka; India played
a central role in each of them. First, there was the war between the
Sri Lankan Army and the LTTE, which the Accord had been tailored
to halt. Second, there was the murderous war between the LTTE and
all other Tamil militant and political groups, which, like the first,
would continue even after the Indians withdrew their troops. Third,
there was the war between the IPKF and the LTTE, which erupted
after the signing of the Accord. Finally, there was the vicious war
between the Sri Lankan security forces and the JVP, which escalated

after the IPKF entered Sri Lanka. India's military involvement greatly expanded the scale of the Sri Lankan conflict. After the signing of the Accord, the IPKF–LTTE war broke out in the north while the Sri Lankan army fought the JVP in the south.

Scattered protests in Tamil Nadu did not prevent India from warring against the LTTE. New Delhi had greater political flexibility vis-à-vis the Tamil Nadu government at this time, and while the plight of the Sri Lankan Tamils continued to command sympathy, public opinion was sufficiently divided about support for the LTTE. (The EPRLF and other Tamil militant organizations had developed their own popular networks in Tamil Nadu.) Immediately after the Accord was signed, India sent about 7,000 soldiers to enforce the cease-fire.

The War in the North

Throughout the peacemaking effort India's principal political problem was to convince the warring factions that the IPKF was a truly neutral and sufficiently powerful force. Between July and October 1987, while the Indians waited for the LTTE to disarm voluntarily, the guerrillas went on another intra-Tamil rampage, massacring members of the Peoples Liberation Organization of Tamil Eelam (PLOTE) and the Eelam Peoples Revolutionary Liberation Front (EPRLF), which were rivals for the planned provincial councils in the Northeast. At this time, Indian troops were accused by the Sri Lankan government and Sinhalese citizens of being too tolerant of LTTE terrorism.

The IPKF deployment rose to 20,000 during Operation Pawan, the IPKF's first major assault against the LTTE in the autumn of 1987. By early 1988, the number of Indian troops had risen to 70,000. Less than three months after the Accord was signed the IPKF launched Operation Pawan, a virtual replay of the June assault by Sri Lankan forces which India had curtailed. The LTTE's recalcitrant behavior and Sinhalese perceptions that the IPKF was partial to Tamils convinced the IPKF it would have to act if it were to assert its credibility as a peacekeeping force. Although it finally routed the Tamil militants, the IPKF inflicted high civilian casualties, severely damaged the city of Jaffna, and failed to capture the LTTE's leaders. (According to one observer, India's generals had expected to quickly round up LTTE members.) Indian casualties were higher than expected, 160 killed and 544 wounded, while civilian casualties have been estimated at between 700–3,000.[21] After the debacle at Jaffna, the LTTE moved its terrorist operations to the Eastern province, which had a mixed population of Tamils, Muslims, and Sinhalese.

What went wrong in this first encounter between the IPKF and the LTTE? The Indian forces were surprised by the well-planned LTTE defenses and by their sophisticated weaponry. While IPKF troops repeatedly disarmed the LTTE, its fighters continued to acquire weapons. India had not expected the LTTE to be able to buy arms on the international market with such ease. Through their expatriate kinsmen, their own drug networks, and the open Sri Lankan coast, the LTTE was able to purchase and bring in large weapons caches to Jaffna. By the spring of 1988, it had become evident that the LTTE had large numbers of weapons that had either been hidden away or were being freshly supplied.[22]

There were other problems. Indian soldiers were accused of committing atrocities against civilians. According to *Asia Watch*, the IPKF "replicated" human rights abuses committed earlier by the Sri Lankan security forces, including massacres, rapes, disappearances, torture, and the extra-judicial killing of detainees. Reportedly, the IPKF also indiscriminately shelled civilian areas.[23]

By the end of 1987, the Sri Lankan ethnic conflict had left about 7,000 persons dead, half a million more displaced, and the economy in ruins. The LTTE was still at large. Rajiv Gandhi had to choose either to commit India to an occupation of northeast Sri Lanka until the LTTE was ousted, or cut his losses and withdraw the IPKF. The latter policy risked tarnishing his reputation as a peacemaker at home and abroad. Gandhi chose the former policy. Until the final decision to disengage was made in 1989, the IPKF became bogged down in what Gandhi's opponents called India's "Vietnam."

After the IPKF's early fiasco at Jaffna, counter-insurgency units were shipped in, inflicting higher casualties upon the LTTE. Over the next two years, the IPKF improved its military performance against the LTTE, driving it out of strongholds such as the Batticaloa District in the Eastern Province.

As the war against the LTTE progressed, India became increasingly committed to particular Tamil clients—to those Tamil militant groups which, under the leadership of the EPRLF, had surrendered their weapons according to the terms of the Accord and had supporters in Tamil Nadu. These groups ran candidates to the provincial councils in the newly-merged Northeast Province in the November 1988 elections. (The LTTE had refused to participate.) Under IPKF supervision, the elections proceeded and an EPRLF-led government won power. India's Tamil proxies would provide another reason for the IPKF to stay mired in the ethnic crisis.

In the following two years, the LTTE and the IPKF each pursued two military goals. The Tamil militants concentrated on defending themselves against the IPKF and eliminating members of rival Tamil groups. The LTTE virtually destroyed PLOTE and TELO, the Tamil Eelam Liberation Organization, but was less successful in annihilating the EPRLF. The IPKF sought to defeat and disarm the LTTE as well as develop new forces: the Tamil National Army, an independent armed force loyal to the EPRLF, and a citizen's volunteer force which could protect its Tamil clients against the depredations of the LTTE. Meanwhile, IPKF casualties mounted. By June 1989, nearly two years after the Accord was signed, the Indian peacekeepers had suffered 900 dead and 2,500 wounded.[24]

In northeast Sri Lanka the IPKF encountered a hostile civilian population that was sympathetic to the LTTE and suspicious of India's intentions. An often-heard Tamil refrain was that the IPKF came to Sri Lanka to protect Indian strategic interests and control Trincomalee harbor rather than to protect them and the LTTE fighters. Noting the "total distrust" of the Sri Lankan Tamil civilians for the IPKF, Major-General Sardesh Pande, Commander of the IPKF, said "90 percent of the population is pro-LTTE."

"What they can't stomach," said General Pande, is that "we have suddenly entered into a conflict with the LTTE." Jaffna's Tamils remained unconvinced that the IPKF could ensure their security and were afraid that if the LTTE were vanquished, Sri Lankan forces would return to the northeast.[25]

This distrust of the local populace for the IPKF handicapped the force. In South Asia, as one analyst commented, it is difficult to find "an ethnically impartial security force . . . . At present there does not appear to be any security force that all communities of Sri Lanka believe will refrain from violating the human rights of one group or another or possibly all of them." In eastern Sri Lanka, for example, as violence between Tamils and Muslims grew, the Sri Lankan police claimed that the IPKF had turned a blind eye to attacks on Muslims.[26]

Not only Tamils and Muslims, but Sinhalese, too, mistrusted the IPKF. In response to Sinhalese complaints that the IPKF could not protect them from the LTTE, the Sri Lankan government deployed security forces in selected Sinhalese villages in the east. In the spring of 1988, the Home Guards (an auxiliary armed force of non-Tamil civilians created by a Presidential directive and subordinate to the

Ministry of Internal Security), as well as the Special Task Force (a police commando unit) continued to operate in the east, in violation of the Accord.[27]

Clearly, the presence of the IPKF had transformed the nature of the conflict. It led to a protracted war in the north, and spurred a deadly war of terror in the south, where its presence provoked the ire of Sinhalese extremists, especially of the JVP.

The War in the South

By the terms of the Accord the Sri Lankan army had been removed from the battlefields of the north (and confined initially to its barracks). The IPKF had gradually assumed its functions. The release of his forces allowed President Jayawardene to mass them in the densely populated south, where, the JVP, a Sinhalese terrorist organization, had begun to wage a bloody war.

The JVP, a left-oriented movement, drew its cadre from educated but unemployed youth. Successive governments had tried to bring the JVP into the democratic process by legalizing its activities, but to no avail. During the 1970s, the JVP had led an insurrection to which the army responded brutally; an estimated 10,000 people died. In the 1980s it draped itself in the flag of Sinhalese nationalism. Led by Rohana Wijeweera, the JVP developed an estimated one million supporters in the late 1980s, and controlled many student bodies and unions. After July 1987 it launched a campaign to get the IPKF out of Sri Lanka and to end all concessions of political autonomy made to the Tamils in the Accord.

The JVP began to execute members of Jayawardene's United National Party, other politicians, and thousands of civilians. Between September and November 1987 alone the armed factions of the JVP killed 50 to 100 local UNP officials and supporters. Between 1987 and 1989, about 50 people were being killed each day.[28] In the first half of 1989 more than 3,000 people were killed and their bodies were left in public places as warnings. The JVP also successfully enforced large-scale public transport strikes (often by killing workers) which crippled the civil administration. It paralyzed Sri Lanka's economy through strikes and threats against shopkeepers carrying Indian merchandise.

In February 1989 parliamentary elections were held. The polls were boycotted by the JVP (and the LTTE), and more than one thousand party workers, candidates, and citizens were killed. Now, Sri Lanka's new President, former Prime Minister Ranasinghe Premdasa, seeing that his pleas to the JVP to enter mainstream politics had fallen on deaf ears, authorized Sri Lankan security forces to retaliate. They did, without inhibition. In a single month, August 1989, about 1,000 people were killed during a government attack on the JVP. Increasingly, vigilante groups controlled by Sri Lankan security forces and "anti-subversive" paramilitary organizations such as the "Black Cats" and the "Peoples Revolutionary Red Army" were implicated in the killings, which included the "necklacing" of JVP suspects. Special legislation was enacted by the Sri Lankan government, granting security forces immunity from prosecution in the conduct of the civil war.

Corpses burned along the road until December 1989, when the Sri Lankan government achieved a critical coup. It decapitated the JVP leadership, thereby largely resolving the crisis of terrorism inspired by the IPKF presence. While the casualties in the Tamil war in the north prior to 1990 have been estimated at around 8,000, the casualties from the JVP insurgency totalled about 30,000. As late as May 1990, the killings continued in the south at the reduced rate of five persons each week. According to military sources, in 1990 about 1,000 JVP activists continued to operate in Sri Lanka's south.[29]

Stage III: Getting Out

In December 1987, an important change in leadership had occurred in Sri Lanka. Presidential elections were held in which Jayawardene, now over 80 years old, decided not run. Ranasinghe Premdasa, the former Prime Minister, was elected to succeed him. Premdasa, who had refused to attend the ceremonies celebrating the signing of the Indo–Sri Lanka Accord, had campaigned on a promise to get Indian soldiers out of Sri Lanka. On June 1, 1989, Premdasa publicly asked Indian troops to leave Sri Lanka within six weeks. The announcement caught the Indians unaware.

The Sri Lankan government was suffering under the extraordinary pressure of the JVP's anti-Indian terrorism in the south. The longer the IPKF stayed in Sri Lanka, the greater the number of new recruits which the JVP could induct.[30] And, barring the few Tamil groups allied with India, President Premdasa could count also on the support of many Tamils and thus on a national consensus on getting the IPKF out of Sri Lanka. Only the EPRLF and its associates in the Northeast Province (including TELO and ENDLF, the Eelam National Democratic Liberation Front) as well as TULF political leaders in Tamil Nadu, were outspoken in their demand that the IPKF stay on. If Indian troops left they would be the LTTE's first victims, unable to sustain their authority in the Northeast provincial councils.

In order to resolve the civil wars, Premdasa took a different gamble from that of former President Jayawardene. He calculated that if the IPKF were evicted from the island he might be able to forge domestic political compromises, bringing the LTTE back into the democratic process and reducing support for the JVP.

Premdasa changed his operational partners, replacing India with the LTTE. On May 12, 1989, the Sri Lankan government opened talks with the LTTE, excluding India's representatives; the parties discussed their common goal of evicting the IPKF. The LTTE needed respite from the continuing IPKF assaults in the north, which were inflicting heavy casualties on the Tamil militants. The IPKF had succeeded militarily to the extent that it had deprived the LTTE of its urban bases and driven it into the jungles. Thus, for its own tactical reasons, the LTTE encouraged Premdasa to believe that it would negotiate seriously only after an IPKF withdrawal. In December 1989 the LTTE even formed a political party: the Popular Front of Liberation Tigers, which did not include "Eelam" in its name.[31]

Premdasa accused the Indians of having failed after trying for two years to disarm the LTTE. The remaining 45,000 IPKF troops, he said, must depart by the end of July 1989: "The Indians came on our invitation and helped us. Now they must go and help us by going."[32] Sri Lanka asserted that the IPKF had failed to implement the terms of the Accord by ensuring neither the cessation of hostilities nor the surrender of weapons by Tamil militants. (During this tense period the LTTE was responsible for assassinating leaders of the TULF and PLOTE, who supported the IPKF's continued presence in Sri Lanka.)

The Sri Lankan government derived political strength in the process of negotiation with India because it commanded broad popular support on the issue of the IPKF withdrawal. It also tried to compensate for its weakness in relation to India by making its demands public. Premdasa boycotted a meeting of regional foreign ministers at the South Asian Association for Regional Cooperation (SAARC) forum in Islamabad, protesting India's alleged intransigence on the withdrawal of the IPKF.

Premdasa's demand that the IPKF depart Sri Lanka raised three concerns for Rajiv Gandhi: he had to determine how to extricate his forces from this dirty war without chaos in Sri Lanka, without a loss of prestige and political support at home during an election year, and without abandoning his Tamil clients to face the wrath of the LTTE.[33]

Shortly after getting into the Sri Lankan ethnic war, India's leaders had become preoccupied with the question of getting their troops out. The Indians were not averse in principle to disengagement. The costs to them, and the complexities of fighting this ethnic war, had become clear. The IPKF could not eradicate the LTTE entirely without high Tamil civilian casualties, and those casualties carried significant political costs in both Tamil Nadu and Sri Lanka. Especially after the assault on Jaffna, the IPKF soldiers had to fight with "our right arm tied behind our back," as one IPKF veteran phrased it.[34] Indian forces were finding it difficult to function in an environment where not only the Tamil population but also the host government was increasingly hostile. Still, because Premdasa's demand was unilateral and public, India could not immediately accept it.

Other factors adversely affected India. The deteriorating civil war was costing India dearly in money (estimated at around $150 million in May 1989) and in men, and frustration was growing over the number of casualties in this "peacemaking" operation. By early 1989 the war against the LTTE was recognized as a stalemate. Even India's oldest ally, the Soviet Union, had become critical. *Izvestia* wrote that India was beginning to look like "a big power trying to impose its will on a small state" and Soviet officials voiced their disagreement with India's policy.[35]

Still, it was an election year. Gandhi, whose political reputation was suffering from the Bofors arms purchasing scandal and significant regional electoral difficulties, could not afford to be perceived as succumbing to Sri Lanka's unilateral demand. Thus, Gandhi stressed India's successes as guarantor of the Accord: it had been instrumental in getting Tamils their rights from the Sri Lankan government and convincing the militants to give up their demand for Eelam. In Sri Lanka, however, Gandhi's political objectives became limited, focusing on measures to "save face," that is, to withdraw according to an Indian timetable rather than that prescribed by Premdasa, and to protect its local Tamil clients. India also wanted to avoid a new stream of refugees heading for Tamil Nadu as a result of the IPKF's withdrawal.

Gandhi insisted that the Accord was a bilateral agreement, and that India was its guarantor. Any withdrawal of the IPKF had to be linked to the terms of the Accord, which included a greater devolution of powers to the pro-Indian Tamil authorities in the Northeast Province. The withdrawal, said Gandhi, had to be "conditional, . . . a joint, parallel, and linked exercise along with the devolution process so that the Tamils and the provincial council can look after their security." Calling Premdasa's demand "unilateral and unrealistic," India iterated its "firm commitment to the phased withdrawal of the IPKF as soon as practicable."[36] Provisions of the Accord that concerned India and that remained inadequately implemented included the creation of conditions which would permit all persons displaced by ethnic violence to return home and the withdrawal of all paramilitary personnel from the north and east.

The government of India argued that as early as January 1, 1989 it had initiated a phased withdrawal. Further, it had announced that as the security situation improved in the Northeastern Province, "as the devolution of power became effective," "as the Indo-Sri Lanka agreements get progressively implemented, and as the mischief-making potential of extremist elements opposed to the agreement is reduced, further withdrawals will be made in consultation with the Sri Lankan government."[37] India pulled out about a third of its forces and roughly 43,000 troops remained in Sri Lanka.

As the July 29, 1989, deadline approached, a diplomatic impasse was reached. President Premdasa broke the standoff between the two governments on July 19 by sending a letter to Rajiv Gandhi. Gandhi responded by making gradual token reductions, withdrawing, for example, 620 soldiers on July 29, 875 soldiers on August 6, and 700 soldiers on August 8.

Negotiations resumed. Initially, India wanted a fifteen-day ceasefire to be observed by the LTTE and the establishment of committees to oversee the withdrawal process, while Sri Lanka wanted IPKF forces to be confined to barracks as of mid-September. On September 18, 1989 an agreement was finally reached in which Sri Lanka and India each achieved some goals. The IPKF would withdraw without any official linkage to the status of devolution in the Northeast Province, but it would do so in phases. Control of security in the Northeast was to be gradually turned over to the Sri Lankan army and police. Institutions to facilitate and monitor the disengagement process were to be established. A coordinating committee would include representatives of the principal political and ethnic groups in the Northeast province. A security coordination group to ensure that a vacuum would not occur after the IPKF withdrawal would include the Chief Minister of the Northeast province (an EPRLF leader and Indian client), an Indian general, and a Sri Lankan defense official. A military observer group would include the commanders of the Sri Lankan army and the IPKF. India agreed to withdraw between 1,500 and 1,600 soldiers each week, ending its deployment seven months later in March 1990.

The months prior to the final departure of the remaining IPKF troops from Sri Lanka were a nervous time for India's Tamil clients. It was widely assumed that the LTTE would turn on the EPRLF as soon as the IPKF left. The Tamil National Army and the citizens volunteer force, trained by the IPKF and created to support the EPRLF government, were expected simply to disintegrate, and it became quickly evident that the various Indo–Sri Lankan disengagement committees were unable to affect the growing turmoil on the ground.

When India began seriously to consider a full military withdrawal, the security of its local Tamil clients had become a priority. The LTTE had a long record of massacring its opponents and India was convinced that the LTTE, rather than Sri Lankan forces, would fill the void when the IPKF left. It was correct. Besides, the EPRLF, which had ridden to electoral success in the November 1988 provincial elections on the IPKF's coattails, had only a small stock of legitimacy among the Tamil population. Before the IPKF's departure, India attempted one final act of mediation to assure the security of its local clients. The new Prime Minister, V.P. Singh, asked the new DMK Chief Minister of Tamil Nadu to try to persuade all the warring Tamil groups to coexist following the IPKF withdrawal.[38] The effort failed. The Chief Minister of the Northeast Province, V. Perumal, fled to India before the departure of the IPKF, and as Indian troops withdrew, the LTTE predictably took over the civil administration of the Northeast Province. As one of their final acts in Sri Lanka the Indians helped members of the EPRLF alliance to escape aboard Indian ships, providing them with sanctuary in Tamil Nadu and the state of Orissa. By March 1990 there were already 3,000 Tamil refugees, many of them fighters from the EPRLF, ENDLF, TELO, and PLOTE, in camps in Tamil Nadu.[39]

In India, a change of leadership guaranteed the steady pace of the withdrawal. In December 1989, Gandhi was defeated in the elections and V. P. Singh, leader of the opposition Janata Dal party (a member of the National Front coalition) became Prime Minister of India. Singh's earliest efforts in foreign affairs were to seek reconciliation with all India's neighbors including Pakistan, Nepal and Sri Lanka. Said President Premdasa, "The National Front government has assured us that the withdrawal is unconditional, and we are happy about it."[40] The troop withdrawal was completed without impediment in March 1990.

In certain respects, then, changes in leadership did affect the processes of intervention and withdrawal. Although neither Jayawardene nor Gandhi lost power as a direct consequence of the ethnic conflict—Jayawardene was extremely old and Gandhi was beset by numerous other problems—the ascent of Premdasa did make the IPKF's presence in Sri Lanka more complicated while V. P. Singh's victory did facilitate India's withdrawal from the island state.

When the last Indian troops left Trincomalee harbor on March 24 1990, Auld Lang Syne was played by a military band. 1,155 Indians were dead and 2,984 were seriously wounded. The IPKF claimed 2,200 LTTE members dead while the LTTE said that only 683 of its cadre were lost. According to some Indian generals the war in Sri Lanka had been " a politician's war fought by soldiers with one arm tied behind their backs."[41]

Yet Another War

India, which first fanned the flames of ethnic violence by providing shelter and support to Sri Lankan Tamil militants in Tamil Nadu, ended its military involvement in the conflict in 1990. It failed to act as a neutral armed force, interposing itself between the government and the Tamil guerrillas in Sri Lanka. It could neither crush nor disarm the LTTE. Throughout the 1980s, a major flaw in India's strategy of intervention was that the leverage it exercised over the parties to the conflict was never sufficient to make it a successful military broker of peace. Still, India did assert its regional dominance in South Asia, successfully eliciting important foreign policy concessions from the Sri Lankan government.

In the short run, the IPKF presence had deterred the secessionists. And, while its presence incited the JVP to killing, it also relieved Sri Lanka's troops from their northern responsibilities to a degree sufficient for them to turn their attention to the war in the south. The Indian troop withdrawal also achieved certain short-term ends. It encouraged the guerrillas to go to the negotiating table and decreased the political pressure on the Sri Lankan government. Yet, the disengagement of India's troops did not resolve any of the fundamental issues dividing the LTTE and the Sri Lankan government. These would have to be negotiated again, without India's military presence.

The Indian troop withdrawal left a stubborn Sri Lankan government negotiating with an erratic and dangerous partner. The LTTE had a shabby record of negotiation. It had not renounced separatism and continued to kill Tamil moderates as well as Tamil militants belonging to groups favored by India. As expected, after the IPKF left, the LTTE quickly became de facto master of the Northeast.

The War in Sri Lanka

An uneasy peace held between the LTTE and the Sri Lankan govern-ment for two and a half months. The terms contained in the Accord were renegotiated, including the staging of new elections in the Northeast, the disarming of the LTTE, and the devolution of powers to provincial authorities. Sri Lankan officers and soldiers were con-fined to their barracks in Tamil areas while the talks progressed. The LTTE, however, with a force still estimated at between 5,000 and 15,000, refused once more to surrender its weapons prior to elec-tions, insisting that the Sri Lankan government was not offering enough concessions.[42] It balked, too, at the government's decision to discuss peace with all the Tamil groups.

In June 1990 the situation was tense. Sri Lankan army officers were chafing to return to battle against the LTTE. While Premdasa negotiated and armed, the LTTE built up its strength and obliterated its Tamil rivals in the Northeast. In the middle of June, the cease-fire collapsed. The LTTE took 800 Sri Lankan policemen prisoner, mas-sacring 200 of them immediately. The war began again, escalating rapidly.

Once more in Sri Lanka, both sides to the conflict chose to use military means to pursue political goals. The LTTE and the Sri Lan-kan government accused one another of negotiating in bad faith and refusing to accede to fundamental political demands.[43] The Sri Lan-kan government, emboldened by its success against the JVP, seemed determined to annihilate the LTTE, regardless of the number of civilian casualties. By August 1990, an estimated 14,000 persons had died since the conflict first erupted, with 2,856 combatants killed since June 1990.[44]

A year later, in August 1991, a brutal, stalemated war continued between Sri Lankan government troops and the LTTE. The militants gained in strength, flaunting new anti-aircraft weapons and armor-plated bulldozers. Says Sri Lankan army Lieutenant General Hamil-ton Wanasinghe, the LTTE "can no longer be considered a guerilla outfit . . . (they are a) conventional force."[45] A military solution to this ethnic conflict seems even less likely now.

India's Role

Shortly after the last Indian soldier departed Sri Lanka, an Indian policy maker said "We're happy to be out of the island. There will be no question of a re-induction ever again, even if the Sri Lankans beg for it."[46] The question, however, remains: How long can New Delhi remain politically neutral or militarily aloof from the war?

While the situation in Sri Lanka reverted largely to that which prevailed in 1987 when the government and the LTTE were at war, the regional political context of the conflict has significantly altered. In India, national public support for the LTTE has fallen. The LTTE has not aided its case across India: it is thought to have massacred nineteen leaders of the EPRLF in Madras. (In Tamil Nadu, however, the LTTE retains significant support among leaders of the state government.) Inside Sri Lanka, such actions have allowed the government to portray its new war as a war waged against LTTE extremists and not against the Tamil people.

In the near term, a number of factors argue against Indian military re-involvement. The IPKF's military misadventure is all too recent, and India's own ethnic wars too inflamed for another IPKF-led intervention. While it is afflicted by communal violence at home, fights for the union in Kashmir (where the potential for a large-scale conventional war with Pakistan exists), against Sikh militants in Punjab, and violence in Assam, the Indian center is unlikely to support Sri Lankan Tamil demands for a separate state.

Still, the domestic political context in India continues to evolve, with each shift affecting policy toward the LTTE. The complex power relations between New Delhi and Madras remain an important factor in determining India's responses to the Sri Lankan crisis. In 1990, the Chief Minister of Tamil Nadu, DMK leader Muthuvel Karanunidhi, supported the LTTE, and his DMK party was a member of V. P. Singh's fragile and short-lived governing coalition in New Delhi. In November of that year, Ranjan Wijeratne (who would be assassinted a few months later, reportedly by the LTTE) complained that the LTTE were still able to ship about 10 shiploads of weapons per day from the Tamil Nadu coastline.[47]

In 1991, however, changes in leadership once more instigated a dramatic shift in New Delhi's policies. In November 1990, the socialist Chandra Shekhar became Prime Minister when Singh failed to survive a parliamentary vote of no confidence. Shekhar's new government rested upon the support of Gandhi's Congress-I party, which was allied, in turn, with the former governing party of Tamil Nadu—and DMK opponent—the AIADMK.

On January 30, 1991, the President of India dismissed the DMK government of Tamil Nadu, dissolved the assemblies, and placed the state under federal rule. (Numerous reports plausibly suggest that Rajiv Gandhi's Congress Party encouraged the dismissal.) The President accused the DMK of failing to maintain law and order and allegedly encouraging political contacts with the LTTE as well as aiding the guerrillas' military activities on Indian soil, particularly along the state's coastal areas. The Sri Lanka government, which had long accused the DMK government of permitting the LTTE to smuggle arms from Tamil Nadu into northern Sri Lanka, welcomed New Delhi's actions.

While the dismissal was bitterly criticized by many in India, it was defended by the Congress Party. Said a spokesman for Gandhi's party: there is an "obvious linkage between the LTTE and the anti-national and secessionist elements in the rest of the country."[48] Gandhi eventually withdrew his party's support from the government of Chandra Shekhar in New Delhi, and new elections were called for May and June of 1991.

While campaigning for these elections, on May 21, 1991, Gandhi himself paid the highest price for the intervention and for Indira Gandhi's and his own earlier armed support of the LTTE. At Sriperumbudur in Tamil Nadu, was brutally assassinated by a suicide bomber, identified later as a young Tamil woman. India's Central Bureau of Investigation and Sri Lankan Lankan authorities both traced the crime to the LTTE. In July 1991, the principal suspect committed suicide when Indian investigators surrounded her hideout.

As this bloody story of India's entanglement in Sri Lanka's war continued to unfold, the extent to which the Tamil war has deeply penetrated India's own body politic became even more apparent. So long as it remains unresolved, India's central and state governments risk once again being drawn in, either as intervenors or victims.

Abbreviations

ENDLF	Eelam National Liberation Front
EPRLF	Eelam Peoples Revolutionary Liberation Front
EROS	Eelam Revolutionary Organization of Students
IPKF	Indian Peace Keeping Force
JVP	Janatha Vimukthi Peramuna (Peoples Liberation Front)
LTTE	Liberation Tigers of Tamil Eelam
PLOTE	Peoples Liberation Organization of Tamil Eelam
SLFP	Sri Lanka Freedom Party
TELO	Tamil Eelam Liberation Organization
TULF	Tamil United Liberation Front
UNP	United National Party

Chronology

1948–1983

April 2, 1948: Independence from Great Britain.

1956: Official Language Act (Sinhala only language law).

1958: Tamil language (special provision) act promises "reasonable use" of Tamil in education.

1970: Standardization of marks policy initiated; discriminates against Tamil students.

1972: New constitutional amendments make Sinhalese official language and give Buddhism a special status in Sri Lanka.

1976: TULF passes resolution demanding establishment of Tamil Eelam.

1977: National elections; fall of Bandaranaika's government; Jayawardene becomes Prime Minister.

August 1977: Riots leave 25,000 Tamils homeless; 112 officially dead.

1978: Article 19 of constitution recognizes Tamil as a national language.

October 1981: First presidential elections.

December 1982: Referendum to extend term of parliament.

July–August 1983: Tamil–Sinhalese riots.

1987

May 26: Sri Lankan government launches offensive against Tamils in north.

June 4: India drops supplies over Jaffna using transport and fighter aircraft.

July 29: Indo–Sri Lanka peace accord.

August 18: Attempt to assassinate Jayawardene.

October 5: Twelve LTTE members attempt suicide after being captured by IPKF; five survive.

October 21: IPKF launches assault against Jaffna.

1989

April 26: LTTE opens talks with the Sri Lankan government.

June 1: Premdasa requests withdrawal of IPKF.

June: Premdasa declares that the IPKF must leave Sri Lanka forthwith.

July: Indians respond by making a few gradual and token troop reductions: 620 soldiers withdrawn on July 26 (the date set by Premdasa), 875 soldiers on August 6, and 700 on August 8.

September 18: Sri Lanka and India reach an agreement on the withdrawal of the IPKF.

December: LTTE forms a political party, the Popular Front of Liberation Tigers.

December: Rajiv Gandhi is defeated in the elections and V.P. Singh of the opposition Janata Dal becomes Prime Minister of India.

1990

March 24: Indian troop withdrawal completed.

Mid-June: Cease-fire between LTTE and Sri Lankan government after the IPKF withdrawal collapses. The LTTE takes 800 Sri Lankan policemen prisoner, massacring 200 of them immediately.

November: Indian Prime Minister V.P. Singh loses vote of confidence. Supported by Rajiv Gandhi, Chandra Shekar becomes new Prime Minister.

1991

January 30: President of India dismisses Tamil Nadu government.

May 21: Rajiv Gandhi assassinated in Tamil Nadu while campaigning for re-election by suicide bomber identified later as a young Tamil woman.

July: Principal suspect in Gandhi's murder commits suicide when Indian authorities surround her hideout.

Notes

1. See Stanley J. Heginbotham, *Sri Lanka's Gamble for Ethnic Peace, CRS Issue Brief,* November 6, 1987, p.6; also S.J. Tambiah, *Sri Lanka: Ethnic Fratricide and the Dismantling of Democracy* (Chicago: University of Chicago Press, 1986); Minority Rights Group, *The Tamils of Sri Lanka,* Report No. 25; and Marshall R. Singer, "Prospects for Conflict Management in the Sri Lankan Ethnic Crisis," in Joseph V. Montville, ed. *Conflict and Peacemaking in Multiethnic Societies* (Cambridge, MA: Lexington Books, 1990), pp. 259–287.

2. Singer, "Prospects for Conflict Management," p. 263.

3. *Far Eastern Economic Review,* (FEER) July 30, 1987, p. 22.

4. Quoted in P. Venkateshwar Rao, "Ethnic Conflict in Sri Lanka: India's Role and Perception," *Asian Survey,* 28, no. 4 (April 1988):419–436, at p. 420.

5. Singer, "Prospects for Conflict Management," p. 273; also see *Christian Science Monitor,* April 16, 1986.

6. *Washington Post,* May 30, 1991; Rao, "Ethnic Conflict," p. 424; and "Sri Lanka Rebels: Ominous Presence in Tamil Nadu." *India Today,* pp. 88–94, March 31, 1984.

7. Rao, "Ethnic Conflict," p. 424. For an assessment of Indira Gandhi's policies toward the Sri Lankan Tamils, see Maya Chadda "Domestic Determinants of India's Foreign Policy in the 1980s: The Role of Sikh and Tamil Nationalism," *Journal of South Asian and Middle Eastern Studies,* 11, nos. 1/2 (Fall/Winter 1987):21–35.

8. Mahnaz Ispahani, "Taming the Tigers," *New Republic,* July 27, 1987, pp.14–16, p. 16; and P. Saravanamuttu, "Instability in Sri Lanka," *Survival,* pp. 455–468, p. 459.

9. See Singer, "Prospects for Conflict Management," p. 270.

10. See "Playing With Fire," *Hindustan Times,* January 10, 1987.

11. *Times of India,* January 9, 1987, and Singer, "Prospects for Conflict Management," p. 276.

12. See Ralph Buultjens, "The Ethics of Excess and Indian Intervention in Sri Lanka," *Ethics and International Affairs,* 3 (1989):73–100, p. 97.

13. For a good legal-political analysis, see M. L. Marasinghe, "Ethnic Politics and Constitutional Reform: The Indo-Sri Lanka Accord," *International and Comparative Law Quarterly,* 37, part 3 (July 1988):551–587. Pakistan did condemn the invasion, calling it a "deplorable infringement of international law." *Washington Post,* June 8, 1987.

14. Jayawardene quoted in *India Today,* August 15, 1989, p.29. Also see Ralph R. Premdas and S.W.R. de A. Samarasinghe "Sri Lanka's Ethnic Conflict: The Indo-Lanka Peace Accord," *Asian Survey,* 28 no.6 (June 1988):676–690, at p. 676.

15. See *The Indo-Sri Lanka Agreement. Hearings before the Subcommittee on Asian and Pacific Affairs of the Committee on Foreign Affairs,* U.S. Congress, August 6, 1987, p. 13.

16. See text of *The Indo-Sri Lanka Agreement to Establish Peace and Normalcy in Sri Lanka.* Embassy of Sri Lanka, Washington, D.C.

17. Gandhi's statement excerpted in *Hindu,* July 31, 1987. According to Gandhi, Jayawardene had formally requested "appropriate Indian military assistance to ensure the cessation of hostilities and surrender of arms in the Jaffna peninsula and, if required, in the Eastern Province. He also requested for [sic] air transport to move some of Sri Lanka [sic] troops from Jaffna to points South [sic]." Said Gandhi: "Let me repeat that our troops have landed in Sri Lanka in response to a specific and formal request of the Government of Sri Lanka, who have invoked our obligations and commitments under the Indo-Sri Lankan agreement."

18. Heginbotham, "Sri Lanka's Gamble," p. 12.

19. See *Times of India,* September 9, 1987; Rao, "Ethnic Conflict," p.434; and Premdas and Samarasinghe, "Sri Lanka's Ethnic Conflict," p. 682. Also see Heginbotham, "Sri Lanka's Gamble," p. 8.

20. Heginbotham, "Sri Lanka's Gamble," p. 9.

21. Ibid., pp. 9–10.

22. *Hindustan Times,* April 6, 1988; also see Major-General Sardesh Pande's remarks in *Hindu,* April 2, 1988. See also *Hindu,* June 10, 1989 and Singer, "Prospects for Conflict Management," p. 274. On India's surprise see Bryan Pfaffenberger, "Sri Lanka in 1987: Indian Intervention and the Resurgence of the JVP," *Asian Survey,* 28 no.2, (February 1988):137–147, at p. 144.

23. *Asia Watch,* News Release, August 17, 1989.

24. *Economist,* June 10, 1989, p. 32

25. Quoted in *Hindu,* April 2, 1988, and *Hindustan Times,* April 6, 1988.

26. *Asia Watch,* News from Sri Lanka, January-April 1988, p. 4.

27. *Asia Watch,* News from Sri Lanka, pp. 3–4.

28. Heginbotham, "Sri Lanka's Gamble," p. 10.

29. *Asiaweek,* May 4, 1990, pp. 28–29 and *New York Times,* September 17, 1989.

30. One estimate made in mid-1989 suggested that the JVP commanded broad-based support in the south. Approximately 70 percent of the Sinhalese population (mainly educated but poor and unemployed persons) were estimated to be sympathetic to the JVP. *India Today,* July 15, 1989, p. 28.

31. A year later, after a new war had broken out between the Sri Lankan government and the LTTE, the minister of state for defense, Ranjan Wijeratne, said in response to a question about why the LTTE had decided to negotiate with his government: "It was a question of survival—the IPKF had nearly decimated them." Interview in *India Today,* July 15, 1990, p. 16. Also see Saravanamuttu, "Instability in Sri Lanka," p. 462.

32. Quoted in *Asiaweek,* June 30, 1989, p. 18. See also *India Today,* July 31, 1989, p. 30.

33. The Indian Foreign Secretary said: "Nobody who has relied on you should be let down." Quoted in *India Abroad,* August 11, 1989, p. 5.

34. Quoted in *India Today,* July 15, 1990, p. 15. After the IPKF had withdrawn, Wijeratne assessed the IPKF's predicament: "The IPKF had come here not to fight but to keep the peace. The IPKF did not want civilian casualties and so did not launch a war." See *India Today,* July 15, 1990, p. 16.

35. See *India Today,* May 31, 1989, p. 51; July 31, 1990, p. 31; *New York Times,* September 17, 1990.

36. Text of Indian Foreign Office statement in *Hindu,* June 13, 1989.

37. *Hindu,* June 13, 1989.

38. *FEER,* January 25, 1990, p. 10.

39. *India Today,* March 15, 1990, p. 34.

40. Quoted by Bhabani Sen Gupta in *India Today,* February 28, 1990, p. 70.

41. *FEER,* April 5, 1990, p. 10. For statistics also see *India Today,* April 15, 1990, pp. 65–66.

42. *Washington Post,* June 17, 1990.

43. Saravanamuttu, "Instability in Sri Lanka," p. 463.

44. *New York Times,* July 24 and August 12, 1990.

45. *Washington Times,* August 8, 1991; and *Asiaweek,* August 9, 1991.

46. *Asiaweek,* March 30, 1990, p. 26.

47. *Washington Post,* May 30, 1991.

48. *Foreign Broadcast Information Service,* FBIS, Near East and South Asia, January 31, 1991, p. 44, and February 5, 1991 p. 59.

8

Getting In: The Initial Stage of Military Intervention

CHARLES A. KUPCHAN

Research support for this chapter was provided by Princeton University Center of International Studies.

The principal aim of this chapter is to draw on the preceding case studies to examine the process of getting in: why and how states decide to engage in direct military intervention. The chapter focuses on the events and considerations that motivate the intervening state to deploy its own ground forces in a combat role on the territory of the target state. The analysis concentrates on two key sets of questions. First, what assumptions motivated decision makers to escalate from indirect to direct intervention? How were broader political goals translated into specific military objectives? Second, does the notion of the "slippery slope" accurately capture the nature of the process through which states found themselves bogged down in costly, protracted interventions? Did elites have a fairly accurate assessment of the likely costs of intervention when they decided to engage their own troops in the conflict, or were they dragged into a quagmire by unforeseen events?

The analysis shows that direct military intervention is precipitated by developments that threaten to alter fundamentally the political status quo in the target state. These developments take the form of a major change in domestic political alignments or in the military balance among actors within the target state. Intervention takes place when these changes have convinced elites that they have been left with a very clear choice: either intervene directly or be prepared to abandon the objectives that had initially motivated indirect intervention.

The analysis also shows that the concept of the "slippery slope" does not present a widely applicable explanation of how protracted military intervention comes about. For the most part, the case studies indicate that elites were aware of the potential magnitude of the operation that they were authorizing. In some cases, division-level assets were introduced at the outset of the intervention. In the cases in which only a small number of troops engaged in the initiation of hostilities, the historical record suggests that decision makers were often aware that the scope of their commitment would likely escalate. The initial assumptions informing the decision to intervene were, however, erroneous in two important respects. First, elites believed that the conflict would be relatively short in duration. Second, they believed that the application of military force would enable them to achieve, in a durable way, their political objectives. These erroneous assumptions appear to be rooted in a tendency among elites both to underestimate the difficulties involved in gathering reliable political intelligence and to overestimate the ability of superior military force to resolve deep-rooted ethnic and political divisions.

The analysis indicates, however, that even a more accurate picture of the difficulties likely to be encountered would not have dissuaded decision makers from proceeding with military intervention. Elites were driven by a strategic logic informed by powerful reputational and intrinsic interests. This logic seemed impervious to warnings of a quagmire and, importantly, to the possibility that domestic politics might come to constrain severely the ability of elites to conduct a foreign war. Nor does cross-national learning seem to have taken place; elites in one state do not appear to have drawn lessons from the previous experiences of other states involved in costly, protracted military interventions.

This chapter, the structure of which follows the same conceptual framework used by the case study authors, begins by considering the broad external environment in which the intervention occurred. It then examines those developments in the target state that precipitated intervention, and finally focuses on the assumptions and decision-making dynamics that lay behind the initial decision to intervene. A chief goal of the chapter is to draw out generalizations from the individual case studies. At the same time, care will be taken to identify outliers and to explain why a specific case differs from the others in some critical dimension.

The final section of the chapter addresses—in a somewhat speculative manner—a series of questions that emerge from the analysis. What were the sources of the erroneous assumptions that informed the decision to intervene militarily. Were elites misled by faulty intelligence? Was the problem a cognitive one? Should elites reasonably have foreseen that they were entering a quagmire or were random events responsible for turning a well-planned and realistic operation into a long and painful struggle?

The Setting

The instances of direct military intervention examined above are, with the exception of Cuba's role in Angola, the culmination of a long-term involvement between the intervener and the target state. Years of effort to shape indirectly the political landscape in the target state usually preceded the decision to introduce combat forces. This interest stemmed from one or two sources. The intervening state was motivated either by global security concerns shaped by the Cold War (the United States and Cuba), or by more immediate security concerns stemming from geographic proximity (South Africa, the Soviet Union, India, Syria, and Israel).

In all of the cases, the discrete decision to intervene was precipitated by a specific event—usually a military setback. But this even served more as an excuse for intervention than a root cause. Direct intervention usually had already been given consideration, and the setback served principally to rally sufficient support among elites for the operation to begin. In all but one case—that of Israel—the momentum for intervention was provided by changes in the target state, not by a shift in the policy goals of the intervener. Put differently, the goals pursued by the intervening state did not change before the decision to introduce military force. Rather, elites perceived that military force was required to achieve the same goals that had previously been sought through indirect means. In some cases indirect efforts had proved inadequate from the start; direct intervention was the culmination of growing frustration. In other cases indirect efforts were deemed no longer adequate because of new conditions in the target state. In either case, elites calculated that only direct military intervention would allow them to achieve their goals. As the following review of the cases shows, it was usually a perceived or anticipated change in the political landscape in the target state that induced the intervening state to step up its level of involvement.[1]

In Angola, foreign intervention was triggered by the civil war that broke out following Portugal's decision to withdraw from its colonies in Africa. South Africa viewed this conflict as posing a threat to its control in Namibia, to its access to hydroelectric power generated in southern Angola, and more generally to the status quo in Southern Africa. When the Marxist, pro-Soviet MPLA appeared poised to defeat its rivals, the South Africans intervened on behalf of UNITA and the FNLA. With the military balance decidedly altered in favor of pro-Western forces, Cuba sent combat troops to prevent the defeat of the MPLA. Both South Africa and Cuba intervened directly only when it became apparent that indirect assistance would not succeed in securing their clients' military superiority.

Before intervening in Sri Lanka, India for years exercised indirect influence over the struggle between Sinhalese and Tamils on the island nation just off its coast. India's interest in resolving ethnic conflict in Sri Lanka was partly a function of domestic politics: southern India contains a sizable Tamil population. But the Indians—

246 CHARLES A. KUPCHAN

staunch proponents of nonalignment—were also worried about Sri Lanka's drift toward strategic cooperation with the United States. Direct military intervention was precipitated by a major offensive launched by the Sri Lankan army against the Tamils. In return for a Sri Lankan pledge to pursue a more non-aligned foreign policy, India agreed to monitor and guarantee an uneasy truce in Sri Lanka, a task that was to require some 100,000 combat troops.

Moscow's interests in Afghanistan stemmed from a long-term preoccupation with security and political stability along the Soviet Union's southern borders. When a coup brought a leftist, pro-Soviet leadership (the PDPA) to Afghanistan in 1978, the Soviets grew committed to ensuring that the country remained in their orbit. Military intervention was precipitated by a power struggle in Afghanistan in which the leader of the PDPA was murdered. The new leadership showed little willingness to acquiesce to dictates from Moscow. The Soviets sent in roughly 100,000 troops, installed a new leader, and set about defending the government against mounting opposition.

The United States in 1954 took over from the French the task of defending South Vietnam against communist North Vietnam. The growing communist insurgency in the south and the instability of South Vietnam's government forced the United States to choose between abandoning its goals or intervening directly. The decision to send combat troops was triggered by Viet Cong attacks on U.S. advisers' barracks at Pleiku in 1965. The United States retaliated by bombing North Vietnam and deploying 3,500 Marines to protect the air base at Da Nang. Division-level assets soon followed.

Syrian interests in Lebanon had deep historical roots; Lebanon had been part of Syria until 1920 and the Ba'ath regime therefore claimed rights of political hegemony. When the Lebanese civil war threatened to splinter the country and create independent PLO and Christian states, Syria intervened against the side that enjoyed military superiority—the leftist Muslim camp. Syria preferred a stalemate—in which it could play the role of power broker—to victory for any of the parties. That the Lebanese president is, by political agreement, always a Christian increased the incentives for Assad to ingratiate himself with the Maronites.

Only in the case of Israel's invasion of Lebanon do we find an instance in which military intervention was the result of changing goals within the intervening state rather than developments with the target state. Lebanon's strategic landscape indeed changed in the late 1970s. The PLO established a mini-state in the south and posed a more formidable security threat to Israel's northern villages. Syria also increased its military presence, raising the possibility that Lebanon could become an invasion route. But Israel initially adjusted to these changes without altering its essentially defensive, retaliatory posture. It was only after the formation of Begin's second government that offensive military intervention became the preferred option. This change of policy was not a simple reaction to events in Lebanon. Rather, the rationale was to drive the PLO from the country, effectively neutralizing the organization as a political force. Pursuit of this goal marked a fundamental shift in Israel's objectives in Lebanon. It was a change in Israel's leadership that brought about this shift. As in the other cases, a discrete event triggered intervention: the murder of Israel's ambassador to London.

The picture that emerges is one in which the intervening state's interests in the target state developed over a long period of time. The effort required to protect these interests gradually mounted as civil strife in the target state worsened. Eventually, elites came to believe that they faced the options of intervening directly or abandoning efforts to achieve a desirable outcome in the target state. It is to the considerations and decision-making dynamics that prevailed during these critical decision periods that the analysis now turns.

The Intervening State: Goals, Objectives, Assumptions, and Domestic Politics

As mentioned in the introduction to this volume, we are examining only cases in which states reached this critical decision juncture and opted to proceed with military intervention. But this does not mean that we are left with cases in which the decision to engage military force was taken without hesitation. On the contrary, elites were generally aware that the costs of direct intervention would be very high. They proceeded only because powerful incentives were at work. How did elites perceive these incentives? Why, in each of our cases, did elites decide in favor of intervention? These questions are addressed by examining four components of the decision process: the overarching goals of the operation; its discrete military objectives; the principal strategic assumptions reigning at the time of decision; and the domestic political milieu in which the decision was made.

Goals

The analysis examines the overarching goals of the intervening state along two dimensions: whether they were reputational or intrinsic in nature, and whether they were essentially defensive or offensive in orientation. Reputational goals stem from a state's desire to project an image of resolve into the international community; intrinsic goals stem from a state's primary security concerns—the safety of its borders, the stability and political orientation of neighboring states, and the maintenance of a non-threatening regional environment. Defensive goals are aimed at preserving the status quo in the target state; offensive goals, at altering the status quo in the target state.

Cuban involvement in Angola and the U.S. involvement in Vietnam were motivated primarily by reputational concerns. Cuba clearly had no strategic interests in Angola; Castro was driven exclusively by the desire to establish himself as a leader of leftist movements in the Third World. American officials on occasion identified intrinsic interests in Vietnam—protection of the sea lanes and the prevention of communist domination of Southeast Asia. But Berman's article (chapter 2) clearly reveals that concern about demonstrating credibility and resolve was the critical variable compelling elites to decide in favor of direct intervention. President Johnson concisely set out the key argument that was repeatedly marshalled to counter George Ball's recommendation that the United States pull out of the war in Vietnam: "But George, wouldn't all these countries [in Asia] say that Uncle Sam was a paper tiger, wouldn't we lose credibility breaking the word of three presidents, if we did as you have proposed? It would seem to be an irresponsible blow."[2]

In the other historical cases examined above, the initial decision to intervene was based primarily on intrinsic interests. The South Africans, Indians, Soviets, Syrians, and Israelis were all seeking to address security problems stemming from continuing conflicts in neighboring states.[3] Reputational concerns were by no means absent, but they tended to play a critical role only after military operations had begun. As dominant regional powers, each of these states was concerned about demonstrating its will and ability to influence the outcome of local conflicts. Once the commitment to secure a specific outcome had been publicly set forth, fulfilling that commitment became an end in itself. This dynamic was particularly pronounced in cases in which the intervening state enjoyed marked military superiority over its adversary. As discussed in Cohen's article (chapter 9), the tendency for reputational concerns to grow during the course of the operation had important implications for both the duration of the conflict and the strategy which the intervening states used to prosecute the war.

All the intervening powers, with the exception of Israel, had primarily defensive goals; they were seeking to preserve the political status quo, not to alter it in a fundamental way. Israel had some defensive goals—preventing attacks on Israeli territory from southern Lebanon. But the Israelis also pursued far more ambitious offensive goals. They were seeking to achieve the political restructuring of Lebanon and to undermine the PLO's role in determining the disposition of the West Bank and Gaza Strip. The difference between defensive and offensive goals provides insight into why most of the interventions examined above were so protracted. The Israelis had very clear goals. They knew when they had failed and were able to withdraw accordingly.[4] The interveners with essentially defensive aims became mired in a stalemate. They were able to achieve their goals of preserving the status quo, but only by maintaining a military presence in the target state. The adversary could be held off, but not defeated, and the local ally, contrary to initial expectations, proved unable to assume primary responsibility for the war. Were the interveners to have suffered outright military defeat, they would likely have withdrawn as the Israelis did. But they became stuck in a situation in which they could neither defeat nor be defeated by the adversary. In these cases, defeat came to the intervenor by virtue of its own political choice to disengage, not through failure on the battlefield. To be sure, choosing defeat is not something that political elites do with enthusiasm or alacrity. Avoidance of such a difficult decision played an important role in turning these interventions into protracted conflicts.

Objective

Translating political goals into military objectives was one of the key difficulties facing elites in the intervening states. The crux of the problem was defining concrete operational objectives which would enable the intervener to achieve its broader political goals. Military force is useful for attaining *military* objectives; using force to attain *political* objectives is far more elusive. The case study chapters reveal an important pattern. At the outset of the intervention, military elites successfully identified narrow, concrete objectives that served as the focal point for operations. As the conflict dragged on, however, military objectives became more amorphous and less narrowly specified. In some cases, initial military operations were frustrated by the adversary. As a result of these initial setbacks, the intervener, rather than focusing on the protection of key cities or strategic points, tended to redefine its mission as destroying the will of the adversary, convincing him that victory was not attainable. This more ambitious objective often played an important role in convincing the intervening state to switch from defensive to offensive tactics and to increase its commitment of combat personnel. In combination with the rising importance of reputational goals, this dynamic provided a key source of escalatory pressure.

The following examples corroborate these generalizations. The first contingent of U.S. ground troops to arrive in Vietnam was charged with protecting specific military installations. Soon, U.S. troops found themselves carrying out a pacification campaign and hunting Viet Cong in the jungle, seeking to demonstrate to the adversary their staying power and resolve. In Afghanistan, initial Soviet operations focused on holding key cities and the road network linking them. When the Mujahadeen resistance proved more intractable than expected, Soviet troops found themselves attacking guerilla strongholds, seeking to demoralize the opposition. Ten thousand Indian soldiers were originally sent to Sri Lanka to disarm the LTTE— a militant Tamil group that refused to lay down its arms. One hundred thousand Indian troops were soon fighting wars against both Tamil and Sinhalese militants. The IPKF essentially occupied the north in order to protect civilians and undermine the militant resistance movement. In the south, Indian soldiers had to cope with widespread insurgency instigated by nationalist Sinhalese extremists. In all of these cases, the mission of the military broadened over time, changing from narrow, concrete objectives to more ambiguous—and ambitious—psychological objectives. Force requirements rose accordingly.

Strategic Assumptions

A state's decision to intervene militarily is based upon several key projections about how the conflict is likely to proceed. Our analysis here focuses on the set of initial assumptions held by elites when they made the critical decision to engage their own military forces. Of particular importance are their assessments of three issues: How many troops will be required? How long will the conflict last? Is military victory possible? Changes in elite thinking about these three issues had a considerable impact on the trajectory of the intervention.

Initial calculations of force requirements vary among the cases. Contrary to common wisdom, however, elites, when making the decision to intervene, were quite often acutely aware that the operation would require a very substantial commitment of military resources. In these cases, the intervenor was clearly not gradually dragged into the conflict by unforeseen events. The Soviets began their operation in Afghanistan with roughly 100,000 troops. Force levels climbed only marginally during the course of the conflict. The Israelis, despite their public claims of seeking only to push the PLO from southern Lebanon, had from the outset very ambitious military objectives that required far more troops than would have been needed to drive guerrillas from southern Lebanon. The U.S. intervention in Vietnam also challenges the notion of the slippery slope. Archival sources presented by Berman reveal that, during the critical policy debates of 1965, top decision makers were informed that the U.S. commitment was likely to reach 500,000. Although U.S. troop levels in Vietnam did increase incrementally, elites were aware of the probable scope of the conflict when they decided to participate fully in the ground war.

The other cases are somewhat more ambiguous, in part because the available information is incomplete. Both South Africa and Cuba ended up sending more forces to Angola than they originally deployed. In comparative terms, however, the number of forces eventually committed by both interveners remained moderate and did not increase substantially from initial force levels. Neither state appears to have been incrementally dragged in by unforeseen developments.

The experiences of Syria and India more closely parallel the "slippery slope" model. Syria's intervention in Lebanon proved to require more troops than were initially deployed. Especially after the 1976 "red line" accord, the Syrians assumed they could maintain their dominant political position in Lebanon at low cost. Syrian forces were to serve as keepers of the peace. The intensification of the civil war and direct clashes with Israeli forces, however, prompted the Syrians to move in more troops and firepower as well as more sophisticated weaponry. Similarly, Indian troops were deployed in Sri Lanka primarily as peacekeeping forces. They were to keep the warring parties apart, not to enter directly into the conflict. When the Indians found themselves fighting both parties in the ethnic rivalry, they increased force levels tenfold. In both Sri Lanka and Lebanon, the disintegration of domestic political order was the key variable drawing the intervenor in more deeply. As testimony to the profound changes taking place in the political landscape, both Syria and India ended up fighting against parties with whom they had originally been allied.

Initial assessments of the likely length of the conflict also vary across the cases. As one might expect, the norm is that elites envisaged a relatively short stay. In Angola, the interveners were hoping that their presence would rapidly turn the tide in favor of their local allies. The Indians assumed that they would have little difficulty disarming the LTTE. Once this was accomplished, Indian forces would have only to monitor the settlement and patrol the waters between the mainland and Sri Lanka. The Soviets foresaw a relatively brief stay in Afghanistan. According to Shevardnadze, "the people who made the decision . . . did not plan to stay in Afghanistan for any length of time."[5] Soviet troops would eliminate the opposition and leave the PDPA on stable ground. So too did the Israelis envisage a relatively short operation in Lebanon. After driving the PLO from Lebanon and stabilizing the Maronite-led government, the Israelis believed they could return home with a friendly country on their northern border.

The Syrians and Americans were the outliers. Although documentary evidence is not available, one can infer from Syrian goals and behavior that, from the outset, they planned a relatively long stay in Lebanon. Their goal was, after all, to establish durable political hegemony. The U.S. case is far more striking and counter-intuitive. American officials recognized that the war in Vietnam would not only require up to one-half million troops, but that it was also likely to be a long conflict. Even Secretary McNamara, one of the most vocal proponents of escalation, admitted in June 1965, that "the war is one of attrition and will be a long one."[6] Military elites agreed with this assessment. That decision makers foresaw a lengthy and costly war but nevertheless proceeded with full-scale intervention speaks to the importance of the interests which they assumed were at stake.

In all of our cases, elites initially believed that military victory was possible. Definitions of victory did vary across the cases, but several commonalities emerge. None of the interveners was intent on physical destruction of the enemy. The goal was to neutralize the adversary through superior force, thereby convincing him that to continue the struggle was futile. In the meantime, the intervener's local ally would consolidate its military and political position and, eventually, be able to establish control over the country with only indirect assistance from outside. The core issue was essentially one of resolve.

The intervenor's military might and staying power would crush the adversary's will. The balance of resolve would shift to the local ally and gradual disengagement could take place.

Before the commencement of operations, elites viewed defensive tactics as sufficient to wear down the adversary's resolve and let him know that his objectives were unattainable. After initial setbacks, elites tended to switch to offensive tactics to punish the enemy and convince him to disengage. When this effort failed, elites began to question whether victory would be possible. They still sought to maintain a military edge, however, assuming that a strategic advantage would offer benefits at the negotiating table. Thinking about military victory thus tended to progress through three stages: at the outset, that victory is possible through defensive tactics; after setbacks, that victory is possible through offensive tactics; finally, that victory is not possible.

The intervenor's initial strategic assumptions—especially those about the length of the war and the possibility of victory—thus tended to change radically after the intervention was under way. For the most part, as detailed in the following chapter, interveners came to see the conflict as a long one and began to doubt that military victory, at least as originally envisaged, would be possible. Why the initial assumptions of elites were so frequently mistaken will be discussed shortly.

Domestic Factors

The effects of public opinion and intra-elite divisions on the decision to intervene vary widely across the case studies. Two generalizations do, however, emerge. First, domestic constraints and opportunities figure less prominently during the initial stage of intervention than at later points in the conflict. This is quite understandable; public attention tends not to be mobilized by foreign conflicts until members of that public are directly involved. Accordingly, domestic opinion becomes a much more potent factor in shaping elite decisions as the intervention progresses. Second, in all the cases where information about the decision-making process was available, significant divisions within the elite community existed over whether intervention was the preferred course of action. Those in favor of intervention thus had to overcome significant opposition. This opposition played an important role in ensuring that decision makers were informed of the risks involved in proceeding with direct military engagement.

In some cases, public opinion abetted the process of getting in; in others, it served as a constraint. The Indian government, for example, was pressured to intervene in Sri Lanka by the large Tamil population in Tamil Nadu. Especially after the Sri Lankan army launched a major offensive against the Tamils, domestic forces played an important role in convincing Rajiv Ghandi to mediate the dispute. Ispahani's analysis suggests that party politics were thus a critical factor leading to the intervention. In the Angolan case, Castro was not pushed by popular opinion to intervene, but he did perceive that intervention might have a positive backlash at home. Standing behind leftist Third World movements served to strengthen both his domestic and his international reputation.

In the U.S. and Syrian cases, popular opinion played more of a constraining role. Domestic politics indeed played some role in precipitating U.S. involvement in Vietnam; no administration wanted to be blamed for allowing South Vietnam to fall to the communists. But U.S. decision makers were also very concerned about potential domestic constraints. President Johnson hid from the American people the full scope of the country's commitment in Vietnam. He feared that complete knowledge of U.S. intentions would undermine public support for the war and might jeopardize his ambitious domestic program. The Syrian government faced popular opposition because it was intervening against a coalition of largely Muslim factions. Domestic backlash in fact convinced President Assad to curtail his initial offensive in Lebanon. In neither of these cases, however, did the public's reaction prevent the intervention from proceeding. Popular opinion does not appear to have been a critical factor shaping elite behavior.

Of more importance than popular opinion during the getting in stage was intra-elite dynamics. As far as civil-military relations are concerned, we would expect to find a divergence between the superpowers and regional powers. The military establishments of the United States and the Soviet Union have been focused on and structured for a major conflict in Europe. Historically, they have resisted taking on low-intensity missions in peripheral areas.[7] In the Afghanistan and Vietnam cases, we would therefore expect to find civilian elites to be more enthusiastic proponents of intervention than military elites. This division should not be as pronounced in the cases involving regional powers. In these instances, the military would be facing a familiar mission, one which suited its principal orientation and structure. Organizational interests would therefore induce the services to support intervention.

The case studies confirm these general propositions. Litwak (chapter 3) provides recently released information which suggests that the Soviet military was in fact opposed to the intervention in Afghanistan. It was the inner circle of civilian elites that strongly favored the operation. So too was there hesitancy within the American military about deepening involvement in Vietnam. Berman shows that top *civilian* elites were the ones vigorously arguing in favor of intervention and escalation.

The constellation of forces was quite different for the regional powers. In Israel, the Chief of the General Staff and the Defense Minister—himself a military man—were the chief proponents of a major operation in Lebanon. They in fact had to deceive the Cabinet in order to overcome civilian opposition to the intervention. In South Africa, the military placed considerable pressure on civilian elites to go forward with the intervention in Angola. In the Syrian case, military officials were involved from the start in shaping policy toward Lebanon. The Chief of Staff and the Commander of the Air Force were part of the team negotiating with the Lebanese prior to direct intervention.

Ultimately, it is difficult to assess the impact of civil-military splits on the decision to intervene. In the United States and the Soviet Union, military opposition did not prevent operations from proceeding. In the other cases, the military may have abetted the process of getting in, but responsibility for making the decision to intervene still rested with civilian leaders. Furthermore the cases suggest that the civilian community, while it contained individuals with strong reservations, tended to be consistently in favor of intervention.

Assessment Errors and the Decision to Intervene

While opposition to intervention within the elite community failed to prevent intervention from occurring, it did broaden the information that decision makers had at their disposal as they considered whether to proceed with military operations. Those against intervention marshalled evidence to show that the costs of direct engagement would be too high; they played a key role in forcing the elite community to confront the risks involved. That such information was available at the time of the initial decision to intervene challenges the notion of the "slippery slope." In all but two of our cases, elites had before them a fairly accurate assessment of the likely scope of the conflict when they decided to proceed.

Assessment errors were, however, prevalent on two other dimensions: the length of the conflict and the likelihood of military victory. The analysis now addresses the key suppositions that underlay these assessment errors and seeks to uncover their sources. The cases suggest that errors in assessment emerged from the following three erroneous suppositions:

1. That the balance of resolve would favor the intervening state.
2. That the local ally would serve as a reliable political/military partner.
3. That the intervention would not fundamentally alter the political landscape in the target state, except as intended by the intervener.

These suppositions are now examined in more detail.

Given that intervention, by definition, occurs on the adversary's territory, it is somewhat surprising that the intervening state regularly considered the balance of resolve to be in its favor. Intuition suggests and the case studies confirm that resolve usually favors the side defending its own territory. Nevertheless, the case studies show that the intervening state, because its goal was to neutralize, and not destroy, the adversary, consistently assumed that it would be able to outlast the enemy. This assumption informed the belief that military victory would be possible: if the intervenor believes that he has superior resolve, and identifies breaking the will of the adversary as his goal, he also believes that military victory will be attainable.

The intervening states also repeatedly overestimated the stability and reliability of their local allies. This assessment bias stemmed, at least in part, from the assumption that the chief threat to the ally was principally a military one. Accordingly, elites in the intervening state believed that the ally would consolidate its political position once the military threat had been neutralized. They failed to see that the ally's instability was chronic, and not simply a function of the ongoing civil strife.

Finally, elites in intervening states tended to underestimate the implications of intervention for the political landscape in the target state. Foreign intervention often complicates and destabilizes pre-existing alignments. The local ally is sometimes discredited among the populace, making more difficult its attempts to establish political order. South Africa's reputation in Black Africa, for example, made it a risky partner in Angola. In Sri Lanka, Indian troops intervened in order to disarm Tamil militants, but ended up fighting against the Sinhalese, who had come to resent the presence of foreign troops.

Foreign intervention can also precipitate the formation of a more unified and militarily potent opposition than had been present at the outset. In Afghanistan, Soviet intervention strengthened the Mujahadeen by forcing rival groups to put aside their differences. It also enabled the opposition to gain access to foreign military assistance. Israel's failed efforts to restructure Lebanon's domestic order further demonstrates the difficulties and irreducible uncertainties involved in using military force to effect durable political change. In all of these cases, the intervenor failed to appreciate the effect that its presence would have on the ongoing domestic turmoil.

What was the root cause of these consistent errors in assessment? Can we assume that psychological distortion was at work—that elites were predisposed to decide in favor of intervention and shaped incoming information to support this outcome? In all of our cases, there clearly was a strong disposition to intervene within the elite community; decision makers in favor of engagement had to overcome a strong opposition armed with good reasons for exercising restraint. Furthermore, the desire to avoid appearing weak or indecisive—the cognitive affect associated with a predisposition to take action—probably played an important role in pushing elites toward a decision for intervention. But psychological explanations do not withstand two important lines of argument. First, top officials in the U.S. government were clearly intent on intervening in Vietnam; we know this because they proceeded despite awareness that the conflict would be long and require hundreds of thousands of men. Nevertheless, in this critical case, psychological pressures did not distort the assessment process. Berman reveals that elites had before them quite sober projects of what the conflict would entail. Second, as discussed in the following chapter, elites, soon after the intervention had begun, did tend to correct the erroneous assumptions outlined above when faced with contradictory incoming information. Given that sunk costs would only add pressure within the elite community to shape information to support the decision to intervene, we would expect psychological pressures, if operating, to continue to distort the assessment process. That they did not casts doubt on psychological explanations of the initial period of assessment failure.

Miscalculation—a failure to foresee the likely course of events—provides a simpler and more compelling explanation. Interventions aimed at achieving political outcomes are, after all, hostage to events and developments that have very little to do with the battlefield. It is therefore plausible that elites fell prey to random events that they could not have been expected to foresee. Given the consistency of assessment failures across the cases, however, random miscalculation is somewhat unsatisfying. Rather, miscalculation appears to have recurred throughout the cases studied along three critical dimensions.

First, intelligence communities demonstrated a glaring inability to gather accurate and reliable information about political, as opposed to military, variables. For the most part, the intervening states were stymied not by an inadequacy of force, but by political developments—involving both the local ally and adversary—that undermined their broad political/military strategy. Even when initial political assessments were accurate, the very act of intervention often altered in a fundamental way the alignment of forces and the domestic position of various actors within the target state.[8]

Second, elites in the intervening states consistently overestimated the value of superior firepower. They assumed that military superiority would allow them to overwhelm the adversary and destroy his willpower. Guerrilla tactics, however, repeatedly offset numerical and technological advantages and took their toll on the willpower of the intervening army. Elites also consistently overestimated the ability of military force to affect the political landscape. Even when the intervening states enjoyed successful military campaigns, they could not translate such success into a stable political outcome. Nor could military force be used to alter domestic alignments or to repair deeply rooted ethnic rivalries. Israel's futile effort to use force to recast Lebanon's political structure is the most glaring case in point. In all of our cases, the complexities and intractable nature of civil war left even the most powerful of foreign interveners strangely impotent.

Finally, elites consistently failed to appreciate the degree to which domestic politics would come to constrain their behavior. Prior to the commencement of military operations, before popular opinion had been mobilized, elites were understandably optimistic about their ability to manage the domestic backlash that usually accompanies foreign intervention. As the operation dragged on and the financial and human toll mounted, domestic costs played a key role in hampering the prosecution of the war and in triggering the disengagement process in most of the historical cases examined in this volume.

The important role of domestic politics in serving as a constraint on military intervention is borne out by the fact that even if they had had at their disposal more accurate political intelligence about the target state, elites may well have nevertheless decided in favor of intervention. In the U.S. case, decision makers were confronted with remarkably sober assessments of the likely course of the war in Vietnam, yet proceeded to pour in troops nonetheless. In many of

the other cases, elites became aware that they were entering a quagmire soon after the intervention began. They did not, however, then
readily decide to withdraw. On the contrary, they tended to prepare
themselves for a costly and protracted conflict. Even when elites
began to doubt that military victory was possible, they did not begin
preparations for withdrawal. The key turning point inducing elites to
pursue a policy of disengagement rather than of escalation appears
to have been the emergence of severe domestic opposition, not
awareness of the length or likely outcome of the war. This analysis
suggests that domestic constraints may play a powerful role in preventing states from engaging in interventions to begin with, a proposition borne out by U.S. behavior in the Angolan conflict in 1976.[9]

Conclusion

In sum, it appears that elites decided in favor of intervention largely
because they were driven by powerful reputational and intrinsic
interests. Elites were generally aware of the financial and human
costs that would be involved in deciding in favor of intervention, but
they proceeded nonetheless. The notion of the "slippery slope,"
while potentially applicable in two of our cases, thus does not provide a compelling explanation for why states regularly find themselves mired in protracted interventions. This is not to suggest that
important assessment errors were not repeatedly made. On the contrary, particularly with regard to the likely length of the war and the
probability of success, initial assessments were far off the mark.
These errors stemmed from underestimation of the difficulties involved in gathering reliable political intelligence and overestimation
of the ability of superior military force to resolve, in a durable manner, intractable civil strife. Even if elites had been provided with
more accurate information, however, the analysis suggests that they
would have nevertheless proceeded with intervention. This conclusion is cause for considerable pessimism about the ability of states, in
the absence of strong domestic opposition, to avoid getting involved
in costly, protracted military interventions.

Notes

1. The point here is similar to that made by Robinson and Gallagher with
respect to British imperial policy during the late nineteenth century. They
argue that the British began to pursue the establishment of a formal, as

opposed to informal, empire because of mounting resistance and opposition in the periphery, not because of a change in the objectives being pursued by the British government. British goals remained the same, but indirect influence was no longer sufficient to attain them. See John Gallagher and Ronald Robinson, "The Imperialism of Free Trade," *The Economic History Review*, 6, no. 1 (1953).

2. Berman, p. 40.

3. As discussed below, the Indian Government also faced domestic political pressures to intervene.

4. The Israelis did not readily disengage from Lebanon altogether, but they did scale back the scope of their operation and withdraw troops to southern Lebanon.

5. Litwak, p. 77.

6. Berman, p. 35.

7. On the attitudes of the American military toward peripheral conflict see Charles Kupchan, *The Persian Gulf and the West* (Boston: Allen & Unwin, 1987), pp. 83–98.

8. This assessment bias may have been the product of bureaucratic considerations. Prior to direct military intervention, the agency or office responsible for covert operations and in-country advising is usually also responsible for intelligence gathering. An assessment bias could result from this group's close contact with the local ally and its effort to present information to decision makers that would bring more resources to bear in the target state. The information necessary to corroborate this hypothesis, however, is not available.

9. We are here getting beyond the scope of this study. A follow-on project should, however, examine cases in which states considered military intervention, but decided against it.

9

Dynamics of Military Intervention

ELIOT A. COHEN

Introduction: The Middle Game

Political scientists have by and large tended to be less interested in the conduct of wars than how they break out or how they are brought to an end. There are a number of reasons for this, perhaps the most important of which is the widely shared belief that the beginnings and ends of war are where the politics are. This is not quite true, as anyone who has studied coalition warfare, in particular, realizes. But the disinclination to study the middle of military conflict has even deeper roots. For many scholars, aside from military historians, what goes on within a war is either too confusing to be understood, or subject to the operation of secular forces not really subject to decision or control. Sometimes this approach leads to a crude determinism, such as that which, upon looking at the raw economic potential of the opposing sides in the American Civil War and the World Wars, declares that this alone is sufficient to explain the outcome. At other times, this line of argument takes a more subtle form, as when scholars declare that the United States could not win the Indochina War because the Vietnamese communists were simply too determined or because no outside power can win a revolutionary conflict.

The traditional, and now generally disdained, approach of historians until the mid-twentieth century was different. It held that decisions made a difference, that war was a struggle whose outcome rested not simply on the forces of production or a constant application of will power, but on choice. Admittedly, this led to other kinds of crudity, and in particular an excessive focus on the Great Captains of history—the Napoleons, Lees, or Grants. This school paid too little attention to the military organizations that they led, and failed to analyze the impact of technology or logistics on the conduct of war. But the core insight remains valid—wars *are* shaped, and in some cases determined, by the "middle game." The analogy is drawn from chess, where this emphasis on the middle certainly makes sense. It is even more valid when one speaks of a political contest such as war, where "winning" and "losing" may have far less clear meanings than soldiers and statesmen would like.

This essay explores that "middle game" in military interventions. It will look at some of the problems that go into the formulation of strategy, operational approaches, and tactics in the kinds of wars that are discussed in this book. Implicitly, it will make the case that what goes on in the middle—the disagreeable details of the way war is waged—can determine the outcome of war. The conceptual task here is complex. We have, first of all, the problem raised by Clausewitz in his treatment of war's conduct, namely how one assesses the component campaigns of a war. Clausewitz asks whether separate campaigns or battles should be viewed as a kind of cumulative game, in which an overall balance of success or failure emerges, or if the only campaign that matters is the last one, and that battles are discrete entities. To understand the failure of American intervention in Vietnam, for example, should we look at the war as an organic whole, beginning with ROLLING THUNDER and the Ia Drang Valley campaign of 1965, or would we learn more from concentrating on the crucial Vietnamese Communist Tet offensive of 1968? Clausewitz argued that war must be viewed as a whole:

> Just as a businessman cannot take the profit from a single transaction and put it into a separate account, so an isolated advantage gained in war cannot be assessed separately from the overall result. A businessman must work on the basis of his total assets, and in war the advantages and disadvantages of a single action [can] only be determined by the final balance.[1]

So too with military intervention. No battle, no matter how dramatic, can be viewed in isolation from the entire course of the war in which it occurs.

The Fog of War

The conceptual problem that Clausewitz raises is compounded by the intrinsic difficulties of understanding the middle game in modern war. In another place, Clausewitz wrote of the fog of war—the sheer difficulty of figuring out what is really happening in wartime. This was true in his era, and despite (in some ways, because of) the vast technological changes in warfare since then the fog still lies thick over modern battlefields.

Modern warfare is not only fiendishly complex but also obscure: it is only now, for example, that military historians are beginning to unravel, in a satisfactory and complete way, how battle was waged on the Western Front in World War I, what role concepts of command and leadership played there. It is difficult enough for military forces to figure out what *they* have done; to understand the enemy as well, and to see how both sides understood the battle, is even harder. The combat dynamic of the World Wars may only now be coming clear, and that is with full access to the necessary records. In the Third World the problems are much greater. Records may be scanty to begin with, since insurgents, for example, are not always capable bureaucrats (some times they are, however: the Israelis captured vast quantities of PLO material during the Lebanon intervention of 1982, and the Philippine Army has achieved similar coups against rebels there). But even when records on both sides exist, they are often regarded as too sensitive, for political reasons or more narrowly military ones, to be shared with researchers. This is particularly true with regards to intelligence documents, which are at once valuable and uniquely sensitive. If we have learned anything from the historiography of World War II during these last two decades, it is the overwhelming importance of intelligence in modern warfare. Without a sense of what each side knew about the other it is very difficult to assess the quality of decisions and actions in war. Some of this information may be very technical—what, for instance, the Israelis knew about the characteristics of Syrian radars in 1982, or the kind of intelligence passed by the Soviets to the Cubans about South African military installations and activities. Furthermore, in cases where only one side is willing to be forthcoming about the details of a war, intelligence reports may be the only way of judging what is going on "on the other side of the hill." In their absence, the student of a contemporary war is reduced to inference from scanty or unreliable published reports.

Measuring Effectiveness

Strategy is best defined as the preparation and use of military power to serve political ends—a classic understanding that goes back to Clausewitz. As the examples of Germany in World War I and Japan in World War II suggest, countries that sacrifice strategic effectiveness for tactical effectiveness often end up losing.[2] This simple truth is not always a palatable one. In a classic statement of American military bafflement at the course of the Vietnam War, Colonel Harry Summers recalls an American colonel telling his North Vietnamese counterpart in 1975, "You know, you never defeated us in battle." The North Vietnamese paused for a moment and said, "That is true. It is also irrelevant."[3] It is a hard thing for a tactically superior force to accept the proposition that it can lose a war even as it inflicts heavy casualties on an enemy or occupies the ground that it desires. The wars in Afghanistan and Lebanon clearly bred self-doubt in the Soviet and Israeli armies, although to varying degrees, for that reason.

Without some kind of capacity for battle, however, it is hard to achieve strategic success. The first problem faced by military organizations, therefore, is understanding their performance. This is a more difficult problem than often realized, for military effectiveness is a matter of relative, not absolute capabilities. Some military organizations may be more adaptable than others, but it is rare to find an army that is omnicompetent. If a force has been equipped and trained for intense armored warfare in Europe it is probably not as ready for guerrilla warfare in the jungle, and vice versa. And, in fact, in the cases that we examine, we generally see conventional forces being thrown into fighting that turned to guerrilla-style conflict for which they were ill-suited.

Military ineffectiveness, then, may be task-specific, rather than general in nature. Beyond the question of specialization, however, are other uncertainties in military effectiveness. For one thing, particularly in conflicts that involve guerrilla warfare, and are waged in large part for the control of civilian populations, it may be hard to discover whether one is winning or losing. In conventional warfare one can point to the trophies of battle—prisoners, captured towns or fortified positions, diminished resistance to one's forces. Guerrilla warfare, by way of contrast, is "strange war," as Marine General Lewis Walt called it. The counterinsurgent side may try to measure its success by counting enemy corpses, or weapons capture, or (most misleading of all) the acreage nominally under government control— but those measures of effectiveness may mean very little. Even the insurgents often have only a limited sense of how well they are doing, which accounts for the frequency with which guerrilla forces attempt, prematurely, to move up the scale of warfare to conventional operations. Success in guerrilla war depends on a host of intangible measures—the loyalty of the contested population (which in turn depends on an unstable mixture of fear and expectation), the willingness of the external power to prosecute the war, the supportiveness of the insurgents' external allies. Modern guerrilla/counter-guerrilla warfare is full of surprises: who would have expected the Soviet Union to withdraw from Afghanistan, unable to crush the primitive tribesmen who opposed them—and conversely, who expected their puppet regime in Kabul to hang on to power once Soviet fighting forces (though not advisers) had withdrawn? Similarly, one frequently finds radically different assessments of the progress of a war among the intervening forces, simply because no clear measure, no line on the map, tells one how the war is going.

The *measures of effectiveness* problem, then, is particularly acute in insurgency warfare, but it is not unique to it. Static or low-level border warfare has the same problem, and at other periods in history the same problem has even occurred in high-intensity combat—during World War II, for example, those in charge of prosecuting submarine and anti-submarine warfare could not be certain what the appropriate measures of effectiveness were. For the anti-submarine side, was it holding merchant-ship losses to a tolerable level, or was it sinking enemy submarines? And for the pro-submarine side, was it sinking a given level of enemy tonnage, or was it destroying particular kinds of ships (e.g., oil tankers)? Even in conventional interventionary warfare measures of effectiveness may prove elusive. The Israelis scored a stunning success in 1982 when they knocked out 82 Syrian aircraft while suffering virtually no losses of their own, yet this spectacular score concealed a much more muddled picture on the ground, leading two experienced Israeli commentators to refer to the advance of the Israel Defense Forces as "a lame blitz." In retrospect it appears that the notorious body count of Vietnam was not necessarily inaccurate; it was merely an inappropriate measure of success or failure. One important area for research is how communist countries have measured progress in counterinsurgent warfare, and whether their numerical indices have been any more useful than those in the West.

Beyond the problem of measures of effectiveness in actual combat is the difficulty of assessing relative strength in the early stages of intervention. The cases that we have examined here include the interaction of forces that had not prepared for conflict with each other—the Cubans and the South Africans, for example, or the United States and the Vietnamese. In both cases the intervening forces brought to bear superior quantities of materiel and, on occasion, even of personnel. Although advisers and intelligence personnel may have had opportunities for observing their new enemies, neither side found itself up against traditional enemies. The ability of the Eelam Tigers to resist the Indian Peacekeeping Force in Sri Lanka surprised the Indian government, even though the insurgents were neighbors, and in some ways even clients of the Indians.

It may be difficult, then, to assess how well the middle game is going because the two sides are new opponents. In some cases the problem is compounded by the newness of one or both of the forces to combat. The Soviet army that marched into Afghanistan was not, by and large, combat-experienced. To be sure, Soviet advisers had controlled and assisted in wars in the Middle East and the Horn of Africa; the rank-and-file and the junior officers of the Soviet forces in Afghanistan, however, were innocent of combat experience. They faced the further difficulty, already noted, of having trained for a very different kind of war than the one in which they found themselves.

War is the most severe and hence the most honest audit of an army. Fundamental flaws in training, officer selection, tactics, or the style of command can be concealed in peacetime, or look less serious than they really are. For this reason the first battles of a military intervention are of particular importance, at least if an army is capable of looking at itself and adapting to what it finds. The slowness with which the Soviets adapted to the war in Afghanistan (though adapt they did) suggested to outside observers deeper weaknesses in the Red Army. Occasionally, however, an initial performance may be misleadingly good—making an army think that its prewar tactics and command system are better suited to a war than they really are. Something like this may have occurred in the Ia Drang battles of 1965, in which American forces inflicted heavy casualties on the North Vietnamese. Those successes, coupled with the predispositions of the commander in South Vietnam, William Westmoreland, led the U.S. military to focus on conventional-style offensives against the North Vietnamese, rather than a mixed strategy emphasizing counterinsurgency as well as battles against the enemy main force.

First battles have a way of creating impressions on both sides in a war that can last a very long time. But it is important to understand just how variable military effectiveness may be over time and over unit types. The U.S. Army in 1966 was an efficient, well-disciplined fighting force; in 1970, with notable exceptions, it was riven by racial tensions, plagued with drug abuse, and in large parts demoralized by its experience in Vietnam. In Lebanon in 1982 Syrian air defense forces performed poorly, outmatched by the Israelis and the victims, in some cases, of poor operational practice. Syrian special forces, on the other hand, gave the Israelis a run for their money, and showed themselves a tough fighting force. Military effectiveness, then, is rarely homogeneous. Both sides in war may make serious errors if they make firm judgments about their opponents on the basis of engagements with only one part of their enemies' forces, or on the basis of engagements early on in a war.

It is difficult to measure strategic effectiveness, then, because the performance of military organizations in combat may be much harder to assess than is often thought. But an even more serious problem stems from the larger purpose for which military forces are used. In most strategic analyses the political objective is often regarded as something relatively simple and fixed—to evict an opponent from a given territory, to force acceptance of another state's independence (or its end), or simply to cease armed resistance. Yet political objectives are just that—political, which means that they are innately ambiguous, complex, and mutable. Even the simplest of objectives has codicils attached to it that shape military action. In the recently ended Persian Gulf War the American objective was to force Iraq out of Kuwait, yet it became clear in the course of the war that attached to the objective were certain other, only hinted at, political aims, including the destruction of the bulk (but not all) of the Iraqi military, the mortal weakening of the personal rule of Saddam Hussein, and the avoidance of civilian casualties. Yet the Persian Gulf war was a relatively simple one, and the objectives did not change much over time, in large part because the opponent was incapable of direct counteraction against the United States.

Wars of intervention, unlike classical confrontations of state on state, create particularly complicated sets of political objectives for the intervening power. In many cases they mandate goals that are difficult to put into operation (e.g., the creation of a stable government) and have a peculiarly open-ended quality—and this, in turn, can lead to civil–military friction of a particularly acute kind. For any intervening power, one political objective that usually insinuates itself into a war is prestige, the desire to come out of a conflict with its reputation for effectiveness as a power still intact. In addition, if casualties have been suffered, it becomes necessary to justify the losses of those who have born the battle. This is especially true, of course, in democratic states, in which casualties cannot be hidden for long, and where opposition politicians will call the government of the day to account for those losses. But our case studies suggest that this may be true even in the case of dictatorships of one kind or another, as in the case of the Soviet Union in Afghanistan.

All this does not prevent a country from liquidating an expensive military commitment. But it will shape the conduct of a war, the kind of destruction inflicted in the latter stages of conflict, and the willingness to maintain lower level commitments of personnel and resources even after the main fighting has ended. Thus, even if the end game—the liquidation of the intervention—becomes clear, its nature will be shaped by the way the middle game went. Evidence to support this can be found in the Christmas bombing of Hanoi and Haiphong in 1972, and in the deliberate Soviet withdrawal from Afghanistan.

Typically we speak of winning and losing in war, and this makes some obvious sense. The closer one looks at any given military intervention, however, the more we see that political objectives are more nuanced and complicated than they at first appear. The amount of time that elapses before a client caves in, the amount of damage actually inflicted on an opponent, as well as the amount of damage that *appears* to be inflicted on an opponent, the degree of losses suffered, the dignity (or lack thereof) in a withdrawal—all become important issues in the latter phases of an intervention's middle game.

Escalation

How those political objectives change, and the way they are pursued, are shaped chiefly by the phenomenon of *interaction* in war. Clausewitz, whose treatment of this subject is considerably richer than contemporary analyses of escalation, argues that the conduct of war is subject to three kinds of spirals: reciprocal increases of will, effort, and fear. These forces, which are fundamental to the act of war, conspire to exert a constant escalatory pressure on warfare; that pressure, however, is retarded by political constraints and the weaknesses of individuals and organizations, which prevents them from exerting their full strength.

There are many different ways to escalate a conflict. The most obvious, is *intensification,* a quantitative increase in military operations—doubling the number of troops, the weight of bombs dropped, the frequency of patrols, etc. This is at once the easiest and the least effective of choices for a general, particularly if what is involved is a mere increment to previous levels of effort. Such a strategy has come into disrepute following the Vietnam War, which is perhaps its classic application. Gradual escalation rarely works because it allows an opponent time to adapt to one's own behavior. After Vietnam, moreover, this strategy has acquired such a bad reputation that no general staff worthy of its name would tolerate it.

But quantitative escalation as a strategy is not always a confession of lack of imagination, or, in fact, doomed to failure. During the British quasi-war with Indonesia during the mid-1960s, for example, a gradual extension of the number, scope, and depth of raids across the border eventually brought about a settlement of the conflict on British terms.[4] When both sides have extremely limited objectives quantitative escalation may make sense. Moreover, the dictum of Soviet military theory that quantity has a quality all its own has some merit. At a certain point in the American buildup in Vietnam, for example, the war fundamentally shifted in character, because the United States had assumed the burden of the war. And when the quantitative change is very great, the "rules of the game" may undergo a profound change, which may not be recognized immediately by the parties. North Vietnam, for instance, took a while to understand that the weight of American air power was so much greater than that of French it completely altered the nature of the war—one day in 1966 in South Vietnam, for example, the United States would fly more attack missions than the French flew during the entire siege of Dienbienphu in 1954.

As the Indonesian confrontation episode suggests, quantitative escalation can be the strategy of either side in a military intervention. Although when we think of escalation in the context of the Vietnam war we usually think of the increase in American effort, we should recognize that the opposition could, and did escalate (and de-escalate) in response. Particularly in dealing with an opponent who is sensitive to casualties or to the duration of the conflict, escalation can make sense as a strategy—it worked, for example, against both the United States in Vietnam and Israel in Lebanon, at points where continued or even increasing human costs seemed out of proportion to the possible political gains of continued military involvement.

Qualitative escalation is a more interesting, and in general a more productive strategy. One form it often takes is the introduction of a new technological dimension into warfare—portable anti-aircraft missiles, for example, radically changed the equation for the Soviets in Afghanistan. An effective new technology not only increases the costs to one side, but also can cause "virtual attrition" by causing him to avoid certain areas or alter patterns of operation. In the Afghan case, for example, the trickle of losses inflicted on the Soviets surely counted, but so too did the difficulty they found in conducting intensive heliborne operations and close air support of their own and Afghan forces. Mine warfare is a classic example of a technology that imposes virtual attrition by causing the opponent to avoid certain areas or making him unable to operate there freely. The Syrian deployment of surface-to-air missiles in Lebanon before 1982 limited Israeli freedom of action over Lebanese air space. Once again, it should be born in mind that both sides in a conflict, even an asymmetrical one, can introduce new technologies: long-range rockets and artillery, for example, enabled the Palestine Liberation Organization to strike at Israel from Lebanon during the 1970s.

Qualitative escalation can take place through a change in the nature of targets that are attacked (sanctuaries and logistical bases vs. forces in the field, for example). The kinds of forces used also reflect escalation: air forces, which hit and run, are usually seen as being lower down on the escalatory ladder than the introduction of land forces. And even when land forces are sent in, it may make some difference whether they are merely advisers or combat forces. Indeed, in some cases, the branch of service may make some difference: the United States sent Marines into Lebanon in 1983 rather than Army troops in part because it was thought that there would be less of an assumption of permanence in the Marine presence.

Escalation is also possible through *extension of the area of combat*— attacking guerrilla sanctuaries, for example, in a nominally neutral country, or conducting raids deep in an enemy's territory. The distances need not be very great—a few score miles, for example, in the case of the Israeli advance to the Damascus–Beirut highway, a few miles in the case of the British response to the Indonesians in 1965 and 1966. Wars of intervention are frequently limited wars, for at least one of the parties, and thus may be fought under tacit or even explicit rules in which so-called "red lines" have been drawn. Crossing those red lines is a way of expanding the war.

A final source of escalation lies in the *introduction of new players* into combat, new national or subnational participants in conflict. The complicated politics of Lebanon provided a fruitful source of escalation by this means for both the Syrians and the Israelis. The direct participation by the Cubans and the South Africans in the Angolan civil war is another example of escalation by this means. An intervening power often has to worry about counterintervention (e.g. the Cubans and the South Africans eyeing each other in Angola, or American worries about Chinese intervention in Vietnam). One potential source of success in these wars comes from sealing off the area of operations diplomatically or directly from foreign counterintervention. The success of the American intervention in Panama, for example, may be attributable to this "isolation of the battlefield."

The four means of escalation—by the intensity of operation, the introduction of new technology, the expansion of the area of conflict, and the introduction of new participants—suggest that "escalation" is no simple phenomenon. Each of these means may take a different form at different times. Moreover, the four types of escalation may be combined in a host of ways, as the papers in this volume indicate. One has to ask whether the distinctive national styles of escalation exist. To some extent countries intensify war in different ways depending on the degree of visibility their actions have domestically and internationally. The Soviet Union could intensify operations in Afghanistan by destroying villages or taking tens of thousands of Afghan youngsters away for indoctrination without any fear of a bad domestic press, and with only slightly more worry about the external repercussions of escalation. The Israelis confronted an opponent with much more access to international television, and were more subject to pressure from Western, and specifically American, public opinion. And Israeli domestic opinion exercised influence as well. The influence of domestic opinion on escalation may be quite different in democratic, open societies, however, than in authoritarian, closed ones. The Soviets did not escalate the size of their troop commitment in Afghanistan sharply after the beginnings of their war there, nor did they attempt to settle the war very quickly. Insulated in some (though not all) respects from public opinion, and inclined to take a long view by the nature of their ideology, the Soviets adopted a long-term strategy. Although public opinion did make itself felt in some way, one could not attribute to it decisive results in forcing a Soviet withdrawal from Afghanistan; and Soviet domestic opposition to the war became important only in the context of a larger national crisis of which it was a part. In Vietnam, by way of contrast, the United States could not, for domestic reasons, tolerate a prolonged medium-level commitment of the kind the Soviets readily turned to in Afghanistan. The result was sharp escalation in terms of numbers of troops, and an avowed impatience to bring the war to a successful conclusion.

Escalation does not necessarily take war to a climactic paroxysm of violence. It may ebb and flow, usually in parallel with negotiations to end or at least suspend hostilities. In most wars of intervention a turning point comes—a moment at which the intervening power decides that it has had enough, or in which the defending power concedes defeat. The most dramatic kind of turning point is a battle, of course, such as the Tet offensive during the Vietnam War, the siege of Cuito Cuanavale in the Angolan War, or the siege of Beirut in the Israeli–Lebanon War. Battles are defining moments, although here too we find a reality much more complex than that of simple "winning and losing." By any normal tactical measure, for example, the United States "won" the 1968 fighting during Tet, disposing of something like 40,000 enemy troops, denying the Viet Cong and the

North Vietnamese permanent gains in South Vietnamese cities, and suffering relatively few losses. Yet the fact of the battle itself—the seeming ability of the communists to strike at will throughout South Vietnam, penetrating so far as the American embassy—seemed to contradict the American high command's description of a war that was gradually being won. It marked a sharp turn in American public opinion which went against the war thereafter.

If the fighting in Saigon shook the domestic basis of the American war in Vietnam, the fighting in Beirut destroyed the permissive international environment for Israeli intervention in Lebanon. Although by comparison with the urban battles of World War II the Israeli onslaught on the city was carefully done and relatively cheap in human lives, opinion in the United States turned against Israel and paved the way for negotiated withdrawal of the Israelis' Palestinian enemies.

In war particular towns, cities, crossroads, or hills may acquire a psychological significance that goes beyond their intrinsic military or political value. Whether or for how long one side can hold on to, or another can seize a Verdun or a Bataan may shape perceptions of relative military power in profound ways. This was true of the South African/UNITA failure to take Cuito Cuanavale, the highwater mark of their joint offensive against the Cuban backed MPLA. Similarly, the failure of the Mujahedeen to take Kandahar and other major Afghan cities in 1988 and 1989 suggested that the pro-Soviet Afghan regime was not bound to collapse, or the Soviets to be humiliated.

Critical battles of these kinds do not by themselves determine the outcome of a war, nor do they necessarily set an irreversible course. More than once both the Sri Lankan government and the Indian Peace Keeping Force thought they had broken the back of their Tamil opposition by occupying the Jaffna Peninsula, only to find their successes short-lived. The failure to take Cuito Cuanavale in no way spelled the end of UNITA as an effective fighting force. Some times critical battles may not even be seen as such by those closest to the action, as may have been the case with General Westmoreland in Vietnam during 1968. In some cases even those well-removed from the scene of the action do not see the full importance of the battle until some time has lapsed. Critical battles may be thought of as crossroads on a difficult path: the ultimate objective may still be reachable no matter which direction one turns, but the travelers have lost some control over the difficulty and length of the trip.

To extend the metaphor: a crossroads can be as important because of where a traveler *thinks* his new path will take him, as the reality that actually does lie before him. A critical siege or battle or mere clash can rightly or wrongly convince a country that a war is now doomed to be long, bitter, and inconclusive, or, alternatively, that success is possible. Tet had that effect on the United States in Vietnam; other, less known battles were probably of equal importance in the other cases that we have examined.

The Problem of Strategic Balance

We have already noted that wars of intervention are rarely total wars, at least from the point of view of one of the parties. In some cases (Syrian and Israeli jousting in Lebanon, for example, or Cuban and South African confrontation in Angola, for instance) this may be true for more than one party. If that is the case, at least one power, usually the intervening one, will face the problem of strategic balance—of preventing an important but ultimately secondary set of military operations from distorting a country's overall strategic posture. Military interventions are, in the broadest strategic sense, usually sideshows, and it is a test of strategic control to prevent them from becoming more than that.

What are some of the distortions created by a sideshow out of control? One obvious one affects personnel: a large war, particularly if it lasts for years, usually requires conscription or mobilization of reservists. This has domestic consequences, as was evidenced in growing public disenchantment with Vietnam, the Israeli war in Lebanon, the Soviet occupation of Afghanistan, and Cuban discontent with the Angola war. Popular discontent normally has greater effects in a democracy than in a dictatorship, of course, and hence one usually assumes that democracies are more casualty sensitive in such wars. The lengths that the Soviets went to conceal casualties in the Afghan War suggests that authoritarian regimes may harbor such sensitivities as well. And the reported incarceration of Cuban soldiers coming back from Angola with AIDS, a move that provoked fear and discontent among the Cuban people, may have been a source of pressure even on the totalitarian regime of Fidel Castro. Conversely, democracies can sustain a steady trickle of casualties in a foreign intervention if it seems unavoidable—the Israeli deployment in southern Lebanon and the losses of the British armed forces in Northern Ireland indicate that. Furthermore, the experience of Vietnam can be read as reflecting a remarkable willingness to bear casualties for years without a decisive result. As students of American public opinion in war have noted, the American public did not turn against the Vietnam War until 1968, and even then a good part of the dissent came from "right wing" opponents of the war—citizens who would have been just as happy to see North Vietnam obliterated if it would get the war over with quickly.

Governments can shield themselves against the domestic political consequences of losses in a war of intervention in various ways. The British example of having a professional force clearly helps, although the American practice of relying exclusively on volunteers is not quite the same thing, since many of the volunteers do not, in fact, intend to make the military a profession. More often, intervening forces often adjust tactical and operational styles to minimize casualties, particularly in the latter phases of an intervention. Reliance on fire-power rather than maneuver is one way to do this, as are the training and extensive use of surrogate forces, and the avoidance of certain areas that are too difficult to occupy without intense fighting. These resorts are usually militarily less desirable than the alternative, but domestic politics may dictate their necessity—frustrating and demoralizing the senior military leadership in many cases.

Manpower anxieties can cause other distortions as well. In order to avoid politically difficult measures such as the recall of reservists or large draft callups, units in other theaters can be stripped in order to maintain the expeditionary force. In the late 1960s and early 1970s the United States gutted its Army in Europe in just this way. In any event, the experience of fighting an expeditionary war usually creates a group of officers whose defining experience has been a particular war of intervention. The "Afghantsy" in the Red Army are a good example of this; in the case of the United States Army in Vietnam virtually all of the officer corps was molded by this experience. Those consequences were both good and bad, in everything from tactical habits to political conceptions.

Doctrinal distortion is another problem that expeditionary armies worry about. The kinds of tactics, but more importantly the tactical mindset suited to, say, the jungles of Southeast Asia or villages of Shi'ite Lebanon are hardly the same that apply in Central Europe or on the Golan Heights. Guerrilla warfare usually requires carefully restrained use of violence on the part of the intervening power—all-out conventional fighting requires just the reverse. Intervening forces can get used to favorable conditions (air supremacy, for example) that they certainly could not hope for in other cases. Cuban officers who thought that a defensive war against the United States (the chief task of the Cuban armed forces) would look anything like the war they waged against UNITA and its South African allies would be proven thoroughly mistaken. It is no wonder, then, that armies self-consciously turn their backs on their expeditionary experiences and begin recasting themselves as soon as they are concluded—this occurred to American forces after Vietnam. The Soviet experience, in which counterguerrilla war abroad proved but a precursor of counterguerrilla war at home, is more rare.

The experience of fighting an interventionary war can create habits of command—the helicopters of American commanding officers circling over battlefields in Vietnam are an example. But they can also shape force structure as well. A modern counterguerrilla army will fit itself out with lots of transport helicopters and light infantry; a more conventional force preparing for all-out war will equip itself with tanks and mechanized infantry. Although a competent military will be flexible—the South Africans, for instance, showed themselves able to alternate between counterinsurgency operations and semi-conventional battles against the Cubans—preparation for one kind of war invariably detracts from the ability to prepare for another.

Finally, an interventionary war shapes the foreign policy of the government waging it, leading it to sacrifice other interests to feed the war. Israel did damage to its fundamental policy of alliance with the United States in its invasion of Lebanon; the United States sacrificed some of its leading position in Europe in order to wage the Vietnam War. Sometimes it can work the other way around: one of the reasons for a Soviet withdrawal from Afghanistan was the imperative of establishing relaxed relations with the West, to slow down the arms race and secure open access to Western credits and aid.

As a general matter, one would have to say that it is much easier to avow the need to maintain strategic balance than to achieve it. If limited war has a natural tendency to escalate in the ways we have discussed, it also has a tendency to unbalance a country's strategy. As a general matter, this was true of all the countries considered here. But there are noteworthy differences among them.

The Soviet Union, for example, never allowed the Afghan War to distort its military nearly as much as the United States did during the Vietnam War. Where Vietnam virtually wrecked the American military for a decade Afghanistan had no such effect on overall Soviet military effectiveness. The Red Army had its difficulties, to be sure, but those had relatively little to do with the Afghan War. It is more difficult to compare Israel's and Syria's performance in Lebanon. Israel plunged in and got badly burned by the Lebanon war; within three years, however, it had managed to liquidate its commitment and get out, thereby restoring a certain strategic balance. Syria's much longer presence has had its ups and downs, but it has certainly exercised a more pronounced effect on the Syrian armed forces. Until recently, however, Soviet willingness to stock the Syrian armed forces prevented the Syrians from suffering overly much from their Lebanon commitment. Of all the cases covered in this book, however, only the Indians in Sri Lanka seem to have been able to make a large military commitment of a messy war of intervention and escape serious strategic imbalance from it. This probably reflects not only the relatively small scale and short duration of their involvement in the Sri Lankan civil war, but also that their army is designed chiefly with this kind of contingency in mind.

Doctrinal and Organizational Aspects of Military Intervention

Military intervention poses a host of novel military challenges to which the intervening power must adapt. The solutions (if any) to the problems posed by these wars rest in doctrine—defined as the fundamental guiding principles that shape how a military organization performs its tasks—and in organization. Even when intervention is ultimately unsuccessful, a military organization may adapt to its problem fairly well. Since, as we have suggested above, it is difficult to define ultimate "success" in any simple way, and since the outcomes of most interventions are mixed, how well armies adapt to the wars in which they find themselves can be of tremendous importance.

What are some of the problems that intervening armies confront? One is technological surprise—occasionally high tech surprise. When the Cubans engaged the South Africans, for example, they found themselves up against an army equipped with one of the best artillery pieces in the world, the long-range G-5 howitzer, indigenously designed. But more often the intervening army finds itself confronted with startling low-tech problems, particularly in guerrilla warfare. The rash of suicide car and truck bombers in Lebanon temporarily baffled the Israel Defense Forces, as did the challenge of dealing with children recruited or coerced into handling rocket propelled grenades. Relatively simple heavy machine guns and light Oerlikon cannon, in the hands of Afghan guerrillas on mountain tops, reduced the effectiveness of Soviet helicopter gunships. Ingenious mines and booby traps are the preferred weapon of the weak in such war, and all counterinsurgent forces come up against them sooner or later. Such challenges are usually controllable, but they may undercut an army's tacit belief that superior technology equates to tactical superiority across the board.

Another surprise concerns the physical environment in which war takes place. Much of tactics concerns the use of terrain; and even in a compact area like the Levant, for example, regions may have very different kinds of geographical formation. For interventions across continents, as for the U.S. in Vietnam, the shock of difference can be much greater. In modern military interventions, unlike those of the eighteenth and early nineteenth century, however, differences in climate and terrain are usually important for their effect on tactical effectiveness; in earlier times disease could virtually wipe out intervening forces before serious fighting began.

Perhaps most difficult for any intervening force is the problem of mastering local politics. And here too, proximity is no guarantee of sophistication. The Israelis clearly misread by mirror-imaging the Christian communities of Lebanon, for example. The Indians appear to have equally failed to understand the character of the Tamil guerrilla groups of Sri Lanka, even though they had been clients of theirs for some time. The United States in Vietnam and the Soviets in Afghanistan were notoriously unable to work within the local political culture, although the Soviets, ironically, may have understood the country better than their doctrinaire puppets in the Afghan government.

Interventionary war is frequently a combination of conventional and unconventional warfare. The American debate about whether Vietnam was one or the other has been a sterile exercise because in fact the war was both. Indeed, the mixture of the two styles of warfare was precisely what caused the greatest difficulty for the United States military. Although some conflicts (the recently concluded Gulf war, for example, or the Soviet War in Afghanistan) have been relatively pure in type, the reverse has been true on more than one occasion (e.g., Vietnam, Angola, Lebanon). In some cases, as Maoist revolutionary warfare doctrine would suggest, one form of warfare precedes another—a guerrilla phase may be followed by a conventional phase, or vice versa.

I have already alluded to some of the difficulties posed by having to fight two kinds of war simultaneously. The profile of anti-guerrilla and conventional forces differs enormously—for counter-guerrilla warfare, for example, a force composed of a large, second rate static garrison force backed by elite commando-type units may make the most sense—something like this was Soviet practice in Afghanistan, as it had been French practice in Algeria. For conventional warfare on the other hand, a "high average" force may be best—a uniformly high quality military for high intensity warfare.

Interventionary warfare may pose unusual intelligence requirements as well. Some of these may be mundane (though nonetheless severe), such as a lack of linguists capable of interrogating prisoners of war or interpreting and analyzing captured documents. Problems may be more severe if what is required is the development not of better technical acquired intelligence, but the development of agent networks for human intelligence. The Gulf War has brought that home, as the United States proved able to deploy its vast imagery and signal intelligence collection apparatus to monitor the Iraqi military, but that still left large holes in intelligence analysis. In wars that involve more guerrilla insurgency, the intervening power may find usually productive sources of information, particularly photographic reconnaissance and signal intelligence, less helpful than in conventional operations.

During a war of intervention the interposing side frequently feels the need to engage in what one might call political-military engineering to augment its own forces. Given the constraints on one's own military effort caused either by domestic political concerns or worries about strategic balance, it is imperative to augment one's force with locally recruited military power. Such forces may be created or reinforced not only to replace one's own army, but to provide capabilities that the intervening country's forces lack (intimate knowledge of the population and terrain, for example) or to provide cover for an eventual withdrawal. The range of political-military engineering projects is wide, from creating large armies to providing modest financial subsidies and small arms to local militias.

The range of success and failure in this enterprise is also wide, even within a particular case. South Vietnamese Marines, for example, trained by their American counterparts, fought valiantly to the end, as did South Vietnamese ranger and airborne units: other components of the Army of the Republic of Vietnam collapsed, despite a full suite of American equipment and training. The lowest cost and most likely successes seem to come when the intervening force co-opts or merely reinforces local informal forces, such as the Lebanese militias. Held together by ethnic or religious ties, such groups frequently need only technical advice and modest financial support to defend their own turf against external threats. The greatest difficulties appear to arise when the patrons of such groups attempt to use them for offensive operations, or when the patron fails to realize that the local group remains an autonomous actor. The

Israeli experience working first with Christian militias near Beirut, and then with the mixed Christian and other groups in the South Lebanese Army illustrates the limits, but also the utility of such organizations.

It is far more difficult for a foreign power to create a conventional force to replace it. Two problems in particular stand out: the recruitment and training of an effective officer corps, and the adjustment of tables of organization and equipment, and doctrine, to the abilities of the client state. Invariably there must be some problem of mixed allegiance for the officers of a newly created client army, and considerations of domestic politics often intrude into officer selection, unless the intervening power simply takes control of its client lock, stock, and barrel. To do that, however, risks undermining the self-respect and motivation of the local force, since few officers worthy of the name are content to be puppets of another nation. Very few armies—mainly colonial ones—have managed to square this circle.

The normal inclination of an intervening power is to model a local army on the pattern of its own forces. This can lead to the introduction of its own forces. This can lead to the introduction of equipment too sophisticated to be handled properly by the local force, or to its adoption of doctrine that is too difficult to implement or only imperfectly suited to its problems. Early on in the Vietnam War, the United States found itself doing the latter, preparing the Army of the Republic of Vietnam for a purely conventional threat from the North.[5]

The problem of creating and supporting one's own clients, be they regular units, militia, or insurgent organizations also merits attention. One obvious difficulty is that of control, as the Israelis found out when their Christian allies in Lebanon began massacring Palestinians in the Sabra and Shatila refugee camps. Even the Soviets had a mixed record early on in controlling the Afghan army and government. Often, it is the intervening power (the two cases cited are examples) that attempts to moderate the strategy of its client. Another difficulty can come in taking the client military from one stage of capability to another—from guerrilla or defensive operations to major conventional offensive, for example.

Conclusion: Some Socio-Political Aspects of
Military Intervention

In the middle phases of military intervention, the question of costs and benefits can be muddy. The costs are obvious and often stark—casualties, heavy expenditures, and domestic or international political stress. The indirect costs can be considerable, such as the AIDS epidemic that Cuba suffered when infected soldiers returned home from Angola. But some benefits of military intervention may also be felt. Leaving aside direct political and military gains in fighting, these can include the combat hardening of military and the development of long-term (or what look to be long-term) relationships with a local ally. Almost all of the cases of military intervention that we have discussed in this book are, in fact, coalition wars, in which two major powers aid, or even do the fighting for, local powers or factions. It is naturally tempting, if occasionally misleading, to make one's allies look more effective and durable than they really are.

During the middle phases of military intervention other, more subtle consequences can be felt. Domestic politics can begin to hinge on the handling of the intervention, crowding other issues off the public screen. In many cases, the war will give birth to neuroses of will (are we determined enough, or merely stubborn?), of strength (are we winning, however slowly, or have we run into a task beyond our capabilities?), and of position (is this war confirming our status as a major power in the region or, ultimately, destroying it?). Almost without exception, one can say that moderate or equivocal positions on these questions become impossible as a war winds on. This is true in dictatorships almost as much as in democracies, and can produce a deadlock either in public opinion or in a ruling elite. But in either case, it means that a moderate view frequently becomes untenable, as the debate begins to turn on a total withdrawal or prosecution of the war to victory.

One group that invariably emerges during these domestic debates consists of what one might call "anti-war hawks"—a faction that has no compunctions about the use of force, or about the justice of a given war, but believes that the costs of the war exceeds its benefits. Sometimes a large part of the public adheres to this view as well, as appears to have been the case of the American public in Vietnam. And characteristically it takes a well-known hawk to begin the process of winding these wars down (Richard Nixon and Yitzhak Rabin are good examples of this).

One of the most intriguing studies that can emerge from a study of the middle phase of military intervention is a comparative study of democratic and authoritarian regimes. The debate about the relative strategic effectiveness of these forms of government has a long lineage, back indeed to Thucydides' treatment of the differences between Athens and Sparta, or at the beginning of modern historiography, to Francis Parkman's comparison of French and British fortunes in waging war in North America. For our present purposes, we can compare liberal-democratic and authoritarian-totalitarian regimes with respect to "toughness," "cleverness," and "balance."

Democratic regimes frequently think of themselves as soft—unwilling to accept high casualties, almost as unwilling to inflict them, and impatient for success. There is surely something to be said for this, although the American experience in Vietnam gives one pause. The United States took between three and four times as many deaths as the Soviets did in Afghanistan, and fought the war, in a fairly intense way, for five or six years. Because liberal democracies have tended to be wealthier and more advanced than their opponents they can be more profligate with firepower, and are inclined to resort to air power as a tool to win a war. Though more discriminating in the way they deal with civilians (neither Israel nor the United States, for example, simply massacred hostile populations or prisoners), they could be quite as ruthless on the battlefield as their opponents. And even their "lack of persistence" can be read as a willingness, born of open politics, to liquidate an unprofitable commitment. Liberal democracy cannot, however, make systematic use of terror directed against civilians. It is deplorable but true that such methods can work, at least in the short run; whether they have a payoff in the long run is not clear. It does appear, however, that the use of terror by Soviet forces in Afghanistan and Syrian forces in Lebanon was useful in intimidating the local population.

In terms of "cleverness"—the relative ingenuity of intervening powers—the evidence is more ambiguous. Typically, liberal democracies come up with more clever gadgets, and dictatorships or totalitarian regimes with more devious ruses or ingenious systems for subversion or counterinsurgency. Tactically, the liberal democracies appear to be the more flexible. The contrast between American adoption of airmobile tactics in Vietnam, for example, and the years required for the Soviets to do the same more than fifteen years later, for example, is remarkable.

It is with regard to strategic balance that democracies appear at a disadvantage relative to dictatorships. The contrast between the United States sending over half a million men to Vietnam, and the Soviet Union refusing to send more than a quarter as many to Afghanistan bespeaks an ability to keep a minor conflict in some overall perspective. The Vietnam War gutted the American army in Europe and threw the American military, as well as American society, into turmoil. The Afghanistan war, hard though it was on both the Soviet military and Soviet society, did not have effects anywhere near as disruptive. On the other hand, democracies appear more inclined to decide earlier on that a war no longer makes sense, and to begin a process of disengagement. This may be read as greater realism or lack of persistence, but either way it tends to bring military interventions to an earlier end.

Notes

1. Carl von Clausewitz, *On War*, Michael Howard and Peter Paret, trans. (Princeton: Princeton University Press, 1976), p. 182. Book III, Ch. 1.

2. This is one of the major themes that emerges from an outstanding work, Allan R. Millett and Williamson Murray, eds., *Military Effectiveness* 3 vols. (Boston: Allen & Unwin, 1988).

3. Harry Summers, *On Strategy* (Novato, CA: Presidio, 1982), p. 1.

4. Raffi Gregorian, a doctoral student at the Johns Hopkins School of Advanced International Studies, has presented a fascinating study of the "CLARET Operations" in an unpublished manuscript, from which I draw, and which will be published shortly.

5. See Ronald H. Spector, *Advice and Support: The Early Years of the U.S. Army In Vietnam* (New York: The Free Press, 1985).

10

The Lessons of Disengagement[1]

GEORGE W. DOWNS

The disengagements that followed the unsuccessful interventions described in the case studies possess three striking characteristics. First, they were motivated to an unusual extent by a series of low probability events. If the determinants of disengagement are any guide to the reason that the interventions failed to achieve their objectives, they indicate that the role of improbable events was at least as important as poor decision-making. Second, there is considerable evidence that the head of state eventually chose to intervene at a higher level of intensity and/or for a longer duration that was consistent with public opinion and with the preferences of critical elites. Third, disengagement did not take place before the administration that had initiated the intervention had been replaced.

The role of improbable events is interesting because it suggests that the amount of miscalculation in the traditional sense may be smaller than retrospective analyses usually imply. It should also temper confidence that any given set of reforms (e.g., increasing intelligence agency performance) will dramatically reduce the probability of intervention failure. If the results of these cases are generalizable, they encourage us to reflect on the critical importance of exogenous events and how poorly we tend to understand local political processes.

The magnitude of intervention and the timing of disengagement are interesting because they suggest the prevalence of "gambling for resurrection"—the phenomenon whereby individuals engage in creasingly high payoff, low probablity wagers to salvage past losses.[2] Inevitably, some percentage of interventions will be failures. When such a failure seems to be occurring, the chief executive will be tempted to escalate the intensity or duration of the conflict for some of the same reasons that the president of a failing Savings and Loan may attempt increasingly risky investments. He or she can do no worse than be replaced—something that may well occur if the intervention is unsuccessfully terminated—and there is some probability of success. As a result, the head of state's estimate of the value of continued (or increased) intervention grows increasingly different from that of the constituency. This acts to extend the duration and intensity of an intervention and helps explain why disengagement does not take place until a different head of state is appointed.

The Impact of Low Probability Events

In the case of these failed interventions, it is easy, as it is with most policy failures, to overestimate the role of human error. Yet policy makers often make mistakes for much the same reason that investors or meteorologists do—their understanding of the phenomena at hand is either sadly incomplete or plagued by the operation of one or more fundamentally unpredictable elements. When this is the case, the attempt to assign responsibility to individuals, organizations, and decision rules can be misleading and even counterproductive. Unless the phenomenon is completely predictable, forecasting mistakes will be made that have nothing whatever to do with the shortcomings of institutions and individuals making the forecasts. To pretend otherwise is not simply to be in error; it can actually lead to decreased performance by leading to poor estimates of the uncertainty associated with forecasts.

"Ex post facto" analysis of the sort used in historical case studies can make this point difficult to appreciate. Once the locus of the decision has been identified and the rationale that drove the incorrect decision has been discovered, it is almost impossible not to jump to the conclusion that the "cause" of the poor outcome has been discovered. If the decision to intervene was made by a vain chief executive who intervened because he believed that the state was an extension of his own personality, the analyst can easily conclude that the subsequent failure was a consequence of vanity and absolute power. The problem is that the implicit counterfactual may be wrong. Intervention may well have occurred in the absence of the vain executive and, even more commonly, failure may have occurred for reasons that the most modest of leaders would not have foreseen.

This tendency is compounded by two other problems. The first lies in the intuitive belief that consistency is a reliable indicator of bias. If each of five interventions is marked by intelligence failures or an underestimation of cost, there is an overwhelming inclination to jump to the conclusion that intelligence or cost estimates must have been biased. This can be misleading. If an intervention fails, we know that *some* expectation was incorrect. However, that expectation could simply be the one about which there was the most uncertainty. The fact that more baseball games are cancelled by rain than by labor walkouts does not mean that meteorologists are more "optimistic" than labor lawyers.

The second problem lies in leaping to the conclusion that a bias must exist whenever someone "knew" the truth and his or her opinion was ignored. If a historian can produce a memo from someone in the bureaucracy that predicts that Shi'ite support of Israeli intervention in Lebanon would rapidly diminish, this is taken as solid evidence of irresponsibility by some decison maker or suppression of information by some bureaucrat. Yet as we all know a correct prediction can be poor evidence of prescience. Uncertainty breeds a variation of opinion, which in turn frequently breeds an accurate forecast of what will happen. Given a group of twenty investment advisory services it is likely that at least one of them will have a prediction record that is far better than one would expect by chance. Unfortunately, investors have learned through painful experience that this record of success can be a poor guide to what will happen in the future. This is not because the successful forecaster has grown indifferent to success, but because the initial success was due largely to luck.

The same phenomenon operates in the realm of intervention. The historical record will almost always show that some individual forecast that the intervention would run into trouble. Does this mean that policy makers were irresponsible for not having listened to this person? Not necessarily. To answer that question we need to know something about the range of advice the policy maker was getting and the quality of the arguments supporting each position.

We can now move on to what the determinants of disengagement of the United States from Vietnam, the Soviet Union from Afghanistan, South Africa from Angola, Israel from Lebanon, and India from Sri Lanka have to tell us about the role played by low probability events.

The Determinants of Disengagement

The list of determinants of disengagement can be short or long depending on the level of abstraction that we choose. At one extreme, there are the aggregate categories of benefits, costs, and resources. At the other extreme there are all of the factors that have some influence on these aggregate categories. Here the approach will be to focus on those determinants that the authors of the case studies suggest are the most important.[3]

Superpower Relations and Exogenous Events

It is difficult to read these five cases without being struck by how frequently the decision to disengage was motivated by a change in the relations between the two superpowers, as well as by changes in other factors that were not directly related to the intervention. Detente with the Soviet Union (and China) not only distracted Nixon and Kissinger from the war in Vietnam but, more importantly, vastly reduced the implications of withdrawal and the eventual fall of the government in South Vietnam.

Increasingly cordial relations with the United States made it easier for the Soviet Union to withdraw from Afghanistan. They also made it more necessary. Better relations with the United States depended on giving foreign policy substance to the new image that Gorbachev was fostering. Two other exogenous events also helped speed disengagement. The Soviet economy was continuing to disintegrate and the fundamentalist revolution in Iran which threatened to engulf the neighboring states was beginning to lose momentum.

Detente played an equally decisive role in the Angolan dispute. In that case, the United States and Soviet Union who together supplied an increasingly large portion of the resources that fueled the war, made it clear that they wanted the conflict to end. South Africa could not easily have predicted the emergence of such cooperation, nor could it have easily predicted that the international embargo against it would have achieved so much success that South Africa would no longer have the ability to chart its own course.

The role of detente was more modest in the case of the Sri Lankan intervention, but an important—even necessary—condition for Indian intervention hinged on Sri Lanka's strategic position and the fear that this small nation might be exploited by a state that intervened on the government's behalf. By 1990 that fear had diminished substantially, in large part because continued rapprochement between the United States and Soviet Union provided the former with little incentive to establish a base for naval operations in the Indian Ocean.

Changes in Enemy Composition, Resources, and Strategy

Kupchan is undoubtedly correct in charging that an inability to accurately anticipate changes in the nature of the opposition was a major reason why the goals of these interventions were not accomplished.

The issue here is, how much of the this inability was due to incompetence and how much to unpredictability?

It would be foolish to argue that incompetence and self-interest were unimportant. The intervention of the Soviet Union in Afghanistan was rife with them. By Litwak's account, the United States military's performance in Vietnam was a study in context sensitivity compared with the Red Army's performance in Afghanistan. The Red Army expected to fight a small scale version of the central front war that they had fought in Germany and Poland primarily because they were inclined to expect nothing else. It is doubtful that the opinions of their regional specialists, who were familiar with the British experience in Afghanistan and knew better, were ever seriously entertained. The Soviets then compounded the problem by believing their own propaganda about their invincibility. This is institutional inertia and hubris at its best.

On the other hand, culpability for not anticipating two of the most militarily crucial developments in Afghanistan is difficult to assign. The first involves the ability of the rebels to coordinate their activity. Should Moscow have known that groups who had an active antipathy toward each other would cooperate in an unprecedented fashion? In retrospect the answer may seem to be obviously yes. With the advantage of hindsight, it seems only reasonable that groups will put aside mutual hostilities to unite against a common outside threat. However, ethnic groups do not always put aside mutual antipathies to unite against the outsider. They have not always done so in Lebanon, Northern Ireland, Kenya, Uganda, or Tanzania. It appears that sometimes ethnic groups exploit a relationship with the invader to gain advantage over other groups and sometimes their inter-group hostilities make cooperation impossible. In retrospect, it is far easier to make a case that Moscow should have been uncertain how these groups would behave than to argue that Moscow should have predicted that they would cooperate effectively against the Soviet Union.

The other major development in Afghanistan was the decision by the United States to supply Stinger anti-aircraft missiles to the rebels. Once again, without the benefit of hindsight, it is difficult to view the failure to anticipate this as evidence of a biased institutional process. The Soviet Union had good reason for believing that the interest of the United States in the success of the Afghanistan rebels was small and better reason for assuming that the United State would adopt the view that the area fell within the Soviet sphere of influence. Moreover, early events suggested that their logic was correct. The Stingers were not supplied until 1986.

The other cases reveal similarly critical changes in the resources, composition, and strategy of the enemy which would have been very difficult to anticipate. For example, the Israeli army marched into Lebanon with the intent of eradicating the Palestinians and, if necessary, defeating the Syrians. Both objectives could have been handled with conventional tactics. What they ended up with was an unconventional war against Shi'ite guerrillas. Perhaps they should have been more concerned about the contingency that the Shi'ites would not remain neutral, but the Israelis had little reason to predict that they would not.

Nor is it clear that Israel should have anticipated the extent to which the Maronites would prove to be weak and unstable allies. The assassination of Bashir Jumayyil may not, as Feldman argues, have been an important cause of Israel's ultimate failure, but in its absence Israel might well have been able to accomplish more in Lebanon and the character of the disengagement might have been quite different. In any event, it was an important event that was possible, but hardly probable.

Improbable events were also a chief source of India's problems in Sri Lanka. It had intervened as the protector of the Tamils in Sri Lanka because of growing pressure from Indian Tamils in the Indian southern province of Tamil Nadu. What it discovered was a morass of Tamil and Sri Lankan parties whose loyalties and appreciation for Indian intervention shifted quickly and unaccountably. In the end, most of the pressure for increased troops ended up coming from the violent LTTE—a radical Tamil party. While the Indian government was aware that LTTE constituted a problem, it is difficult to hold the government accountable for not predicting how bitterly the LTTE would eventually respond to its intervention or how formidable a foe the LTTE would become. It had, after all, originally intervened to prevent the LTTE from being exterminated. It is still more difficult to fault the Indians for not having anticipated that the Sri Lankan government would ally itself with the LTTE for the purpose of evicting the Indians. Given the history of their relations and their disparate goals, short-term cooperation between the two seemed unlikely and long-term cooperation seemed impossible.

Whether the United States should have foreseen that a guerrilla war against the Viet Cong would turn into a conventional war against the North Vietnamese is also debatable. This outcome probably should not be viewed as being as unexpected as the transformation of the Shi'ites from neutrals to enemies or cooperation between the LTTE and the Sri Lankan government for the purpose of expelling India, but it was far from certain.

South Africa's intervention in Angola also held its surprises. While the South Africans can probably be faulted for underestimating the effectiveness of the Cuban ground forces and the magnitude of the Soviet commitment, they had no reason to anticipate that they would have to cede air superiority to the Cubans. That fact, made glaringly clear at Calueque Dam, was as much a consequence of the embargo as anything directly connected to the intervention itself.

Cost

It is not difficult to argue that the cost of intervention was often increased by the uncertain events just described and that their impact was further exacerbated by general economic conditions that were sometimes difficult to predict. The successful collaboration of Mujaheedin elements and the availability of Stinger missiles had substantial cost implications for the Soviet Union, and the cost to the United States of fighting an extended conventional war against North Vietnam regulars was also high. The ineffectiveness of Maronite forces in Lebanon and LTTE actions in Sri Lanka created similarly unexpected costs for Israel and India. South Africa had to cope with not only the unexpected shift in air superiority but also the general economic effects of the embargo.

Public Opinion

All of the authors note the role of public opinion in precipitating disengagement, Litwak and Berman emphasize it as one of the most critical factors. In the Soviet Union the war had become universally unpopular and was most despised by the very groups that Gorbachev depended on to spearhead a restructuring of the economy and Soviet society. In the United States, public opinion against the war was responsible for nearly defeating a sitting President in his party's first primary and ultimately caused him not to seek reelection.

Yet none of the cases reveals a grossly biased initial estimate about the extent to which the public would support the war. With the possible exception of Israel, the public was either indifferent to, or very supportive of, these interventions when they first took place.

The fact that an ever larger portion of the public came to believe that these interventions should be abandoned and began to speak out against them, raises the possibility that the public was learning at a faster rate than the government or that the government had developed an evaluative bias that was absent at the time of intervention. This issue is treated in some detail in the next section.

Uncertainty, Reputation, and Gambling for Resurrection

In every case, disengagement was preceded by a change in the administration of the intervening state.[4] Does this mean that we should view the initial intervention and the subsequent delays in disengagement as the actions of particular administrations' eccentric policies?

Feldman provides a strong argument that this is true in the case of Israel's intervention in Lebanon, but there is good reason to be skeptical of this explanation in the other cases. One must first consider in each instance how plausible it is to believe that another head of state would have acted differently and, if so, would his reasons for doing so have been better than those of the original leader? The qualification about having a good reason for acting differently is important because it keeps us from falling into the trap of confusing variation inspired from uncertainty with bias. Evidence that two stockbrokers disagree with my stockbroker may be more indicative of mutual uncertainty than of any error on her part.

Except in the case of Israel, there is very little evidence in most of these cases that a different executive—specially from within the same party—would have acted differently and still less that the underlying rationale for the different policy would have been more justifiable. In the case of the Soviet Union, the policy of keeping surrounding buffer states on a short leash had been part of the Russian grand strategy since the nineteenth century and had been pursued with success since the beginning of the Cold War. There is no doubt that skepticism about the wisdom of this policy was scattered among the elite, but it would not be until Andropov assumed power that this skepticism began to diffuse through the party to any serious extent. Even Gorbachev evidenced little distaste for the logic that motivated intervention in Afghanistan when he first took office.

Gandhi's decision to intervene in Sri Lanka was also more mainstream than eccentric. Tamil support in the south of India was an important source of electoral support for the Congress party and a commitment to not having a great-power presence on Sri Lanka superseded party lines. The same is true of the South African decision to intervene in Angola. South Africa had a long standing relationship with the MLPA before the intervention and its propensity for aggressively intervening in neighboring states (e.g., Mozambique) was well established. There is no reason to believe that another leader of South Africa's dominant party would have acted differently.

The extent to which the decision to intervene is identified with Lyndon Johnson tends to obscure the fact that most other plausible candidates for office would also have intervened. It is true that Berman effectively documents the variation of opinion that existed within the highest circles of the administration, but for every George Ball there was a Robert McNamara and a Dean Rusk. It is unlikely that another Democratic President would have been advised differently or made a different decision. It is even more unlikely that a Republican President—with the possible exception of Goldwater—would have refrained from intervention. Moreover, had the decision been made to refrain from intervention, the arguments justifying that choice would have been no stronger.

Yet there is still an interesting leadership question here. Regardless of how typical their attitudes toward intervention were when they took office, the refusal of heads of state to disengage in the face of growing public disapproval, and the fact that their successors succeeded in disengaging while they did not, suggest that their attitudes had become less typical by the time they left office. What had occurred?

One explanation is that there was a difference in the value that the head of state and the constituency assigned to the goal of successful intervention which had existed from the very beginning. Members of the constituency may have felt that it was sensible to intervene, but there was a limit to the price they were willing to pay that was lower than that of the head of state. This would lead them to push for disengagement at an earlier point. Perhaps Ghandi was more committed to Tamil civil rights and Johnson more fearful of communist insurgence in Southeast Asia than most other members of their parties and the general public.

There may be some truth in this claim, but it is not well supported by the case studies. With the possible exception of Israel, there is no indication that the head of state's commitment to the goals of the intervention was markedly greater than other potential leaders from the same party or the general public.

Another, more plausible, explanation is that we are witnessing an instance of "gambling for resurrection!" One way of viewing such behavior is that it is designed to protect reputation: of an individual to herself; of an individual to others; of an organization to itself and its public; and of a nation. While a number of these motives can operate simultaneously, identifying the reputation that is primarily involved in a given instance can be helpful in thinking about the possibilities for reform. Problems of self-image, for example, are unlikely to yield to the same solutions as those of national reputation.

While the case studies do not focus on individual psychology, they depict less of the denial behavior and distaste for bad news that is usually present when the primary concern is self-image. Berman's account in particular makes it clear that Johnson went to extraordinary lengths to keep up with the flow of events and to fairly assess their implications—even with respect to mounting costs and the deterioration of political support.

The argument that disengagement was delayed because of a preoccupation with organizational reputation is undermined by the fact that new administrations were able to disengage without organizational reforms. There is no evidence that changes in administration occurred coincident with important changes in the military, intelligence agencies, or other bureaucracies. The ability of new administrations to disengage also argues against the sort of preoccupation with national reputation that George Ball believed would create a slippery slope from which there would be no recovery. By definition, "national humiliation" is not administration specific. It scars an entire nation. If national reputation were dominant, new administrations would be almost as anxious to avoid its effect as the administration that initiated the intervention. Yet they were not.

While it would be counterproductive to overemphasize the point, the evidence from these case studies suggests that the head of state's concern for his reputation as a decision maker dominated others. Moreover, this concern probably had less to do with the social embarrassment of admitting failure than with the decision maker's ability to retain office and execute his policy agenda.

To see what might be going on, consider the intervention control problem as one where a principal (i.e., the constituency) faces the problem of how to design an incentive scheme or set of punishments that will encourage its agent (the head of state) to intervene at a rate and magnitude that reflects its preferences. Here the "moral hazard" problem lies less in preventing the agent from performing at a low level of effort, than in preventing "adventurism"—intervention for the sake of personal glory. Given the difficulty of assessing the extent of adventurism directly, the most effective way of curbing the influence of this motivation lies in establishing the expectation that the head of state will be punished for an unsuccessful intervention.

The constituency also has a interest in assessing a head of state's judgment and leadership skills. Except in those cases when a military leader is elevated to the position of head of state, direct information about a head of state's competence to act effectively in a wartime environment is extremely scarce. Performance during an intervention—particularly whether the intervention has succeeded or failed—provides some of this information. An intervention failure is a signal, however imperfect, that an important aspect of executive competence may be lacking and will inevitably lead to some punishment or erosion of support.

The result is that as long as there is uncertainty about the congruence between the motivations of the constituency and those of the head of state and uncertainty about why an intervention failed—as there almost always will be—there will be reason to punish the head of state for the intervention's failure.[5] Not to do so will inspire the adventurism that the constituency would like to avoid.

Of course, an incentive structure that punishes only failures could easily produce a level of conservatism on the part of the head of state that is irresponsible. Why would such an executive ever intervene? One answer is that success is also probably rewarded: the head of state is more likely to be reelected and her ability to accomplish a domestic agenda is likely to increase. Even if the punishment for failure were quite harsh, some interventions (i.e., those with a high expected benefit) could still appear to be attractive propositions. Another answer lies in the ability of the constituency to gauge the opportunity costs of *not* intervening and delving out punishments accordingly. There is doubtless a price to be paid for opening oneself to the charge of *not* intervening when it was necessary.

Thus, it is reasonable to assume that some percentage of potential interventions will be unavoidable and some of the set will be unsuccessful. When this occurs the executive must choose between disengagement with the accompanying punishment and either persisting in or escalating the level of intervention.

It is not difficult to appreciate why the second option may be the most attractive. For a punishment to be significant enough to prevent adventurism the penalty is probably substantial enough to jeopardize continuance in power or critical portions of a leader's policy agenda.

The head of state can attempt to convince the constituency that the failure was unforeseeable, but the self-serving nature of the argument that it was a good decision that was upset by a bad outcome usually results in such arguments being heavily discounted. The fact that rival aspirants for leadership will be arguing that incompetence alone was the reason the intervention failed is unlikely to help matters.

The situation is not helped by the fact that further intervention is not likely to produce a harsher punishment since there is limited liability. Except in extraordinary circumstances, the worst that can eventually happen is eviction from office. The head of state finds herself in a position that is roughly comparable to that of a failing Savings and Loan executive. Increased investment in intervention or housing is unlikely to lead to good results, but postponing bankruptcy or disengagement holds out the possibility of a good outcome (resurrection) and makes the penalty for failure no worse.

Conclusion

The list of factors that the case authors believe prompted disengagement includes changes in superpower relations, the composition, resources, and strategy of the enemy, and public opinion. While predictions regarding these factors were often wrong, there is little reason to believe that most of the error was due to an individual or institutional bias of the sort often responsible for international debacles such as World War I. The fact that there were individual and organizations who may have put forth different estimates that subsequently proved more correct does not disprove this. For the most part, these estimates are like those of many successful stockbrokers. They possess the post facto advantage of having come true, but were inspired by evidence that was no more persuasive than that which supported very different predictions.

On the surface, it is hard to think of better evidence for the belief that intervention and escalation was eccentrically motivated than the knowledge that the replacement of those in power was followed by withdrawal. Yet we have seen that such a conclusion might well be incorrect. This situation can easily be brought about by nothing more than the fact that the leader who initiated the unsuccessful intervention would have to suffer a penalty for failure. This gives the old leader an incentive to gamble for resurrection that the new leader does not have.

There are a variety of possible explanations for why the interests of the heads of state and their constituencies diverged over time, but one based on the political economy of intervention seems quite plausible. A leader's interest is not always synonymous with national interest or even with the interest of whoever will hold the position next. In this case, uncertainty about the sources of failed intervention may leave a constituency with little alternative apart from holding leaders responsible for the failure. This provides leaders with an incentive to continue the intervention far longer than seems "rational" in order to salvage their reputations and careers. The limited liability of leaders makes such gambling for resurrection an attractive proposition.

Thinking about these personal incentives helps us evaluate the superficially attractive prescription that if an intervention proves unsuccessful, the policy maker should simply lower his goals and disengage. This advice is based on the quite correct observation that the worst-case scenario that was often used to justify the initial intervention never took place. After the departure of the Indians, Sri Lanka did not murder all of its Tamils and become a staging area for another power. The fall of Vietnam did not precipitate communist takeovers throughout Southeast Asia. Afghanistan did not join a fundamentalist power bloc hostile to the interests of the Soviet Union.

The problem with this advice is that it ignores the fact that the worst-case scenario for the leader who initiated the intervention involves more than what will happen to the nation's interests if disengagement takes place. It also includes what will happen to the leader's *personal* interests. These interests refer not simply to macho self-image and the desire to be a successful leader (although these may matter), but to the prospects for electoral success and success in accomplishing a political agenda. If disengagement takes place, the chief executive's personal interests may not fare as well as those of the state he represents.

Notes

1. I would like to thank Alexander George and the editors of this volume for their helpful comments.
2. For an excellent review of some of this literature see Barry M. Staw and Jerry Ross, "Understanding Behavior in Escalation Situations," *Science* 246 (1989):216–220.

3. My knowledge of the Israeli intervention into Lebanon was further enhanced by a lengthy conversation with Professor Levite.

4. While in the Indian case Gandhi was responsible for both intervention and disengagement, a new administration had taken office in the interim.

5. This is particularly true if it is difficult for the constituency to discriminate among intervention failures. If it cannot discriminate between a small failure, a large failure, and a disaster, it may be forced to punish them all in a similar fashion.

11

Foreign Military Intervention in Perspective

BRUCE W. JENTLESON,
ARIEL E. LEVITE, LARRY BERMAN

As noted at the outset, two principal questions have guided this study: What do these six cases have in common? What can be learned more generally about foreign military intervention from these commonalities?

Many of the answers to these questions have already been provided both in the case studies themselves and in the cross-case analyses of each of the three stages of foreign military intervention. In this final chapter we have three principal concerns. First, we offer some overarching generalizations about the pattern of protracted foreign military interventions. Second, we consider the broader research agenda of which this study is a part. Finally, we assess the prospects for foreign military interventions in the post–Cold War era.

General Observations

Bringing together and building on many specific points that have been made throughout this study, five overall conclusions can be drawn.

First, foreign military interventions are an especially *dynamic* phenomenon. A nation that commits combat troops into another nation's internal conflict is introducing a powerful new catalyst in an already unstable and often volatile mix. The differences among prior or alternative commitments (diplomatic, economic, indirect military) are differences of degree; the crossing of the threshold to the introduction of large numbers of ground forces on an open-ended basis is a difference of kind. Unless it can be carried out quickly and decisively, it is highly likely to trigger a set of reactions along all three dimensions—international, intervenor-domestic and target-indigenous—and from previously dormant as well as already active forces, which alters the environment in and over which the intervenor seeks to exert influence. Thus the conditions under which the foreign military intervention was originally calculated at an initial point in time (T_1) are subject to alterations as the intervention proceeds over time (T_2, T_3 . . . . T_x). Moreover, many of those changes—often critically important ones—are ones which the intervenor did not (and in many cases could not) expect at all, or ones to which it attached low probability.

Thus, for example, the Soviets (for reasons common to other intervenors in the other five cases) did not calculate either that the Mujaheddin would mount organized resistance, or later that they would
possess weaponry such as the Stinger missiles which substantially
enhanced their military capability to mount counterattacks. Israel
similarly proved unable to foresee the consequences of its military
action removing the Palestinian reign in Southern Lebanon on the
attitude and conduct of the heretofore deprived but dormant Shi'a
population.

This dynamism of the process thus creates a constant or at least
recurring need for reassessment of goals, objectives, strategies and
tactics. Yet this is a need which policy makers have had difficulty
meeting, for reasons of both capability and disposition. Once troops
have been committed, the dominant pressures have been for intensification of military activity, rather than either a reassessment of the
political objectives or of the on-the-ground military tactics. Decision-
making and strategizing have tended to run "behind the curve" at
all three stages of the intervention.

Second, and further complicating the dilemma, is the high degree
of *uncertainty* inherent to undertaking foreign military intervention.
This point comes through all the case studies and is stressed by
Kupchan, Cohen, and Downs. It is not meant to alleviate the criti-
cisms of poor intelligence, flawed or biased decision-making, and
other controllable factors. Rather it is to differentiate that which could
have been known, but was not, from the irreducible uncertainty
which by definition would remain even if intelligence agencies be-
haved optimally, decision makers used the intelligence effectively,
and the decision processes were both unbiased and open to alternative options. We are struck by the contrast between the extent to
which case study authors initially were inclined to advance explanations based on flawed processes, yet how through the comparative
perspective a consensus emerged that much greater weight ought to
be assigned the dilemmas inherent in such an undertaking.

Third is the sheer *complexity* of the enterprise. Remaking the internal political order of another state is perhaps the most formidable
task that can be undertaken. Defeating the armed forces of another
state through direct military action or other classical means of warfare
is of course no small task. It has rarely been the case—not in ancient
Greece, not even in medieval Europe, not in the world wars of the
twentieth century, not in Operation Desert Storm—and it doubtfully
ever will be. But to send troops into states ridden by deep divisions
and torn by violent conflicts, which often are matters of fundamental

identity (ethnicity, religion, culture) even more than of politics as traditionally understood in the West, is to take on goals and objectives of a much greater magnitude of complexity. This involves not just restraining or otherwise changing the behavior of another state, but remaking the essential nature and structure of the domestic political order as well. Winning over hearts and minds of a people is a much more complex undertaking than defeating an opposing army.

The magnitude of the task assigned to military intervention appears even more formidable when we take into consideration that often for the intervenor the intervention is largely perceived as a sideshow. It is consequently both designed and expected to attain the desired result of a limited expenditure and moderate cost in both human casualties and material. This perception also translates sooner or later into political reluctance and public resistance to commit more than a certain amount of resources, and frequently also into delays and difficulties in breaking this limit. Herein lies not only a sharp contrast with classical military warfare but also with the motivation to resist the intervention which opposing forces in the target country manifest. For them the outcome of the intervention is a matter of life and death. This asymmetry of motivation is not to be underestimated as an independent variable that explains, in part, both the course and outcome of an intervention.

A fourth point is the extensive *destructiveness* wrought by all six of these foreign military interventions. One need not calculate separate accountabilities for how many casualties and how much destruction is to be attributed to foreign intervenors and how much to the indigenous parties. Nor does it matter that we cannot be certain about the counterfactual of whether death and destruction would have been less without foreign military intervention. The point is that the foreign intervention adds to the already explosive mix a large number of well armed soldiers. Moreover, the very nature of the operation that does not allow for easy distinction between innocent civilians and terrorists or freedom fighters, or between fighting grounds and populated areas, makes the violence even more bitter and widespread. The longer the intervention lasts, the greater the volume of destructiveness it wreaks, not merely as a mathematical function of the duration of the fighting, but also due to the self-feeding dynamic of the intervention itself which requires or legitimizes (as the case may be) less restrictive use of force on all sides to get results.

Other studies, in addition to our own, have identified similar results. Among those studies cited earlier, Singer and Small found "internationalized civil wars" to have much higher casualties than noninternationalized ones, and Pearson shows that foreign military interventions tend to increase levels of violence and exacerbate instability.[1] In a recent comparative study of contemporary revolutions, Ted Gurr and Jack Goldstone concluded that "the most deadly of our ten revolutionary conflicts are those that have attracted foreign intervention." They further note, in assessing the types of domestic political regimes which come out of revolutions, that

> the most inimical condition for democracy is a protracted and violent revolutionary conflict. Intense conflict hardens on all sides and convinces the victors that they must rely on force to suppress potential opponents. It takes a full political generation or more to overcome battle-hardened revolutionaries' habits of relying on force to maintain power. *We know of no clear exception to this principle in this century.*[2]

Violence not only intensifies in the moment, but also begets further violence, and lives on beyond the actual fighting of revolutions and foreign military interventions.[3]

A final general observation concerns *the lack of comparative thinking* and the resulting *limited learning* by intervenors and prospective intervenors one from the other. Policy makers, other elites, and the general public do, however, consider or are otherwise emotionally affected by their own country's previous experiences. Thus, for example, the Vietnam experience has influenced U.S. attitudes toward intervention (e.g., in the Angolan civil war in the 1970s, Central America and the Weinberger-Shultz debate more generally in the 1980s) to the point where some lamented it as a "syndrome."[4] Similar influence was evident in recent Israeli and Indian decisions not to reintervene in Lebanon and Sri Lanka, respectively.

That policy makers may not draw these lessons or make the analogies effectively, and otherwise misuse historical analysis, is a separate point.[5] They also show a tendency to feel bound by earlier decisions pertaining to the country in question, whether made by themselves or by their predecessors. Yet there is little evidence in any of the cases, whether because they deemed them irrelevant and/or for lack of knowledge, about questions asked or analyses posed based on other country's experiences. The Soviets just assumed that they would "do it right" this time, not like the Americans in Vietnam. Ariel Sharon never stopped to assess whether there was something to be learned about Lebanon from Syria's prior experience there. South Africa, Cuba, and India all were primarily inwardly motivated in their interventions, responsive to their own versions of domestic imperatives with little sense of the possible relevance of comparative learning. Yet the central point of this book is precisely the value that comparative analysis can have. The value of the comparative perspective in this context is rather considerable, as it may sensitize analysts as well as policy makers and their advisers to the features of and dilemmas inherent in the very nature of foreign military interventions. This would make it more difficult for them, cognitively and otherwise, to attribute other people's intervention experience to idiosyncratic or *sui generis* factors. This, in turn, could lead on the one hand to devising an integrated politico-military strategy for intervention that takes into account the complications that might otherwise be expected to arise along the way, or on the other hand to a conscious choice to forego military intervention and pursue some alternative strategy.

To be sure, none of these generalizations are to be taken as fixed or all pervasive. Each case had its exceptions and unique features. Moreover, as the rich description of the case studies shows, there is some diversity in both the processes leading to intervention and the intervention strategies pursued, and ultimately also in the outcomes of the interventions, varying as they did from relative success (Syria in Lebanon) to all but total failure (U.S. in Vietnam), with other cases falling somewhere in between. Here, conscious of the problem of equifinality, we are circumspect in claiming any single causal model. Yet at the same time the limitation of equifinality does not deny the scope of the considerable similarities that do exist among the cases. Thus the patterns as traced and the explanations offered for such a broad range of cases do provide important insights, for scholars and statesmen, into the dynamics of protracted military intervention.

The Broader Research Agenda

Our research design, as noted at the outset, has emphasized variation within one subset of cases—namely, protracted military intervention, rather than variation across types of cases. Our study thus offers more depth than breadth. In the first chapter we defined and delimited our case set. We also differentiated it from (a) other uses of military force (e.g., classical wars), (b) other forms of intervention, and (c) quick-decisive military interventions.

It is useful now, to conclude this study and to address the broader research agenda, to consider both the scope and the limits of the insights gained herein. In doing so we shall offer some working propositions on the relationship between our generalizations and the three other subsets of the intervention universe, as identified in the first chapter.

On the Goal and Utility of Employing Military Force

If there truly were any doubts, events in the Persian Gulf in 1990–91 proved that the obituaries for war and military force were, at best, premature. On August 2, 1990, Saddam Hussein showed that military force would continue to be used aggressively and in pursuit of territorial conquest. From January 16 through February 27, 1991, the United States and its coalition partners showed that military force could still be used quite effectively to defeat aggression and reverse conquest. But this observation should not lead us to confuse the distinction between classical war and foreign military intervention.

The 1990–91 Persian Gulf war did prove that notwithstanding the fall of the Berlin Wall, the increased importance of economic power, and other transformations of the international order, military power still has relevance and utility. Yet as emphasized by former Defense Undersecretary William J. Perry, the military capabilities demonstrated in Desert Storm

> will be quite limited in effectiveness in any regional conflicts that are basically civil wars or dominated by guerrilla warfare. No one should be deluded into believing that the military capability that can easily defeat an army with 4,000 thanks in a desert is going to be the decisive factor in a jungle or urban guerrilla war.[6]

The utility of any policy instrument (military, foreign, or domestic) to achieve an objective does not necessarily imply its utility for the achieving of some other and very different objective. As stressed in chapter 1, there is a fundamental difference in the nature of the central objectives to be achieved through classical warfare (defeat the armed forces of an adversary) and through foreign military intervention (remake the internal political order of another state). It is inherently more difficult, as a matter of basic instrumental fit between political ends and military means, to devise military strategies capable of achieving the latter. The lines of battle and conditions of warfare are less conventional and require tactics and operations for which large-scale combat forces are less well suited. Targets are less easily identifiable, either in an operational sense or in assessing their significance. Setbacks inflicted on the enemy are harder to convert into firm and enduring gains. Even gaining military control over territory may not bring effective and enduring political control. On the other hand, setbacks suffered make it harder to endure, both with respect to sustaining domestic support and to maintaining military morale. Little comes easily either in itself or in terms of coordinating the multiplicity of factors which must go into foreign military intervention strategy.[7]

Moreover, the dependent nature of the relationship with the local ally further constrains the utility of interventionary military force. The whole notion of indirect political control that separates foreign military intervention from invasions and outright efforts at conquest requires that the military action be limited to supporting a local indigenous ally. The objective is not to gain power directly, but to remove from power one faction or individual and install or maintain another in power. But while this may enhance claims of legitimacy, it may well simultaneously undermine the local credibility of the ally. Moreover, it also means that the ability of the intervenor to achieve his objectives is significantly dependent on the abilities and indigenous appeal of the local ally.

Yet as is readily observable across the cases, the relationship with the local ally is notoriously problematic, as the latter on many occasions becomes a liability rather than an asset. In quite a few cases the local ally is unreliable in the first place, in fact appealing for external assistance precisely in order to make up for his lack of domestic political support, not just his military weakness. In other cases the ally may have had a measure of credibility and reliability at the outset but increasingly loses it in the process of the involvement, either because his association with the external power discredits him locally, and/or because it reinforces his inclination to brutality or complacency once the external power appeared increasingly committed to his cause (yet another version of the "free rider" problem). Thus, for example, both the United States and the Soviet Union found it necessary to depose local allies (Diem, Karmal) who proved unreliable. The Israelis lost theirs to an assassin while Syria switched its local partners on several occasions. India's initial local ally (the Tamils) became over time the principal inflicter of casualties on the IPKF.

Thus there is nothing contradictory or mutually exclusive about the lessons of the Persian Gulf War and the lessons of Vietnam (or Afghanistan, Lebanon, etc.). Despite the misleading rhetoric of President Bush suggesting that "by God, we have kicked the Vietnam syndrome once and for all,"[8] the actions of the Bush administration in response to the Iraqi civil war which followed in the wake of Operation Desert Storm indicated that it was somewhat cognizant of the distinction. It resisted the facile calls for "marching to Baghdad" and instead opted for a form of multilateral peacekeeping as an alternative strategy. While this strategy has had its own problems, it can be just as dangerous to overestimate the scope of the utility of military power as it can be to underestimate it.

Why Military Intervention?

A second distinction made at the outset was between military and other forms of foreign intervention. If one takes as a given that state A's interests are affected by developments internal to state B, and that therefore it is rational for state A to seek to influence developments within state B, the question is why does state A choose one particular form of intervention rather than another? It is not simply an action/inaction situation or choice, but rather which type of action to choose from among a number of alternatives. Put differently, even if we follow Richard Little's distinction between "push" and "pull" explanations of intervention, and attribute it to the latter, we are still left with the need to explain why and when military intervention is ultimately decided upon as the preferred course of action.[9]

The choice for direct military intervention was a criterion for selecting our subset of cases. Our analysis reveals a number of commonalities that seem to characterize these cases. First, at the brink of crossing the threshold from political commitment to military intervention, it was more the desirability of the objectives being pursued than the prospects for success which motivated the key decisions. The rationale for intervention had by this time grown to be considered overwhelming, in part because current policy makers perceived their choices as being so constrained by earlier commitments that they had no other choice but to take the next step. Thus there was little inclination to subject the decision to cross the threshold to systematic cost-benefit calculus. The common assumption was that more was to be lost by not militarily intervening than by doing so. This was a very different assumption, and a harder one to refute, than had it been a matter of what was to be gained. And it mostly was an assumption, not a proposition. The burden of proof at best was on those who favored not moving toward military engagement. This made for standards of evidence that were neither uniform nor neutral. And while, as Kupchan points out, decisions to intervene may have been made anyway, irrespective of their cost assessment, a greater openness in the debate on cost-gain expectations seems at least a necessary condition for any prospect of a choice of an alternative strategy.

Second, and as part of the explanation for this skewed structuring of the decision process, in all of the cases it was not just the intrinsic importance of the target state but broader international concerns about the regional/global balance of power and credibility which motivated the intervenor. This consideration obviously complicated further a strict cost-benefit calculation. The intervention may have been targeted at the internal politics of a particular country, but the calculations had much to do also with exogenous global and/or regional considerations. Moreover, these systemic calculations were commonly made in a zero or at least fixed sum fashion in which the minimal objective was to prevent even the perception of gains by others, if not for the intervenor to make net gains for himself. Beyond even such direct balance of power calculations, there was persistent concern (especially in the U.S. and Israeli cases) over the implications of (non)intervention for the broader perceptions of other adversaries and other allies alike which could affect the credibility of the intervenor's other commitments, and overall deterrence posture.

The implications for the "slippery slope" thesis are mixed. On the one hand, the deterministic nature of the metaphor is tempered. These were not decision-makers who had either lost control or were not consciously making choices. Moreover, they had more options than a single intervention/nonintervention dichotomy allows. Direct military intervention through combat troops, as we stress, is not the only form that intervention can take. The United States was intervening in other ways in Vietnam well before 1965; similarly for the Soviets in Afghanistan, and Israel in Lebanon. And then there are the numerous cases outside our subset of what, as with the United States in Vietnam in 1954, are often referred to as decisions "not to intervene," but really amounted to decisions for alternative strategies of intervention.

On the other hand, once embarked, the ground is not perfectly level. Precedents are set, credibility is staked, options are narrowed, and sacrifice becomes value. Decision points for shifting policy are still there. It isn't like falling off a precipice. But there is a slope, the footing can be treacherous and momentum can gather.

Once the military intervention is launched, but when immediate victory proves elusive, concerns over credibility can assume even greater importance. As the intervention drags on, and increasing resources are expended in an attempt to attain the desired result, the political stakes also grow. More sacrifice becomes more value. The intervenor accordingly tends to strengthen his belief that his international position (whether global or regional) would be more adversely affected by withdrawal than by staying in, accounting for the difficulty and delay in reaching a decision to seek disengagement.

One of the key factors explaining the shift to getting out in those cases in which military disengagement did occur was the restructuring of the international context because of fundamental changes in superpower relations and/or relations of the small power intervenor with the superpower that was its principal ally. The United States considered its loss in Vietnam more bearable in the context of the early 1970s detente than in the context of Cold War. The Soviet Union under Gorbachev in the late 1980s wanted to improve relations with the United States and realized that both its own military withdrawal from Afghanistan and its ally Cuba's military withdrawal from Angola were necessary conditions. Red, yellow, or green lights aside at the outset of the intervention, Israel found itself under pressure from the United States to withdraw from Lebanon. The Syrian case, on the other hand, points to the role of changes in the international and/or regional scene as a key independent variable explaining not only disengagement, but also consolidation of the intervenor's control over the target country. The Syrians initially benefitted from the Israeli and U.S. decisions to disengage from military involvement in internal Lebanese affairs following their traumatic experiences of the early 1980s. The U.S. pulled out its Marines from Lebanon, while Israel confined its military involvement to the "security zone" it had established in Southern Lebanon. Then, in late 1990 and early 1991, Syria took advantage of the additional changes in the international scene to all but consolidate its control on the Lebanese political scene. Exploiting its improved ties with the U.S., especially in the context of the anti-Iraqi coalition in the Gulf crisis, Syria proceeded to launch the military moves that finally dislodged from power the opposing Christian forces and forced the different Lebanese factions to endorse a Syrian sponsored political settlement.

The influence of domestic political pressures follows a similar trajectory. One is struck by how domestic political pressures, or at least the perception thereof by leaders, initially pushed toward military intervention. The particular source of these domestic pressures varied from case to case, but they often were from elites even more than from the general public. In the Soviet Union, Israel and the United States, it was civilian elites and some political factions, or at least key figures within them, even more than military elites. In the

U.S. case public pressure also appeared to play a role, but less through direct pressure than in the perceptions and assumptions made by Johnson. In India, the political link was the most direct, with the pressures for intervention coming primarily from the citizens of the State of Tamil Nadu, a key ethnic group in a key state vital to the political base of Rajiv Gandhi and his Congress Party.

Yet domestic political pressures reversed themselves and at equal if not greater intensity made staying in increasingly difficult. But this did not happen primarily as a result of the disillusionment of those factions, elites, or individuals supporting the original intervention decision, many of whom (e.g., Ariel Sharon in Israel) remained hawks. Rather, the balance of forces changed because of the awakening and legitimation of forces previously dormant or weak, whether because of the absence of a strong policy preference or for fear of a political backlash. Johnson became the first American president to choose not to seek reelection since Calvin Coolidge in 1928. Menachem Begin suffered an even greater tragedy, not just political but personal. Sri Lanka helped defeat Rajiv Gandhi politically and, tragically, led to his assassination. And while Brezhnev, Andropov, and Chernenko all died in office, the effects of Afghanistan in undermining the old Soviet order were pervasive and profound.

As to the influence of leaders as individuals, the conclusions are mixed. Clearly in some cases, such as Israel in Lebanon, the influence of a particular individual such as Ariel Sharon was a critical factor. This, however, may be the exception so far as getting in is concerned. Personality idiosyncrasies do have to be taken into account: LBJ's insecurities, Asad's vision of a "Greater Syria," Castro's revolutionary messianism. Overall, though, as Downs points out, the interventions were less a function of the individual or psychological traits of leaders than the factors already noted stressing the dynamics of the decision environment.

Where leadership was more important, however, was in the staying in and, ultimately, getting out. As Downs also stresses, and as with the shift in the international context, in every case it was a different leader who got out than got in. This finding is consistent with Craig and George's observation regarding the difficulty of leaders who initiate classical wars to terminate them when results fall far short of goals.[10] There is an irony in this, in that the leader who committed military troops so often feels constrained and even compelled by the political commitments made by predecessors. Yet even as the interventions became protracted, such leaders persisted in seeing their personal credibility as at stake and at risk by anything

314 JENTLESON, LEVITE, BERMAN

short of staying the course. Undoubtedly psychological as well as other political factors enter in to a full explanation of this phenomenon. As in other cases of war termination, these include such considerations as general concern for national and international credibility, the pursuit of a position of strength from which to negotiate, and the influence of military commanders. Whatever the particulars, the key point is that quite frequently political leaders find it more difficult to back out of a war than they originally envisaged, and that a change of leadership appears to be a necessary condition for ending protracted foreign military interventions.

Further research could test these patterns as demonstrated by these cases, in all of which military intervention did occur, against cases in which military intervention did not occur. Some such comparisons can be done on an intra-case basis, as with the contrast within the Vietnam case between the 1954 decision not to intervene militarily and the 1965 decision to do so,[11] and within the Israel–Lebanon case between the limited interventionary strategy of the Litani operation and the full-scale launching of the invasion.

A particularly interesting case would be Gorbachev's decisions (n.b., the plural) not to intervene militarily anywhere in Eastern Europe in 1989. Clearly Soviet interests were affected by internal political developments within these countries. Why then did the tanks not roll as they did in Afghanistan in 1979 (and in Czechoslovakia in 1968 and in Hungary in 1956)? The patterns identified herein could provide a useful theoretical framework within which to analyze this case (as well as others) in non *sui generis* terms, and in turn to continue the theory building process.

Why Protracted?

This too is a question that cannot be conclusively answered here. But some propositions again can be offered for further testing, based on the commonalities in our cases in contrast to some of the major historical examples of quick-decisive foreign military intervention cited earlier (such as the U.S. interventions in the Dominican Republic in 1965, Grenada in 1983, and Panama in 1989; the Soviet interventions in Hungary in 1956 and Czechoslovakia in 1968).

One readily evident difference is in the preexisting relationship between the intervenor and the target state as intra-bloc or extra-bloc. Intra-bloc means a relationship in which the target state is at least de facto recognized by other key states in the international system as part of the sphere of influence or hegemonic domain of the intervenor. This may not be a formalized or even explicitly articulated recognition, but even when it is tacit, it is significant. Extra-bloc means that the sphere of influence claim is weaker or disputed by other powers.

All five of the quick-decisive cases mentioned involved intra-bloc military interventions: Latin America (Dominican Republic, Grenada, Panama) for the United States, Eastern Europe (Hungary 1956, Czechoslovakia 1968) for the Soviet Union. The protracted cases, however, all involved interventions which from one perspective or another were extra-bloc. In the eyes of the Soviets and Chinese, Vietnam was not Latin America. In the eyes of the United States, Afghanistan 1979 was not Hungary 1956 or Czechoslovakia 1968. It was considered a Soviet effort to expand their bloc, not just maintain it, to convert that which was extra- into intra-.

India's claim to hegemonic dominance over Sri Lanka was stronger but still less than de facto recognized. The whole point of the Cuban and South African troops in Angola was that they each disputed any such claims the other made. Israel found even its U.S. ally unwilling to accede to its effort to pacify Lebanon while the Syrian success in Lebanon came about not only because of its own perseverance but also as noted because of the failure of the Israeli intervention and the tacit willingness of the United States to acquiesce to Syrian control in Lebanon as a price for Syrian cooperation in the war against Iraq.

The intra-bloc systemic context gives the intervenor two crucial advantages. First, it reduces the likelihood of a counter-intervention by another outside power, both because of the tacit rules of the great power game and the greater risks to a counter-intervenor of either defeat or escalation. The intervenor can thus very likely politically and/or physically "seal off" the domain of his intervention. The importance of the vulnerability to counter-intervention should not be underestimated. It may well make the difference between success and failure. Herein also lies another principal difference between military intervention and classical military action. In intervention, negative gains appear significantly easier to attain than positive ones. In fact, our case studies lead us to conclude, albeit tentatively, that counter-intervention may *suffice* to deny the original intervenor success, while its absence may well be one *necessary* condition for success. Other historical instances, such as the French counter-interventions, most recently in 1991 in Chad (against Libya), further reinforce this conclusion.

Second, in intra-bloc cases the intervenor is more able both to arrange to be "invited in" by the government or other local political authority, and to line up support from other nations or multilateral bodies in the region. In many instances (e.g., the U.S. in Panama, the Soviets in Hungary and Czechoslovakia) there is even the advantage of having a prior military presence. Troops already are there; they have been for a long time. This allows operationally for enormous military advantages, including pre-positioning (both troops and hardware), familiarity with the terrain, and better information. Politically it also can facilitate the legitimizing claim that the intervention is not, as Andrew Scott puts it, of a "precedent-breaking nature."[12] In extra-bloc interventions, however, it is inherently more difficult both to seal off involvement by other foreign powers and to lay credible claim to not having broken precedent, even as so defined by realpolitik.

A second distinction which helps explain the quick-decisive/protracted contrast is in the distinct variants of military interventionary strategies characterizing the two sets of cases, what adapting from Alexander George can be termed "war winning" and "coercive diplomacy" interventionary strategies. In the war-winning variant, as seen in all the quick-decisive cases, the emphasis is on "ample force to be applied promptly . . . to destroy a significant portion of the opponent's military capability."[13] There is no gradualism; the numbers of military forces are overwhelming from the outset, and they are employed with concrete and immediate military objectives. This strategy contrasts with the coercive diplomacy variant, which characterizes the protracted cases in which, as Kupchan brings out in his chapter, "none of the intervenors was intent on physical destruction of the enemy." Instead they all pursued strategies of using military force for purposes of political coercion. Even when the number of the interventionary forces was rather massive from the outset (Soviets in Afghanistan, Israel in Lebanon), their mission was originally defined more in terms of helping the local ally prevail politically than directly militarily defeating the adversary. Moreover, as we also saw, in at least some of the cases, at least some of the decision-makers knew from the outset that these interventions would not be quick ones and that they were in for the long haul.

A third postulated factor concerns the distinction in the scope of the principal political objective as "leader-centric" (i.e., installing, maintaining, or removing a particular leader or leadership from power) or "body politic-centric" (i.e., having also or instead to reshape the broader political environment). The former is less ambitious in scope, more readily translatable into operational military terms, and less susceptible (at least in the short term) to the risks of an unreliable local partner. The United States went into the Dominican Republic, removed the pro-Bosch regime and installed a pro-Balaguer one; into Grenada and removed the New Jewel Movement and reinstalled a Governor General; and into Panama and removed Manual Noriega and installed Guillermo Endara. The Soviets did the same in Hungary (Imre Nagy out, Janos Kadar in) and Czechoslovakia (Alexander Dubcek out, Gustav Husak in).

Setting out to reshape the body politic, however, is a much broader, more ambitious and even open-ended undertaking. While this too involves installing or maintaining in power favored leaders, even if successful this is much less of a sufficient basis for achieving the principal objectives of the intervention. This, as previously discussed, is where the "hearts and minds" problem of translating political goals into military objectives becomes so especially problematic. Consequently, there also is a much greater need for the local ally to have both an independent base of power and an indigenously credible basis of legitimacy and political appeal to his own people. Yet one of the major problems seen in all six protracted cases was the unreliability and/or political weakness of the local ally (e.g., Diem, Karmal, Gemayel, the Tamils). The local allies proved much weaker, politically as well as militarily, than the intervenors assumed, hoped or calculated—in part, in its own vicious cycle, as a result of the open association with the intervenor.

Moreover, the relationship between the intervenor and its local ally often had the perverse "tail-wagging-the-dog" quality of the intervenor's leverage over the local ally being inversely correlated to the extent of the commitment.[14] This point is often made with respect to the United States and Diem, whom the Eisenhower administration initially helped create as a nationalist leader, yet whom the Kennedy administration found both ineffective and hardly compliant, such that it felt it had no choice but to collude in his assassination—an action that in turn left Johnson to feel even more committed and ultimately prepared to intervene on behalf of Diem's successors with American military forces. Years later, when the Nixon administration sought to disengage, it had so little leverage over Thieu that he had to be coerced, deceived, and in some respects abandoned. Similar limits of leverage over recalcitrant or otherwise unreliable local allies, as Litwak shows, also not only led the Soviets into their military intervention in Afghanistan but also complicated their disengagement.

India never had to assassinate a local ally, but as Ispahani shows, it actually switched local allies repeatedly in its search for a reliable partner for peacemaking. Bashir Gemayel had managed to demonstrate how quickly Israel's leverage over him had waned following the intervention. Shortly after Israel intervened militarily in Lebanon on his behalf, helping him get elected as the Lebanese President, Gemayel not only failed to honor his commitment to contribute his share to the military operation around Beirut, but also rebuffed Begin's explicit demand that he immediately sign a peace treaty with Israel. Gemayel's assassination at the hands of the Syrians shortly thereafter further demonstrated the reliability problem of a local ally. Although he was succeeded by his own brother, Amin, and Israel remained almost another three years in Lebanon with a formidable military presence, Israel lost virtually all of its remaining leverage over the politics of Lebanon in the aftermath of Bashir's assassination.

Further research involving more systematic and in-depth comparisons between protracted and quick-decisive cases is necessary before firm conclusions can be reached about these (and potentially other) factors. Classifying the above conditions for success (intra-bloc/extra-bloc, war winning/coercive diplomacy interventionary strategies, leader-centric/body politic-centric objectives) into necessary and sufficient conditions is a crucial task for further research. It is, however, possible to acknowledge that many of them are becoming increasingly difficult to meet in the emerging post-Cold War world order. With the possible exception of Latin America for the United States, there are few if any remaining de facto recognized spheres of influence in the post-Cold War world. The problem of a reliable local ally is perhaps the most often underestimated yet the most pervasive problem encountered by intervenors. The lesson of the war winning strategy may still be one more within the control of an intervenor— i.e., to make the decision to commit forces at a massive level— but it is a sobering one about the levels of force that may be needed.

Nevertheless, it should again be stressed that the distinction between quick-decisive and protracted foreign military interventions bears resemblance to, but is not synonymous with, attributions of success and future. On the one hand, some claim to a degree of success can be made (and has been made, usually by proponents of the intervention in the first place) in virtually every one of the six protracted cases. Many of these claims do not stand up to an objective net assessment (i.e., not just was at least some objective achieved, but how do the gains made balance against the costs incurred). Yet there nonetheless is significant variance in the degree of success and failure among our cases. If, for heuristic purposes only, we were to place each of the cases on a failure-success continuum based on net assessments of their outcomes, we would see that the Syria in Lebanon case comes closest to the success pole, whereas the U.S. in Vietnam case would come closest to the failure pole. The other cases would be somewhere in between, with the Cuban-Angolan case closer to the Syrian one and the Israeli, Indian, and Soviet ones much further along toward the U.S. case. On the other hand, the decisiveness of several of the quick-decisive cases has proven less than ironclad over time. In Panama, while the Endara government has endured, problems set in, and instability returned within a year, already raising questions about its future. Soviet interventions in Eastern Europe proved quite enduring, but ultimately, despite continued massive Soviet military presence there, even they turned out to be neither complete nor permanent, albeit for rather complex reasons.

Beyond the cases themselves is the more inherent methodological problem regarding the measurement of success. Given that success and failure are not a strict dichotomy, what are valid criteria for assessing the degree of success? If you measure success in relationship to intervention goals, how do you determine these in any valid manner: declared ones, "real ones," initial ones, ultimate ones? Even then, how are net assessments factoring in the price paid to attain the goals to be made: in comparison to the expected price, to the actual price? What is the appropriate time horizon for such assessment? And what of interventions that were terminated briefly and completely but without visible positive results: are they to be considered total failures? Conversely, is every decision not to intervene militarily necessarily qualified as a success?

The research agenda relating to foreign military intervention thus remains a rich and complex one, both empirically and theoretically, given these as well as many other open questions. What makes it even more important and engaging is the likely continued and even increasing salience of such matters in the new era of international affairs into which we are just entering.

Foreign Military Interventions in the Post-Cold War Era

What does the future hold? Is there really some "new world order" emerging, which will make foreign military interventions obsolescent? If so, than a study such as this could be considered useful as analytic history, and not much more.

However, as noted in the first chapter, while particularly frequent during the Cold War, foreign military interventions are neither a new international phenomenon, nor are they tied necessarily to any particular international system structure. While no definitive answer can obviously be given to what the post-Cold War era will bring, there does not appear to be any reason to believe that the future will be fundamentally different from the past. Five crucial factors conducive to foreign military intervention—opportunities, incentives, capabilities, weak prohibitions, and limited alternative strategies—are likely to persist, and potentially even be exacerbated, in the years ahead.

First, as we have seen, opportunities to intervene are created by internal political instability. It is, as Oran Young has stressed, "the relative internal viability of the actors in an international system" which is the key determinant of the opportunities for intervention. "The less viable an actor is, the more susceptible it will be to intervention by outside powers."[15] Clearly, as one surveys the world of the late twentieth century, the number of states low in relative internal viability is all too obvious. Indeed, the number of such states has grown dramatically, as a result of the disintegration of the Soviet Union and its empire, as well as other ramifications of the end of the Cold War. Nor is this just a matter of listing global "hot spots." It is even more telling to consider the broader historical forces which have given rise to explosive "politics of identity" in many parts of the world that are not only threatening the domestic stability of numerous existing governing regimes, but also calling into question the very legitimacy of the structure and identity of many nation-states. This has a number of different manifestations, including Islamic fundamentalism in the Middle East, tribal-ethnic conflicts in Africa, religious-ethnic conflicts on the Indian subcontinent, and nationality-ethnic conflicts in the Balkans, Eastern Europe, and former Soviet Union. Because such conflicts tend to be defined in zero sum terms (who am I, who are you, and how are we different?) and because they tend to carry with them long and often bitter historical legacies, they are less susceptible to orderly, nonviolent political compromises and reforms.

Moreover, the persisting if not worsening socioeconomic tensions and conflicts in the Third World must also be taken into account. Latin America, for example, recently has been relatively quiescent and orderly in its internal political processes, with the 1970s military governments having given way to civilian governments and most (although not all) of the 1980s civil wars having wound down. However, so long as economic problems continue to worsen, political corruption runs rampant, and drug cartels and other forces undermine the basic societal fabric, the roots of instability will remain.

Second, it is almost stating the obvious that as long as there are the opportunities to intervene, states will have an incentive to do so. Instability is only "domestic" or "internal" in the descriptive sense of its locale. Its effects do not necessarily stop at state boundaries. The interests of other states *are* affected by developments internal to another state. These interests may be political, military, strategic, and/or economic. Values and humanitarian concerns also often are affected. And whatever the other benefits of increasing global interdependence, the increasing interconnectedness via commerce and communications can add to the sensitivity to what happens elsewhere on the globe and consequently also to the incentives to intervene. Metternichian calculations also may enter in for leaders who perceive their own stability as threatened by examples set or movements ignited elsewhere, or by potential security threats posed by evolving fundamentalist renegade regimes (e.g., Iran, Iraq, Libya, North Korea, potentially Algeria), particularly if they possess or seek to acquire weapons of mass destruction or other major military capabilities.

Third, the capabilities part of the mix is that more and more states possess greater and greater military power and thus are (or believe themselves to be) capable of projecting sufficient military power to undertake military interventions. The United States first made the development of military capabilities for Third World interventions, then called counter-insurgency warfare, a priority in the Kennedy administration. The terminology changed over time (e.g., low-intensity conflict), but the mission remained largely the same. Soviet interventionary capabilities became quite formidable in the 1970s, as their navy gained "blue water" capabilities, their air force enhanced its troop and equipment airlift capacity, and the huge profits from their OPEC-inflated oil exports financed the projection of their power beyond Eastern Europe. Clearly, as Litwak stressed even before the Union crumbled, the Soviets were in an inward mode, more than burdened at home, pulling back from old external commitments, and showing few signs of interest in new ones. Nevertheless, the Russian republic in particular does retain certain capabilities which could again be activated and mobilized. Moreover, as our own cases demonstrate (but by no means exhaust), a number of regional powers also have developed substantial interventionary capabilities.

Yet (fourth) international controls, while arguably stronger than in the past, remain well short of strict prohibitions. The United States as well as regional multilateral organizations such as the Conference on Security and Cooperation in Europe (CSCE), the European Community (EC), and the Organization of American States (OAS) have been seeking to develop both stronger norms against unilateral military interventions and more effective mechanisms for multilateral peacekeeping. The unprecedented debate that has begun recently in the United Nations Security Council on the possibile rethinking of the principle of nonintervention in the internal affairs of member states, and even the possible creation of a permanent UN interventionary peacekeeping force, is perhaps the most significant manifestation of this trend. At the same time, the incentive to take unilateral action remains inherent in both the quasi-anarchic nature of international relations and in the "self-help principle" to which governments resort, when they deem necessary. It may be called national defense or national security or international solidarity or collective security or some other term. But nation-states always have—and, without a doubt, always will—reserve the right to take whatever action they ultimately deem necessary to defend themselves and along broad operational interpretations of self-defense. As Craig and George have observed, "despite repeated attempts to define aggression and to limit the conditions in which resort to arms is justified, agreement on these matters has proved to be elusive, and nations have been unwilling to surrender the sovereign right to decide for themselves when to use military force to protect or advance their interests."[16] There are signs of attenuation, but not (yet) of a full sublimation of this aspect of the claim to sovereign action.

Part of the problem, as we already have discussed, is defining what types of actions constitute intervention. But even if there could be agreement on the parameters between intervention and nonintervention, there would remain the debate over conditions legitimizing intervention. In addition to the self-help principle, there is the "altruistic" principle, which postulates that some situations are so dire (e.g., genocide, to free people from political or religious persecution, or to provide relief from famine) as to create a consensus among concerned individuals and nations that intervention is the only moral thing to do, and that nonintervention would in fact be shameful and ought to be condemned. For those who are inclined to allow for altruistic exceptions, the counterarguments stress the dangerous precedents that are set. For those who take a firm prohibitive view, there is always the case of whether intervention to overthrow Adolf

Hitler would not have been justified. Our point, though, is not to take sides in this debate. What we do mean to suggest, however, is that because of the strength of the self-help principle and the weakness of the norm of nonintervention, military intervention is not considered a prohibited undertaking.

Finally there is the question of if not military intervention, then what? What other alternative strategies are available and viable? If there is a major difference in these first years of the post–Cold War world, it is in the increased resort to alternative strategies of intervention. In Liberia and Kurdish Iraq, military interventions were undertaken but on both a limited scale and multilateral basis. And in Yugoslavia, the European Community attempted a political-economic rather than military strategy, as did the Organization of American States in Haiti.

All these cases are still going on as of this writing. The record thus far is mixed. The very attempts in themselves are significant as demonstrations of a shift away from unilateral military interventions toward multilateral and political-economic ones. Yugoslavia marks the first instance of the EC emerging as the lead actor in a major international security issue. The September 1991 coup in Haiti drew attention to the resolution passed by the OAS a few months earlier authorizing "any measures deemed appropriate" by the multilateral body to restore constitutional rule if democratic processes in any member country were overturned. The Liberian case showed the role that can be played even by a sub-regional group of smaller nations (i.e., the West African Ceasefire Monitoring Group) to help end a civil war. And the Kurdish case showed the reluctance of the United States, even in the wake of overwhelming victory in an interstate war, to get unilaterally militarily involved in another nation's internal conflict.

Ultimately, of course, the efficacy demonstrated (or not) will matter most, but clearly there are some hopeful signs. Perhaps the historical record of cases may provide some incentives for scholars and policy makers alike to explore and develop these further. For the dilemma of reconciling strategic interests with limits of influence is a crucial one, but not an easy one, for states to resolve.

The point, to put it another way, is that history is far from over. And foreign military interventions may still be a major part of the history which is to come. It is our hope that this study will contribute to a better understanding of the dynamics and potential consequences of that option.

Notes

1. Melvin Small and J. David Singer, *Resort to Arms: International and Civil Wars* (Beverly Hills: Sage Publishers, 1982); Frederic S. Pearson, "Foreign Military Intervention and Domestic Disputes," *International Studies Quarterly* 18 (December 1974) :259–89.

2. Ted Robert Gurr and Jack A. Goldstone, "Conclusions: Patterns and Prospects," in Jack A. Goldstone and Ted Robert Gurr eds., *Revolutions of the Late Twentieth Century* (forthcoming 1991), ms. pp. 17, 25 (emphasis added).

3. See also Robert A. Pastor, "Preempting Revolutions: The Boundaries of U.S. Influence," *International Security*, 15 (Spring 1991) :54–86.

4. In a November 1984 speech, Secretary of Defense Caspar Weinberger laid out "six major tests to be applied when we are weighing the use of U.S. combat forces abroad." The speech is included as an Appendix in his memoirs, *Fighting for Peace* (New York: Warner Books, 1990).

The influence of the Vietnam experience also could be seen in two respects in the U.S. Persian Gulf War strategy. First was the absolute rejection of any form of gradualism and the emphasis on rapid overwhelming force in the military strategy of Operation Desert Storm from the outset. Second was the reluctance, the overwhelming war victory notwithstanding, to do anything militarily more than "provide comfort" to the Kurds in the internal war that followed.

5. Ernest R. May, *"Lessons" from the Past: The Use and Misuse of History in American Foreign Policy* (New York: Oxford University Press, 1973); Richard E. Neustadt and Ernest R. May, *Thinking in Time: The Uses of History for Decision Makers* (New York: Free Press, 1986).

6. William J. Perry,"Desert Storm and Deterrence," *Foreign Affairs*, 70 (Fall 1991) :81.

7. A similar argument is made by Robert O'Neill, "The Use of Military Force: Constant Factors and New Trends," *The Changing Strategic Landscape: Part II*, Adelphi Paper #236; International Institute of Strategic Studies (Spring 1989):3–17.

8. Quoted in E.J. Dionne, "Kicking the 'Vietnam Syndrome'," *Washington Post*, March 4, 1991, p. A1.

9. Richard Little, *Intervention: External Involvement in Civil Wars* (London: Marten Robertson, 1975).

10. Gordon A. Craig and Alexander L. George, *Force and Statecraft: Diplomatic Problems of Our Time* (New York: Oxford University Press, 1990), p. 233.

11. John P. Burke and Fred Greenstein, with Larry Berman and Richard Immerman, *How Presidents Test Reality: Decisions on Vietnam, 1954 and 1965* (New York: Russell Sage, 1989).

12. Andrew M. Scott, *The Revolution in Statecraft: Intervention in an Age of Interdependence* (Durham, N.C.: Duke University Press), p. 182.

13. Alexander L. George, *The Limits of Coercive Diplomacy* (Boston: Little, Brown, 1971), pp. 16–17.

14. Bruce W. Jentleson, "American Commitments in the Third World: Theory vs. Practice," *International Organization* 41(Autumn 1987):667–704.

15. Oran R. Young, "Intervention and International Systems," *Journal of International Affairs*, 22 no. 2(1968):177–78.

16. Craig and George, *Force and Statecraft*, p. 289

Index